<u>EP Exam Review</u>

3rd Edition

Volume 1 of 2

Paul Haas, M.D.

April Felton
Scot Felton
Wes Todd

Published by KDP
www.kdp.amazon.com

Over the past 20 years, the treatment for complex cardiac arrhythmias has evolved from primary medical therapy to more frequent, invasive, and definitive therapies with ablations. As such, the number of ablations performed has increased substantially. Electrophysiology, once a niche field, has become a well-established specialty throughout hospitals around the world. There is now a tremendous need for lab staff, industry personnel, and physicians trained in the intricacies of electrophysiology.   Unfortunately, there are very few formal educational opportunities for trainees. Education is frequently done "on the fly" by more experienced lab members, industry members, and practicing electrophysiologists. This is inadequate. This text is designed to be broad—appropriate for EP lab staff, individuals studying for the RCES and IBHRE exams, industry personnel, and new fellows.

Paul Haas, M.D.

EP Essentials LLC

EP Exam Review

Table of Contents

EP Essentials LLC

Volume 1:

Volume 2:

EP Essentials LLC

Chapter 1
Cardiac Foundation

EP Essentials LLC

Terminology:

1. **Match the general class of ECG rhythm with its name below:**
   1. **Slowed or interrupted Conduction**
   2. **Cessation of activity**
   3. **Chaotic rapid beating**
   4. **Rapid, but regular beating**
   5. **Beat which occurs too soon, early.**
   6. **Delayed beat, from lower pacemaker**
   7. **Rate over 100 bpm**
   8. **Rate less than 60 bpm**
   9. **Sudden rhythm or rate change**

   a. **Flutter**
   b. **Fibrillation**
   c. **Arrest**
   d. **Tachycardia**
   e. **Bradycardia**
   f. **Premature**
   g. **Escape**
   h. **Block**
   i. **Paroxysmal**

CORRECTLY MATCHED ANSWERS ARE:
1: h. Block = Slowed or interrupted Conduction (as in BBB or 3rd deg. HB)
2: c. Arrest = Cessation of activity (as in SA arrest)
3: b. Fibrillation = Chaotic rapid beating (over 400 bpm)
4: a. Flutter = Rapid, but regular beating (usually over 200 bpm)
5: f. Premature = Beat which occurs too soon, early (as in PVC)
6: g. Escape = Delayed beat, from lower pacemaker (as in junctional escape)
7: d. Tachycardia = Rate over 100 bpm (as in ventricular tachycardia)
8: e. Bradycardia = Rate less than 60 bpm (or <50 in young athletes)
9: I. Paroxysmal = Sudden rhythm or rate change (as in paroxysmal atrial tachycardia)
See: Dubin, chapter on "Rhythm."

2. Medical terms are commonly built by adding a prefix in front of a root word. Match the prefix with its meaning.

1.	PERI-	a.	Behind
2.	ENDO-	b.	Deficient
3.	RETRO-	c.	Excessive
4.	HYPER-	d.	Within
5.	HYPO-	e.	Surrounding
6.	TRANS	f.	Across

CORRECTLY MATCHED ANSWERS:
1. PERI- e. Surrounding or around (E.g., Pericardium)
2. ENDO- d. Within or inward (E.g., Endocardium)
3. RETRO- a. Behind or backward (E.g., Retroperitoneal)
4. HYPER- c. Excessive, above, beyond, or more than normal (E.g., Hyperkalemia)
5. HYPO- b. Deficient, beneath, under, or below normal (E.g., Hypothermia)
6. TRANS- f. Across or beyond (E.g., Trans-thoracic) Be able to match all prefixes above.

See: Medical Dictionary

3. Medical terms are commonly built by adding a prefix in front of a root word. Match the prefix with its meaning. Note a (o) indicates an o may be added to the combining form.

1.	Vaso _____	a.	Vessel
2.	Phlebo _____	b.	Systemic vessel containing deoxygenated blood.
3.	Arterio _____		
4.	Ather(o) _____	c.	Fatty degradation
5.	Cholangi(o) _____	d.	Systemic vessel containing oxygenated blood.
		e.	Bile duct

CORRECTLY MATCHED ANSWERS:
1. Vas(o):   a. Vessel or canal for carrying a fluid (E.g., vasoconstriction)
2. Phlebo: b. Systemic vessel containing deoxygenated blood (E.g., phlebitis)
3. Arteri(o): d. Systemic vessel containing oxygenated blood (E.g., arteriosclerosis)
4. Ather(o): c. Fatty degradation (E.g., atheromatous plaque)
5. Cholangi: e. Bile duct (E.g., cholangiogram)

See: Medical Dictionary Keywords: prefix

4. Medical terms are commonly built by adding a suffix to the end of a root word. Match each suffix with its meaning.

1.	Blood condition	a.	-poiesis
2.	Formation	b.	-pathy
3.	Enlargement	c.	-emia
4.	Disease condition	d.	-penia
5.	Deficiency	e.	-megaly
6.	Inflammation	f.	-itis

CORRECTLY MATCHED ANSWERS:
1. Blood condition   c. -emia (E.g., anemia)
2. Formation   a. -poiesis (E.g., erhythropoiesis)
3. Enlargement   e. -megaly (E.g., cardiomegaly)
4. Disease condition b. -pathy (E.g., neuropathy)
5. Deficiency   d. -penia (E.g., thrombocytopenia)
6. Inflammation   f. -itis (E.g., phlebitis)

5. Surgical terms are commonly built by adding a suffix to the end of a root word. Match each suffix with its meaning.

1. **Surgical repair**
2. **Surgical removal or incision**
3. **Surgical tap**
4. **Surgical opening between organs**

a. **-centesis (E.g., thoracentesis)**
b. **-ostomy (E.g., colostomy)**
c. **-plasty (E.g., angioplasty)**
d. **-ectomy (E.g., pericardiectomy)**

CORRECTLY MATCHED ANSWERS:
1. Surgical repair: c. -plasty (E.g., angioplasty)
2. Surgical removal/incision: d. -ectomy (E.g., Pericardiectomy)
3. Surgical tap: a. -centesis (E.g., thoracentesis
4. Surgical opening between organs: b. -ostomy (E.g., colostomy pericardiostomy)
See: Medical Dictionary

6. A patient with oliguria may be treated with a:
a. **Foley catheter**
b. **Fogarty catheter**
c. **Urethroscope**
d. **Kidney catheter**

ANSWER: a. Foley catheter is a dual lumen rubber catheter which is positioned in the bladder to drain it when patients are unable to void adequately. This condition of decreased urine output in relation to the intake is termed oliguria, hypouresis or oligouresis. Oligmeans "deficient."
See: Mosby's Comprehensive Review of Nursing for NCLEX-RN, Chapter on "Urinary systems"

7. Infiltration of IV fluids from an IV access site into tissue is termed:
a. **Extravasation**
b. **Extravenous irrigation**
c. **Extramural tamponade**
d. **Extra-parenteral discharge**

ANSWER: a. Extravasation or infiltration is the accidental administration of fluids into the surrounding tissue, either by leakage or direct infusion. Extravasation occurs commonly with geriatric patients, whose vessels are hardened by atherosclerosis. Extravasation of blood around a vascular access site is usually termed hematoma.

8. An ambulatory patient is:
   a. **Able to walk.**
   b. **Unable to walk.**
   c. **Breathing adequately**
   d. **Not breathing adequately**

ANSWER: a. Patients can walk, means the patient is ambulatory or able to "ambulate." An ambulatory lab is one where patients can get up and walk soon after their procedure.
See: Medical dictionary

9. Match each medical directional term with its anatomic meaning.
   1. **Ventral**   a. **Anterior**
   2. **Dorsal**   b. **Posterior**
   3. **Cranial**   c. **Superior**
   4. **Caudal**   d. **Inferior**

CORRECTLY MATCHED ANSWERS:
1. Ventral = a. Anterior, the face is anterior.
2. Dorsal = b. Posterior, the butt is posterior.
3. Cranial = c. Superior, The head or higher
4. Caudal = d. Inferior, Toward feet or lower
All directions are labeled as shown like a fish. See: Spence, chapter "Intro to A&P"

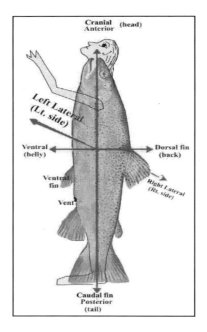

10. Match the medical directional terms with their anatomic meaning.
   1. **Toward the midline**   a. **Distal**
   2. **Away from the midline**   b. **Proximal**
   3. **Closer to a point of reference**   c. **Medial**
   4. **Farther from a point of reference** d. **Latera**

CORRECTLY MATCHED ANSWERS ARE:
1. Toward the midline: c. Medial (E.g., Heart is medial to the lungs)
2. Away from the midline: d. Lateral (E.g., Lungs are lateral to the heart)
3. Closer to a point of reference: b. Proximal (E.g., Arm is proximal to the hand)
4. Farther from a point of reference: a. Distal (E.g., Hand is distal to the arm)
See: Spence, chapter "Introduction to A & P"

11. A patient tells you that he has "awful palpitations" meaning he:
   a. **Feels a sensation of heat and flushing.**
   b. **Feels that his heart rate is rapid or irregular.**
   c. **Feels that he cannot get his breath.**
   d. **Feels a sense of impending doom.**

ANSWER: b. Feels that his heart rate is rapid or irregular. Palpitations are a patient's subjective awareness that his heart rate is unduly rapid, irregular, or fluttering. This is usually an arrhythmia or series of PVCs. See: Medical Dictionary

12. The admitting nurse reports that your patient has tachypnea. This means that your patient has:
   a. **Rapid heart rate**
   b. **High blood pressure**
   c. **Rapid respiratory rate**
   d. **Labored breathing**

ANSWER: c. Rapid respiratory rate. Tachy means fast, as in tachycardia. Tachypnea means rapid respiration. Dyspnea is a term to describe labored or difficult respirations. Noisy respirations are referred to as stertorous breathing. Moist respirations are often associated with pulmonary edema and may be termed rales. There is no term for describing shallow respirations.
See: Medical Dictionary

13. Evaluate a patient's blood pressure of 80/45 and heart rate of 56 bpm.
   a. **Hypertensive with tachycardia**
   b. **Hypertensive with bradycardia**
   c. **Hypotensive with tachycardia**
   d. **Hypotensive with bradycardia**

ANSWER: d. Hypotensive, bradycardia. Normal blood pressure is 120/80. Below 100 is hypotensive. Normal HR is 60-100. Bradycardia is below a heart rate of 60 bpm. However, in resting athletic young people the rate may normally go as low as 50 bpm. See: Lippincott's State Board Review NCLEX-PN.

Anatomy:

1. This valve may be present at the GCV (great cardiac vein) ostium.
   a. **Eustachian**
   b. **Vieussens**
   c. **Thebesian**
   d. **Tricuspid**

ANSWER: b. Vieussens. The Vieussens valve is present in about three-quarters of autopsied hearts. However, it is infrequent that this valve prohibits catheter/lead advancement. Noheria, et al, Anatomy of the Coronary Sinus and Epicardial Coronary Venous System in 620 Hearts: An Electrophysiology Perspective. Journal of Cardiovascular Electrophysiology

2. Where is the ligament of Marshall located?
   a. **Near the junction of the great cardiac vein and the coronary sinus**
   b. **Near the anterior interventricular vein**
   c. **Near the lateral marginal branches**
   d. **Near the posterior vein**

ANSWER: d. Near the junction of the great cardiac vein and the coronary sinus.
The ligament of Marshall (or persistent left superior vena cava, when present), and the valve of Vieussens (where present) is located at the junction of the great cardiac vein (GCV) and the CS.

3. Which cardiac chamber has three papillary muscles?
   a. **Right Ventricle**
   b. **Left Ventricle**
   c. **Right Atrium**
   d. **Left Atrium**

ANSWER: a. Right Ventricle. Papillary muscles are found in the ventricles. There are three papillary muscles in the RV, each one will attach to a valve leaflet. The AV valve on the right side of the heart is the tricuspid with three leaflets. The mitral valve on the left side of the heart has two leaflets; therefore, there will be two papillary muscles in the LV. Although, papillary muscle anatomy is variable and can have single or multiple heads.
2019 HRS/EHRA/APHRS/LAHRS expert consensus statement on catheter ablation of ventricular arrhythmias. Journal of Arrhythmia

4. This structure within the left ventricle may impede catheter manipulation.
   a. **Aortomitral Curtain**
   b. **Sinus of Valsalva**
   c. **Aortic Vestibule**
   d. **False Tendon**

ANSWER: d. False Tendon. The false tendon (or LV moderator band) is a fibrous or fibromuscular chord-like band that crosses the LV cavity, attaching to the septum, papillary muscles, trabeculations, or free wall of the LV. It may contain conduction tissue and may impede catheter manipulation in the LV. The RV moderator band is a muscular band in the RV, typically located in the mid to apical RV, connecting the interventricular septum to the RV free wall, supporting the anterior papillary muscle. It typically contains a subdivision of the right bundle branch (RBB).

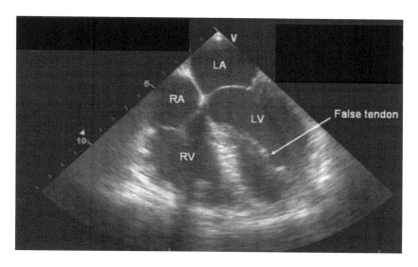

2019 HRS/EHRA/APHRS/LAHRS expert consensus statement on catheter ablation of ventricular arrhythmias. Journal of Arrhythmia

5. In this RAO projection of the heart identify the structure labeled at #6.
   a. **Right subclavian artery**
   b. **Right pulmonary artery**
   c. **Right pulmonary vein**
   d. **Right main stem bronchus**

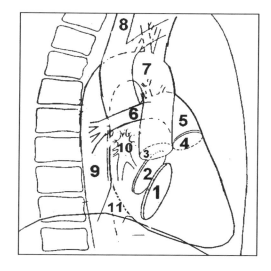

ANSWER. b. right pulmonary artery. This view RAO Film clearly shows the long axis of the heart. This RAO view is the best view for separating the atria and ventricles. The RV chamber and PA are the most anterior structures. Note the right PA beneath the aortic arch supplying the right lung. Be able to match all answers above.

6. In this RAO view, identify the structure labeled at #1.
   a. **Aortic valve**
   b. **Mitral valve**
   c. **Pulmonic valve**
   d. **Tricuspid valve**

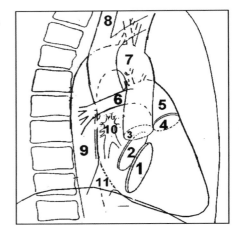

ANSWER d. Tricuspid valve. The tricuspid valve is larger and slightly lower than the mitral valve. It is lower partly because the heart is tilted at 60 degrees. But the tricuspid attachment to the AV septum is slightly lower than the mitral valve attachment. The mitral valve is attached to the aortic valve.

CORRECTLY MATCHED ANSWERS ARE:
   1. Tricuspid valve
   2. Mitral valve
   3. AO valve
   4. PA valve
   5. Main PA
   6. Right PA
   7. Aorta
   8. SVC
   9. Descending AO
   10. Pulmonary Veins
   11. IVC

See: Braunwald, chapter on "Radiographic Examination of the Heart."

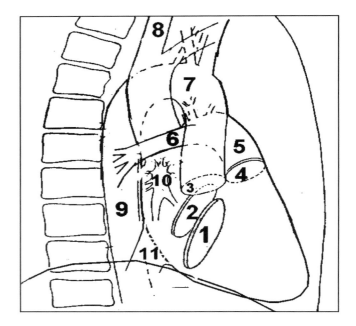

7. On view of the BACK of the heart identify the structure labeled at #11.
   a. Ascending AO
   b. Descending AO
   c. SVC
   d. IVC
   e. Right PA

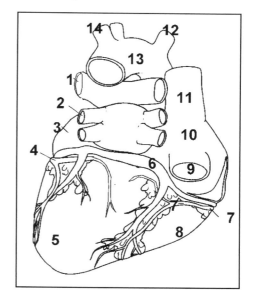

ANSWER c. SVC. This view clearly shows the vessels leading to and from the base of the heart. See: Braunwald, chapter on "Radiographic Examination of the Heart."

8. Identify the structure labeled at #6.
   a. Left anterior descending coronary artery
   b. Circumflex coronary artery
   c. Posterior descending coronary artery
   d. Coronary sinus

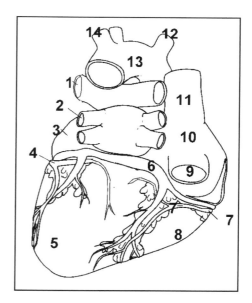

ANSWER d. Coronary sinus. The coronary venous blood returns via the great cardiac vein (beneath the LA) and coronary sinus (#6). Here the CS dumps its black blood into the RA near the crux of the heart. Note the larger size of the CS and how it collects blood from the left side of the heart, the right side of the heart (small cardiac vein) as well as from the inferior wall near the PDA artery (middle cardiac vein).

CORRECTLY MATCHED ANSWERS ARE:
1. Left PA
2. LSPV
3. LAA/LA
4. Circumflex artery
5. Left ventricle (LV) Apex
6. Coronary sinus
7. Right coronary artery
8. Right ventricle (RV)
9. Inferior vena cava (IVC)
10. Right atrium (RA)
11. Superior vena cava (SVC)
12. Innominate (Brachiocephalic artery)
13. Aortic arch (AO)
14. Left subclavian artery

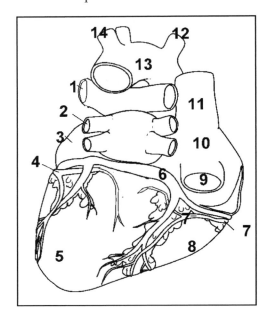

See: Netter's, Collection of medical illustrations or Braunwald, chapter on "Radiographic Examination of the Heart."

9. Which valve (or valves) are open during ventricular systole?
    a. **Bicuspid valve**
    b. **Tricuspid valve**
    c. **AV valves**
    d. **Semilunar valves**

ANSWER d. Semilunar valves. Ventricular contraction causes systolic squeezing. This opens the aortic and pulmonary semilunar valves as shown in the right diagram. S, S, S = systole, squeezing, & semilunar valves. During diastole or relaxation, shown in the left diagram, the two AV valves open and the ventricles fill. See chapter on hemodynamics. See: Underhill, chapter on "Cardiac Physiology."

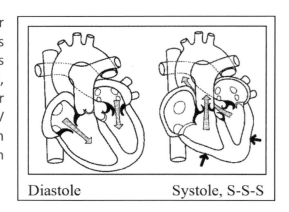

Diastole   Systole, S-S-S

10. In this superior view of the cardiac valves, the atria have been removed. The most anterior heart valve labeled #1 on the diagram is the:
    a. **Mitral**
    b. **Tricuspid**
    c. **Aortic**
    d. **Pulmonic**

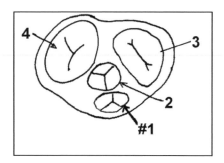

ANSWER d. The Pulmonary valve is the most anterior cardiac valve, nearly touching the sternum. It exists anteriorly and slightly left of midline. (You'd think it would be right-ward, since the RV is right-ward, but it's NOT!) For this reason, pulmonary valve murmurs are usually heard to the left of midline and aortic valve murmurs to the right of midline. (Note the crossing of aorta and pulmonary vessels.)

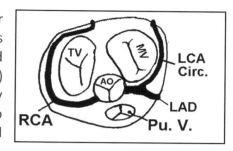

A superior view of the cardiac valves forms a kind of "cat face" shape - with the large AV valves forming the eye sockets, the AO the nose, and the PA valve the mouth. Note the two coronary arteries arise from the AO to form a moustache. See: Netter's collection of medical illustrations, "The Heart."

11. Where is the fibrous skeleton of the heart located?
   a. **Around the heart valves**
   b. **At the IVC - SVC annuli**
   c. **At the pericardial attachments**
   d. **In the interventricular septum**

ANSWER a. Around the heart valves. These four fibrous rings encircling the four valves at the base of the heart form the cardiac skeleton. Except through the AV node area, there is no electrical conduction through this fibrous ring. These four rings are joined by triangular pads of fibrous tissue (trigones). This makes the AV rings a rigid structure into which the cardiac muscles anchor. This ring may have become calcified in old age and in valve disease blocking AV electrical conduction.
See: Grays anatomy.

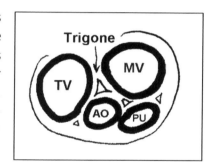

12. The largest cardiac valve is the:
   a. **Mitral**
   b. **Tricuspid**
   c. **Aortic**
   d. **Pulmonic**

ANSWER b. Tricuspid. Both AV valves are large 4-5 cm2. But the tricuspid valve has a slightly larger orifice. It will admit three fingers, whereas the Mitral will only admit two fingers. You can remember this because the Mitral valve has two leaflets (two fingers) while the tricuspid has three leaflets (and admits three fingers). The RA does not normally generate as much pressure as the LA so the orifice area must be larger to admit the same amount of blood. See: Underhill, chapter on "CV Anatomy."

13. Match every number in this picture of the right heart with its anatomic name.

    a. CS
    b. RV
    c. SVC
    d. IVC
    e. Fossa Ovalis
    f. Eustachian valve/ridge
    g. Thebesian valve
    h. Tricuspid valve
    i. Crista terminalis
    j. Atrial appendage

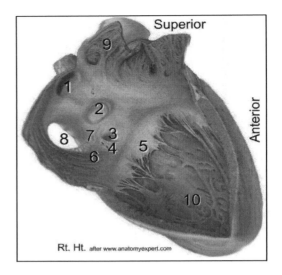

Rt. Ht. after www.anatomyexpert.com

CORRECTLY MATCHED ANSWERS ARE:

1: c. SVC
2: e. Fossa Ovalis
3: a. CS
4: g. Thebesian Valve
5: h. Tricuspid Valve
6: i. Crista Terminalis
7: f. Eustachian Valve
8: d. IVC
9: j. Right Atrial Appendage
10: b. RV

"The tricuspid annulus lies anterior to the body of the RA. The RA endocardium is architecturally divided into the anterolateral trabeculated RA, derived from the true embryonic RA, and the posterior smooth-walled RA, derived from the embryonic sinus venosus. These distinct anatomical regions of the RA are separated by the crista terminalis on the lateral wall and the eustachian ridge in the inferior aspect."

"The crista terminalis is formed at the junction between the sinus venosus part of the RA and the "true" RA contributing to the RA appendage and free wall. The crista runs from the high septum, anterior to the orifice of the SVC superiorly, and courses caudally along the posterolateral aspect of the RA. In its inferior extent, it courses anteriorly to the orifice of the IVC. As it reaches the region of the IVC, it is extended by the eustachian valve ridge (the remnant of the embryonic sinus venosus valve), which courses superiorly along the floor of the RA to the coronary sinus ostium (CS ostium), to join the valve of the CS and form the tendon of Todaro. "

"The inferior portion of the tricuspid annulus lies a short distance (approximately 1 to 4 cm) anterior to the eustachian ridge..." See: Issa, chapter on "Isthmus Dependent Atrial Flutter"

14. Match each RA anatomic feature with its location:

1. **CS ostium is located:**
2. **Fossa ovalis is located:**
3. **Crista terminalis is:**
4. **Atrial appendage is:**

a. **Anterior to the IVC**
b. **Superior - posterior to the CS ostium**
c. **Posterior to the tricuspid valve**
d. **Superior to the Fossa ovalis**

CORRECTLY MATCHED ANSWERS ARE:
CS ostium: c. Posterior to the tricuspid valve
Fossa ovalis: b. Superior posterior to the CS ostium
Crista terminalis: a. Anterior to the IVC
Atrial appendage: d. Superior to the Fossa ovalis

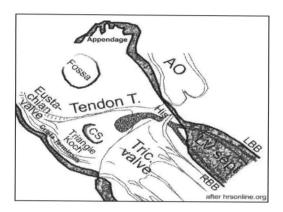

15. What is the valve over the CS ostium that may interfere with CS catheter placement?
a. **Eustachian valve**
b. **Thebesian valve**
c. **Valve of Valsalva**
d. **Atrioventricular valve**

ANSWER: b. Thebesian valve may close when probed with a catheter. The valve of the coronary sinus (Thebesian valve) is a semicircular fold of the tissue at the orifice of the coronary sinus. It is commonly fenestrated and may vary in size or be completely absent. It may help prevent the regurgitation of blood into the sinus during the contraction of the atrium. Also note the Eustachian valve which attached to the IVC helped redirect flow in uterine into the LA through the Foramen Ovale (now closed - Fossa Ovalis). Both valves may present some obstacle to OS cannulation.
OF = Fossa Ovalis
App= RA appendage
TT=Tendon Todaro
TV=Tricuspid Valve leaflet
AV = AV node

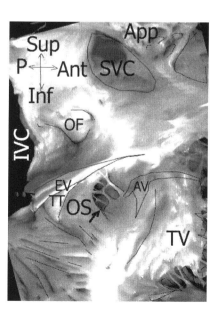

16. The sides of the triangle of Koch are formed by the tricuspid annulus, AV node, and
_____.
    a. IVC
    b. SA node
    c. Crista terminalis
    d. Tendon of Todaro

ANSWER: d. Tendon of Todaro. Fogoros says, "The three sides of Koch's triangle are defined by the tricuspid annulus, (the portion of the annulus adjacent to the septal leaflet of the TV), the tendon of Todaro, and the ostium of the CS. The His bundle is located at the apex of Koch's triangle .... the fast and slow pathways are readily discernible and can be localized within Koch's triangle... The fast pathway is an anterior and superior structure and lies near the compact AV node along the tendon of Todaro. The slow pathway is a posterior and inferior structure and can usually be identified along the tricuspid annulus near the OS of the CS."

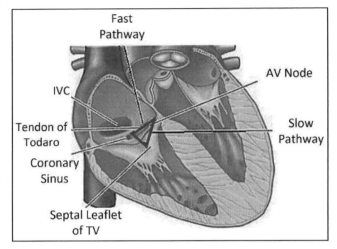

17. The posterior border of the triangle of Koch is the:
    a. CS ostium
    b. Tendon of Todaro
    c. Compact AV node
    d. Slow AV node pathway

ANSWER: a. CS ostium. Issa says, "The triangle of Koch is bordered by the CS ostium posteriorly and the attachment of the septal leaflet of the tricuspid valve inferiorly. The compact AVN is located anteriorly at its apex, where the tendon of Todaro (the superior margin of the triangle of Koch) merges with the central fibrous body. Slightly more anteriorly and superiorly is where the HB penetrates the AV junction through the central fibrous body and posterior aspect of the membranous AV septum. The triangle of Koch is septal and constitutes the RA surface of the muscular AV septum." This anatomy is extremely important when you ablate an AVNRT slow pathway in the triangle of Koch, along the annulus of the tricuspid valve. See Issa, chapter on AVRT Ablation

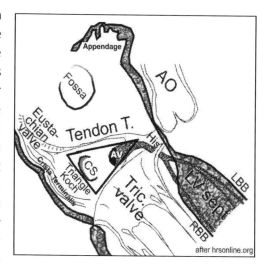

18. The superior border of the triangle of Koch is the ___ and it normally contains the _____.
    a. Tendon of Todaro, Fast AV node pathway
    b. Tendon of Todaro, Slow AV node pathway
    c. Tricuspid valve annulus, Fast AV node pathway
    d. Tricuspid valve annulus, Slow AV node pathway

ANSWER: a. Tendon of Todaro, Fast AV node pathway
The Triangle of Koch is defined by the following structures within the right atrium:
(1) The ostium of the coronary sinus, posteriorly.
(2) the anterior portion of the tricuspid valve annulus; and
(3) the tendon of Todaro (connecting the valve of the IVC ostium to the central fibrous body)

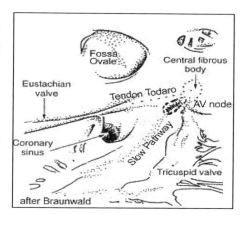

19. The ridge of tissue in front of the IVC that functions as a valve in utero is the:
    a. Eustachian ridge
    b. Crista terminalis
    c. Moderator band
    d. Atrial appendage

ANSWER: a. Eustachian ridge. The valve of the inferior vena cava (Eustachian valve) lies at the junction of the inferior vena cava and right atrium. Most commonly, it is a crescentic fold of endocardium arising from the anterior rim of the IVC orifice. The lateral horn of the crescent tends to meet the lower end of the crista terminalis, while the medial horn joins the thebesian valve, a semicircular valvular fold at the orifice of the coronary sinus. You can see why this valve might get in the way during a femoral approach to CS.

In fetal life, the Eustachian valve helps direct the flow of oxygen-rich blood through the right atrium into the left atrium via the foramen ovale (preventing blood flowing into the right ventricle) While the Eustachian valve persists in adult life, it does not have a specific function.

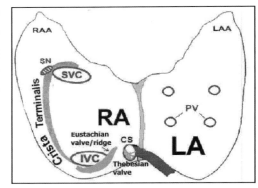

20. Match the normal location of each pulmonary vein to its closest anatomic neighbor:

1. LSPV
2. RSPV
3. LIPV
4. RIPV

a. Closest to SVC
b. Hardest to access & ablate
c. Closest to LPA & LAA
d. Closest to descending aorta & circumflex artery

CORRECTLY MATCHED ANSWERS ARE:
1. LSPV c. Closest to LPA & LA Appendage
2. RSPV a. Closest to SVC and closest to phrenic nerve
3. LIPV d. Closest to descending aorta & circumflex
4. RIPV b. Hardest to access & ablate because the transseptal catheter must turn 180 degrees

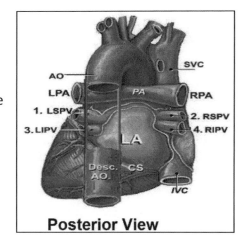

Posterior View

21. Where are the pectinate muscles in the left atrium?
a. LA isthmus
b. LA appendage
c. All walls of the LA
d. Posterior to the Crista Terminalis
e. The LA has no pectinate muscles

ANSWER: b. LA appendage. Zipes say, "In contrast with the right atrium, virtually all the pectinate muscles in the left atrium are confined within the appendage. The major portion of the atrium, including the septal component, is smooth walled."

In this photo of the lateral LA, note the smooth wall surfaces - all except for the LA appendage. It is little wonder clots originate there. Note in this the lateral   LA wall specimen how close the LSPV is to the LA appendage (LAA) See: Zipes chapter on Supraventricular Arrhythmias

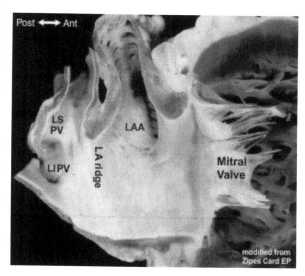

22. What is the name of the muscular bands lining the anterior walls of the RA and atrial appendages? (Labeled C in the diagram)
   a. **Pectinate muscles**
   b. **Trabeculae**
   c. **Papillary muscles**
   d. **Auricular muscles**

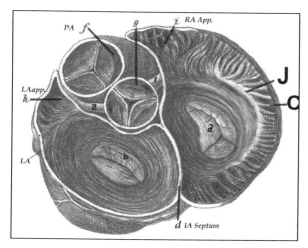

ANSWER: a. Pectinate muscles. The pectinate muscles are parallel ridges in the walls of the atria of the heart. They resemble the teeth of the comb. Pecten in Latin means comb. The pectinate muscles form parallel ridges in the walls of the atria. Like the trabeculae in the ventricle, these muscular ridges make it possible to anchor pacemaker leads in the heavily pectinated RA appendage. These pectinate muscles may be useful in increasing the power of RA contraction. Pectinate muscles make up the part of the atrial wall superior to the crista terminalis. See Gray's Anatomy

This diagram shows a superior view of the heart with vena cava and pulmonary veins removed. Note the pectinate muscles labeled with 'C' above the crista terminalis 'J.' Labeled structures are:

a. Tricuspid valve
b. Mitral Valve
c. Pectinate muscles of RA
d. Interatrial septum
e. -
f. Pulmonic valve
g. Aortic valve
1. RCA
2. LCA
h. LA appendage
I. RA appendage
j. Crista Terminalis

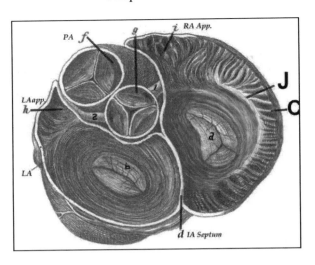

23. The vena cava has a smooth inner endothelial lining, but the RA is heavily pectinated. What RA structure separates smooth muscle from pectinated muscle?
   a. **Limbic ridge**
   b. **Crista terminalis**
   c. **Chordae tendineae**
   d. **Cavotricuspid isthmus**

ANSWER: b. Crista terminalis. "The line of union between the right atrium and the right auricle is present on the interior of the atrium in the form of a vertical crest, known as the crista terminalis. The crista terminalis is a smooth-surfaced, thick portion of heart muscle in a crescent shape at the opening into the right auricle. The Crista Terminalis provides the origin for the pectinate muscles" Because conduction does not usually occur across the crista terminalis, its location may be defined by identifying split potentials recorded from catheters placed on the lateral wall.

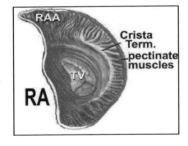

24. The main parasympathetic nerve that innervates the heart is the:
   a. **Phrenic**
   b. **Vagus**
   c. **Cardiac plexus**
   d. **Brachial plexus**

ANSWER b. The Vagus is the largest parasympathetic nerve of the heart. When a patient has a Vasovagal response or VAGAL discharge, this depressant system slows or "bradys" the patient's heart rate down. See: Berne and Levy, Chapter on "Regulation of the Heartbeat."

Conduction System:

1. To record the earliest depolarizations from the SA node, you should position the EP electrode near the RA _____ wall near the junction of the _____.
   a. **High lateral wall, CS**
   b. **High medial wall, CS**
   c. **High lateral wall, SVC**
   d. **High medial wall, SVC**

ANSWER: c. High lateral wall near junction of SVC. Fogoros says: "In the right atrium, catheters are most commonly positioned in the high lateral wall, near the junction of the superior vena cava. The position approximates the location of the SA node and is the region of the atrium depolarized earliest during normal sinus rhythm. Pacing from this area results in P wave configurations that are similar to normal sinus beats."
See: Fogoros chapter on Principles of the Electrophysiology Study

2. Bachman's bundle connects the?
   a. **RA to RV**
   b. **RA to LA**
   c. **CS to PV**
   d. **CS to RA**
   e. **RV free wall and RV septum**

ANSWER: b. RA - LA. Bachmann's bundle, also known as the anterior interatrial band, is a broad band of atrial muscle that runs just behind the ascending aorta and connects the top of the right atrium with the top of the left atrium. Bachmann's bundle is, during normal sinus rhythm, the preferential path for electrical activation of the left atrium. It is therefore considered as part of the atrial conduction system of the heart." The CS also provides rapid electrical conduction between inferior RA and LA. (Not shown) The moderator band connects the RV free wall and RV septum.

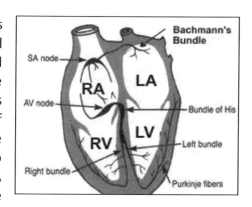

3. What are the two major electrical connections between the RA & LA?
   a. **Moderator band**
   b. **Bachman's bundle**
   c. **Coronary sinus**
   d. **Atrial appendages**

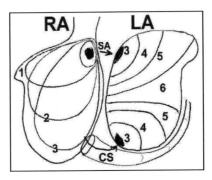

ANSWER b. Bachman's bundle; d. Coronary sinus. Moulton says, "it is readily apparent that one site is activated earlier than another. ...once the impulse wavefront is set into motion, it propagates as a single wavefront in all directions throughout the atria.... And remember, if there is no electrode pair there, you won't see that region's timing of activation." This drawing shows how those wave fronts are timed, and how the earliest activation of the LA is at #3 superior and inferior, Bachman's bundle and CS. See, Moulton, Electrophysiology Review Course

4. The SA node lies at the junction of the SVC and the _____.
   a. **Lateral end of Thebesian valve**
   b. **Lateral end Tendon of Todaro**
   c. **Superior end of Eustachian ridge**
   d. **Superior end of crista terminalis**

ANSWER d. Superior end of crista terminalis. The SA node lies near the superior Crista Terminalis at the anterior junction of the SVC and RA. "The sinus node is located near the superior anterolateral portion of the RA near the SVC junction and the superior end of the crista terminalis." See: Abedin chapter on Sinus Node

5. The SA nodal pacemaker is surrounded by a rim of tissue which _____.
   a. **Conducts slowly**
   b. **Conducts rapidly**
   c. **Blocks retrograde conduction**
   d. **Blocks antegrade conduction**

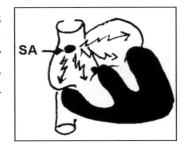

ANSWER: a. Conducts slowly. Fogoros says, "The SA node consists of a patch of pacemaker cells surrounded by a rim of perinodal tissue, which conducts electrical impulses slowly (similar to the AV node)." If this tissue conducts too slowly SA exit block may occur resulting in no P wave. See: Fogoros chapter on EP Testing for Bradyarrhythmias

6. Which fibers of the autonomic nervous system innervate the SA node?
   a. **Sympathetic**
   b. **Parasympathetic**
   c. **Both**
   d. **Neither**

ANSWER: c. Both. Heart rate goes either up and down, depending on sympathetic tone (speeds HR) and Parasympathetic tone (slows HR).

7. Compared to ventricular conduction system, the AV node richly supplied with:
   a. **Parasympathetic nerves**
   b. **Sympathetic nerves**
   c. **Coronary blood supply**
   d. **Collateral coronary blood supply**

ANSWER: a. Parasympathetic nerves. Vagal nerve discharge slows AV conduction, whereas the ventricles are sparsely supplied with parasympathetic fibers. Fogoros says: "Autonomic maneuvers offer an important method for localizing the site of AV block. This is true because the AV node has a rich autonomic (especially parasympathetic) innervation, whereas the distal conduction system does not. Maneuvers that decrease vagal tone or increase sympathetic tone can be expected to improve AV nodal block but not infranodal block. Maneuvers that increase vagal tone or decrease sympathetic tone will worsen AV nodal block but not infranodal block. These maneuvers are most helpful when Mobitz type I or 2:1 second degree block is present. If the level of block is at the AV node, exercise or atropine administration will usually result in resolution of the block. If the block is located in the His-Purkinje system, with exercise or atropine administration the AV block will usually not resolve and, in fact, the ratio of block often worsens to 3:1 or higher." See: Fogoros chapter on EP Testing for Bradyarrhythmias

8. The principal delay in the cardiac depolarization impulse as it passes from the SA Node to the ventricular myocardial cells occurs in the:
   a. **Atrial Muscle**
   b. **Specialized atrial conduction fibers**
   c. **AV node (upper regions AN-N)**
   d. **AV node (lower region – NH)**

ANSWER: c. The AV node (upper region) is where the principal AV delay occurs. The slowed conduction occurs in the upper ("AN" and "N") regions of the node. The conduction velocity here is ten times slower than in the Ventricular Purkinje cells. The proper AV delay (PR interval) allows the atrial kick to pack the ventricle with just enough blood (preload) before contraction to optimize systole. With increased sympathetic tone (E.g., exercise) the AV conduction speeds, and the PR interval shortens (dromotropism = increased AV conduction).

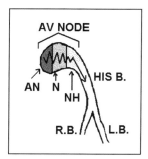

9. Which of the following is the normal conduction sequence after an electrical impulse has traveled through the AV node?
   a. **Bundle branches, Bachmann's bundle, Purkinje fibers**
   b. **Bundle branches, bundle of His, Purkinje fibers**
   c. **Bundle of His, bundle branches, Purkinje fibers**
   d. **Purkinje fibers, His bundle, AV junction**

ANSWER: c. Bundle of His, bundle branches, Purkinje fibers. The sequence is:
   1. SA node
   2. Inter-atrial tracts (including Bachmann's bundle)
   3. AV Node
      a. AN = Transitional tissue between Atria and AV Node.
      b. N = Mid AV nodal tissue (most of the AV time delay occurs in these upper two regions of the AV node)
      c. NH = region where nodal fibers gradually merge with bundle of His tissue.
      d. His = the upper portion of ventricular conduction tissue
   4. Bundle of HIS
   5. Right and Left Bundle branches (Left has two fascicles, ant. & post.)
   6. Purkinje System - to myocardium
See: Underhill, chapter on "Cardiac Electrophysiology."

10. Normal interventricular conduction proceeds from the bundle of HIS through three major fascicles. All of following are major interventricular fascicles EXCEPT the:
   a. **Right bundle branch**
   b. **Right posterior fascicle**
   c. **Left anterior fascicle**
   d. **Left posterior fascicle**

ANSWER: b. The right posterior is NOT one of the three major fascicles. The three branches of the conduction system are the: right bundle branch, left anterior fascicle, and left posterior fascicle. The two branches of the left bundle go to the two papillary muscles attached to the anterior and posterior mitral valve leaflets. This division of the left bundle into two is analogous to the 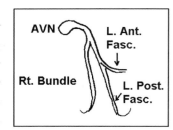 way the main left coronary divides into two major branches to supply the LV. There is also a common Main left bundle between the His and left fascicle division analogous to the left main coronary artery. As with the right coronary, the right bundle branch supplies the RV. See: Davis, Chapter on "IV conduction Abnormalities."

11. What is it called when one of the three conduction fascicles is blocked?
   a. **First degree block**
   b. **Unidirectional block**
   c. **Hemiblock**
   d. **Bifasicular block**

ANSWER: c. Hemiblock. If any one of these fascicles is blocked, it is a hemiblock. When any two fascicles become blocked, it is termed a bi-fascicular block. Any type of bundle branch block (BBB) prolongs the QRS complex and deviates the QRS axis from normal. A right bundle branch block is a type of hemiblock. See: Underhill, chapter on "Cardiac Electrophysiology."

Physiology:

1. Alterations in heart rate evoked by changes in blood pressure are dependent upon the baroreceptors located in the:
   a. **Circle of Willis**
   b. **Vertebral arteries**
   c. **Aortic arch and carotid sinuses**
   d. **Coronary sinus and Sinus of Valsalva**

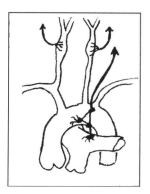

ANSWER: c. Aortic arch and carotid sinuses. Baro means pressure. Pressure receptors in the carotid sinuses and aortic arch regulate the blood pressure by sensing the pulsations regardless of body position, blood volume, or contractility, etc. Rubbing the carotid sinus is the main vagal maneuver (CSM).

The chemoreceptors (O2, CO2, & pH) are in the same general areas as the baroreceptors - the carotid and aortic bodies. See: Berne & Levy, Chapter on "Regulation of the Heartbeat."

2. The naturally occurring neurotransmitter liberated at the parasympathetic nerve junctions is:
   a. **Adrenalin**
   b. **Norepinephrine**
   c. **Atropine**
   d. **Acetylcholine**

ANSWER: d. Acetylcholine is the naturally occurring neurotransmitter liberated at parasympathetic neural junctions. From the word "ACETYLCHOLINE" comes the word "CHOLINERGIC" which refers to parasympathetic system of depressant nerves. Cholinergic sites may also be called "Muscarinic." Acetylcholine's effect is to stimulate the parasympathetic receptors that decrease the heart rate and as a result lower BP. Overstimulation of the vagal nerve leads to over-secretion of acetylcholine, overstimulation of the cholinergic/Muscarinic receptors, and finally a "vasovagal reaction. "
See: Berne and Levy, Chapter on "Regulation of the Heartbeat."

3. The two primary cardiac responses associated with a PARASYMPATHETIC neural discharge are ____ heart rate and _____.
    a. Increased HR, Increase AV Conduction
    b. Increased HR, Reduced AV Conduction
    c. Reduced HR, Increased AV Conduction
    d. Reduced HR, Reduced AV Conduction

ANSWER: d. Reduced HR, reduced AV conduction. The vagus nerve inhibition is mainly supraventricular. It depresses the SA node, atrial myocardium, & AV conduction. It's depressing effect on ventricular myocardium is less pronounced. That is why a vagal response usually appears initially as bradycardia and only later as low BP or hypotension. See: Berne and Levy, Chapter on "Regulation of the Heartbeat."

4. Which <u>two</u> of the following would be most likely to cause the vasovagal reaction shown?
    a. Pain
    b. Patient anxiety
    c. Dyspnea
    d. Cyanosis

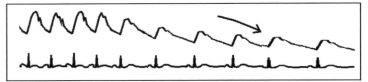

ANSWER: a. Pain, b. patient anxiety. An anxious patient is ripe for a vasovagal or bradycardia reaction. Relaxing and preparing most patients for invasive procedures includes premedication with sedatives and/or hypnotics. The first painful needle sticks (before Lidocaine has taken effect) or holding pressure at the arterial puncture site may trigger this bradycardia. Be able to match all answers above.
See: Braunwald's paragraph on "vagal reactions" in his chapter on "Heart Catheterization."
& Todd, Ch. F6,

5. Increased vagal tone causes: (Note: + indicates increasing)
    a. + Inotropism, + Chronotropism
    b. + Inotropism, - Chronotropism
    c. - Inotropism, - Chronotropism
    d. - Inotropism, + Chronotropism

ANSWER: c. - Inotropism, - Chronotropism. The vagal system is the depressor or vegetative system. When vagal nerve tone increases all cardiac function parameters decrease. The heart slows (-chronotropism), conducts slower (- dromotropism), and the atria decreases their force of contraction (- inotropism). The ventricular contractility does not change much because there are very few parasympathetic receptors there. These result in lower CO and BP. The balance between these two opposing systems (sympathetic and parasympathetic) determines the HR, PR interval, and dP/dT.
See: Berne and Levy, Chapter on "Regulation of the Heartbeat."& Todd, Ch. F6,

6. What autonomic neural effect would result in the greatest tachycardia?
   a. Sympathetic stimulation & Parasympathetic stimulation
   b. Sympathetic stimulation & Parasympathetic blocked
   c. Sympathetic blocked & Parasympathetic stimulation
   d. Sympathetic blocked & Parasympathetic blocked

ANSWER: b. Sympathetic stimulation & Parasympathetic blocked - for example, if both epinephrine and atropine were given together. Both stimulate the heart rate, but by different mechanisms. Epinephrine stimulates the sympathetic system (fight or flight response) and may result in tachycardia. In contrast, parasympathetic nerve stimulation slows the heart rate (vasovagal effect). But when atropine is administered, this depressor system is blocked, resulting in exaggeration of the tachycardia.

In contrast, sympathetic blocking & parasympathetic stimulation would result in bradycardia. It is the balance of these two systems in a push-pull relationship that determines the overall autonomic effect. This push-pull of the two systems is like a car, with the brake (parasympathetic) and gas pedals (sympathetic). The greatest speed would be from releasing the brake and pressing the gas pedals. See: Alexander, Human Anatomy and Physiology, chapter on "Nervous System"

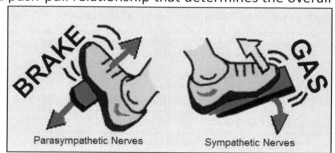

7. What is the effect of pressing on the neck at the junction of the internal and external carotid arteries (carotid sinus massage)?
   a. + Chronotropic
   b. – Chronotropic
   c. Cholinergic
   d. + Adrenergic

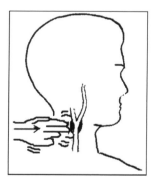

ANSWER: b. - (Negative) Chronotropic. "Chrono" means "time" (as in chronometer). Thus "negative chronotropic" means slowing of heart rate. Pressure on the baroreceptor in the neck fakes them into thinking the blood pressure is high. This stimulates a parasympathetic vagal response and slows the heart rate. For this reason, the use of vagal maneuvers may break supraventricular tachycardias. Other activities that increase vagal tone are eye rubbing, carotid sinus massages, Valsalva, nausea, vomiting and endotracheal intubation. These maneuvers may depress the SA & AV node enough to break supraventricular tachycardia, sometimes a desired side effect.

Chrono = Heart Rate or Speed
Dromo = AV conduction or PR interval
Ino = Contractility or dP/dT
See: Braunwald's chapter on "Heart Catheterization."

8. Inspiration normally causes _____ heart rate and _____ RV stroke volume.
   a. **Increased HR, Increased SV**
   b. **Increased HR, Decreased SV**
   c. **Decreased HR, Decreased SV**
   d. **Decreased HR, Increased SV**

ANSWER: a. Increases its rate and increases RV stroke volume. Marked cyclic variation in heart rate with breathing is called "Sinus Arrhythmia." With inspiration more blood is sucked into the RA, thus increasing venous return. The Bainbridge stretch receptors in the RA then cause reflexive drop in vagal tone which speeds the heart rate. This is seen while monitoring PA pressures. Remember, inspiration causes both the diaphragm and blood pressure to drop. Within seconds venous return, HR, and CO increase.

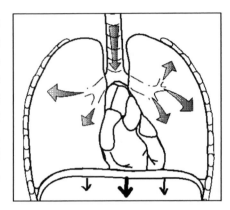

Deep inspirations drop the negative pressure in the thorax and may double venous return. The Starling mechanism then stimulates the heart to pump harder and increase the RV stroke volume. This respiratory pump is the "auxiliary venous pump." Inspiration thus dramatically increases both the rate and output of the heart. This effect reverses on expiration. Heart rate and stroke volume drop. The venous valves prevent reflux of blood back into the veins. See: Berne and Levy, Chapter on "Electrical activity of the heart.

9. Inspiration normally results in an immediate _____ in intracardiac pressure and a/an _____ in venous return.
   a. **Increase, Increase**
   b. **Increase, Decrease**
   c. **Decrease, Increase**
   d. **Decrease, Decrease**

ANSWER: c. Decreased, Increased.

The intracardiac pressures all drop immediately by the amount of the negative inhalation. Pressures drop with the diaphragm. This negative pressure sucks blood into the thorax and RA with inspiration and increases venous return. It also reflexively increases the heart rate. Within a few seconds the increased venous return will increase the output of the left heart and BP (unless followed immediately by another inspiration).

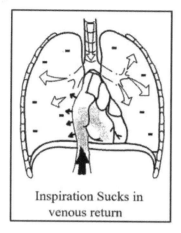

Inspiration Sucks in
venous return

10. Trace the normal flow of blood after it leaves the RA.
   a. **RA, TV, PA, PV, RV**
   b. **RA, TV, RV, PV, PA**
   c. **RA, PV, RV, TV, PA**
   d. **RA, RV, TV, PV, PA**

ANSWER: b. Right atrium through tricuspid valve, to right ventricle, through the pulmonic valve into the pulmonary artery and finally the lungs. These forward flow patterns are important to know. The bronchial arteries supply lung tissue and dump it into the PV. The Coronary circulation dumps into the RA. See: Underhill, chapter on "Cardiac Anatomy."

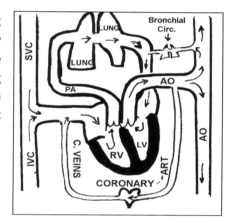

11. Most ventricular filling results from:
   a. **Closure of the AV Valves**
   b. **Opening of the semilunar valves**
   c. **Active atrial contraction**
   d. **Initial rapid inflow**

ANSWER: d. Initial rapid inflow. Most (60%) of the filling volume enters due to diastolic recoil of the ventricle. This rapid filling is the "suction cup effect." Although the pressure does not actually go negative, the ventricle recoils like the release of a suction cup, drawing in blood from the atria.

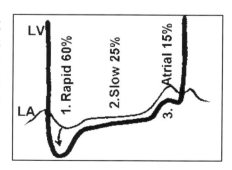

The phases of diastolic filling are:
   • Rapid inflow: Suction cup effect, 60%
   • Diastasis: Slow inflow, 25%

- Atrial kick: Active filling, 15-20%

See: Braunwald, chapter on "Cardiac Catheterization -pressures."

12. When a patient goes from sinus rhythm into atrial fibrillation and the heart rate stays the same, the cardiac output should:
   a. **Increase 5-10%**
   b. **Increase 15-25%**
   c. **Stay the same.**
   d. **Decrease 5-10%**
   e. **Decrease 15-20%**

ANSWER: e. Decrease 15-20% with loss of atrial kick. During diastole, atrial contraction kicks 15-20% more blood into the filling ventricle. Loss of P waves and atrial kick drops the cardiac output by the same amount. When a patient suddenly goes into atrial fibrillation and loses atrial kick, the stroke volume and cardiac output will drop 15-20%.

This phenomenon is ventricular pacemaker patients in bradycardia. When the pacemaker begins firing, the heart rate may increase. Because the patient loses atrial kick these patients may feel worse with VVI pacing. This is called pacemaker syndrome. These patients benefit from modern DDD pacemakers which assure AV synchrony. In the diagram, AF usually has more variability of RR intervals than shown. See: Underhill, chapter on "The Cardiac Cycle."

13. How does a PVC normally affect blood pressure? The systolic BP associated with the PVC will _____ in pressure, and the following sinus beat will _____.
   a. **Increase, Decrease**
   b. **Increase, Increase**
   c. **Decrease, Decrease**
   d. **Decrease, Increase**

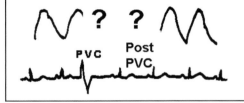

ANSWER: d. PVC BP decreases, Post PVC BP increases. The long compensatory pause following the PVC allows for more LV filling and thus a stronger ejection according to Starlings law. Patients normally don't feel PVCs - but instead the large surge of blood pumped during the post-PVC beat.
See: Braunwald, chapter on "Electrocardiography."

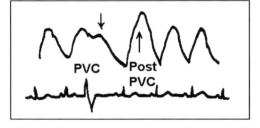

14. The second heart sound is caused by closure of what two valves?
   a. **Mitral and Tricuspid**
   b. **Mitral and Aortic**
   c. **Aortic and Pulmonic**
   d. **Pulmonic and Tricuspid**

ANSWER: c. Aortic and Pulmonic. The closure of semilunar valves is the main cause of the second heart sound. Each semilunar valve has a distinct component of the second heart sound. Understand the causes and components of all four heart sounds.
See: Braunwald chapter on "Heart Sounds and Murmurs."

15. Closure of the AV valves produces the:
   a. **First heart sound - S1**
   b. **Second heart sound - S2**
   c. **Third heart sound - S3**
   d. **Forth heart sound - S4**

ANSWER: a. The first heart sound (S1) begins in systole. The AV valves snap shut, followed immediately by the semilunar valves opening. Be able to label and describe all four phases of the heart sounds, as well as the abnormal murmurs, valvular clicks, and snaps. Relate each to the phases of the cardiac cycle. See: Braunwald's chapter on "Heart Sounds."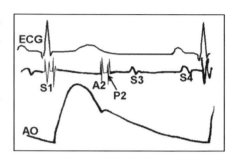

16. The amount of blood pumped from each ventricle during a single systole is the:
   a. **Cardiac output**
   b. **Cardiac index**
   c. **Stroke volume**
   d. **Stroke index**

ANSWER: c. Stroke volume is the amount of blood the heart pumps with each beat. This is calculated from the Cardiac Output (CO) and Heart Rate (HR) SV = CO/HR
E.g.: (4900 ml/min) / (70 beats/min) = 70 ml/beat
Stroke index is the stroke volume adjusted for the body size. It is stroke volume divided by the person's body surface   area. SI = SV/BSA. See: Kern, chapter on "Hemodynamics."

17. The formula to calculate cardiac output from hemodynamic data is:
   a. **CO = (LVEDP) x SVR**
   b. **CO = SV / EDV**
   c. **CO = SV x HR**
   d. **CO = HR x mean BP**

ANSWER: c. CO = SV x HR. Stroke volume times heart rate. Since SV is the amount pumped per beat, and HR is the number of beats/min, the product is the amount pumped/min. SV is measured in ml/beat, HR in beats/min. CO = SV ml/beat x HR b/min = ml/min
To change into L/min, divide by 1000 ml/L. E.g., CO = SV x HR = (70 ml/beat) x (70 beats/min) / (1000 ml/L) = 4.9 L/min. The cardiac output divided by the person's body surface area gives the cardiac index. CI = CO/BSA. See: Braunwald, Chapter on "Evaluation of LV Function."

18. These Starling curves are from a patient in CHF. He is at point A. and is experiencing symptoms of mild dyspnea. Which management regimen below would move him to point #1 on the curve?
   a. **VOLUME EXPANSION: or increased salt intake**
   b. **DECOMPENSATION: continued deterioration**
   c. **DIURETIC: or Na restricted diet**
   d. **DIGITALIS: or another inotropic drug**

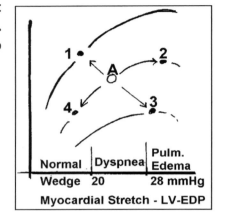

ANSWER d. DIGITALIS: or another inotropic drug such as Dobutamine. The vertical axis of these curves is CO or SV. Each Starling curve represents one contractile state for a patient. This state is determined by the strength of their myocardium (Energy state) and the size of their heart. Large baggy hearts are poorly contractile. Inotropic drugs move a patient from a lower to a higher curve. Giving fluid moves a patient to the right along one curve. These curves can be divided into four quadrants called the "Forrester Subsets" described below.

DIGITALIS - Increased Contractility: or other inotropic drug such as a catecholamine. This will move him to a higher contractile state - a whole higher "supercharged" curve. Dig. will move up the CO and down the wedge pressure which will help the dyspnea. Subset #1.

VOLUME EXPANSION - Increased Preload: or increased salt intake, venoconstriction, continued IV infusions. These do not move him to a new contractile state - only moves up the preload along the same curve to point #2. This may increase CO slightly but also moves up the wedge pressure above the acute pulmonary edema point. Subset #2.

DECOMPENSATION- Decreased contractility and continued deterioration - no therapy. Point #3 is at the peak of this lower LV function curve. Therapy would include cardiotonic drugs to increase contractility. Changing fluid status would only move this patient down to a lower CO on the curve. Subset #3.

DIURETIC - decreased preload: or Na restricted diet or venodilator to pool venous blood away from the main circulating volume. Moving down the same contractility curve will reduce wedge pressure and CO. The patient will breathe better but may feel more tired. Subset #4. Note how the best therapy may be to combine #one (Digitalis) with #4 (Diuretic). This would move the patient to the higher curve and move him down that curve to a new point not shown on the diagram, but on the far left of the upper curve. Know these abnormalities of the Starling curve, as therapy is based on it. See: Underhill, chapter on "Heart Failure" Todd, Vol. I, Chapter on Frank Starling curves

19. What is the end-diastolic filling or stretching of the ventricle?
   a. **Preload**
   b. **Afterload**
   c. **Inotropism**
   d. **Chronotropism**

ANSWER a. Preload refers to the filling of the ventricular chambers in diastole. The more you stretch it (like a rubber band) the harder it will contract. This relationship is the "Starling's Law."
   • Preload = filling (rubber band stretch)
   • Afterload = Resistance
   • Dromotropism = Conduction
   • Inotropism = Contractility
   • Chronotropism = HR   See: Underhill, chapter on "CV Physiology."

20. LV preload occurs entirely during:
   a. **Atrial systole**
   b. **Atrial diastole**
   c. **Ventricular systole**
   d. **Ventricular diastole**

ANSWER: d. ventricular diastole. Diastolic filling is the ventricle is preload. How much the LV is stretched determines how hard it will contract. Just like a rubber slingshot - the more it is stretched the harder it shoots. The LV filling occurs throughout diastole. Atrial kick contributes only a fraction of the LV filling volume and occurs only during the last part of ventricular filling.
See: Medical Dictionary.

21. Cardiac filling pressure (CVP) increases with: (Select all true statements)
   a. **Contracting the calf muscles**
   b. **Sympathetic vasomotor activity**
   c. **Standing to an upright position**
   d. **Hemorrhage**
   e. **Exercise**

ANSWERS: 1, 2, 5. Anything that increases venous return into RA increases central venous pressure (CVP) and preload. CVP is the same as RA mean pressure.
T - The calf muscle pump shifts venous blood into the thorax, raising CVP.
T - Sympathetic venoconstriction shifts flood into the central veins and thorax, raising CVP.

F - By standing upright, gravity distends the veins in the lower body, shifting blood out of the thorax into the legs and lowering CVP.

F - Blood volume is a major determinant of CVP, because two-thirds of the blood is in the venous system. A fall in blood volume therefore reduces CVP.

T - The calf muscle pump, sympathetic discharge, and peripheral venoconstriction together increase the central blood volume, which increases the diastolic filling pressure. This increases cardiac output according to Starlings law.

See: Berne and Levy, Chapter on "Cardiac Pump." > CVP

22. What is the intrinsic ability of the heart to contract with a particular intensity?
   a. Inotropism
   b. Dromotropism
   c. Chronotropism
   d. Psychotropism

ANSWER: a. Inotropism. Positive Inotropic effect defines this state of "hyped up" chemical contractility that can be induced by cardiotonic and catecholamine drugs. E.g., digitalis, epinephrine, and Dobutamine. Remember the term "contractility" is reserved for these chemical effects. Increased preload increases the force of contraction but not the "contractility" because it is not a chemical effect. See: Todd's CV Review Book: Vol. I chapter on "Hemodynamics."

23. What is the intrinsic ability of heart muscle and automatic tissue to generate its own depolarization?
   a. Inotropism
   b. Chronotropism
   c. Rhythmicity
   d. Automaticity

ANSWER: d. Automaticity causes heart tissue to beat regularly. Even when removed from the heart, and placed in a nutrient bath, heart tissue regularly depolarizes itself. Normally the sinus node tissue beats the fastest (60 bpm) and cardiac muscle tissue the slowest (40 bpm). Occasionally an ectopic focus will trigger tachycardia - all due to automaticity. See: Braunwald chapter on "Electrocardiography"

24. If all other factors are constant, INCREASING _____ will DECREASE Cardiac Output. (Note: Inversely relationship)
   a. Preload
   b. Afterload
   c. Contractility
   d. Heart Rate

ANSWER: b. Afterload. These all will increase the CO except afterload. The higher the afterload the lower the stroke volume. Afterload is the force opposing the ejection of blood. Note the inverse relationship - the heavier the load the slower it moves.

Nitroglycerine and other vasodilators relax the arterioles and reduce the load on the LV (usually by lowering BP). This allows the heart to work less. Whereas vasoconstrictor drugs such as Neo-Synephrine and Dopamine increase the load on the LV and thus increase cardiac work (usually by raising BP). Afterload is measured by the SVR. The Systemic Vascular Resistance equation shows this inverse relationship between afterload (resistance) and CO.

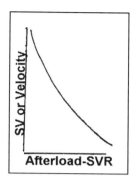

SVR = BP/CO

Note: this equation is like Ohm's law R=V/I.

See: Underhill, chapter on CV Physiology (role of afterload).

25. What is an increase in the contractile state of the sarcomere usually caused by a stimulant such as epinephrine (adrenalin)?
   a. - Inotropism
   b. + Inotropism
   c. - Preload
   d. + Preload

ANSWER: b. + inotropism. Cardiotonic and catecholamine drugs induce a state of augmented cardiac contractility. E.g., digitalis, epinephrine, and Dobutamine. Contractility represents the performance of the heart at a given preload and afterload. Positive Inotropic effect defines this increased "hyped up" chemical state of contractility. I liken this "hyped up state" to Popeye's super-powers when he gulps down his can of spinach. See: Berne and Levy, chapter on, "Cardiac Pump."

26. Most physiologic measurements are adjusted to a patient's body size (indexed) by:
   a. Multiplying it times body surface area (BSA)
   b. Dividing it the body surface area (BSA)
   c. Multiplying it times body weight in Kg.
   d. Dividing it by body weight in Kg.

ANSWER: b. By dividing it by the body surface area (BSA) you will have the index. Most physiological measurements increase as the size of the person increases. Indexing adjusts the measurement for comparison to a normal population of people irrespective of body size. For example, cardiac output (CO) adjusted to body size is termed cardiac Index (CI). It is simply cardiac output divided by the person's body surface area: BSA is a more accurate index of body size than just weight alone. Any term with the word "index" behind it means it was divided by BSA. Some hemodynamic measures are not indexed, such as: HR, BP, and ratios such as Qp/Qs. See: Braunwald, Chapter on "Evaluation of LV Function." Physiology & Pathophysiology

27. LV contractility is a measure of the hearts_____ state.
   a. Chronotropic
   b. Barotropic
   c. Chemotropic
   d. Inotropic
   e. Dromotropic

ANSWER: d. Inotropic. Another way to say this is, the inotropic state is the intrinsic ability of the heart to contract harder. Contractility is occasionally misinterpreted to mean increased force or velocity of contraction. Many things influence the force of contraction (preload, afterload...), but only the inotropic state influences myocardial contractility.
See: Braunwald, chapter on "Assessment of Cardiac Function."

28. At peak exercise, a normal individual's mean blood pressure may not significantly elevate, even though CO may increase up to seven times. This regulation of BP on exercise is due to _____ vascular resistance.
   a. Increased systemic
   b. Decreased systemic
   c. Increased pulmonary
   d. Decreased pulmonary

ANSWER: b. Decrease systemic vascular resistance (↓SVR). With exercise, the increase in CO will raise the BP, unless peripheral vasodilation occurs. Because BP = CO X SVR, to keep a constant BP while the CO increases seven times, the SVR must decrease by a factor of seven. This peripheral vasodilation allows blood to pass the capillary bed more easily and not significantly elevate the BP. Note that the pulmonary resistance (PVR) primarily affects PA pressure, whereas systemic resistance (SVR) affects the systemic BP. The BP equation above is a variation on Ohms law. See: Berne & Levy section on exercise.

CO=18 L/min
BP=130/80

29. Trained athletes have a lower resting heart rate than nonathletes; because of:
   a. Increase parasympathetic tone to SA node.
   b. Decreased sympathetic tone to SA node.
   c. Decreased intrinsic SA node rate.
   d. Decreased humoral epinephrine.

ANSWER: c. Decreased intrinsic SA note rate associated with longer repolarization time and lower slope of phase four. Zipes says, "As is well known, trained athletes have a lower heart rate than nonathletes; this is solely the result of a decrease in the intrinsic heart rate, rather than an increase in parasympathetic tone. .... The explanation of the difference in the intrinsic heart rate is training induced differences in ion channel expression in the SA node." See: Zipes chapter on the SA Node.

30. The hemodynamic effect of increasing a patient's peripheral vascular resistance is to: (Assume constant CO)
   a. Increased BP
   b. Decreased BP
   c. Increased HR
   d. Decreased HR

ANSWER: a. increased BP. The formula BP = CO X SVR demonstrates the direct proportionality between CO and SVR. If CO doubles so does BP. If resistance doubles so does BP. That is why administration of vasoconstrictors raises the BP. Therefore, kinking a hose increases its pressure, and it may rupture.

The resistance is normally closely regulated by the baroreceptor reflex, through vasoactivity. Reflexes also regulate the CO by alerting the HR and SV. For example, the SVR lowers in exercise to allow increased blood flow with only slight elevation of the BP. Note that this is also a rearranged Ohm's Law (V=IR) for fluids where:
BP = aortic mean Pressure = Voltage
Q = Cardiac Output = Electric Current flow
See: Berne & Levy, chapter on "Hemodynamics."

Chapter 2
<u>ECG Foundation</u>

EP Essentials LLC

Waves & Measurements

1. **Match each segment, wave or interval labeled in the diagram with its name.**
   a. **P wave**
   b. **ST segment**
   c. **PR interval**
   d. **R wave**
   e. **RS (QRS)**
   f. **QT interval**
   g. **T wave**
   h. **S wave**

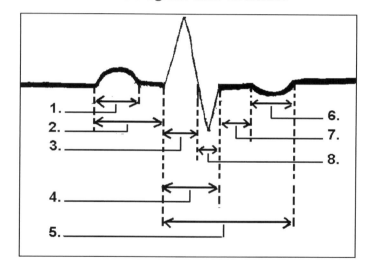

CORRECTLY MATCHED ANSWERS ARE:
   1. a. P wave
   2. c. PR interval
   3. d. R wave (is always above the baseline)
   4. e. RS (QRS) is always above then below the baseline
   5. f. QT interval
   6. g. T wave (this is a negative T wave)
   7. b. ST segment
   8. h. S wave (is always below the baseline)

Note: QT interval. Note that ECG "intervals" are combinations of "waves" plus "segments." E.g., QT interval = QRS waves + ST segment + "T" wave. See: Davis, Chapter on "IV Determination of HR and Normal Heart Rhythms."

2. **Each wave on a QRS complex has a name. Match each QRS complex with how it would be named?**
   a. **QR**
   b. **QRS**
   c. **QRSR'**
   d. **QS**
   e. **RS**

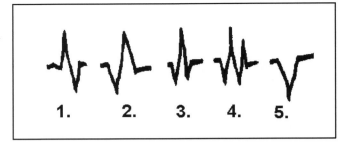

CORRECTLY MATCHED ANSWERS ARE:
1. e. RS
2. a. QR
3. b. QRS
4. c. QRSR'
5. d. QS

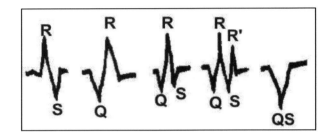

The "Q" wave is the first negative deflection, the "S" wave is the second. "R" is the first positive deflection, R' the second, R" the third, etc. In addition, some authors use upper- and lower-case letters to show the relative size of the complexes. Classic rSR' is termed "rabbit ears" and is seen in RBBB. A "QS" complex has both negative waves rolled into one single negative deflection. See: Davis, Chapter on "IV Determination of HR and Normal Heart Rhythms."

3. **On this magnified ECG, measure the PR interval.**
   a. **0.06 seconds**
   b. **0.10 seconds**
   c. **0.14 seconds**
   d. **0.18 seconds**

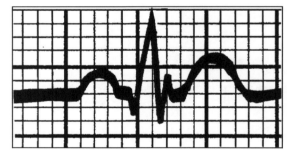

ANSWER: c. 0.14 seconds. Measure from the beginning of the "P" wave to the beginning of the QRS and find 3.5 boxes. Each box is .04 sec. interval = 3.5 x .04 = .14 sec. PR interval is key to evaluating AV node conduction. Normal Adult PR interval = .12 - 2.0 sec. See: Davis, Chapter on "IV Determination of HR and Normal Heart Rhythms."

4. **On this magnified ECG measure the QRS duration.**
   a. **0.08 seconds**
   b. **0.12 seconds**
   c. **0.16 seconds**
   d. **0.24 seconds**

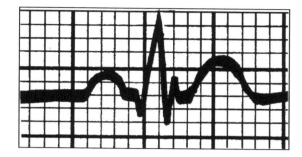

ANSWER: b. 0.12 seconds. From the beginning of the Q wave to the end of the R' wave there are three boxes (leading edge to leading edge). Interval = # boxes x .04 sec/box = 3 x .04 = .12 sec. QRS duration is key to evaluating abnormally conducted ventricular complexes. Normal Range for QRS duration in the limb leads is 0.04 - 0.10 sec. See: Davis, chapter on "ECG Graph Paper and Measurements."

5. **On this magnified ECG measure the R wave voltage:**
   a. **0.6 mV**
   b. **1.0 mV**
   c. **1.6 mV**
   d. **3.2 mV**

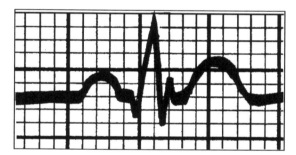

ANSWER: a. 0.6 mV. Voltage is measured vertically. Remember the calibration signal is 1 mV = 1 cm. Each small box is 0.1 mV. The "R" wave deflects six boxes above the baseline or 0.6 mV. R wave voltage is key to evaluating hypertrophy of a chamber. See: Davis, chapter on "ECG Graph Paper and Measurements."

6. **Taken on a standard ECG, measure this R wave.**
   a. **1.5 mV by 0.08 seconds**
   b. **1.5 mV by 0.12 seconds**
   c. **15 mV by 0.04 seconds**
   d. **15 mV by 0.12 seconds**

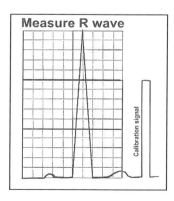

Measure R wave

Calibration signal

ANSWER: a. 1.5 mV by 0.08 sec. Standard ECG paper runs at 25 mm/sec. Each small 1 mm box is 0.4 sec wide and 0.1 mV high. This R wave is fifteen boxes or 1.5 mV, and two boxes wide for 0.08 sec. The calibration signal is normally 1 mV that deflects 10 mm on the paper.

7. **On a standard ECG an R wave that is 1 cm high and four boxes wide measures:**
    a. **mV by 0.12 seconds**
    b. **mV by 0.16 seconds**
    c. **mV by 0.12 seconds**
    d. **mV by 0.16 seconds**

ANSWER: d. 1.0 mV by 0.16 seconds. 1 cm = 10 mm = 10 mm x 0.1 mv/mm = 1 mv
4 boxes x 0.04 sec/box = 0.16 (This is a wide QRS since normal is < 0.12 sec)

8. **On this ECG, measure the cycle length and heart rate.**
    a. **700 ms, 70 bpm**
    b. **860 ms, 70 bpm**
    c. **920 ms, 60 bpm**
    d. **1025 ms, 60 bpm**

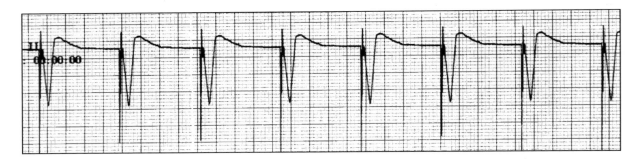

ANSWER: b. 860 ms., 70 bpm. There are 21.5 boxes between spikes. (21.5 boxes) x (40 ms/box) = 860 ms. which is a rate of 70 beats/min. Rate = 60,000/RR interval. Rate = 60,000/ (860) = 70 bpm. This strip shows ventricular pacing since pacemaker artifacts (negative spikes) precede each QRS complex. Whether it is rate or ms you want, always divide into sixty thousand - the number of milli-Seconds in a minute. See: Underhill, Chapter on "Electrocardiography..."

9. **Convert a heart rate of 250 bpm into its cycle length in milliseconds?**
    a. **150 ms**
    b. **185 ms**
    c. **240 ms**
    d. **280 ms**

ANSWER: c. 240 ms. Whether you want bpm or ms, you always divide into 60,000, the number of milliseconds in a minute. Here: 60,000 /250 = 240 ms., Formula is CL = 60,000/heart rate. Whether it is rate or ms you want, always divide into sixty thousand - the number of milliseconds in a minute.

10. **Convert a 620 ms cycle length into beats per minute?**
    a. **62 bpm**
    b. **97 bpm**
    c. **103 bpm**
    d. **372 bpm**

ANSWER: b. 97 bpm. Whether you want bpm or ms, you always divide into 60,000, the number of milliseconds in a minute. Here: 60,000 / 620 = 97 bpm. Formula is HR = 60,000/CL

11. **How is the standard corrected QT interval calculated (Bazett's formula)?**
    a. **QT x square root of RR interval in sec.**
    b. **QT x RR interval in sec**
    c. **QT / square root of RR interval in sec.**
    d. **QT / RR interval in sec.**

ANSWER c. QT / square root of RR interval in sec. A lengthened QT interval is a biomarker for ventricular tachyarrhythmias like torsades de pointes and a risk factor for sudden death. QT interval and VERP both measure length of the ventricular action potential. They are dependent on the heart rate. The faster the heart rate the shorter the QT interval and ERP. This is termed peeling of refractoriness, the opposite of decremental conduction.

To figure out whether the QT is normal, we need to adjust it for heart rate. The standard clinical correction is to use Bazett's formula, where the QT interval is divided by the square root of the RR interval in seconds. If the HR = 60 bpm it is easy, because the RR=1 sec, and the square root of 1 is 1.

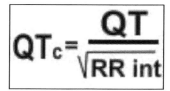

$$QTc = \frac{QT}{\sqrt{RR\ int}}$$

Another example: If QT = 480 ms and HR=100 bpm, then RR = 600 ms or 0.6 sec. The square root of 0.60 = 0.77 then QTc= 600 ms/0.77 = 779 ms. This is a long QT int. An abnormal QTc in males is a QTc above 450 ms, and in females, above 470 ms.

12. Match each ECG measurement to its normal value.

- a. <200 ms
- b. <120 ms
- c. <450 ms

1. PR Interval
2. QRS Duration
3. QTc

CORRECTLY MATCHED NORMALS ARE:

1.a. PR Interval: < 200ms. Longer is first-degree block.

2.b. QRS Duration: <120ms. Longer is BBB or PVC

3.c. QT Interval (QTc < 450 ms) Longer is Long QT syndrome (or Hypocalcemia)

13. Match the type of ambulatory monitoring device to its description:

1. **Records internal ECG continuously < two yrs., allows remote transmission of data.**
2. **Analyzes rhythm & transmits for analysis. Battery lasts about one month.**
3. **Must be activated by patient when they feel symptoms. Battery lasts about 1 month.**
4. **Stores all ECG data, battery lasts about 48 hours.**

- a. **Holter**
- b. **Event Recorder**
- c. **Real-time continuous**
- d. **Insertable loop recorder**

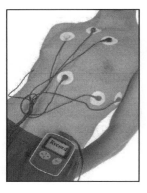

CORRECTLY MATCHED ANSWERS ARE:

1.d. Insertable loop recorder: Records internal ECG continuously <2 yrs., allows remote transmission of data.

2.c. Real-time continuous: analyzes rhythm & transmits for analysis. Battery lasts about 1 month.

3.b. Event recorder: (External) must be activated by patient when they feel symptoms. Battery lasts about 1 month.

4.a. Holter: Stores all ECG data, battery lasts about 48 hours.

See: (Circulation. 2010; Ambulatory Arrhythmia Monitoring, Choosing the Right Device, Peter Zimetbaum,

14. What anatomic landmark is consistently found at the second intercostal space and can be used to begin accurately counting the intercostal spaces for V lead placement?

- a. **Axilla**
- b. **Nipple**
- c. **Clavicle**
- d. **Angle of Louis**

ANSWER d. Angle of Louis. This is the junction between the manubrium and the sternum); so, count down two more spaces to the 4th ICS. Know how to place all 12 ECG leads using proper landmarks. Common mistakes include incorrect sternal space (start counting either from the clavicle or the angle of Louis), placing limb leads too medial (place below tip of clavicle, not mid clavicle), placing V4 & V5 on a woman's breast (place below breast, if they are large, as adipose tissue reduces voltage).

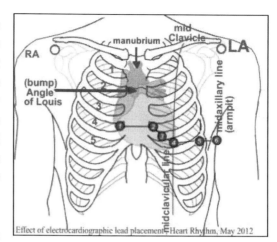

Effect of electrocardiographic lead placement Heart Rhythm, May 2012

- V1 is placed at the right sternal border fourth intercostal space.
- V2 is at the left sternal border fourth intercostal space.
  (Note, the second intercostal space can be found at the sternal bump termed the "angle of Louis." This is the junction between the manubrium and the sternum) So, count down two more spaces to the fourth intercostal space.
- V3 goes between V2 and V4. (So, first place V4)
- V4 is placed in the fifth intercostal space (mid-clavicular line).
- V5 goes between V4 and V6
- V6 is placed at the same level as V4 & V5 mid armpit (midaxillary). This is not actually in the fifth intercostal space.
- V6 is nearer the sixth intercostal space in the mid axillary line (armpit).
  See: Braunwald, chapter on ECG and Marriott, chapter on "Recording the ECG"

15. Where is precordial lead V4 placed?
   a. **Left Sternal Border 4th intercostal space**
   b. **Left Sternal Border 5th intercostal space**
   c. **Fourth intercostal space (midclavicular line)**
   d. **Fifth intercostal space (midclavicular line)**

ANSWER: d. 5th intercostal space (mid-clavicular line) is where V4 is placed. Some labs are so exact about placing these leads that they use a ruler to measure the length of the clavicle, and then divide that in half. Then use the ruler to go straight down to the fifth intercostal space. See diagram above. See: Braunwald, chapter on ECG

16. After having applied the ECG electrodes to a patient, lead I looks unusual as shown. The cause of this is usually:

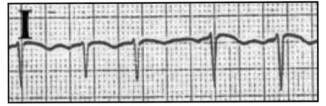

   a. Dextrocardia

   b. Atrial fibrillation

   c. ECG gain or paper speed error

   d. Right arm & left arm leads reversed

ANSWER: d. Right arm & left arm electrodes reversed. Lead I is the voltage measured between the two arms, with the left arm being positive. Lead I normally has an upright R wave configuration, but if the arm lead wires are reversed, where the left arm is incorrectly connected to the right arm electrode, the reading will be inverted. P waves and QRS will deflect downward, instead of upward. It's quite easy to recognize. To remember which lead goes to correct position remember, "White/right & smoke (black) over fire (red)" See: Dubin, Rapid Interpretation of ECGs.

17. How many lead wires or electrodes are used in taking a standard 12-lead ECG?

   a. 2

   b. 6

   c. 10

   d. 12

   e. 20

ANSWER: c. 10: RA, LA, RL, LL, V1-2-3-4-5-& V6. Count them. These are the ten wires and electrodes on the skin - four limb leads, and six chest leads. Various combinations of these give us the standard 12-lead ECG. See: Dubin, Rapid Interpretation of ECGs

18. How could you reduce the artifact seen on this ECG?

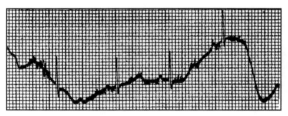

   a. **Relax and quiet the patient**

   b. **Check ground**

   c. **Increase the damping on the machine**

   d. **Move ECG limb electrodes distally**

ANSWER a. Relax and quiet the patient. This artifact is a somatic muscle tremor with wandering baseline due to motion. Make the patient comfortable and ask him to relax all over. If this does not eliminate the noise, the electrodes should be moved more proximally, onto the shoulders and hips after thoroughly prepping the skin. This noisy ECG signal can interfere with ECG interpretation.

See: Davis, chapter on "12-Lead ECG Interpretation." also, Todd, Vol. II, Chapter on "ECG."

19. Your patient's monitor alarm has just sounded. You come running and see this ECG. What do you do?
    a. **Defibrillate**
    b. **Call for help and begin CPR**
    c. **Awake the patient**
    d. **Check ECG electrodes**

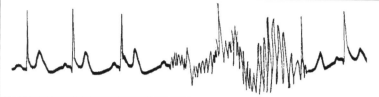

ANSWER: d. Check ECG electrodes and leads. This is a normal sinus rhythm disturbed by motion artifact. Noisy ECG artifacts may occur due to patient motion or a loose electrode. Although this artifact resembles Ventricular Fibrillation it returns to sinus rhythm at the end of the strip. No patient should be resuscitated or treated, based on the ECG alone. Treat the patient, not the monitor. See: ACLS Manual also, Todd, Vol. II, Chapter on "ECG."

20. You see a muscle tremor artifact on ECG leads I and II, but NOT on lead III. Which ECG electrode is causing this artifact?
    a. **Left arm**
    b. **Left leg**
    c. **Right arm**
    d. **Right leg**

ANSWER: c. Right Arm. The electrode resistance is increased on the right arm electrode. The RA is the only electrode common to lead I and II. Draw an Einthoven triangle and note how lead I and II intersect at the right arm. Try prepping that RA electrode to improve the artifact. Poor skin prep is the usual cause of ECG artifacts. With a roughening of the skin, removing hair, application of ECG prep, and checking that the electrodes have good contact with conductive paste, a good ECGs can even be obtained during exercise. Also, move the electrodes up to the shoulders, where arm motion will not be sensed.

Moulton says, "The cause can be narrowed down to either one of the two electrodes belonging to that lead... You may also see only two leads with artifact. Here, the cause is still usually a single electrode (or cable wire), but it is the one shared by both leads.... Problems showing up on an intracardiac channel is usually easier to solve and invariably due to a poor connection due to a broken wire (one of the two wires of the bipolar recording) or to a fault in the connection between the catheter, the connecting cable, or the jack into which the wire connects on the bedside pin box.... Sometimes a cable destined for a skin electrode is simply stretched to its limits and causes a tethering effect which generates artifact" See: Moulton, "Troubleshooting artifact"

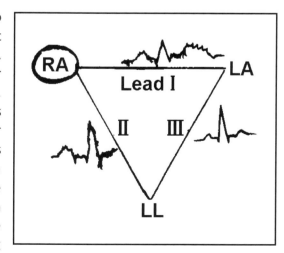

21. How many ECG leads does the implantable loop recorder monitor and record?
    a. 1
    b. 2
    c. 3
    d. 12

ANSWER: a. 1. An implantable loop recorder (ILR) is usually implanted under the left clavicle in a position for optimal P & QRS amplitude, leading to a single ECG lead, usually like ECG lead I. Its main advantage is that it can watch the patient for 2-3 years.

"Medtronic 9525 continuously monitors a single lead electrogram using two sensing electrodes 38 mm apart on the device shell.... The main advantage over conventional Holter monitoring or external loop recorders is that cardiac rhythm is monitored continuously until syncope recurs and the evidence implicating or excluding a cardiac arrhythmia is direct, despite syncope being infrequent and unpredictable." See: Seidl, et. Al., "Diagnostic assessment of recurrent unexplained syncope with a new subcutaneously implantable loop recorder" Europace (2000) 2, 256–262

22. The irregularity seen in the baseline of the ECG tracing below is:
    a. **DC interference**
    b. **AC (60 Hz) interference**
    c. **Muscle tremors**
    d. **Wandering baseline**

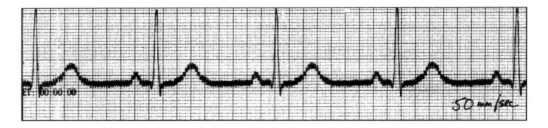

ANSWER: b. AC (60 Hz) interference. This is due to 60-cycle interference from such appliances as: electric motors (beds), transformers (fluorescent lights), or improper electrical ground. Turn off all electrical appliances close to the patient and check all machine grounding. On slower paper speeds this may appear as a very wide regular baseline. But if you look closely there are tiny sine wave vibrations within the baseline. A notch filter can eliminate frequencies at a certain frequency - like 60 Hz. See: Davis, chapter on "12-Lead ECG Interpretation.

23. From this ECG recorded with 0.1 second timelines, determine the heart rate:

a. 30 bpm
b. 45 bpm
c. 50 bpm
d. 56 bpm

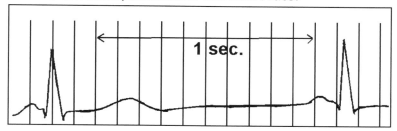

ANSWER b. 45 bpm. RR interval is 1.33 sec. If the paper speed is 100 mm/sec or the timelines are 0.1 as shown, it is EASY to calculate the RR interval and heart rate. Just use the timelines to count the RR time interval, as shown. Note how easily the 1.33 sec (1,330 ms) is measured on the graph. Know the formula: HR = 60/ R-R interval   or 60,000 ms/R-R in ms.
HR (beats/min) = 60 (sec/min) / R-R interval in (sec) HR = 60 sec/min /1.33 sec = 45 bpm
Note the unit cancellation resulting in beats/min.

You may include an ECG recorded at timelines 0.1 sec paper speed factor in the numerator to convert the R-R interval measurement from mm. to seconds. Then you can use a mm ruler to measure the paper speed and R-R interval.
HR (beats/min) = 60 (sec/min) x Paper speed (mm/sec)/ R-R (mm)
See: Grossman, chapter on "Assessing Valvular Stenosis."

ECG and Pathology:

1. The ECG changes most associated with transmural myocardial infarction is:

a. Pathologic Q-wave
b. Inverted T wave
c. Prolonged QT interval
d. Depressed ST segment

ANSWER: a. Pathologic Q waves appear in the first day of an MI. Although they may resolve with time, they usually remain on the ECG throughout the patient's life as telltale markers of the dead myocardium. Q waves are pathologic when they are significantly large - both deep and wide. Significant Q waves are seen in any of the first three V leads or if they are over >0.04 sec (1 box) in duration (or over ⅓ the height of the R wave) in leads I, II, aVL, aVF, V4, V5, or V6.

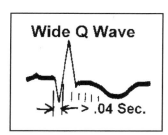

The negative Q wave means that the depolarization forces are traveling away from the electrode. Think of it as the infarcted dead tissue beneath the electrode as a window looking into the opposing LV wall. Through this window you are watching the remaining viable LV wall depolarize. Thus, Q wave vectors point away from the area of infarction. The term Q-wave infarct describes a significant transmural infarct with pathologic Q waves that remain even after the infarct has healed. See: Braunwald, chapter on "Electrocardiography."

2. In the progression of a myocardial infarction as seen on an ECG, the first sign of acute injury to the myocardial cells is seen as:
    a. **Inverted T waves**
    b. **An inverted QRS**
    c. **ST segment elevation**
    d. **Q waves of significant size**

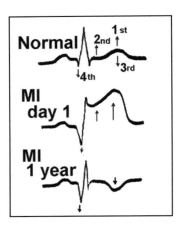

ANSWER: c. ST segment elevation is the first sign of acute injury to the myocardium. Sometimes called a current of injury because the cell wall is destroyed, and the ECG begins to resemble an action potential with ST elevation. Electrodes facing the injury register ST elevation. Those on the opposite side of the heart may register ST depression, termed reciprocal ST changes.

Some authors say that hyperacute T wave elevation is an even earlier sign than ST elevation. These hyperacute T waves are often tall and narrow and are termed peaked. The T waves flip and invert soon after the acute injury begins, signs of continued ischemia in the area around the injury. See: Dubin, chapter on "Infarction."

3. When a positive ECG electrode is placed over an area experiencing myocardial infarction, four basic patterns can be seen. Match each ECG pattern in the diagram with the condition of the myocardium near it.
    a. **Infarction**
    b. **Injury**
    c. **Ischemia**
    d. **Hyperacute ischemia**

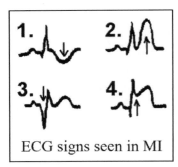

ECG signs seen in MI

CORRECTLY MATCHED ANSWERS ARE:
    1. Inverted T wave: c. ischemia
    2. T wave elevation/broadening: d. hyperacute ischemia
    3. Q waves: a. infarction
    4. ST elevation: b. injury

Q Waves must be deep and wide to be significant for MI (>1/3 the height of the QRS and >0.04 sec wide). Significant Q waves indicate a transmural infarction and remain on the ECG even after it scars over. No ECG lead normally displays large Q waves unless infarct or BBB is present.
See: Kern, chapter on "Electrophysiology."

4. All the following ECG changes are associated with CAD and myocardial infarction EXCEPT:
   a. Q waves
   b. Heart blocks
   c. Preexcitation
   d. ST depression
   e. T wave inversion

ANSWER: c. Preexcitation comes through accessory pathways that bypass the AV node and excite the ventricle early. Accessory pathways are normally congenital and not associated with MI.

5. Which of the following ECG changes results from acute myocardial INJURY?
   a. Pathologic Q-wave
   b. T wave inversion
   c. ST segment elevation
   d. ST segment depression

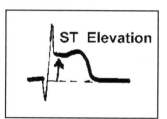

ANSWER c. Elevated ST segments signal an acute INJURY to the heart. ECG complexes with extreme ST elevation are termed "tombstones" because of their appearance and severity. They are seen in the first hours after MI, also during PTCA inflation. Injury is a reversible process that may lead to infarction if allowed to progress. IF this diagram were from lead II, it would signify acute inferior wall injury. STEMI patients are those with acute MI's that ST - Injury we rush to revascularize. See: Braunwald, chapter on "Electrocardiography"

6. Which of the following ECG changes results from myocardial ischemia?

1.	Pathologic Q-wave	a.	1, 2
2.	T wave inversion	b.	2, 3
3.	ST segment elevation	c.	2, 4
4.	ST segment depression	d.	3, 4

ANSWER c. T wave inversion, & ST segment depression. Ischemia is the lack of sufficient oxygenated blood to the LV. It shows on the ECG as symmetrically inverted T waves or ST depression.

Normally the T waves should be upright in all leads (except III, aVR, and V1). When inverted T waves are present in several leads it means that an infarction has occurred some time ago, how long is uncertain. It is neither an "acute" infarction or an "old" infarction but   Ischemic ↓T, ↓ST waves somewhere in between. These are termed "age indeterminate" inverted or ischemic T waves.

ST depression is a common symptom of ischemia on exercise. Treadmill testing relies heavily on ST depression markers. They may also be seen as reciprocal" ST changes of an acute MI. Remember the leads OVER an acute infarction show ST elevation. This forces the opposite leads beneath an infarction to be depressed. It's like looking at a vector from the opposite direction. It is going the other way. An acute inferior MI will show ST elevation in lead III, but inversion in lead aVL (which is an almost opposite lead direction). See: Davis, chapter on Ischemia, Injury, and Infarction.

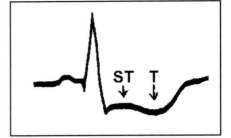

7. Match each abnormal ECG measurement with its most probable cause.

1.	Long PR Interval	a.	BBB or PVC
2.	Short PR Interval	b.	Hypocalcemia
3.	Long QRS Duration	c.	Hypercalcemia
4.	Long QT Interval	d.	First-degree heart block
5.	Short QT Interval	e.	WPW or LGL syndrome

CORRECTLY MATCHED ANSWERS:
1. Long PR Interval = d. First degree heart block
2. Short PR Interval = e. WPW or LGL Syndrome *
3. Long QRS Duration = a. BBB or PVC
4. Long QT Interval = b. Hypocalcemia**
5. Short QT Interval = c. Hypercalcemia

* WPW = Wolff-Parkinson-White. LGL = Long-Ganong-Levine. Both are preexcitation syndromes. This is a premature excitation of the ventricles. The sinus impulse is conducted into the ventricle through an AV bypass tract. Delta waves are seen in WPW sinus beats with a short PR interval.

HYPERCALCEMIA: Abnormal heart rhythms can result, and ECG findings of a short QT interval and a widened T wave suggest Hypercalcemia. Significant Hypercalcemia can cause ECG changes mimicking an acute myocardial infarction.
Hypercalcemia has also been known to cause an ECG finding mimicking hypothermia, known as an Osborn wave.

** HYPOCALCEMIA: QT prolongation, or intermittent prolongation of the QTc (corrected QT interval) on the ECG (electrocardiogram) is noted. The implications of intermittent QTc prolongation predisposes to life-threatening cardiac electrical instability (and this is therefore a more critical condition than constant QTc prolongation). This type of electrical instability puts the patient at elevated risk of torsades de pointes.
See: Davis, chapter on "IV Conduction Disturbances."

FIRST DEGREE BLOCK: Long PR interval (>0.20 sec) associated with slowed AV conduction.
BBB or PVC have long QRS duration (>0.12 sec) associated with slowed ventricular conduction.
BBB often shows an RSR' pattern. PVCs show a wide bizarre QRS, with T in opposite direction.

8. Match each tachycardia mechanism to an arrhythmia it causes.

1.	**Automatic**	a.	**AVRT**
2.	**Triggered**	b.	**RVOT**
3.	**Micro-reentry**	c.	**Junctional Escape**
4.	**Macro-reentry**	d.	**AVNRT**

CORRECTLY MATCHED ANSWERS ARE:
1. Automatic = c. Junctional Escape
2. Triggered = b. RVOT
3. Micro-reentry = d. AVNRT
4. Macro-reentry = a. AVRT

AVNRT is a small reentry loop conducted within or close to the AV node. Larger reentry loops like AFL and AVRT are termed macro-reentry. Junctional tachycardia is an automatic escape rhythm. RVOT is a triggered DAD arrhythmia.

9. Sick sinus syndrome is associated with _____.
 a. **Sinus bradycardia**
 b. **Sinus tachycardia**
 c. **A nodal (junctional) pacemaker escaping**
 d. **A ventricular pacemaker escaping**

ANSWER a. Sinus bradycardia. The term "Sick Sinus Syndrome" is loosely used to describe any severe bradycardia at rest that does not speed appropriately with exercise. Sick Sinus Syndrome (SSS) also has an absence of escape rhythms, so the rate may drop incredibly low. This SA node disease is often treated with an atrial (AAI or DDD) pacemaker. See: Marriott, Chapter on "Decreased Automaticity."

10. An OLD myocardial infarct is seen on the ECG as a significant:
 a. **Q wave**
 b. **Inverted T wave**
 c. **Elevated ST segment**
 d. **Depressed ST segment**

ANSWER: a. Q waves never go away. Since dead myocardial tissue does not conduct, it makes an electrically silent area. The Q wave looks through this window at the remaining myocardium depolarizing away from it. Note how the infarction enlarges the Q wave and drags down the QRS complex. To be significant the Q wave must be wide (>1 box) and deeper than 1/3 of the QRS complex. See: Braunwald, chapter on "Myocardial Infarction."

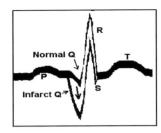

11. The ECG rhythm shown demonstrates an R wave height abnormality. This is termed ___, which is associated with____.
   a. **Bigeminy, CHF**
   b. **Bigeminy, Cardiac tamponade**
   c. **Electrical Alternans,**
   d. **CHF**
   e. **Electrical Alternans, Cardiac tamponade**

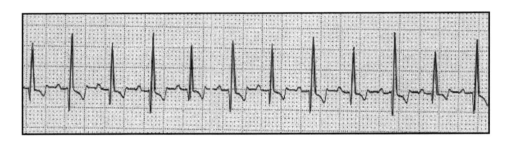

ANSWER: d. Electrical alternans is an alternating QRS complex amplitude between beats. It is seen in cardiac tamponade and is thought to be related to changes in the ventricular electrical axis due to fluid in the pericardium. The heart is swinging back and forth in the fluid filled pericardial space, so the QRS voltage vector varies, beat-to-beat depending on the heart's orientation.

"Pulsus Alternans" (not seen here) is when this happens to the arterial pulse -high systolic, low systolic, hi, lo, hi, lo... This is associated with CHF. There is also T-wave alternans which is associated with risk of VT and sudden death.

12. What cardiac surgery can result in this type of ECG?
   a. **Heart transplant**
   b. **Mini-maze procedure**
   c. **Mitral valve replacement**
   d. **Surgical AV node ablation**

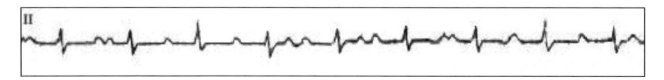

ANSWER: a. Heart transplant. In lead II notice that there is more than one P wave per cycle. Some P waves are timed correctly preceding the QRS complexes whereas the others seem to march through at a slower rate. This is due to remnants of the patients own atrial tissues (native SA node) and the new transplanted heart (new SA node). See diagram below of a donor heart sewn to a native atrium.

Characteristics of a transplanted heart include:
- Two sets of P waves where the recipients native P waves are of a small amplitude, and the donor P waves have normal amplitude and configuration.
- The suture line between the donor and the recipient atria blocks any interchange of the electrical impulses from the two sources.
- Atrial dissociation is present. The donor P wave is conducted and stimulates the ventricles. The recipient's atrial impulses are not conducted. The rate of the donor's heart is normally faster than that of the recipient's atrial remnant rate.
- Since all the nerves were cut during transplant (denervation), heart transplant patients don't experience angina; neither do they have autonomic response to exercise. Heart rate increases are delayed and only due to Frank Starling and hormonal influences (catecholamines).
- In one study two sets of P waves were identified in 86% of patients. But P waves of the recipient atrial remnants may not be seen because of their small amplitude or the presence of sinus node dysfunction or atrial fibrillation prior to the transplantation. Some recipients may lose the sinus node artery during transplant surgery.

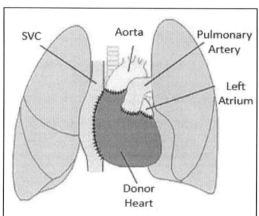

13. Extreme bradycardia or asystole frequently leads to syncope or "seizure-like" convulsion. What is this syndrome termed?
    a. **Stokes-Adams**
    b. **Cushing's**
    c. **Maladie de Roger**
    d. **Eisenminger's**

ANSWER a. Stokes-Adams (or Adams-Stokes syndrome). When insufficient blood supplies the brain, the patient convulses and goes unconscious. Frequently the eyes roll back, and the patient swallows his tongue and gags. The physical convulsion, impact of falling, or recumbent position may be enough to restore consciousness.
See: Medical Dictionary

14. In AF, what is the name of an aberrantly conducted ventricular beat that occurs when a short ventricular cycle is preceded by a long cycle?
   a. PVC
   b. IVCD
   c. Ashman's Phenomenon
   d. Raynaud's phenomenon
   e. Compensatory Aberrancy

ANSWER: c. Ashman's Phenomenon. This is commonly asked on the IBHRE.

Issa says, "Ashman's phenomenon refers to aberration occurring when a short cycle follows a long one (long-short cycle sequence) Aberrancy is caused by the physiological changes of the conduction system refractory periods associated with the R-R interval. Normally, the refractory period of the HPS

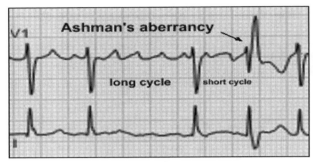

lengthens as the heart rate slows and shortens as the heart rate increases, even when heart rate changes are abrupt. Thus, aberrant conduction can result when a short cycle follows a long R-R interval. In this scenario, the QRS complex that ends the long pause will be conducted normally but creates a prolonged ERP of the bundle branches. If the next QRS complex occurs after a short coupling interval, it may be conducted aberrantly, because one of the bundles is still refractory because of a lengthening of the refractory period." This is also termed "rate related BBB" and it is just another example of how tissues react based on their ERP. See: Issa, chapter on Interventricular Conduction Abnormalities

15. Non-compensatory pauses are most often seen after a _____ and compensatory pauses are seen after a/an:
   a. PAT; PVC
   b. PVC; PAC
   c. PJT; PAT
   d. PAC; PVC

ANSWER d. PAC; PVC. Since PACs Premature Atrial Complexes) originate in the atria they often penetrate and "reset" the SA node. This is the same thing we do when entraining an AFL loop. The SA pacemaker then starts over and resumes firing at the set rate.

PVCs (Premature Ventricular Contractions) are not usually conducted retrograde into the atria and may not reset the SA node. The normal "P" wave usually falls in the refractory period of the AV node and is not conducted. This makes the long "compensatory pause" following most PVCs. In PVCs, the SA node is not usually reset, and the SA node keeps firing as if unaware of the ventricular rate. Here, the period from the last sinus beat to the next sinus beat will be exactly two R-R intervals. See: Dubin, Chapter on "Rhythm."

16. Match each general class of ECG rhythm in the box with its name below:

a.	Flutter	1.	Slowed or interrupted conduction
b.	Fibrillation	2.	Cessation of activity
c.	Arrest	3.	Chaotic rapid beating (over 300 bpm)
d.	Tachycardia	4.	Rapid, but regular (over 200 bpm)
e.	Bradycardia	5.	Beat which occurs too soon, early
f.	Premature	6.	Delayed beat, from lower pacemaker
g.	Escape	7.	Rate over 100 bpm
h.	Block	8.	Rate under 60 bpm
i.	Paroxysmal	9.	Sudden rhythm or rate change

CORRECTLY MATCHED ANSWERS ARE:
a. Flutter = 4. Rapid, but very regular beating (usually over 200 bpm)
b. Fibrillation = 3. Chaotic rapid beating (over 400 bpm)
c. Arrest = 2. Cessation of activity (as in SA arrest)
d. Tachycardia = 7. Rate over 100 bpm (as in ventricular tachycardia)
e. Bradycardia = 8. Rate less than 60 bpm (or <50 in young athletes)
f. Premature = 5. Beat which occurs too soon, early (as in PVC)
g. Block = 1. Slowed or interrupted Conduction (as in BBB or 3o heart block)
h. Escape = 6. Delayed beat, from lower pacemaker (as in junctional escape)
i. Paroxysmal = 9. Sudden rhythm or rate change (as is paroxysmal atrial tachycardia)
See: Dubin, chapter on "Rhythm."

17. Name the irregular ECG conduction pattern at #3 in the ECG and ladder diagram.
a. **Normal sinus rhythm (NSR)**
b. **AV junctional beat (PJC)**
c. **Ectopic atrial beat (PAC)**
d. **Ectopic ventricular beat (PVC)**

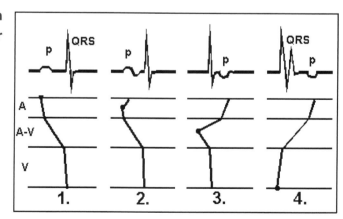

ANSWER: b. AV junctional beat (PJC). The ladder diagram depicts depolarization and conduction schematically. Straight or slightly slanting lines drawn on a tiered framework represent electrical events occurring in various cardiac structures (SA or atrium, AV node and junction, and ventricle. The diagram represents electrical activity against a time base. Conduction is indicated by the lines of the ladder diagram sloping in a left-to-right direction. A steep line depicts rapid conduction. This drawing shows the ECG tracing that would be associated with each ladder diagram.

Activity originating in an ectopic site such as the AV junction, is indicated by a dot in that tier of the ladder. Depolarization proceeds rapidly down into the ventricle with a narrow QRS, indicated by the steep line in the V region. Depolarization also proceeds slowly up into the atrium with a delayed and inverted p wave. The T waves are not depicted in a ladder diagram.
See: Braunwald, chapter on "Specific Arrhythmias: Diagnosis and Treatment."

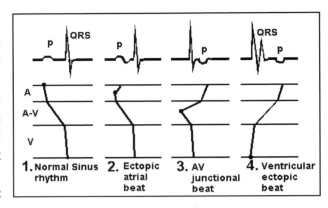

18. After a myocardial infarction has healed and the patient has recovered, what sign usually remains on the ECG for the rest of that patient's life?
   a. **Frequent PVCs**
   b. **Larger than normal "Q" waves**
   c. **ST elevation in some leads**
   d. **T wave inversion in some leads**

ANSWER: b. Larger than normal Q waves. The necrotic or dead tissue leaves an electrically silent area. ECG leads over this area look through the silent area at the rest of the myocardium depolarizing away from it (Q waves). The Q waves develop within one day over the area of dead (infarcted) tissue. They seldom resolve but remain as telltale signs of the old transmural infarction. See: Dubin, chapter on "Infarction."

19. Match each ECG in the diagram to its electrolyte imbalance?
   a. **Moderate hyperkalemia**
   b. **Moderate hypokalemia**
   c. **Hypercalcemia**
   d. **Hypocalcemia**

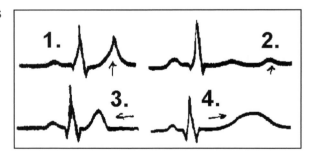

ANSWER: a. Moderate hyperkalemia Electrolyte imbalance patterns show peaked or tent shaped "T" waves during repolarization. Remember hyperkalemia exists whenever the serum K+ exceeds 5.0 mEq/L. In extreme hyper K+ the P waves flatten and the QRS broadens. (Too many bananas and you too will live in a "tent" in South America.)

BE ABLE TO MATCH ALL ANSWERS BELOW:
   • Moderate hyperkalemia = peaked/tented T wave
   • Moderate hypokalemia = prominent U wave
   • Hypercalcemia = short QT interval

- Hypocalcemia = prolonged QT interval

See: Marriott, Chapter on "Hypertrophy."

20. Hyperkalemia is an elevated _____ and is most associated with _____.
   a. **Calcium level > 5.5 mEq/L, Renal failure**
   b. **Calcium level > 15 mg/dL, Heart failure**
   c. **Potassium level > 5.5 mEq/L, Renal failure**
   d. **Potassium level > 15 mg/dL, Heart failure**

ANSWER: c. Potassium or K level > 5.5 mEq/L, Renal failure. Braunwald says, "Hyperkalemia is associated with a distinctive sequence of ECG changes. The earliest effect is usually narrowing and peaking (tenting) of the T wave. The QT interval is shortened at this stage, ... The QRS begins to widen and P wave amplitude decreases. PR interval prolongation can occur, followed sometimes by second- or third-degree AV block. Complete loss of P waves may be associated with a junctional escape rhythm .... Very marked hyperkalemia leads to eventual asystole, sometimes preceded by a slow undulatory (sinewave") ventricular flutter-like pattern. The electrocardiographic triad of (1) peaked T waves (from hyperkalemia), (2) QT prolongation (from hypocalcemia), and (3) LVH (from hypertension) is strongly suggestive of chronic renal failure." See, Braunwald chapter on ECG, Electrolyte Abnormalities

21. The earliest sign of hyperkalemia is:
   a. **Inverted T waves**
   b. **QT interval widens**
   c. **QT interval shortens**
   d. **Tall and sharp T waves**

ANSWER: d. Tall and sharp T waves. Garcia & Holtz say, "1. T wave changes are the earliest sign of hyperkalemia. 2. They are seen when the K+ exceeds 5.5 mEq/L 3. Classic T waves that are tall, peaked, and narrow occur in only 22% of cases...." See: Garcia & Holtz chapter on Electrolyte and Drug Effects

22. How does the "string theory of hyperkalemia" illustrate its changes on the ECG? "Pulling up" on the T wave demonstrates:
   a. **ST elevation**
   b. **T wave narrowing**
   c. **All ECG intervals widening**
   d. **All ECG intervals narrowing**

ANSWER: c. All ECG intervals widening. Garcia says, "The String Theory of Hyperkalemia. The following should help you visualize the T wave shape in hyperkalemia. Imagine an entire complex made of string. Now picture yourself grabbing the string just before the start of the P wave, and at the top of the T wave. The T wave begins to peak. If you continue to pull on the string from both sides, the intervals will widen and start to become smaller. The P waves disappear. Eventually, you would end up with a straight line.... The rhythm can convert to a sine wave and asystole at any point.... This and other arrhythmias are the main dangers of hyperkalemia." See Garcia & Holtz, chapter on "Electrolytes and Drug Changes"

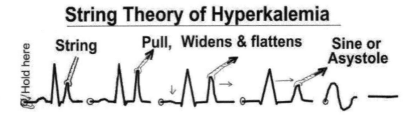

23. Which electrolyte abnormality with ECG shown, is most dangerous because it can lead to lethal arrhythmias at any time and prevents response to the drugs used in resuscitation?
   a. Hyperkalemia
   b. Hypokalemia
   c. Hypercalcemia
   d. Hypocalcemia

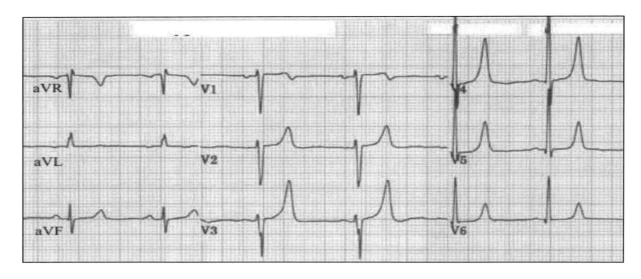

ANSWER: a. Hyperkalemia. Note the small P waves and large pointed T waves. Dr. Garcia says, "Of all the electrolyte changes that can occur, hyperkalemia is the most dangerous. Hyperkalemia can not only kill, but it can kill in seconds- and it prevents response to the drugs used in resuscitation.

The main changes found in hyperkalemia include:
   • T wave abnormalities, especially tall, peaked T's
   • Interventricular conduction delays (IVCD's)
   • P waves missing or decreased in amplitude
   • ST segment changes simulating an injury pattern
   • Cardiac arrhythmias, all varieties....

Electrographically, T wave abnormalities are the first changes noted in a patient developing hyperkalemia. The T wave changes begin to appear when the potassium level exceeds 5.5 mEq/L." See: Garcia & Holtz, chapter on Electrolyte and Drug effects

Interpretation

1. **What is the diagnosis in this ECG?**
   a. **Accelerated Mid Junctional Rhythm**
   b. **Sinus Rhythm with Couplet PVCs**
   c. **Sinus Rhythm with BBB**
   d. **Sinus Rhythm with two PJCs**

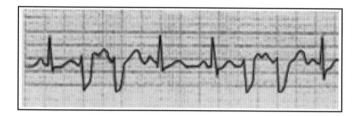

ANSWER: b. Sinus Rhythm with Couplet PVCs. PVCs have a wide QRS complex. Two in a row are called couplets and every other is bigeminy. They have the same morphology, so they are considered monomorphic.

2. **The sinoatrial node serves as the pacemaker in the normal heart because it:**
   a. **Has direct contact with the Purkinje system**
   b. **Is closest to the AV node**
   c. **Produces the strongest electrical impulse**
   d. **Has the highest inherent rate**

ANSWER d. Has the highest inherent rate. The fastest firing cells will become the pacemaker for the entire heart. Normally the SA node sets the fastest pace (see bandleader in diagram). But ectopic foci and pacemakers may develop a rate fast enough to take over. See: Berne & Levy, chapter "ECG."

3. **Slight Sinus Arrhythmia occurs normally and is due to:**
   a. **Erratic pacemakers**
   b. **Occasional PVCs**
   c. **Occasional PACs**
   d. **Respiration**
   e. **Sinus node anoxia**

ANSWER d. Respiration. Breathing affects HR. Inspiration increases the rate as shown in the diagram. When inspiration causes the heart rate to vary more than 10 % it is termed "sinus arrhythmia." It is a normal phenomenon in young people. See: Dubin, chapter on "Rhythm."

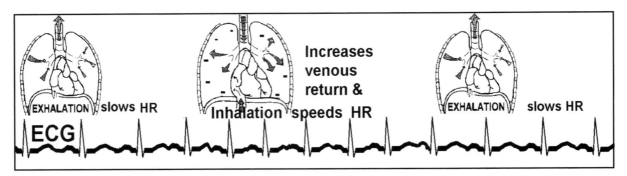

Sinus Arrhythmia with inspiration/expiration

4. **What is the rhythm?**
    a. **Sinus Tachycardia**
    b. **Typical AVNRT**
    c. **Sinus Rhythm with PACs**
    d. **Sinus with 1st degree HB**
    e. **Atrial fibrillation**

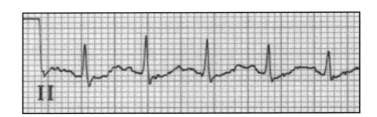

ANSWER: a. Sinus Tachycardia.
*   P waves are upright and preceding each QRS complex eliminating AVNRT.
*   No PACs, although the baseline is irregular it is not AF.
*   PR interval is normal – no heart block (HB)
*   Sinus tachycardia is a heart rhythm with elevated rate of impulses originating from the sinoatrial node, defined as a rate greater than 100 bpm in an average adult. The normal heart rate in the average adult ranges from 60–100 bpm. Note that the normal heart rate varies with age, with infants having normal heart rate of 110–150 bpm to the elderly, who have slower normal rates.

5. **On this ECG, the sinus beats show:**
    a. **Mobitz I HB**
    b. **Sinus bradycardia with first degree HB**
    c. **Sinus bradycardia with second degree HB, type II**
    d. **Sinus Rhythm with ST depression & first-degree HB**

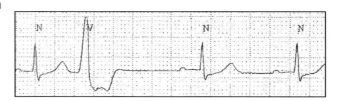

ANSWER: d. Sinus Rhythm with ST depression and first-degree HB. Sinus Rhythm with upright P waves for every QRS complex, long PR interval (0.25 sec) indicating first-degree heart block. The sinus heart rate on the last beat is normal, around 62 bpm. The regular sinus rhythm is interrupted by one PVC with compensatory pause. ST segment is depressed one mm which may be normal in the limb leads.

ST segment depression may be determined by measuring the vertical distance between the patient's trace and the isoelectric line from the PR segment. It is significant if it is more than 1 mm in V5-V6, or 1.5 mm in AVF or III. In a cardiac stress test, ST depression suggests reversible cardiac ischemia. It is often a sign of myocardial ischemia, of which coronary insufficiency is a major cause. Other ischemic heart diseases causing ST depression include: Subendocardial ischemia or even non-Q-wave myocardial infarction.

Test yourself with the arrhythmia quizzes at:

http://www.fammed.wisc.edu/medstudent/pcc/ecg/quiz/rhythm.quiz.1.html

6. **What is observed in the following ECG?**
   a. **First degree HB with acute MI**
   b. **Junctional Rhythm with old MI, ST pattern**
   c. **Sinus rhythm with ST elevation**
   d. **Sinus bradycardia with ST elevation**

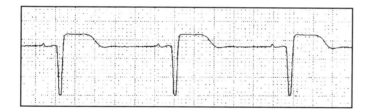

ANSWER: d. Sinus bradycardia with ST elevation. The rate is 52 bpm, so bradycardia is present. Upright P waves for every QRS complex, narrow QRS complexes, and ST elevation of 3 mm. ST elevation is associated with acute injury, and the earliest stages of MI. You have heard of STEMI, ST elevation Myocardial Infarction. These are acute MIs that we rush to revascularize/stent within 3 hours of symptoms. Here there is a large QS wave, suggesting myocardial infarction, but it depends on the lead. This could be V1 which normally may have a Q wave and be negative. "An ST elevation is considered significant if the vertical distance between the ECG trace and the isoelectric line at a point 0.04 seconds after the J-point is at least 0.1 mV (usually representing 1 mm) in a limb lead or 0.2 mV (2 mm) in a precordial lead. The ST segment corresponds to a period of ventricle systolic depolarization when the cardiac muscle is contracted. Subsequent relaxation occurs during the diastolic repolarization phase."

7. **The long pause in this ECG is probably:**
   a. **A compensatory pause**
   b. **A non-compensatory pause**
   c. **Mobitz type I heart block**
   d. **Sinus pause**

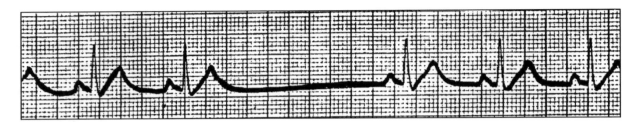

ANSWER d. Sinus pause. There are no "P" waves during the 2 ½ sec period of asystole. Since the asystolic period is not an even multiple of the normal R-R interval this is called a sinus pause. If the asystolic period had been exactly two or three times the R-R interval this would be called "SA block." Usually, an escape pacemaker will take over, unless there is failure of all lower pacemaker cells. When these pauses are brief, no treatment is usually needed. See: Marriott, Chapter on "Decreased Automaticity."

8. **Non-compensatory pauses are most often seen after a _____ and compensatory pauses are seen after a/an:**
   a. **PAT; PVC**
   b. **PVC; PAC**
   c. **PJT; PAT**
   d. **PAC; PVC**

ANSWER d. PAC; PVC. Since PACs Premature Atrial Complexes) originate in the atria they often penetrate and "reset" the SA node. This is the same thing we do when entraining an AFL loop. The SA pacemaker then starts over and resumes firing at the set rate.

PVCs (Premature Ventricular Contractions) are not usually conducted retrograde into the atria and may not reset the SA node. The normal "P" wave usually falls in the refractory period of the AV node and is not conducted. This makes the long "compensatory pause" following most PVCs. In PVCs, the SA node is not usually reset, and the SA node keeps firing as if unaware of the ventricular rate. Here, the period from the last sinus beat to the next sinus beat will be exactly two R-R intervals. See: Dubin, Chapter on "Rhythm."

9. **If an idioventricular pacemaker "escapes" it will usually fire at a rate of:**
   a. **10-20 bpm**
   b. **30-40 bpm**
   c. **60-80 bpm**
   d. **100-200 bpm**

ANSWER: b. 30-40 bpm. The idioventricular pacemaker is the slowest escape rhythm. It is the heart's last resort when all other pacemakers fail. Our hearts have different levels of automatic "escape" pacemakers to prevent asystole. These "potential" escape pacemakers and the usual rates are:

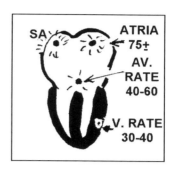

- Junctional (nodal) = 40-50 bpm
- Ventricular = 30-40 bpm

The SA node is like a teacher in control of the class. Myocardial cells are like students; they only pay attention to the fastest leader. When the teacher speaks at a normal rate (SA node rate around 60 bpm) everyone follows. But if a fast jazz band were to prance through the hall it would take the students' attention, like an ectopic focus. The teacher then loses control. Also, if the teacher is too slow, he loses the class's attention - as in sinus bradycardia. A quicker student may stand up and take over. This is analogous to a lower pacemaker that "escapes" at a rate faster than the SA node. A junctional rate of 50 can take over when the sinus node rate falls below 50 bpm. See: Dubin, chapter on Rate "

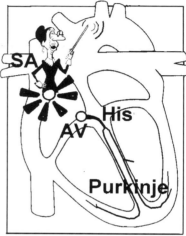

10. What is the rhythm?
   a. **Sinus Rhythm with PJC**
   b. **Sinus Bradycardia**
   c. **Normal Sinus**
   d. **Rhythm**
   e. **Sinus Rhythm with PAC**

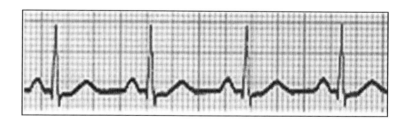

ANSWER: c. Normal sinus rhythm. P wave for every QRS, PR – normal, QRS – normal, QT. Sinus rhythm, more commonly referred to as Normal Sinus Rhythm (NSR), is the normal rhythm of the heart. Several requirements must be met for an electrocardiogram to be classified as normal sinus rhythm. Criteria for a Normal Sinus Rhythm include:

- A heart rate between 60-100 beats per minute.
- Regularity- Regular
- The SA node is pacing the heart. Therefore, a "P" wave must be present for every "QRS" complex in a ratio of 1:1.
- PR interval is between .12 second and .20 second.
- QRS complex width should be less than .12 second.

11. What is the rhythm?
   a. **Sinus Bradycardia**
   b. **Junctional Rhythm**
   c. **NSR with 1st degree AVHB**
   d. **Normal Sinus Rhythm**

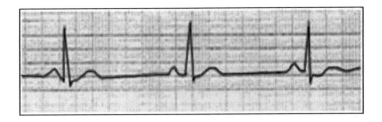

ANSWER: a. Sinus Bradycardia. Upright P wave for every QRS, PR is normal (.12-.20), QRS is normal (<.12), QT appears normal. Just like normal sinus rhythm only with a rate less than 60 bpm.

The decreased heart rate can cause a decreased cardiac output resulting in symptoms such as lightheadedness, dizziness, hypotension, vertigo, and syncope. The slow heart rate may also lead to a trial, junctional, or ventricular ectopic rhythms. Bradycardia is not necessarily problematic. People who regularly practice sports may have sinus bradycardia at rest, because their trained hearts can pump a large stroke volume. Sinus bradycardia is a sinus rhythm of less than 60 bpm. It is a common condition found in both healthy individuals and those who are considered well-conditioned athletes. Studies have found that 50 - 85 percent of conditioned athletes have benign sinus bradycardia, as compared to 23 percent of the general population studied.

12. SVT is defined as an arrhythmia having a cycle length of _____ and QRS duration of

   _____.
   a. **<600 ms, <120 ms**
   b. **<600 ms, <200 ms**
   c. **<1000 ms, <120 ms**
   d. **<1000 ms, <200 ms**

ANSWER: a. <600 ms, <120 ms. This is a fast heart rate of >100 bpm, with a narrow QRS <120 ms. Issa say, "Narrow QRS complex supraventricular tachycardia (SVT) is a tachyarrhythmia with a rate more than 100 bpm and a QRS duration of less than 120 milliseconds.[1] Narrow QRS complex SVTs include sinus tachycardia, inappropriate sinus tachycardia, sinoatrial nodal reentrant tachycardia, atrial tachycardia (AT), multifocal AT, atrial fibrillation (AF), atrial flutter (AFL), junctional ectopic tachycardia, non-paroxysmal junctional tachycardia, atrioventricular nodal reentrant tachycardia (AVNRT), and atrioventricular reentrant tachycardia (AVRT)." See: Issa chapter on PSVT

13. What is the heart rhythm shown?
   a. **Atrial fibrillation**
   b. **Atrial flutter**
   c. **Sinus Tachycardia**
   d. **Junctional Tachycardia**
   e. **Wenckebach**

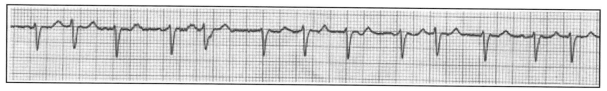

Lead I ECG

ANSWER a. Atrial fibrillation (AF) is an irregular undulation of the baseline with an "Irregularly irregular" ventricular rhythm. Don't confuse the T waves after each QRS with P waves. Here the flutter waves are fine, and barely discernable. The key is the irregular R-R interval. Atrial fibrillation ("f" waves) occurs at atrial rates between 300-600 bpm. The undulations may be distinct or barely perceptible (coarse or fine fibrillation). AF. is best diagnosed by noting the irregular RR intervals, because sometimes you cannot see the AF waves.

Only when a large enough "f" wave enters the AV node is a beat conducted. As shown in this ladder diagram, most "f" waves are blocked. Although it may look musical, it does not. There is no meter or "beat" to atrial fibrillation. Ventricular response varies irregularly between 100-160 bpm. Many supraventricular tachycardias can be terminated by DC Cardioversion.

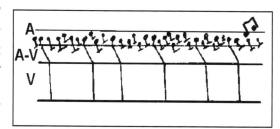

See: Marriott, chapter on "Atrial Fib/Flutter."

14. The tachycardia shown on the last half of this ECG is:
   a. **Ventricular Tachycardia**
   b. **Accelerated Junctional Escape rhythm**
   c. **Paroxysmal Supraventricular Tachycardia**
   d. **Torsade de Pointes**

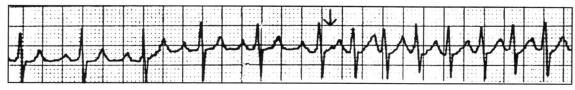

ECG - Lead II

ANSWER c. Paroxysmal Supraventricular Tachycardia. The tachycardia develops suddenly at the arrow, so it is termed "paroxysmal." Since the QRS complexes appear narrow and normal, the rhythm comes from above the ventricles (supraventricular). This is an atrial tachycardia as opposed to a junctional tachycardia because at the end of the strip, the "T" waves contain P' waves, or AVNRT. See: ACLS Manual chapter on "Arrhythmias."

15. This healthy 45-year-old patient presented with palpitations. His BP is 136/75 and all diagnostic tests were normal except for this ECG. He has:
   a. Lone AF
   b. Slow AF
   c. Sinus arrhythmia
   d. Sinus exit block

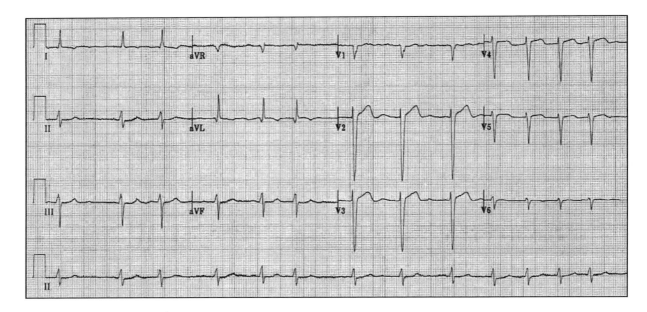

ANSWER: a. Lone AF. In AF, the flutter waves may be small or unnoticeable on ECG. Don't rely on the undulating baseline to diagnose AF. Fine fibrillation waves may be too small to see on the surface ECG. Here, the heart rate is irregularly irregular, typical of AF, with HR averaging 65 bpm. The irregular rhythm is best seen in the rhythm strip. The most common cause of AF is structural heart disease, but when there is no known cause for the AF it is termed "primary" or "lone" atrial fibrillation.

AFbers.org says, "Many cases of atrial fibrillation are not connected with heart disease or hypertension at all and not too long ago were described as "idiopathic", that is, with no known cause. In recent years however, intensive research has uncovered many conditions, which may trigger atrial fibrillation, and the diagnosis "idiopathic atrial fibrillation" is now much less common. Atrial fibrillation not caused by an underlying heart disease is referred to as primary or lone atrial fibrillation" See: http://www.AFbers.org/atrial_fibrillation.htm

16. The early third beat seen on this ECG is a/an:
   a. Atrial Premature Complex
   b. Ventricular Premature Complex
   c. Premature sinus beat
   d. Junctional escape beat

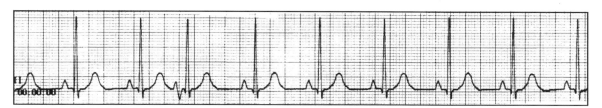

ANSWER: a. Atrial Premature Complex (APC/PAC). APCs are recognized by these criteria:
- Premature abnormal looking P' wave. Here the P' wave appears biphasic.
- QRS is like the sinus beats - not broad.
- No compensatory pause.

Note the same R-R interval after the PAC. These beats commonly occur while manipulating a catheter in the atria. See: Marriott, chapter on "Atrial Fib/Flutter."

17. This ECG strip shows sinus slowing. What type of rhythm takes over during the end of the ECG strip?
    a. **Ventricular escape**
    b. **Junctional escape rhythm**
    c. **Sinus bradycardia**
    d. **Electro-mechanical dissociation**

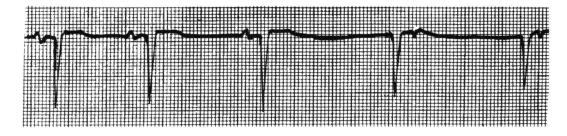

ANSWER b. Junctional escape rhythm. As the sinus rhythm slows from 60 to 40, the 4th beat loses its leading "P" wave. P waves become inverted and after the QRS. These last beats are junctional or nodal escape beats. The QRS configuration remains narrow and normal, so the rhythm is supraventricular. Junctional rhythms may have an inverted "P" wave in lead II (retrograde) that may be buried within the QRS or behind it - as seen in the last two beats. See: Marriott, chapter on "Decreased Automaticity."

18. This lead II ECG shows____.
    a. **Sinus tachycardia**
    b. **Atrial fibrillation**
    c. **Wandering atrial pacemaker**
    d. **Accelerated junctional rhythm**

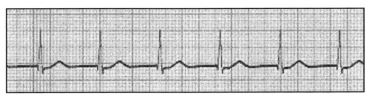

ANSWER: d. Accelerated junctional rhythm. P waves are not seen or are buried in these narrow QRS complexes. In junctional rhythms P waves may be upside down or late because they conduct superiorly from the AV junction. Here the heart's atrioventricular node (junction) takes over as the pacemaker. The atria will still contract by retrograde conduction, but since they arrive too late, they do not aid in ventricular filling, and may cause cannon venous A waves. The junctional rate is normally slow - 40-50 bpm. This rate is 85, much faster than expected for the junction. Thus, it is accelerated. This is a supraventricular arrhythmia with narrow QRS complexes.

19. Match each atrial heart rate range to its SVT.
   a. **100-180 bpm**   1. **Atrial Fibrillation**
   b. **150-250 bpm**   2. **Atrial Flutter**
   c. **250-350 bpm**   3. **Atrial Tachycardia with block**
   d. **300-600 bpm**   4. **Sinus Tachycardia**

CORRECTLY MATCHED ANSWERS BELOW:
Of all supraventricular tachycardias, the atrial rate is the most rapid in atrial fibrillation. It may be so fast that it only shows on the ECG as a small irregular baseline undulation of variable amplitude, called "f" or flutter waves. No effective atrial contraction is present.

TACHY-ARRHYTHMIA RATE RANGES SHOWN ARE IN ORDER:
   1. Atrial Fibrillation: 300-600 bpm
   2. Atrial Flutter: 250-350 bpm
   3. Atrial tachycardia with block: 150-250 bpm
   4. Sinus tachycardia: 100-180 bpm
See: Braunwald, chapter on "Specific Arrhythmias: Diagnosis and Treatment."

20. This ECG (Lead II) shows:
   a. **Frequent PACs**
   b. **Atrial flutter**
   c. **Atrial fibrillation**
   d. **AV nodal reentrant tachycardia**
   e. **Accelerated junctional rhythm**

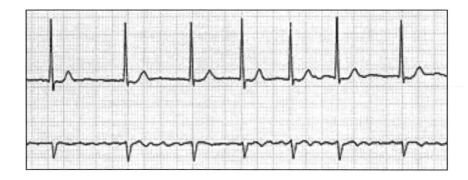

ANSWER: c. Atrial fibrillation is characterized by an irregularly irregular ventricular response, and the absence of discrete P waves. The atrial activity seen in the lower lead resembles old saw-teeth (as opposed to the new, sharp saw-teeth of atrial flutter). See: Marriott, chapter on "Atrial Fibrillation"

21. All the following are vagal maneuvers commonly used to reduce heart rate and increase AV block EXCEPT:
   a. **Rubbing the eyeballs**
   b. **Carotid Sinus massage**
   c. **Cold ice pack on face**
   d. **Valsalva maneuver**

ANSWER: a. Rubbing the eyeballs. ACLS current manual says, "The old practice of pressing on the eyeballs to achieve a strong vagal effect has been discredited. Eliminate this practice from your list of acceptable vagal maneuvers. Carotid sinus massage (CSM) is contraindicated in those who are known to have - or who are at significant risk for - carotid atherosclerosis; most experts avoid CSM in patients who are elderly or even in late middle age. In such cases consider other vagal techniques such as the Valsalva maneuver." Ice packs or putting the patient's face in icy water also initiates the vagal "diving reflex" which slows heart rate and increases AV block.

22. This arrhythmia is an example of:
   a. **Atrial flutter with 2:1 conduction**
   b. **Atrial flutter with 4:1 AV conduction**
   c. **Second degree AV block, Mobitz I**
   d. **Second degree AV block, Mobitz II**

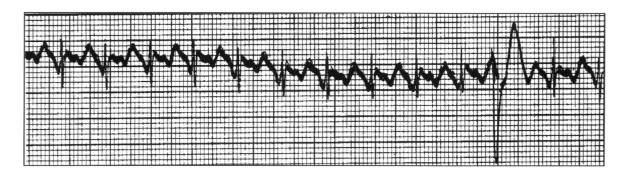

ANSWER: a. Atrial flutter with 2:1 AV conduction. The regular shaped Flutter (F waves) appear as a "sawtooth" baseline. Here 2 "F" waves are seen for every QRS. One is buried in the QRS complex. This indicates a 2:1 AV Block. Atrial rate is 280 ventricular response is ½ of this or 140 bpm. What appears to be a down-sloping ST segment is really the end of a Flutter wave. See: Dubin, chapter on "Rhythms."

23. In a patient with atrial flutter increased AV block and slowing of the ventricular rate may occur with:
   a. **Mild aerobic exercise**
   b. **Mild anaerobic exercise**
   c. **Neck vein massage**
   d. **Valsalva maneuver**

ANSWER d. Valsalva maneuver. Patients often learn to Valsalva with these arrhythmias because they feel more comfortable with a lower heart rate. The Valsalva maneuver increases the vagal tone and the amount of AV block. So instead of 2:1 block, the AV node may block 3:1 or 4:1. This lets fewer "F" waves pass into the ventricle and lowers the ventricular rate. Carotid artery massage (not vein) is another maneuver that may increase vagal tone and reduce the ventricular rate. Watch for trick wording.
See: Marriot, chapter on "Accelerated Automaticity."

24. What is this ECG rhythm?
   a. **Sinus Rhythm with PACs**
   b. **Sinus Rhythm with PJCs**
   c. **NSR with first degree AVHB**
   d. **Wandering Atrial Pacemaker**

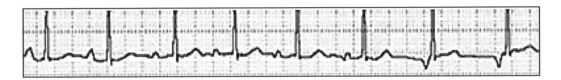

ANSWER: d. Wandering Atrial Pacemaker. Notice the different P wave morphologies throughout the strip, first upright, then biphasic, then inverted.

Wandering pacemaker is an atrial arrhythmia that occurs when the natural cardiac pacemaker site shifts between the sinoatrial node (SA node), the atria, and/or the atrioventricular node (AV node). This shifting of the pacemaker from the SA node to adjacent tissues is identifiable on ECG Lead II by morphological changes in the P-wave. Sinus beats usually have smooth upright P waves, while atrial beats have flattened, notched, or biphasic P-waves. Ventricular conduction is normal with wandering pacemaker, and thus the QRS complex is narrow. Wandering pacemaker is usually caused by varying vagal tone. With increased vagal tone the SA Node slows, allowing a pacemaker in the atria or AV Nodal area, which may briefly become slightly faster. After vagal tone decreases, the SA Node assumes its natural pace. It may be seen in the young, old, in athletes and rarely causes symptoms or requires treatment.

25. Calculate the heart rate of an ECG when the RR interval averages 20 mm running on 25 mm/sec paper speed as shown.
a. 60
b. 75
c. 85
d. 100

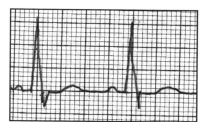

ANSWER: b. 75 beats/min. To measure heart rate easily remember the numbers "300-150100-75-60-50". Each of those numbers estimates the HR when you measure one RR interval by counting the 5 mm timelines on the ECG paper. Each time you jump 5 mm you recite these numbers. Here there are four 5 mm intervals (20 cm) between R waves, so recite 300150-100-75, and stop at the fourth number. Here there are 4 boxes between R waves, so the HR = 75 bpm. It is most accurate to start with an R wave on one of the dark ECG paper lines, then count dark lines as you recite these numbers. If the next R wave is exactly on a dark line, the HR is exactly that number.

Or use the formula HR =60 / RR int. = (60 sec/min) / .8 sec = 75 b/min. See: Dubin, Rapid Interpretation of ECGs

26. What is the rhythm?
a. **Normal Sinus Rhythm**
b. **Wenckebach**
c. **Junctional Escape Rhythm**
d. **Sinus with First-Degree HB**

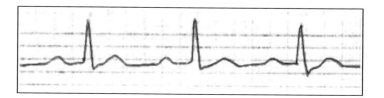

ANSWER: d. Sinus Rhythm with first degree AVHB. Prolonged PR interval: however, it is fixed not progressive like in Wenckebach. Bradycardia is present at 50 bpm.

The most common causes of first-degree heart block are AV nodal disease, enhanced vagal tone (for example in athletes), myocarditis, acute myocardial infarction (especially acute inferior MI), electrolyte disturbances and medication. The drugs that most commonly cause first-degree heart block are those that increase the refractory time of the AV node, thereby slowing AV conduction, like calcium channel blockers, beta-blockers, cardiac glycosides, and anything that increases cholinergic activity.

Heart Block

1. **What is the rhythm?**
   a. **Sinus Bradycardia**
   b. **Wenckebach**
   c. **Mobitz Type II**
   d. **3rd degree HB**

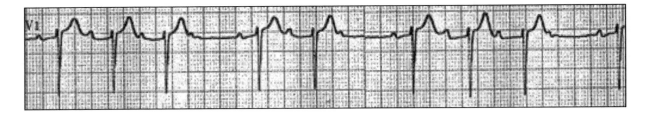

ANSWER: b. Wenckebach. Progressive lengthening of the PR interval until it blocks....
Next beat comes in with a normal PR interval.

Type 1 Second-degree AV block, also known as Mobitz I or Wenckebach periodicity, is almost always a disease of the AV node. Mobitz I heart block is characterized by progressive prolongation of the PR interval on the electrocardiogram (ECG) on consecutive beats followed by a blocked P wave (i.e., a 'dropped' QRS complex). After the dropped QRS complex, the PR interval resets and the cycle repeats. One of the baseline assumptions when determining if an individual has Mobitz I heart block is that the atrial rhythm must be regular. If the atrial rhythm is not regular, there could be alternative explanations as to why certain P waves do not conduct to the ventricles. This is almost always a benign condition for which no specific treatment is needed. In symptomatic cases, intravenous atropine or isoproterenol may transiently improve conduction.

2. **A patient presents with frequent syncope and intermittent 2nd degree heart block. The most dangerous site causing this type of block is:**
   a. **AV Node**
   b. **Bachmann's bundle**
   c. **SA node perinodal tissue**
   d. **His-Purkinje system (Infra-Hisian)**

ANSWER: d. His-Purkinje system (infra-His) is most dangerous. This EGMs has a large H wave that is not conducted to the ventricle. This is an infra-hisian block. The 2nd beat is normally conducted- A, H, V.

Fogoros says, "Although block occurring at the level of the AV node is considered benign, heart block occurring more distally (infra-nodal block) is potentially life-threatening. Block occurring in or distal to the His bundle often leads to serious hemodynamic compromise because subsidiary pacemakers distal to the His bundle are unreliable and escape heart rates usually in the 20 to 40 bpm range. Thus, syncope or hemodynamic collapse leading to death is likely to occur from blocking the His-Purkinje system." See: Fogoros chapter on EP Testing for Bradyarrhythmias

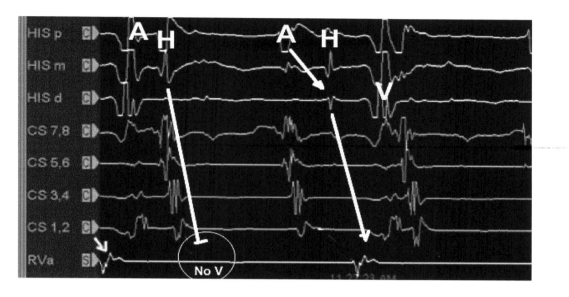

3. **This ECG shows:**
   a. **First degree HB**
   b. **Mobitz I HB**
   c. **Second degree HB type II**
   d. **Sinus Tachycardia with ST depression**

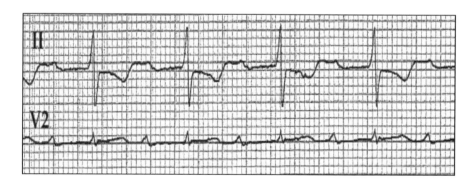

ANSWER: a. First degree HB. The P waves are seen in the upper strip as a small deflection at the end of the T wave, way out in front of the QRS. The lower strip more clearly shows the P waves between each QRS. This is like an electrogram where you can better understand the P waves (A waves) and their relationship to the surface ECG.

4. **What is the rhythm in lead V1?**
   a. **Sinus Tachycardia with RBBB**
   b. **Sinus Tachycardia with LBBB**
   c. **Sinus Rhythm with RBBB**
   d. **Sinus Rhythm with LBBB**

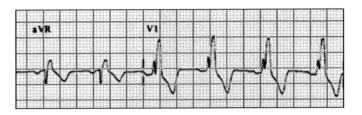

ANSWER: c. Sinus Rhythm with RBBB. QRS is broad with V1 showing positive rSR' suggesting RBBB. Rate of 94 bpm is fast but not tachycardia. This bundle is an important part of the electrical conduction system of the heart as it transmits the impulse from the AV node to the ventricles. Here the right ventricle depolarizes last because the right bundle is blocked. Remember, rabbit-ears and the right sided car blinker you push "up."

5. **This ECG and ladder diagram is an example of:**
   a. **First degree AV block**
   b. **Second degree AV block – Type I**
   c. **Second degree AV block – Type II**
   d. **Third degree AV block**

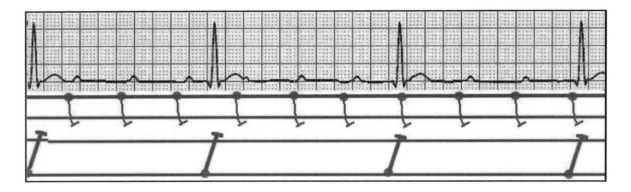

ANSWER d. Third degree AV block. P waves arise from the SA node at a constant rate. QRS complexes arise from the ventricle with a broad complex, not conducted by purkinje system, as indicated by the upward sloping line. See: ACLS Manual chapter on "Arrhythmias."

6. **Mobitz I type heart block is another name for:**
   a. **First degree heart block**
   b. **Sick sinus syndrome**
   c. **Wolff-Parkinson-White syndrome**
   d. **Wenckebach Phenomenon**

ANSWER: d. Wenckebach Phenomenon = Second degree AV block type I or Mobitz I. Progressive lengthening of PR interval until one beat is dropped.
See: ACLS Manual chapter on "Arrhythmias."

7. **First degree AV block usually leads to:**
   a. **Second degree AV block, type II**
   b. **Third degree AV block**
   c. **Junctional escape rhythms**
   d. **Ventricular escape rhythms**
   e. **No symptoms (asymptomatic)**

ANSWER: e. No symptoms (asymptomatic). Fogoros says, "First-degree AV block is asymptomatic because all atrial impulses are transmitted to the ventricles.... First-degree block is diagnosed from the surface ECG when the PR interval is greater than 0.20 seconds in duration. The PR interval in first-degree AV block is usually in the 0.20 to 0.40-seconds range, but PR intervals of greater than one second has been documented. The slowed conduction in first-degree AV block usually occurs at the level of the AV node but occasionally occurs in the His-Purkinje system. " See: Fogoros chapter on EP Tests for Brady...

8. **Which type of hemiblock is rare because that fascicle fans out in many directions over a large area of the heart?**
   a. **Left anterior hemiblock**
   b. **Left lateral hemiblock**
   c. **Left posterior hemiblock**
   d. **Right bundle hemiblock**

ANSWER: c. Left posterior hemiblock. From the diagram you can see the many divisions of the left posterior bundle. There is no main bundle. Garcia says, "The left posterior fascicle also originates from the left bundle. However, the fibers are not organized into a tight fascicle [like the left anterior fascicle]; instead, they disperse loosely and fan out.... The left posterior fascicle is difficult to block because the fibers are not organized as a discrete bundle, but instead are spread throughout the posterior and inferior walls of the LV. Because of this spread, the lesion that could cause this type of block would have to be quite large. These hemiblocks are rare. They are also difficult to diagnose." See, Garcia & Holtz, chapter on "BB and Hemiblocks"

9. **After myocardial infarction, type I Second degree HB is most common in _____ with a _____ prognosis.**
   a. **Anterior MI (LAD), good**
   b. **Anterior MI (LAD), poor**
   c. **Inferior MI (RCA), good**
   d. **Inferior MI (RCA), poor**

ANSWER: c. Inferior MI (RCA), good prognosis, because it usually resolves. This is Mobitz I or Wenckebach with lengthening PR intervals until one P wave is blocked at the AV node.

Moses says, "Inferior MI follows occlusion of the artery supplying the inferior wall of the LV. This is usually the right coronary artery and is the origin of the artery to the AV node, it is characterized by a Mobitz I pattern." See, Moses, chapter in "Indications for Pacing"

Issa says, "First-degree and type 1 second-degree (Wenckebach) AV block occurs more commonly in inferior MI,... Wenckebach AV block in the setting of acute inferior MI is usually transient (resolving within 48 to 72 hours of MI) and asymptomatic, and rarely progresses to high-grade or complete AV block....In the setting of acute inferior MI, the site of the block is usually at the level of the AVN, resulting in a junctional escape rhythm with a narrow QRS complex and a rate of 40 to 60 bpm. The block tends to be reversed by catecholamines and usually resolves within several days." See: Issa, chapter on AV conduction abnormalities" Temporary pacing is seldom needed.

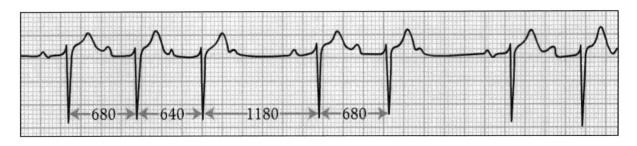

10. In myocardial infarction, type II second-degree AV block is most common in____ with a _____ prognosis.
   a. **Anterior MI (LAD), poor**
   b. **Anterior MI (LAD), good**
   c. **Inferior MI (RCA), poor**
   d. **Inferior MI (RCA), good**

ANSWER: a. Anterior MI (LAD), poor prognosis. Note in the diagram, how the LAD branch supplies the area just below the AV node leading to the second level of AV block and a junctional escape rhythm.

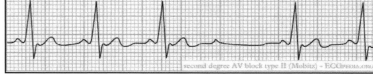

Issa says, "Type 2 second-degree (Mobitz type II) AV block occurs in only 1% of patients with acute MI (more commonly in anterior than inferior MI) and has a worse prognosis than type 1 second-degree block. Type 2 second-degree AV block occurring during an acute anterior MI is typically associated with HB or bundle branch ischemia or infarction and frequently progresses to complete heart block. Complete AV block occurs in 8% to 13% of patients with acute MI. It can occur with anterior or inferior acute MI." See: Issa, chapter on AV conduction abnormalities

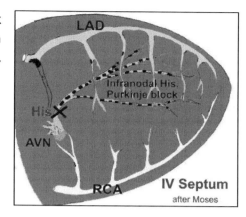

11. Anterior MI and infarction of the HB usually results in __ with a heart rate of____.
   a. Junctional escape rhythm, <40 bpm
   b. Junctional escape rhythm, 40-60 bpm
   c. Ventricular escape rhythm, <40 bpm
   d. Ventricular escape rhythm, 40-60 bpm

ANSWER: c. Ventricular escape rhythm, <40 bpm. Since all conduction from above the His is blocked, complete heart block is likely, and a slower pacemaker will take over. Note in the diagram above, how the LAD branch supplies the His/Purkinje area below the AV node and is thus infranodal and more serious.

12. What type of heart block is this?
   a. First Degree
   b. Third degree
   c. Second degree (Wenckebach)
   d. Second degree (2:1) fixed ratio

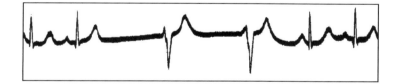

ANSWER b. Third degree or complete heart block with ventricular escape rhythm. The QRS complexes a broad and bizarre with T waves opposite in direction to the RS waves. The ventricular rate is a "ventricular escape" or "Idioventricular" rhythm. Note how the "P" waves have no relation to the QRS complexes. (This was generated by a machine so some relation may exist). Although the atrial rate is 100, ventricular rate is 35 bpm (normal ventricular escape rate is 30-40 bpm). Use a caliper to "walk" out the nonconducted "P" waves. Some "P" waves are buried in the QRS-T complexes. See: ACLS Manual

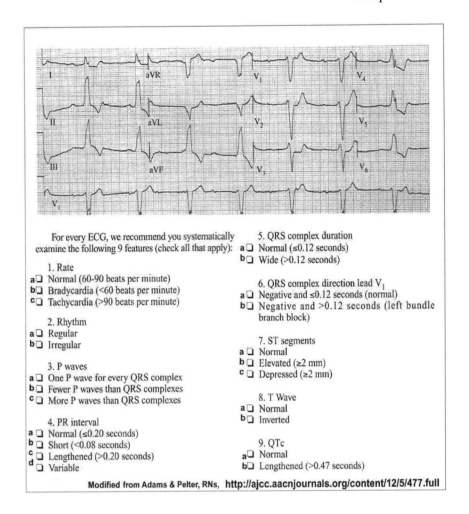

For every ECG, we recommend you systematically examine the following 9 features (check all that apply):

1. Rate
a☐ Normal (60-90 beats per minute)
b☐ Bradycardia (<60 beats per minute)
c☐ Tachycardia (>90 beats per minute)

2. Rhythm
a☐ Regular
b☐ Irregular

3. P waves
a☐ One P wave for every QRS complex
b☐ Fewer P waves than QRS complexes
c☐ More P waves than QRS complexes

4. PR interval
a☐ Normal (≤0.20 seconds)
b☐ Short (<0.08 seconds)
c☐ Lengthened (>0.20 seconds)
d☐ Variable

5. QRS complex duration
a☐ Normal (≤0.12 seconds)
b☐ Wide (>0.12 seconds)

6. QRS complex direction lead V_1
a☐ Negative and ≤0.12 seconds (normal)
b☐ Negative and >0.12 seconds (left bundle branch block)

7. ST segments
a☐ Normal
b☐ Elevated (≥2 mm)
c☐ Depressed (≥2 mm)

8. T Wave
a☐ Normal
b☐ Inverted

9. QTc
a☐ Normal
b☐ Lengthened (>0.47 seconds)

Modified from Adams & Pelter, RNs, http://ajcc.aacnjournals.org/content/12/5/477.full

13. Patients with 3rd degree AV block are most likely to be symptomatic when:
a. The patient has type 1 diabetes
b. The patient has a dilated heart
c. An AV junctional pacemaker takes over
d. A ventricular escape pacemaker takes over

ANSWER: d. A ventricular escape pacemaker takes over. Fogoros says: "Third degree AV block is defined as complete failure of the conduction of atrial impulses to the ventricles. The ventricular rhythm, then, is dependent on subsidiary escape pacemakers. As noted earlier, the reliability of those escape pacemakers is dependent on the site of block - with AV nodal block, the escape pacemakers tend to be relatively dependable; with infranodal block, the escape pacemakers tend to be unreliable and slow. Symptoms depend on the rate of the escape pacemaker. Thus, infranodal third-degree block is much more likely to be symptomatic than third-degree block located in the AV node." See: Fogoros chapter on EP Testing for Bradyarrhythmias

14. Disease in the distal ventricular conduction system (Purkinje) produces a:
 a. Short AH interval
 b. Long AH interval
 c. Short HV interval
 d. Long HV interval

ANSWER: d. Long HV interval. Fogoros says: "Disease in the AV node will often produce prolongation in the AH interval, whereas disease in the distal conduction system produces a prolongation in the HV interval." Disease below the AV node is usually much more serious. See: Fogoros chapter on EP Testing for Bradyarrhythmias

15. Heart block occurring distal to the His bundle is associated with:
 (Select two best answers)
 a. Reentry VT
 b. A junctional rate of 40-50 bpm
 c. A ventricular rate of 20-40 bpm
 d. Deterioration and increased heart block
 e. Wenckebach

ANSWER: c. A ventricular rate of 20-40 bpm & d. Deterioration and increased heart block. Heart block occurring distal to the His bundle is termed infra-nodal block. Fogoros says: "In contrast to AV nodal block, infranodal block tends to be chronic and progressive in nature. Thus, infra-nodal blocks tend to become worse over time. Ischemia and myocardial infarction are common causes of infranodal block, usually associated with disease in the left anterior descending artery, which supplies blood to the His-Purkinje system." and "subsidiary pacemakers distal to the His bundle are unreliable and escape heart rates usually in the 20 to 40 bpm range." As coronary disease progresses, infranodal blocking increases. See: Fogoros chapter on EP Testing for Bradyarrhythmias

16. Disease in the AV node most often produces a:
 a. Short AH interval
 b. Long AH interval
 c. Short HV interval
 d. Long HV interval

ANSWER: b. Long AH interval. Fogoros says, "Disease in the AV node will often produce prolongation in the AH interval, whereas disease in the distal conduction system produces a prolongation in the HV interval." AV node disease is seldom serious unless symptoms develop. Normal AH interval varies markedly with heart rate, but the upper limit of normal is 120 ms.

Diagram shows a long interval, however RBBB is also present. See: Fogoros chapter on Principles of the Electrophysiology Study

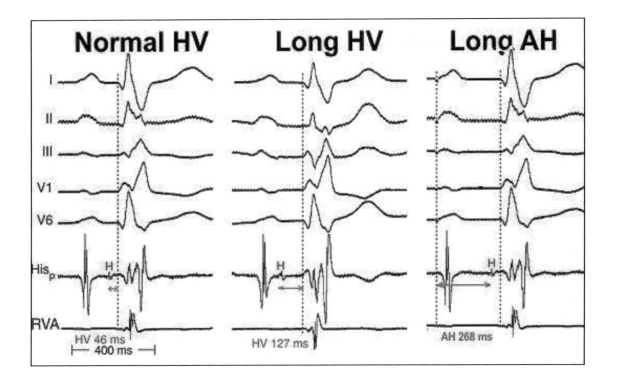

17. This patient's BP is 60/40 mmHg. His arrhythmia is _____ with a definitive treatment of _____.

   a. Complete heart block; Defibrillation
   b. Complete heart block; Pacemaker
   c. Wandering pacemaker; ECG lead II Defibrillation
   d. Wandering pacemaker; Pacemaker
   e. Second degree AV block; Antiarrhythmic drugs

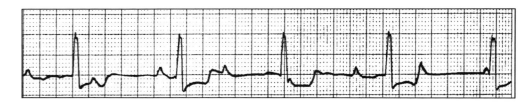

ANSWER b. Complete Heart Block (3rd Degree); Ventricular Pacemaker. This shows an idioventricular bradycardia with ventricular rate of 45. "P" waves are seen with a rate of 75 and no relation to the QRS complexes. Blood pressure was 60/40 mmHg. A patient with such a low BP would be in a decreased state of consciousness. Stimulant drugs and temporary ventricular pacemaker are needed to increase the heart rate and cardiac output. See: Davis, chapter on "Interventricular Conduction Disturbances."

18. Match each ECG complex with its lead and typical morphology.
- a. **V1, LBBB**
- b. **V6, LBBB**
- c. **V1, RBBB**
- d. **V6, RBBB**
- e. **V1, Normal**
- f. **V2, Normal**

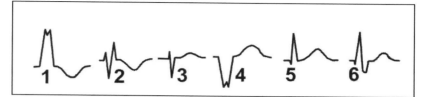

CORRECTLY MATCHED ANSWERS ARE:

a. =4.   V1, LBBB, Broad S, opposite T

b. =1.   V6, LBBB, Broad R, opposite T

c. =2.

d. =6.

e. =3.

f. = 5.

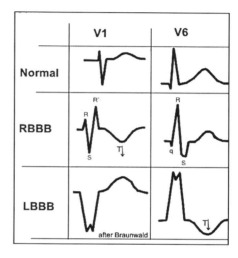

19. In LBBB the _____ ventricle fires first, causing a characteristic V1 _____ pattern.
- a. **Left; Broad QS**
- b. **Left; Narrow QR**
- c. **Right; Broad QS**
- d. **Right; Broad Rr'**

ANSWER: c. Right, Broad QS. Since the Left bundle is blocked the conduction proceeds down the His bundle into the Right bundle branch. Since the RV depolarizes first the depolarization wave must travel across the septum to depolarize the LV. This makes a slow posterior traveling wave of depolarization. Note the broad QS pattern in V1, and the broad Rr' in V6.

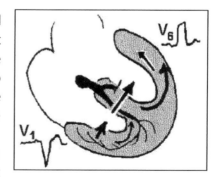

Remember the car blinker crutch to tell what V1 looks like in BBB: "To turn left (LBBB) push car blinker down, to turn right (RBBB) pull the car blinker up."

See: Davis, chapter on "Interventricular Conduction Disturbances."

20. This ECG shows what abnormality?
   a. Atrial hypertrophy
   b. Left ventricular hypertrophy
   c. Right ventricular hypertrophy
   d. RBBB
   e. LBBB

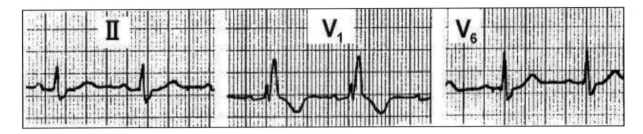

ANSWER: d. RBBB = Right Bundle Branch Block. When the Right Bundle branch becomes blocked the depolarization wave is rapid in the LV. The impulse must travel slowly through IVS, and into the RV last. This makes an anterior traveling wave of depolarization. The following signs are seen in the QRS with RBBB:

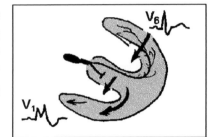

- Broad distorted QRS (>0.12sec)
- Biphasic rSR' complex in V1
- Broad negative "S" wave in V6

See: Davis, chapter on "Interventricular Conduction Disturbances."

21. This precordial lead ECG pattern (rSR' Rabbit Ears in lead V1) is associated with:
   a. Acute anterolateral MI
   b. Right bundle branch block
   c. Left ventricular hypertrophy
   d. Sinus bradycardia; left bundle branch block

ANSWER: b. Right bundle branch block. Precordial lead V1 and V6 are all that are needed for RBBB. Dubin uses the shortcut method of looking for broad QRS and a "Rabbit Ear" pattern. If the rabbit ears are in V1 it is RBBB (Rabbit & Right). If the rabbit ears are in V6 it is LBBB.

In RBBB there is a wide QRS complex and T wave inversion in lead V1. Note the typical wide and deep S wave in V6. The small q wave in V6 may not always be present. Below each QRS complex is its designation (rSR' and QRS) according to standard nomenclature. Remember the car blinker crutch to tell what V1 looks like: "To turn left (LBBB) push car blinker down, to turn right (RBBB) pull car blinker up." See: Braunwald, chapter on, "Electrocardiography"

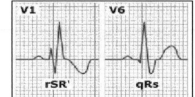

22. In typical second-degree type I AV block the His electrogram shows gradual _____ interval before the nonconducted atrial impulse.
   a. Shortening of the AH
   b. Shortening of the HV
   c. Prolongation of the AH
   d. Prolongation of the HV

ANSWER: c. Prolongation of the AH interval. Fogoros says, "With second-degree AV block of the Mobitz I type, the intracardiac electrogram shows a gradual prolongation of the AH interval in the beats immediately prior to the nonconducted atrial impulse (indicating a gradual prolonging conduction through the AV node before the dropped beat). With the dropped beat, the A deflection is not followed by an H spike, pinpointing the site of block to the AV node." Since the block occurs above the level of the His bundle, it is seldom serious. See: Fogoros chapter on EP Testing for Bradyarrhythmias

23. In second degree type I (Wenckebach) AV block the P waves occur:
   a. Irregularly, The R waves occur regularly
   b. Irregularly, The R waves occur irregularly
   c. Irregularly, The R waves occur regularly
   d. Regularly, The R waves occur irregularly

ANSWER: d. The P waves occur regularly, The R waves occur irregularly. The atrial rate is regular, but the PR interval increased progressively until one P wave is not conducted through the AV node. This drops a QRS making the ventricular rhythm. One straightforward way to identify type I or Wenckebach AV blocks is to look for the groups of QRS complexes, separated by a lone non-conducted P wave, which leaves the non-conducted P-wave alone in the pause.

In the diagram, note how three QRS complexes group together. Note the PR interval increases in three beats until it is blocked every fourth beat. This makes a pause in the ventricular rate making it irregular. Whereas in second degree type II AV block, the PR interval remains constant prior to the blocked P wave. See: Braunwald, chapter on "Specific Arrhythmias"

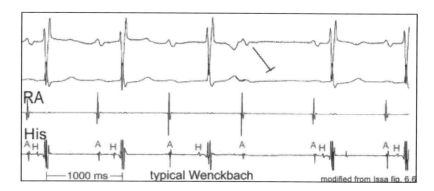

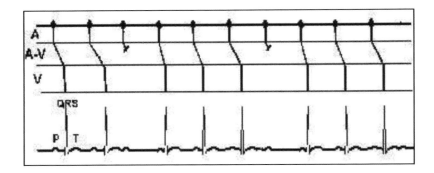

24. Second degree Mobitz II block is usually:
   a. **Supra-nodal block (AV node block)**
   b. **Supra-nodal block (His-Purkinje block)**
   c. **Infranodal block (AV node block)**
   d. **Infranodal block (His-Purkinje block)**

ANSWER: d. Infranodal block (His-Purkinje block). Fogoros says, "Second degree AV block is defined as intermittent conduction through the AV conduction system. Some but not all atrial impulses are conducted across the AV node to the ventricles. Mobitz II second degree AV block is defined as intermittent block in which an atrial impulse suddenly fails to conduct to the ventricle, without any change in the PR interval in the conducted beats preceding the dropped beat. Mobitz type II block virtually always implies infranodal block.... Mobitz type II block is virtually always located in the His-Purkinje system." See: Fogoros chapter on EP Testing for Bradyarrhythmias

25. Complete third-degree heart block:
   a. **Always represents AV dissociation**
   b. **Usually represents AV dissociation**
   c. **Seldom represents AV dissociation**
   d. **Never represents AV dissociation**

ANSWER: a. Always represents complete AV dissociation. Fogoros says, "AV dissociation is present whenever the atria and the ventricles are each being controlled by two separate and independent rhythms. That is, two separate pacemakers are present; one is controlling the atrium, and the second is controlling the ventricle. All complete heart block represents AV dissociation." If any atrial beats are conducted there is NOT complete AV dissociation.... (But) As a general rule AV dissociation represents complete heart block only when the atrial rate is faster than the ventricular rate."
See: Fogoros chapter on EP Testing for Bradyarrhythmias

26. Which of the following would present the greatest risk of leading to a Stokes Adams attack?
   a. LBBB
   b. Mobitz I
   c. Mobitz II
   d. Mobitz III
   e. Atrial Fibrillation

ANSWER: c. Mobitz II occurs when some P waves are not conducted to the ventricle. It may progress to complete heart block. Stokes-Adams attack is a sudden loss of consciousness due to heart block and bradycardia. The ECG for second-degree type 2 AV block, also known as Mobitz II, shows intermittently nonconducted P waves.

The significance of Mobitz II heart block is that it may progress rapidly to complete heart block, where no escape rhythm may emerge. In this case, the person may experience a Stokes-Adams attack, cardiac arrest, or Sudden Cardiac Death. The definitive treatment for this form of AV Block is an implanted pacemaker. In the alternatives, Mobitz I is Wenckebach. There is no Mobitz III - they meant third degree or complete heart block. See: Dubin, Rapid Interpretation of ECGs

27. Where is heart block usually located when the conduction ratio worsens with exercise or isoproterenol administration?
   a. In the SA node
   b. Below the SA node
   c. In the AV node
   d. Below the AV node

ANSWER: d. Below the AV node. Fogoros says, "A fairly simple and accurate way to evaluate AV block is to exercise the patient. Heart block that resolves during exercise is usually located in the AV node, whereas block that remains unchanged or worsens is usually located in the His-Purkinje system." Exercise, isoproterenol, or atropine usually improves conduction in AV nodal block, but usually worsens with infranodal block. Vagal maneuvers have trivial effects below the AV node because of the minimal distribution of parasympathetic nerves on the ventricular structures and the His-purkinje system. See: Fogoros chapter on EP Testing for Bradyarrhythmias

28. Second degree Mobitz II block has a His electrogram with a "dropped" beat showing:
   a. A, H, no V
   b. A, no H, no V
   c. A, normal AH interval, long HV interval
   d. A, long AH interval, normal HV interval

ANSWER: a. A, H, no V. In this EGM, note distinct A and H waves that do not conduct to the ventricle. Fogoros says, "Second degree AV block is defined as intermittent conduction through the AV conduction system. Some but not all atrial impulses are conducted across the AV node to the ventricles. See: Fogoros chapter on EP Testing for Bradyarrhythmias

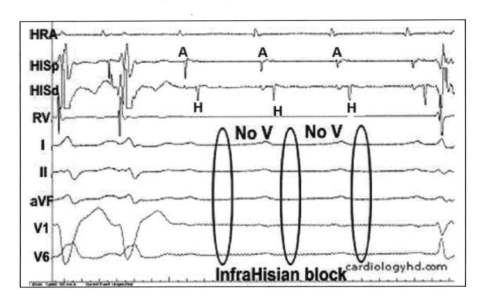

29. In bundle branch block when the T wave is in the same direction as the terminal portion of the QRS complex it is termed_____ and it suggests_____.
    a. Concordance, Myocardial ischemia
    b. Concordance, Magnesemia
    c. Discordance, Myocardial ischemia
    d. Discordance, Magnesemia

ANSWER: a. Concordance, Myocardial Ischemia. The adage that you cannot diagnose MI or ischemia if the patient has a BBB is incorrect. You can check for concordance. Remember how a PVC has its T wave opposite to the QRS -that's normal. But if the T wave is in the same direction as the S wave - it suggests ischemia.

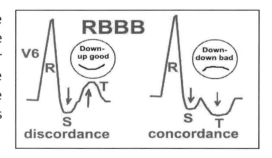

Dr. Garcia says, "The final word is this: in a bundle branch block, the T wave is always in the opposite direction of the terminal portion of the QRS. This is called discordance. If the T wave travels in the same direction as the last part of the QRS, it is known as discordance. Concordance is bad, a sign of ischemia in a bundle branch block, unless chronically present in old ECG." See: Garcia & Holtz, chapter on "ST segment and T wave" also PPT by Dr. Langdorf http://emcongress.org/2007/presentations/1Langdorf.pdf

30. Diagnosis of RBBB requires a QRS >0.12 and a rabbit ears pattern in Leads VI and V2. One other important criterion to diagnose RBBB is:
a. **Wide S wave in lead I and V6**
b. **Wide Q wave in inferior leads**
c. **Broad, monomorphic R waves in I and V6**
d. **Broad, monomorphic S waves in V1**

ANSWER: a. Wide S wave in lead I and V6. Garcia says in RBBB, "We have already seen why the QRS is prolonged, ... Under normal circumstances, the left ventricle gives rise to the vector that accounts for the QRS complex. The late innervation of the septum and the right ventricle in RBBB creates a new slower vector (vector 4 in the Figure) that is unopposed by the vectors from the left ventricle (vectors 1, 2 and 3). This new vector produces a variation in the normal ECG pattern. A new R wave appears in the right precordial leads of V1 and V2 because there is a new vector headed toward those leads. A deeper S wave is also seen in the leads that face the left side of the heart (V5, V6, and I). The S wave is slurred because of the slow transmission of the vector. This slurring [broadening] of the S wave in I and V6 is, in our opinion, the most important criterion for diagnosing RBBB. You will hear many people say that the RSR' complex in V1 is the key, but because there are hundreds of different presentations for that complex, it can prove confusing in many cases." In the diagram note that the first half of the QRS is normal, followed by the large RV late depolarization wave (#4) that creates the R' in V1 and the slurred or broad S in V6. See, Garcia & Holtz, chapter on RBBB

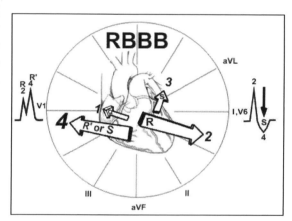

31. LBBB shows as a broad QRS with:
a. **Monomorphic R waves in V1 and Monomorphic S waves V6**
b. **Monomorphic S (or QS) waves in V1 and Monomorphic R waves V6**
c. **Polymorphic R waves in V1 and Polymorphic S waves V6**
d. **Polymorphic S (or QS) waves in V1 and Polymorphic R waves V6**

ANSWER: d. Polymorphic S (or QS) waves in V1 and Polymorphic R waves V6. Monomorphic means the QRS occurs in one direction, either all positive, or all negative. The QRS in V1 is one big ugly S or QS wave with opposite T waves. Remember that V1 is down in LBBB, like the left blinker control (LBBB) on your car gets pushed DOWN to turn LEFT. This ugly ECG is termed the "hunchback of Notre Dame" ECG. We see LBBB in most CRT cases and when an RV pacemaker fires.

Garcia says, "The pathology involved in LBBB is caused by a block of the left bundle or of both fascicles of the left bundle. This block causes the electrical potential to travel down the right bundle first. Then ventricular depolarization proceeds from right to left by direct cell-to-cell transmission. The left ventricle is so big that the transmission is delayed, hence the 0.12 seconds or more criterion, and the complexes are not initially sharp as they were in the RBBB pattern. This slowed transmission gives rise to the broad, monomorphic complexes classically seen in LBBB. Furthermore, because the

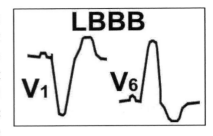

vector is proceeding from right to left, those complexes are negative in leads V1 to V2, and positive in I and V5 to V6. In other words: if you look at V1 and V6, you will note that the complexes are all positive or all negative, respectively." See Garcia & Holtz chapter on BBB.

AXIS Deviation and Misc. ECG

Use Mr. Jones FULL PAGE 12-lead ECG below for the following **seven** questions.

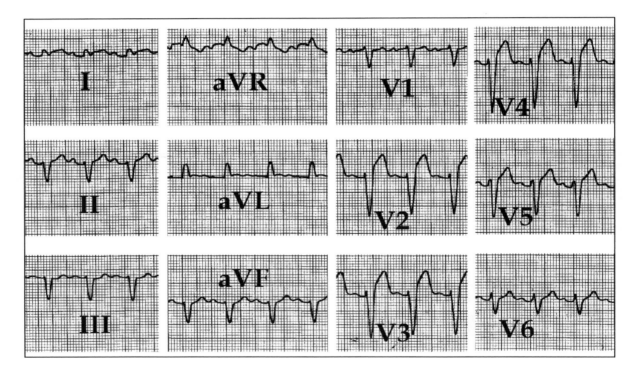

1. Measure the mean QRS axis.
   a. **-90°**
   b. **-45°**
   c. **+60°**
   d. **+90°**
2. Evaluate the mean QRS axis.

    a. Normal
    b. Left axis deviation
    c. Right axis deviation
    d. Extreme right axis deviation

3. Determine the average heart rate on the 12-lead ECG.
    a. 80 bpm
    b. 100 bpm
    c. 120 bpm
    d. 140 bpm

4. What arrhythmia does the patient have?
    a. Sinus tachycardia (with first-degree block)
    b. Atrial flutter (2:1 block)
    c. Slow Ventricular Tachycardia
    d. VVI pacing

5. Determine the QRS duration of the ECG.
    a. 0.08 sec
    b. 0.10 sec
    c. 0.14 sec
    d. 0.20 sec

6. What does the QRS duration of the ECG suggest?
    a. Pacemaker rhythm
    b. Ventricular tachycardia
    c. RBBB
    d. LBBB

7. Measure the PR interval on the ECG.
    a. 0.08 sec
    b. 0.12 sec
    c. 0.18 sec
    d. 0.22 sec

ANSWER #1: a. -90°. Look for the largest positive QRS or R wave. It is in lead aVL. This tells you that the mean QRS axis is upward and to the patients left. The most negative is either II or III. To fine-tune the axis, look for the isoelectric or equiphasic (= up and =down) lead - with smallest or most equiphasic QRS. The smallest QRS is in lead I. This lead is perpendicular to the mean QRS axis. Lead aVF is perpendicular to lead I. Lead aVF is strongly negative, indicating the axis away from the foot or straight upward at -90o. Use Davis's three ways to find the axis:

Tallest ECG points toward the axis. Most negative points away from the axis. The equiphasic QRS is at right angles (perpendicular) to the QRS. See our section on ECG axis and ECG vector determination. See: Davis, Chapter on QRS AXIS.

ANSWER #2: b. Left axis deviation. Since the LV receives the conduction impulse last, LV depolarization continues slowly from the septum posterior and leftward. This shifts the axis leftward. Note the negative RS complex in aVF.
See: Davis, Chapter on "Interventricular Conduction defects."

ANSWER #3: b. 100 beats/min. The RR interval is three large boxes or 100 beats/min.
See: Davis, Chapter on "IV Determination of HR and Normal Heart Rhythms."

ANSWER #4: a. Sinus tachycardia. The heart rate was just slightly over 100. P waves precede each
QRS (positive in lead II), indicating sinus rhythm. First degree heart block is present as indicated by long PR interval >.20 sec.
See: Davis, Chapter on "IV Determination of HR and Normal Heart Rhythms."

ANSWER #5: c. 0.14 sec. Look at lead II. The RS complex is 3.5 boxes wide. 3.5 x .04 = .14 sec. The QRS even looks broad. Normal QRS complex is less than .12 seconds wide.
See: Davis, Chapter on "IV Determination of HR and Normal Heart Rhythms."

ANSWER #6: d. Bundle branch block. The broad QRS (0.14 sec) is primarily negative in V1. The RV depolarizes first (small "R" wave in lead V1). The LV depolarizes last, with strong leftward forces (RS or RR' in V6). This LBBB pattern is like that seen with an RV pacemaker. Remember the car blinker method: V1 down=Left.
See: Davis, Chapter on IV Conduction disturbances.

ANSWER #7: d. 0.22 sec. In lead II the distance from beginning of "P" wave to beginning of QRS is 5.5 boxes. 5.5 x 0.04 = 0.22 sec. Normal is less than 0.20 sec. So, first degree AV block is present. See: Davis, Chapter on "IV Conduction disturbances."

8. **Describe the expected ECG morphology during BIV threshold testing while pacing from only the LV lead?**
   a. **Lead I will be negative and Lead III positive**
   b. **Lead I will be negative and Lead III negative**
   c. **Lead I will be positive and Lead III positive**
   d. **Lead I will be positive and Lead III negative**

ANSWER: a. Lead I will be negative and Lead III positive. Abbott says, "LV pacing looks like an LV PVC with a RBBB pattern. The QRS is a rightward, anterior, and upwards directed vector showing negative in lead I and directed positive in lead III. When measuring the LV electrode threshold, the LV is paced, and it conducts moving rightward into the RV. Since lead I is directed at 0 degrees (Left Arm) it sees the wave moving away showing a negative QRS. Lead III is positive on the other side so as the depolarization wave approaches the + (Right Leg) electrode, it will make a positive QRS. Pacing on the RV lead will provide an oppositely directed QRS resulting in switching of the mean QRS directions on these leads." All CRT devices manufactured today offer independent ventricular outputs. Different output settings are available for LV and RV and can be timed differently (RV before LV, for example) .... [In newer devices] the tip electrodes on both RV and LV leads are the cathodes (negative poles). Capture testing can be performed by programming the device to RV only or LV only pacing. It's handy to know these morphologies if you lose capture on one of the V leads, you can find the bad lead. Graphic changed from abbott.com See: abbott.com, PPT download, Cardiac Rhythm Management CRT EGMs

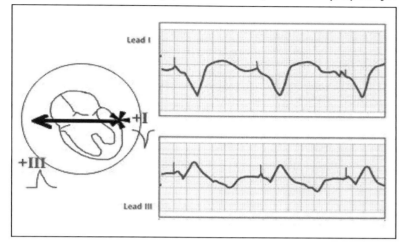

9. **What is the surface ECG like during proper BIV pacing?**
   a. **Lead I will be positive and Lead III negative**
   b. **Lead I will be positive and Lead III positive**
   c. **Lead I will be small or isoelectric and Lead III negative**
   d. **Lead I will be small or isoelectric and Lead III positive**

ANSWER: c. Lead I will be small or isoelectric and Lead III negative BIV pacing of both ventricles simultaneously will conduct upward and result in a superiorly directed vector. It will be the sum of the RV & LV paced vectors. Since it is perpendicular to Lead I it will result in a small or biphasic (RS) QRS. It is directed away from the right leg so it will result in a negative QRS in lead III as shown. You need to be able to understand vectors and their components on each axis of the hexaxial reference system. Graphic changed from abbott.com See: abbott.com, PPT download, Cardiac Rhythm Management CRT EGMs

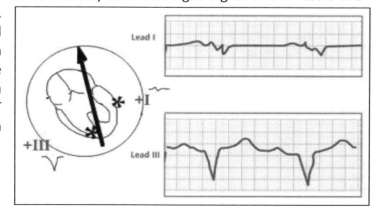

10. **In the following types of paced beats, match the mean QRS direction of each to its expected morphology in leads I and aVF. Note: + indicates positive R wave, - indicates negative QRS wave, 0 indicates isoelectric (Equal up and down)**

   1. **(Lead I=0, F=+) conducts mostly downward**
   2. **(Lead I=+, F= 0) conducts mostly leftward**
   3. **(Lead I=0, F=-) conducts mostly upward**
   4. **(Lead I=-, F= 0) conducts mostly rightward**

   e. **LV Pacing**
   f. **RV Pacing**
   g. **BiV Pacing**
   h. **Sinus Conducted Beat**

CORRECTLY MATCHED ANSWERS ARE:

1.d, Sinus (Lead I=0, F=+) e.g., conducts mostly downward
2.b. RV pacing (Lead I=+, F= 0) e.g., conducts mostly leftward
3.c. BiV pacing (Lead I=0, F=-) e.g., conducts mostly upward
4.a. LV pacing (Lead I=-, F= 0) e.g., conducts mostly rightward

See circular diagram, showing the four orthogonal directions. Of course, this is an oversimplification, because you never see perpendicular cardiac vectors like this at 0, 90, 180 and 270 degrees. The heart is more aligned along a 60-degree axis; and the paced vectors vary depending on the location of the pacing electrode. But, in general these are the main QRS axes in pacing. Lead I and V1 tell whether the ventricular vector is RV or LV. The Lead aVF and III tell whether the depolarization is starting in the atrium and conducts down (+ in aVF) or whether the depolarization starts in the ventricle (BiV) and conducts upward (- in aVF). If the vector is perpendicular to a lead, that lead will be isoelectric with either a small deflection or a biphasic deflection.

Note lead I is perpendicular to the LV paced QRS with a small biphasic RS wave. You must know your hexaxial reference system and where each lead is positive. Start with Einthoven's triangle (I, II, & III), then add the augmented leads (aVR, aVF, aVL). One way to remember this is that in normal sinus beats the mean QRS is upright in all limbs leads except aVR (the upside-down lead). This is the same reasoning you use to localize the site of a VT. See: Abbott.com, PPT download, Cardiac Rhythm Management CRT EGMs

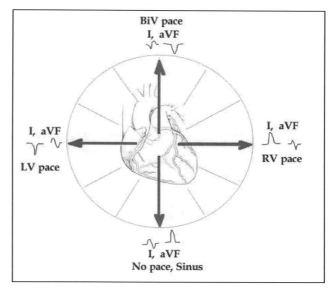

11. In a 12-lead ECG which two ECG leads are usually similar in configuration, because they measure along the same horizontal axis?

    a. I and V1
    b. I and V6
    c. II and aVF
    d. V1 and aVF

ANSWER: b. I and V6. Note on the Einthoven triangle lead I point to the left side, and in the precordial leads V6 points to the left side. V6 is on the chest and closer to the heart than lead I that is on the shoulder, so V6 is usually larger but with the same configuration.

13. The mean QRS vector normally points _____.

    a. **Leftward and inferior**
    b. **Leftward and anterior**
    c. **Rightward and inferior**
    d. **Rightward and anterior**

ANSWER: a. Leftward and inferior. Dr. Garcia says, "The QRS complex is composed of three different waves: the Q, R and S waves. Depending on the angle and size of these vectors, part of the complex may be isoelectric, they are therefore invisible to the ECG. The first area of the ventricles to depolarize is the septum. This area depolarizes in an anterior and rightward direction, ... The main ventricle then begins to depolarize, creating a large vector that is focused posteriorly and inferiorly. Finally, the basilar aspect of the ventricle then begins to depolarize in a posterior-superior direction.... Note how the three vectors flow into each other to create the QRS complexes in the

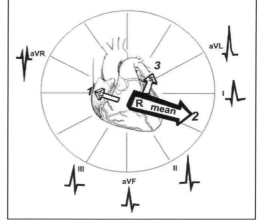

various limb leads." The large R wave moves posteriorly making lead V1 and V2 mostly negative and at about 120 degrees inferior. In the frontal plane, the normal mean QRS axis is between 0 and 90 degrees downward to the left. That's why lead II usually has the largest QRS. See Garcia, chapter on "The QRS Complex."

13. Normally the first part of the ventricle to depolarize is the _____ in a _____ direction:
   a. **LV apex, Left to right**
   b. **LV apex, Right-to-Left**
   c. **IV Septum, Left-to-Right**
   d. **IV Septum, Right-to-Left**

ANSWER: c. IV Septum, Left-to-Right. Note in the graphic how the first depolarization wave starts just in the septum and depolarizes rightward creating the small r wave in aVR. Note how it is perpendicular (isoelectric) to the inferior leads resulting in no or only a small Q wave. Shortly after the apex of the RV depolarizes and moves up the free walls toward the base. Thus, normal contraction proceeds from the apex to the base as blood is "milked" out of the ventricle. See, Braunwald chapter on ECG

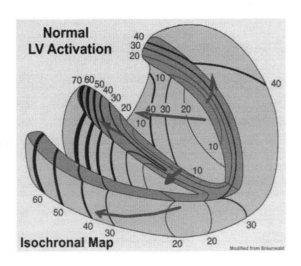

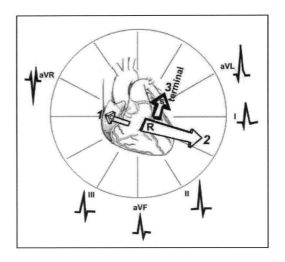

14. On the Einthoven triangle which lead is labeled #6?
   a. **I**
   b. **II**
   c. **III**
   d. **aVR**
   e. **aVL**
   f. **aVF**

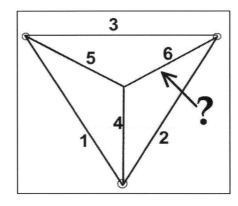

ANSWER e. AVL. Lead AVL points towards the patient's left arm and is oriented at -30 degrees above the Einthoven Triangle horizontally. The positive electrode is at the left arm while the negative pole is the sum of the RA and foot. Thus, it is a unipolar lead and is augmented to make the AV arm leads the same size as the limb – bipolar leads. In fact, aVR lead complexes are typically opposite in direction to the other leads. Knowing these are essential for locating infarctions and finding the vector axis.

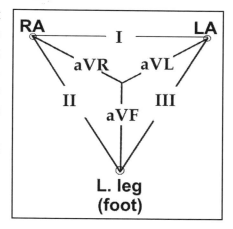

CORRECTLY MATCHED ANSWERS ARE:
1. II
2. III
3. I
4. aVF
5. aVR
6. aVL

See: Dubin, chapter on "Basics."

15. What scalar bipolar limb lead is measured between the right arm and the left arm?
   a. I
   b. II
   c. AVR
   d. AVL

ANSWER a. Lead I. The standard limb leads are commonly used in monitoring - especially Lead I & Lead II (Lead II usually gives the largest P & QRS waves). Study Einthoven's triangle. These + polarities were chosen so that all three limb leads would normally show upright QRS complexes (Although a normal lead III QRS may occasionally be biphasic, or even slightly negative (QRS). See: Berne & Levy, chapter on "Electrical Activity of the Heart."

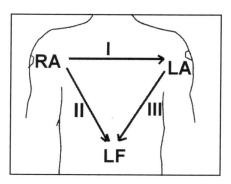

16. The ECG lead labeled #3 on this Hex-axial reference system diagram is lead _____.
   a. aVR
   b. aVL
   c. aVF
   d. I
   e. II
   f. III

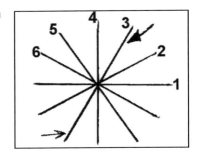

ANSWER: f. Lead III is at 120o in the second quadrant (down and to right) and is a bipolar lead normally positive at the left leg. Know this reference system. It is essential for axis and lead direction.

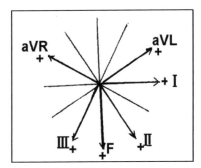

CORRECTLY MATCHED ANSWERS ARE:
   1. +I
   2. +aVL
   3. -III
   4. -aVF
   5. -II
   6. +aVR

Note that as you move around the circle the leads alternate between bipolar (I, II, III) and augmented (aVR, aVL, aVF). Also, the top half of the circle is only positive for the augmented arm leads. In fact, aVR is typically always opposite in direction from most other leads because of its vector polarity. For this reason, lead aVR is usually ignored when checking for infarction patterns. See: Braunwald, chapter on ECGs.

17. The positive pole of the aVR ECG lead on the hexaxial reference diagram is oriented in what vector direction?
   a. 0 degrees
   b. 60 degrees
   c. 90 degrees
   d. 120 degrees
   e. -150 degrees
   f. -30 degrees

ANSWER e. -150 degrees. The aVR positive lead electrode is measured from the right arm electrode. This electrode points upward to the patient's right and is oriented at -150 degrees. Its negative pole is the sum of LA & Right foot electrodes which join at the central pole. Because this negative lead combines electrodes, it reduces their voltage. All augmented leads are augmented in voltage to make them comparable to the bipolar leads. Thus, the term "augmented."

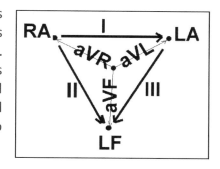

CORRECTLY MATCHED ANSWERS ARE:

aVL = -30 degrees

I = 0 degrees

aVR = + Pole at -150 degrees

II = 60 degrees

aVF = 90 degrees

III = 120 degrees

See: Braunwald, chapter on ECGs.

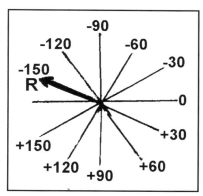

18. A mean QRS axis of the angle labeled #2 (+130o) in the frontal plane is indicative of:

    a. **Normal axis**

    b. **Right axis deviation**

    c. **Left axis deviation**

    d. **Extreme or indeterminate axis**

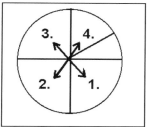

ANSWER b. Right axis deviation (RAD). It is important to understand the vector directions in ECG, because these same vector methods are used to localize VT and WPW in the EP lab. Mean QRS axis plotted in the lower right quadrant have Right Axis Deviation (RAD). RAD is between +90 and +180 degrees in the lower right quadrant. RAD may be found in hearts with

Right Ventricular Hypertrophy (RVH) and RBBB. The mean QRS axis is always close to the frontal lead with the most positive deflection. E.g., lead 2 is usually the largest QRS, so the normal mean QRS is at +60o.

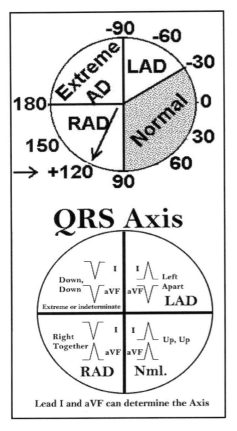

CORRECTLY MATCHED ANSWERS ARE:
1. NORMAL AXIS: = -30 to 90 degrees
2. RIGHT AXIS DEVIATION: +90 to +180o
3. EXTREME AXIS: = +180 to -90o (Also Termed Indeterminate or Extreme Right Axis Deviation)
4. LEFT AXIS DEVIATION: = -90o to -30o See: Davis, Chapter on "QRS AXIS."

19. The mean QRS axis shows Left Axis deviation when the largest frontal plane QRS complex is a large:
   a. **Upright R wave in lead III**
   b. **Negative QS wave in lead III**
   c. **Upright R wave in lead II**
   d. **Negative QS wave in lead II**

ANSWER b. Large negative "QS" wave in lead III. It is important to understand the vector directions in ECG, because these same vector methods are used to localize VT and WPW in the EP lab. Since the greatest QRS deflection is measured along a lead parallel to it. A straightforward way to find the axis is to find the biggest QRS in the frontal plane (limb leads). A negative or downward "QS" wave in lead III means depolarization is AWAY from the lead III positive electrode - which is at the right leg. So, the depolarization is away from the right leg or upwards to the patient's left (-60o). This axis is Mean QRS Axis within the left axis deviation quadrant. See: Davis, Chapter on "QRS AXIS."

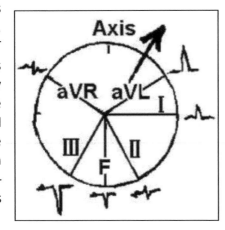

VT ECG Mapping

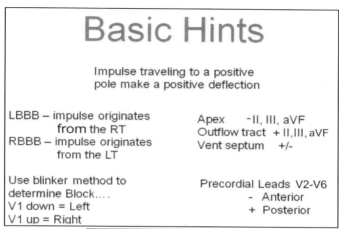

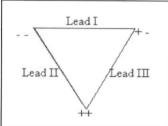

VT mapping from the 12-lead ECG is like finding the mean QRS direction using vector analysis, except we are seeking the starting focus of the ventricular beat - opposite to the direction of depolarization. So, instead of a vector with arrow pointing in direction of depolarization we want the blunt end of the arrow, from which the depolarization originates.

Use the car blinker method to name the RBBB or LBBB pattern. If V1 is up, you are making a right turn (pushing blinker up) -RBBB, the impulse originates from the left side. If V1 is down, you are making a left turn (pushing blinker down) - LBBB, the impulse originates from the right side.

Use limb leads II, III and aVF to find whether it starts high (outflow tract), or low (apex), or in the septum if isoelectric (=up and down). Remember that leads II, III and aVF are positive at the foot. Thus, + depolarizations down towards the foot will be from the outflow tract area. Similarly, - depolarizations up away from the foot originate from the apex.

Kusumoto says, "the right ventricular outflow tract is the most common site for idiopathic ventricular tachycardias (>70%). The 12-lead ECG can be helpful for identifying an arrhythmogenic focus within the RVOT and further localizing the exact arrhythmogenic site. The ECG in patients with a RVOT will be characterized by a left bundle branch block morphology with broadly positive QRS complexes in the inferior leads (inferior axis)" See: Kusumoto, chapter on VT.

Use this ECG for the next two questions.

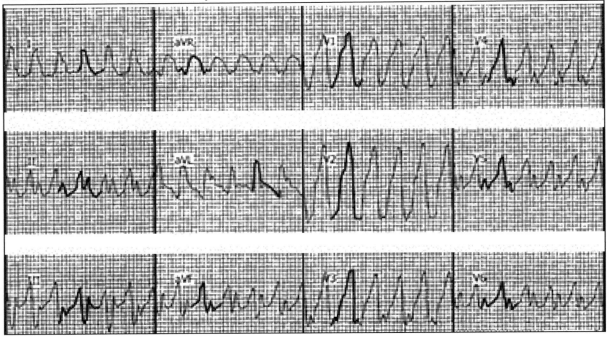

1. **This 52-year-old patient presented to the local emergency department. The following ECG was faxed to the electrophysiologist. Where does the rhythm originate from?**
    a. RVOT
    b. LVOT
    c. Right Ventricular Apex
    d. Left Ventricular Apex
    e. Left septal
    f. Right septal

2. **Specify the starting location of the VT.**
    a. Anterior
    b. Posterior

ANSWER: #1. b. LVOT #2 b. Posterior. According to Murgatroyd, "Monomorphic ventricular tachycardia is of principal interest for EP studies as it is the only ventricular arrhythmia that can be studied by conventional methods. EP testing is of much less value in patients with non-sustained VT, polymorphic VT (such as Torsades) or primary ventricular fibrillation." See: Murgatroyd, chapter on VT.

It is helpful to look at the clinical ECG (as seen above) to help find the origin of tachycardia. At this point, an EP study may be beneficial to precisely map and ablate the VT (if hemodynamically stable).

The indications for EP testing in VT patients are evolving rapidly, but in general, programmed ventricular stimulation is used: to evaluate the inducibility of VT in patients thought to be at risk, to characterize the VT and assist in the choice of therapy, for the purposes of catheter mapping and ablation, and to evaluate the efficacy of treatment. See Murgatroyd, Ventricular Tachycardia in the Electrophysiology Laboratory. Not all VT is amendable to ablation, many VT studies are performed to see if VT is inducible when the patient otherwise would not meet the qualifications for an ICD.

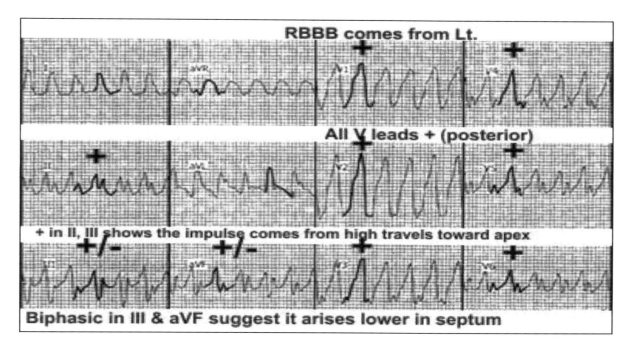

USE THIS ECG FOR NEXT 2 QUESTIONS:

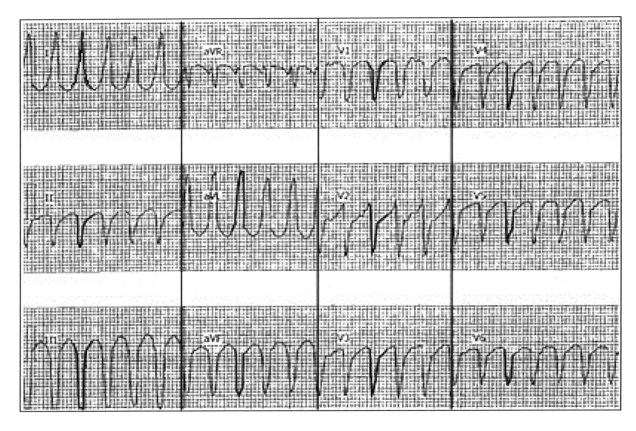

3. A 67-year-old male presented to the ER with palpitations and near syncope. The patient is stable, and ECG was performed revealing VT. Where does the rhythm originate from?
    a. RVOT
    b. LVOT
    c. Rt Vent apex
    d. Lt Vent apex
    e. Rt Septal
    f. Lt Septal

4. Specify the location of the VT.
    a. Anterior
    b. Posterior

ANSWER: #3 c. Right Ventricular Apex. #4 b. Anterior. Always make sure your patient is stable when dealing with any tachycardia; especially wide complex tachycardias that may need defibrillation. Murgatroyd says, "The differential diagnosis of a wide complex tachycardia is: supraventricular origin, with aberrant conduction; supraventricular origin, with ventricular preexcitation; and VT. Several pieces of evidence support the diagnosis of VT: inducibility from the ventricle but not the atrium; QRS morphology that is highly atypical for BBB or pre-excitation; and lack of response to adenosine." See: Murgatroyd, chapter on VT.

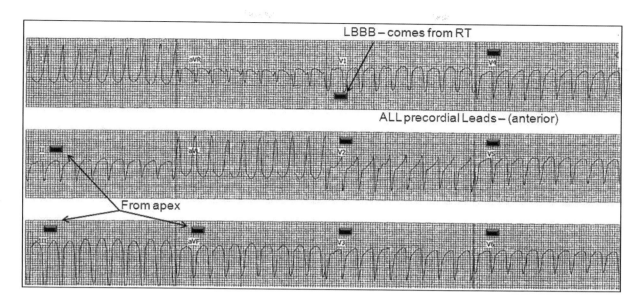

5. Where is the origin of this VT?
   a. **RVOT**
   b. **LVOT**
   c. **Rt Ventricular Apex**
   d. **Lt Ventricular Apex**

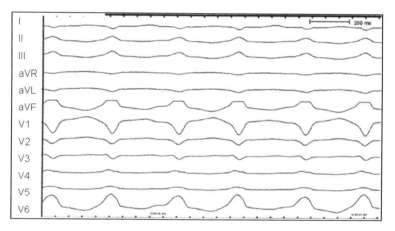

ANSWER: a. RVOT. Murgatroyd says "the key to a positive diagnosis of VT is the demonstration that the atria are not part of the tachycardia mechanism. Once VT is induced if it causes hemodynamic collapse the patient should be defibrillated. If the VT is well tolerated, the operator should try pace-termination (ATP). Keep in mind, the more aggressive the pacing intervention, the more likely it is to accelerate rather than terminate the VT." See: Murgatroyd, chapter on VT. Note in the diagram how the V lead vectors point to the patients right, and the frontal place vector points down.

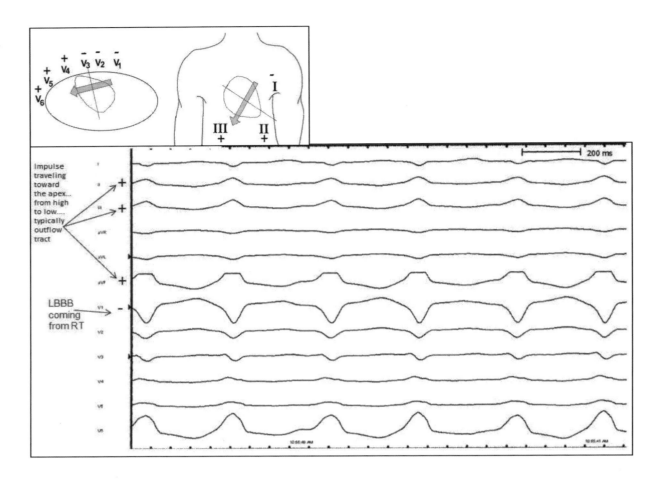

Delta Wave Mapping

You can get an idea about where a WPW accessory pathway is from the 12-lead ECG. This is analogous to finding the mean QRS direction, except instead of the average depolarization direction, you are seeking the initial delta wave. We want to know where the initial V from the AP starts. Then you can narrow it down with mapping from there.

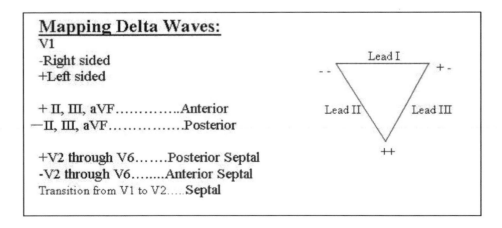

1. **On this 18-year-old patient with Delta waves, we were able to get an idea of where the pathway was found with 12-lead mapping. Where is the pathway?**
    a. Right Posteroseptal
    b. Left Posteroseptal
    c. Anteroseptal
    d. Left Mid Anterior

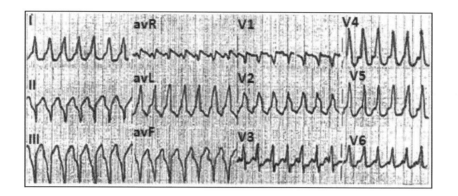

ANSWER: a. Right Posterior Septal. WPW (Wolff-Parkinson-White) is a preexcitation syndrome since it activates the ventricles early. An accessory pathway is an abnormal electrical connection between the atrium and the ventricle. Many people with WPW are asymptomatic; however, there is still a risk of SCD (sudden cardiac death). Using this pathway, a patient may go into AVRT (Atrioventricular reentrant tachycardia) which is a form of SVT.

The incidence of WPW is between 0.1% and 0.3% in the general population. Sudden cardiac death in people with WPW is rare (incidence of less than 0.6%) and is usually caused by the propagation of an atrial tachy-rhythm to the ventricles by the abnormal accessory pathway. Some individuals may experience palpitations, dizziness, shortness of breath, or syncope during episodes of supraventricular tachycardia.

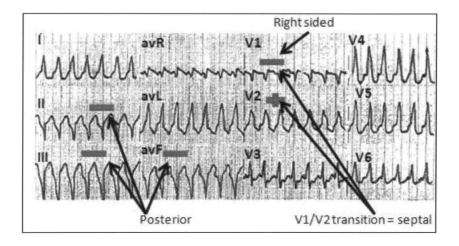

2. This patient came to the lab with complaints of palpitations. On the clinic ECG, delta waves were noticed. Where is the pathway?

   a. **Right Posteroseptal**
   b. **Left Lateral / Anterior aspect**
   c. **Anteroseptal**
   d. **Left Mid Anterior**

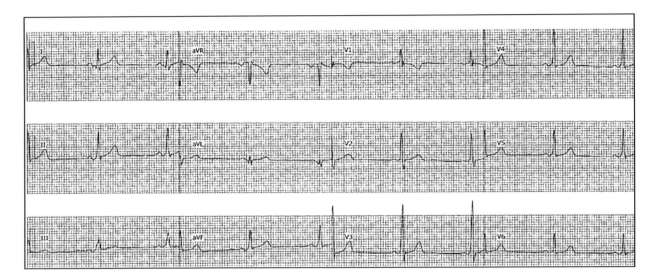

ANSWER: c. Anteroseptal. The delta wave isn't quite as obvious as in some examples. Mapping out the pathway by use of the surface ECG is just to get you close to the right area or the right "zip code". Extensive pacing maneuvers and mapping for the earliest activation and AV fusion is needed to find the precise location.

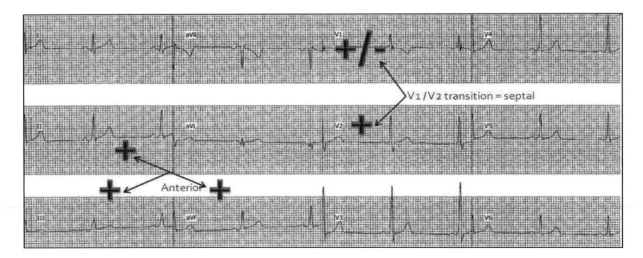

The AV node serves an important function as a "gatekeeper", limiting the electrical activity that reaches the ventricles. In situations where the atria generate excessively rapid electrical activity (such as atrial fibrillation or atrial flutter), the AV node limits the number of signals conducted to the ventricles. For example, if the atria are electrically activated at 300 beats per minute, half those electrical impulses may be blocked by the AV node, so that the ventricles are stimulated at only 150 beats per minute—resulting in a pulse of 150 beats per minute).

Another important property of the AV node is that it slows down individual electrical impulses. This is manifested on the electrocardiogram as the PR interval (the time from electrical activation of the atria to electrical activation of the ventricles), which is usually less than 200 milliseconds in duration.

Individuals with WPW have an accessory pathway that communicates between the atria and the ventricles, in addition to the AV node. This accessory pathway does not share the rate-slowing properties of the AV node and may conduct electrical activity at a faster rate than the AV node. For instance, in the example above, if an individual had an atrial rate of 300 beats per minute, the accessory bundle may conduct all the electrical impulses from the atria to the ventricles, causing the ventricles to contract at 300 beats per minute. Extremely rapid heart rates such as this may result in hemodynamic instability or cardiogenic shock. In some cases, the combination of an accessory pathway and cardiac dysrhythmias can trigger ventricular fibrillation, a leading cause of sudden cardiac death.

3. This patient presented with delta waves on a presurgical ECG. Where is the pathway?
   a. **Left Lateral / Anterior aspect**
   b. **Right free wall**
   c. **Anterior septal**
   d. **Posterior septal**

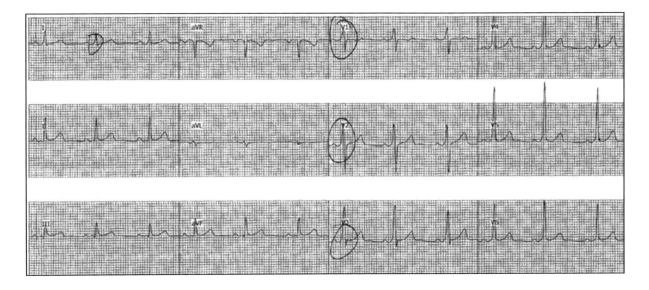

ANSWER: a. Left Lateral / Anterior aspect. If the AV node conducts very rapidly and the pathway is far away the delta wave will not be as prevalent as this example. If conduction is slowed down through the AV node with drugs or if you atrial paced the patient closer to the pathway, the delta wave would be more noticeable.

According to Fogoros, "Bypass tracts can occur virtually anywhere along the AV groove (except in the space between the aortic valve and the mitral valve) and can also occur more or less parallel to the AV conducting system in the septal area." See: Fogoros chapter on SVT

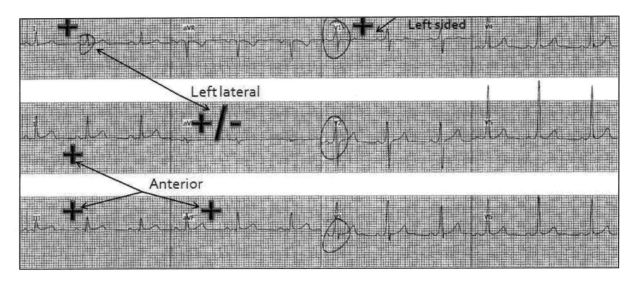

4. Where is the AVRT pathway located?
   a. **Right Posteroseptal**
   b. **Left Posteroseptal**
   c. **Anteroseptal**
   d. **Left Mid Anterior**

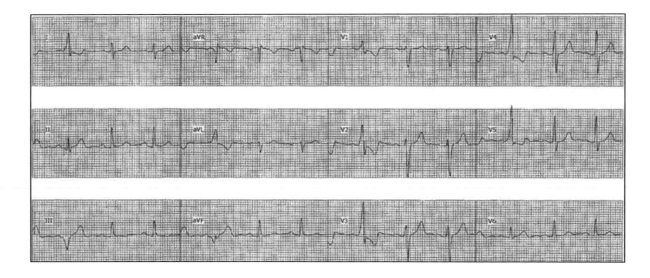

ANSWER: b. Left Posterior Septal. Notice there was only one beat on each of the leads in which the pathway manifested itself. Fogoros says, "Bypass tracts may or may not conduct in the antegrade direction. When they do (in the case of WPW), the surface ECG often shows preexcitation of the QRS complex. Preexcitation refers to antegrade conduction over a bypass tract that stimulates the ventricle prematurely. This ventricular stimulation is premature because the bypass tract conducts rapidly, like most myocardial tissue. Thus, and impulse traveling over the bypass tract does not display the delay seen when an impulse encounters the AV node." See: Fogoros chapter on SVT

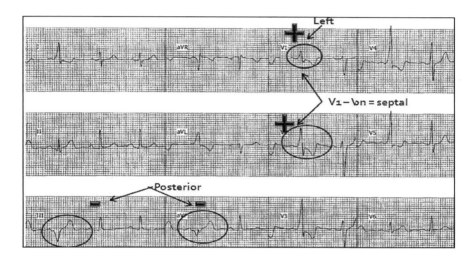

5. The following 12-lead ECG was taken on a 15-year-old WPW patient. Where is the pathway?
- a. **Right Posteroseptal**
- b. **Left Lateral/ Anterior Aspect**
- c. **Right Free Wall**
- d. **Left Mid Anterior**

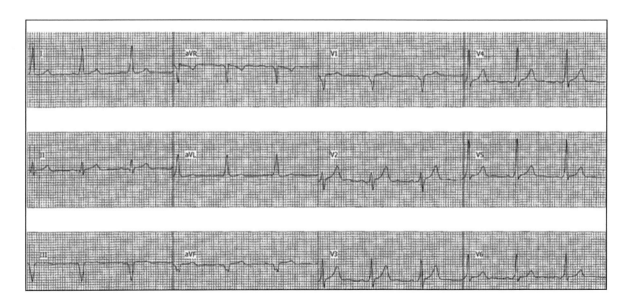

ANSWER: a. Right Poseroseptal. This is WPW, you can tell this by the presence of delta wave, the slur on the upstroke of the QRS. In patients whose bypass tracts are capable of antegrade conduction, most QRS complexes are fusion beats between ventricular stimulation via the normal AV conduction
system and ventricular stimulation via the bypass tract. The degree of preexcitation then depends on several factors, including the AV nodal conduction time; the conduction velocity and refractory period of the bypass tract; and how close the bypass tract is to the SA node. See: Fogoros: Supraventricular Tachycardias

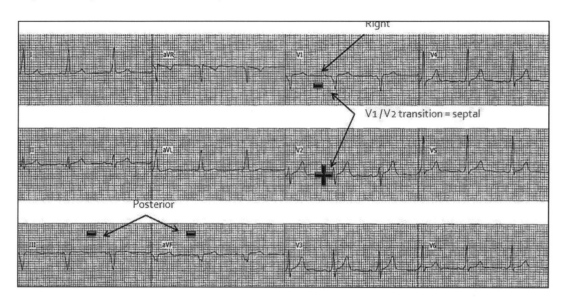

6. This 18-year-old patient had a history of palpitations and dizzy spells. In the ER the above ECG was taken. Where is the pathway?
  a. **Right posteroseptal**
  b. **Left Lateral**
  c. **Right free wall**
  d. **Left mid septal**

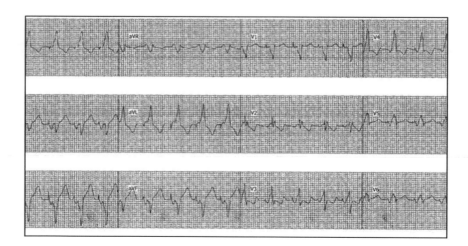

ANSWER: a. Right Poseroseptal. This ECG reveals AVRT. More specifically WPW which is AVRT in the Antidromic direction. Notice the one normal beat on the bottom strip. On that beat it went down the AV node rather than the pathway. Fogoros says, "Bypass tracts are clinically significant for three reasons. First, they can confuse the clinician. Delta waves can masquerade as Q waves and lead to the false diagnosis of myocardial infarction. Marked preexcitation that occurs during an atrial tachycardia can lead to the mistaken diagnosis of ventricular tachycardia. Second, bypass tracts often function as one pathway of a macro reentrant circuit (the normal AV conduction system acting as the second pathway). Thus, macro reentrant supraventricular tachycardia is common in patients with bypass tracts. Third, bypass tracts can bypass the normal protective mechanism of the AV node during atrial tachyarrhythmias. In bypass tracts with short antegrade refractory periods, extremely rapid ventricular rates can result during atrial tachyarrhythmias. This may be

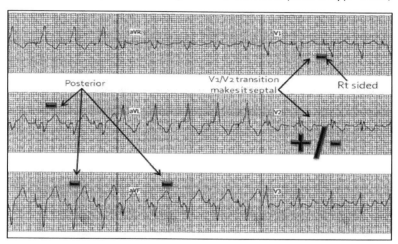

life threatening." See: Fogoros chapter on SVT

7. When mapping the delta wave from this ECG, where is the accessory pathway?
   a. **Left Lateral / Anterior aspect**
   b. **Right free wall**
   c. **Posteroseptal**
   d. **Left Mid Anterior**

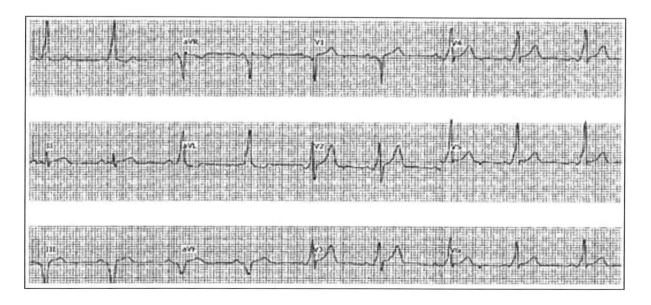

ANSWER: c. Posteroseptal. AVRT is a form of macro reentrant tachycardia. It is often induced by PAC at a time when the bypass tract is still refractory from the previous impulse, but when the AV node has recovered. This circuit needs all the following components to continue tachycardia: Atria, accessory pathway, ventricle, and AV node. If there is block in the AV node the tachycardia may not continue. One will not see AVRT in a patient without retrograde conduction (V to A). When the tachycardia goes down the bypass tract and up the AV node it is said to be Manifest or Antidromic (WPW). When the tachycardia goes down the AV node and up the bypass tract it is said to be Concealed or Orthodromic (ortho meaning correct). Orthodromic AVRT is not called WPW simply AVRT. So, all WPW reentrant tachycardias are called AVRT, but not all AVRT is considered WPW.

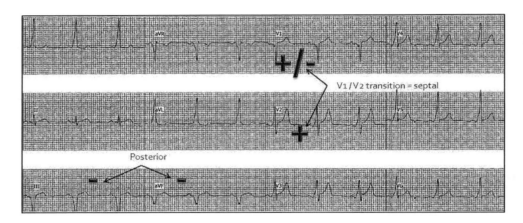

Chapter 3
Electrophysiology Building Blocks

1. Electricity (pg. 113)
2. Math & Units (pg. 118)
3. Action Potential (pg. 120)
4. Impulse Formation, Filters, & Mechanisms (pg. 130)
5. Signals & Measurements (pg. 138)

EP Essentials LLC

Electricity:

1. The flow of electric current is measured in:
    a. **Ohms**
    b. **Volts**
    c. **Watts**
    d. **Amperes**

ANSWER: d. Amps = 1 coulomb/sec   Electric current flow is like fluid flowing through tubes. Current (I) is analogous to fluid flow, except when the units change. Hemodynamic flow is expressed in L/min. Electric current flow is in coulombs/sec. See: Electronic text

2. What is the term used to denote the total opposition to flow of alternating current in a circuit:
    a. **Reactance**
    b. **Impedance**
    c. **Inductance**
    d. **Capacitance**

ANSWER: b. Impedance or resistance (ohms). Resistance is the term used to denote opposition to DC current flow. Impedance is the complex resistance to alternating or pulsating flow. Impedance changes with the frequency, amount of capacitance, resistance, and inductance - as shown in the diagram. The same is true in fluid systems composed of pulsatile flow, compliant vessels, and dynamic inertial forces. When the impedance rises during RF ablation it means something is increasing the resistance to current flow, like char on the electrode tip or loss of tissue contact. See: Aston, Chapter #1 on Definitions, components.

3. What is the most common DC electric power source?
   a. 60 cycle wall outlets
   b. A charged capacitor
   c. Transformer
   d. Battery

ANSWER: d. Battery. Batteries are an electrochemical source of direct current. DC current only travels in one direction. Defibrillators use batteries to charge a capacitor. See: Physics text

4. Electric battery current has a frequency of:
   a. 0 Hz
   b. 60 Hz
   c. 120 Hz
   d. 1000 Hz

ANSWER: a. 0 Hz. DC current flows steadily from - to +. It does not alternate back and forth like AC current does. See: Aston, Chapter #1 on "Definitions, components..."

5. The elimination of vibrations at certain frequencies is accomplished using electronic devices known as:
   a. Diodes
   b. Grids
   c. Filters
   d. Rectifiers

ANSWER: c. Filters. Most amplifiers have high and low limits beyond which they do not amplify. ECG amplifiers typically incorporate a band pass filter that cuts off low frequencies < 0.1 Hz and high frequencies >100 Hz. Pressure amps. use only a low pass filter, because they pass all low frequencies - down to 0 Hz or DC. The upper limit may be changed to increase fidelity and/or reduce motion artifacts. See: Aston, Chapter #1 on "Definitions, components..."

6. When a DC defibrillator charges it stores electrical energy in its_____.
   a. Batteries
   b. Capacitors
   c. Transformers
   d. Photovoltaic cells

ANSWER: b. Capacitors. Large capacitors store the charge. When you charge a defibrillator, large capacitors become polarized and charged up to several thousand volts. This allows for a large amount of electricity to be temporarily stored. When the shock button is depressed, this charged capacitor is suddenly discharged into the patient. See: Aston, Chapter #1 on "Definitions, components..."

7. EP lab external defibrillators should be tested by:
   a. **Discharging paddles into a dummy load**
   b. **Discharging paddles against each other**
   c. **Measuring paddle & cable resistance**
   d. **Evaluating a defibrillation threshold**

ANSWER: a. Discharging paddles into a dummy load. Test firing a defibrillator can be dangerous. It must be fired into a resistance like that of a human thorax. Many defibrillators have dummy loads built into the paddle rests for this purpose. Discharging paddles against each other or in the air can damage the defibrillator. See: Company Literature

8. The watt second (or Joule) is a unit of:
   a. **Current**
   b. **Energy**
   c. **Resistance**
   d. **Rate of power usage**

ANSWER: b. Energy. Defibrillators are charged from 50-360 Joules. Watt second units are like the units on your home electricity/energy bill in Kilowatt hours. A watt is the product of voltage and current. 1 Watt = 1 volt x 1 amp.

Common units are:
Frequency = Hertz = cycles / sec
Force = Newton = m kg/sec2 (also weight in grams - CGS)
Energy or work = Joule =m2 kg/sec2 (also Ergs or Watt Sec)
Power = Watt =m2 kg/sec3 (also rate of doing work)
See: Curry, Chapter on "Radiation"

9. What is the current drawn by a resistor of 100 ohms, if a 10-volt battery is applied across it?
   a. **0.1 amp**
   b. **10 amp**
   c. **100 amp**
   d. **1000 amp**

ANSWER: a. 0.1 amp. I = V/R = 10v/100Ω = 0.1 amp or 100 milliamps. This is used to measure pacemaker lead impedance. Ohms law relates current, voltage and resistance just the way cardiac output relates to driving pressure and resistance. If you can't remember Ohm's law, use this triangle. Cover up the letter you want to solve for. E.g., Cover up the V on top, to get the formula I x R on the bottom of the triangle. To solve for current (amps) cover I, to get V/R. See: Aston, Chapter #1 on
"Definitions, components..."

10. Using Ohm's law calculate the amount of current drawn by a pacemaker if it's lead resistance is 200 Ohm's and the pacing voltage is 1 volt (Use Ohm's law):
   a. 0.5 mA
   b. 2 mA
   c. 5 mA
   d. 20 mA

ANSWER: c. 5 mA. Simple Ohm's law. $I = V/R = 1000$ mV/200 ohm = 5 mA. Know how to calculate current, voltage, and resistance. You can use the little triangle image to remember the formula. Cover up the unknown, to get the formula. To solve for V, cover it up and you see I R. So, $V = I R$ To solve for I, cover it up, and get the formula V/R. So, $I = V/R$. Note that I is current. Watson says: "Current is measured while pacing at a fixed output (5.0 V and 0.5 millisecond). It is the rate the electrical charge passes through any point within the circuit. Its unit of measurement is milliamperes (mA) and can be obtained using the PSA. "See: Watson, Chapter on Cardiac Pacing

11. In electrical injury, the pathway of current most likely to be fatal is:
   a. Hand-to-hand
   b. Hand-to-foot
   c. Foot-to-foot
   d. Foot-to-ground

ANSWER: a. Hand-to-hand. Most of the current passes though the chest and heart using much the same path as defibrillation. It is the path most likely to cause ventricular fibrillation. Hand-to-foot current path is more associated with cardiac muscle damage. To prevent shock, electricians avoid the practice of working with both hands-on live circuits. Lightning strikes on an individual are DC current that is less hazardous than 60 cycle AC current. Also, protective in lightning strikes is a "flash over" phenomenon, where the current travels along the outer surface of the body. See: ACLS manual, Chapter on Special Resuscitation Situations.

12. For maximum electrical safety, the ECG monitored patient should be _____, and the monitor chassis should be _____ or nonconductive.
   a. Grounded, Grounded
   b. Grounded, Ungrounded
   c. Ungrounded, Ungrounded
   d. Ungrounded, Grounded

ANSWER: d. Ungrounded, Grounded. Patients should never be connected directly to the ground. This is analogous to standing in a pool of conductive water. A grounded patient becomes a lightning rod available to conduct any potential leakage currents. Whereas, if the patient is ungrounded, or floating, he does not provide himself with a ready conductor to ground. Most medical instruments at a patient's bedside are encased in a metal box (chassis). For safety these should always be grounded through the third prong of the plug (green wire). Properly grounded medical equipment safely conducts stray leakage currents away from the patient to ground. Some new devices are encased in a plastic non-conductive case which makes leakage current flows negligible. Plastic cases, especially battery operated, need not be grounded because they are insulated and cannot conduct leakage currents. See: Aston, Chapter on Electrical Shock.

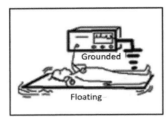

13. In the ICU when recording an intracardiac ECG from a pacing electrode or pericardiocentesis needle in the heart, it is safest to _____.
   a. **Ground the ECG monitor to a water pipe**
   b. **Ground the patient to a water pipe**
   c. **Use a battery powered monitor**
   d. **Use low resistance defibrillation pads as the limb electrodes**

ANSWER: c. Use a battery powered monitor. This will reduce micro shock hazard. Underhill says, "To record the electrocardiogram from a pacing wire, or to help guide a pericardiocentesis needle, it is safest to operate the monitor on battery power, if possible. Otherwise, only use an instrument known to have a leakage current of less than 10 µA..." Because batteries are not referenced to ground, battery power provides a safe method of preventing leakage current. See: Underhill, chapter on Electrical Hazards in the Cardiac Care Unit.

14. When you plug in an electric instrument, you are alarmed when sparks fly from the wall outlet as shown. The most likely electrical safety problem is a:
   a. **Outlet incorrectly wired**
   b. **Broken insulation on the power cord**
   c. **Machine off-on switch was left turned-on**
   d. **Machine fuse shorted out**

ANSWER: c. Machine off-on switch was never turned off. Electrical equipment should not be turned off (or on) by pulling the plug from (or plugging it into) an electric outlet. Switches are designed to safely do this. Pulling the plug of a piece of equipment while it is operating can also damage the equipment, melt the plug, and present a fire hazard. Consider how computers can be damaged if turned off incorrectly. See: Aston, Chapter on Electrical Shock.

Math & Units:

1. The prefix "centi" corresponds to:
   a. **1/10**
   b. **1/100**
   c. **1/1000**
   d. **1/1,000,000**

ANSWER: b. 1/100 = "centi"

2. Which prefix listed below is correctly arranged from smallest to largest?
   a. **Milli, deci, centi, nano**
   b. **Nano, micro, milli, centi**
   c. **Nano, centi, micro, milli, deci**
   d. **Micro, nano deci, centi, milli**

ANSWER: b. Nano, micro, milli, centi. nano= 10-9, micro=10-6, milli = 10-3, centi = 10-2. These prefixes are used in measurements of ultrasound waves and microscopic measurements. See: Reynolds, chapter on Elementary Principles.

3. Convert 30 Kg into pounds:
   a. **44 lbs**
   b. **55 lbs**
   c. **66 lbs**
   d. **77 lbs**

ANSWER: c. 66 lbs. 30 kg (2.2 lb/kg) = 66 kg. To remember which is larger, you will be happy to learn you weigh less in metric kg, about half as much. 220 lb = 100 kg

4. A PR interval measures 4 mm long on an ECG strip which was run at paper speed 25 mm/sec. How long is the PR interval?
   a. **160 ms**
   b. **200 ms**
   c. **250 ms**
   d. **400 ms**

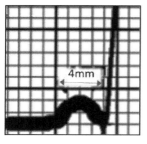

ANSWER: a. 160 ms

$$4 \text{ mm} \left(\frac{1 \text{ sec}}{25 \text{mm}} \right)\left(\frac{1000 \text{ms}}{\text{sec}} \right) = 160 \text{ ms}$$

5. **In electrophysiology, the formula for calculating heart rate is:**
    a. **Programmed base rate/upper rate**
    b. **60 sec/min x (Time period in seconds)**
    c. **60,000 ms/min / (Time period in milliseconds)**
    d. **Time period in milliseconds / (60,000 ms/min)**

ANSWER: c. 60,000 ms/min / (Time period in milliseconds) Rate = 60,000/RR interval. E.g., if the RR interval is 860 ms, Rate = 60,000/ (860) = 70 bpm. This formula uses the fact that there are 60 sec in a minute or 60,000 ms in one minute. See: Moses, chapter on "Types of Pacemakers and Hemodynamics of Pacing"

6. **Match the cycle length of the following heart rates.**

    1. **300 bpm**   **a. 10 ECG boxes (1 cm) cycle length at standard ECG speed**
    2. **150 bpm**   **b. 500 ms cycle length**
    3. **120 bpm**   **c. 200 ms cycle length**

CORRECTLY MATCHED ANSWERS ARE:
    1. 300 bpm = c. 200 ms cycle
    2. 150 bpm = a. 10 ECG boxes (1 cm) cycle length standard ECG speed
    3. 120 bpm = b. 500 ms cycle length

The formula is HR = (60 sec/min)/ (RR in sec.) or (60,000 ms/min)/ (cycle length in ms.) for
#1   300 bpm = 60,000/200 = 300

Fogoros says, "When electrophysiologists talk about heart rate, they typically speak in terms of cycle length, the length of time between each heartbeat. Thus, the faster the heart rate, the shorter the cycle length: an arrhythmia with a rate of 100 beats/min has a cycle length of 600 ms, while an arrhythmia with a rate of 300 beats/min has a cycle length of 200 ms. " See: Fogoros chapter on Principles of the Electrophysiology Study

7. **Calculate the heart rate (HR) if the R-R interval is 920 ms?**
    a. **42 bpm**
    b. **51 bpm**
    c. **65 bpm**
    d. **72 bpm**

ANSWER: c. 65 bpm   Use the basic formula (you should memorize): HR = 60/RR, or
HR = (60,000 ms/min)/ (r-r interval in ms) (60,000 ms/min)/ 920 ms = 65/min.
EP study and Pacemaker rates are now calculated not with ECG boxes, or seconds but in milliseconds. Since there are 1000 ms/sec, the standard HR formula uses 60,000 in the numerator. Note how the units cancel to give beats/min. See: Braunwald, chapter on Electrocardiography.

Action Potential:

1. When the heart is insensitive to stimuli and cannot be depolarized by stimulation (such as pacing), it is said to be:
   a. Aberrant
   b. Blocked
   c. Arrested
   d. Refractory

ANSWER: d. Refractory. This is the period of the cardiac cycle when the myocardium cannot respond to a second impulse because it has not fully recovered. That is why a ventricular pacing impulse in the ST segment (refractory period) is ineffective. The refractory period has two parts: absolute and relative refractory periods. Absolute refractory period includes the entire action potential plateau (ST segment) as shown. However, during the relative refractory period the heart is somewhat sensitive to extrastimuli. An extrastimuli or PVC here may initiate VT or VF. See: Berne and Levy, Chapter on Electrical activity of the heart.

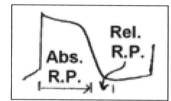

2. Purkinje and ventricular cells have their own automaticity and intrinsic rate. These lower pacemaker rates are usually suppressed if:
   a. Enough calcium is available
   b. The AV node conduction rate is normal
   c. The SA node rate is fast enough
   d. The conduction system is normal

ANSWER: c. The SA node pacemaker rate is fast enough. It is normally the fastest in the heart. Only when the SA rate slows or another pacemaker speeds up, does it relinquish its control of the intrinsic pacemaker's heart rhythm. Pacemaker control goes to the one with the fastest rate.

These lower pacemakers with slower intrinsic rates are found in the atrium (60), junctional (50), & ventricular tissue (30-40). They are normally suppressed until they escape the control of the SA node - and pace the heart at their own intrinsic rate (60, 50, or 30-40 ppm respectively). Note the lower in the heart the pacemaker, the lower its intrinsic rate. See: Dubin, chapter on Heart Rate.

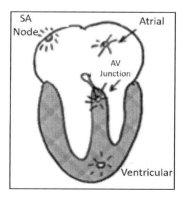

3. Sympathetic nervous stimulation of the heart primarily affects the heart rate by altering what phase of the SA node action potential?
  a. Phase 1
  b. Phase 2
  c. Phase 3
  d. Phase 4

ANSWER: d. Phase 4. A mechanism to speed the sinus rate is to increase the slope of phase 4, so that the cell reaches firing threshold sooner. The other mechanisms that change the heart rate are altered threshold and resting potential. NSR is Normal Sinus Rhythm. See: Berne and Levy, Chapter on Electrical activity of the heart.

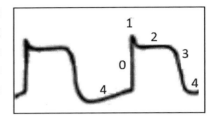

4. Which of the below is NOT one of the three things which change the rate (automaticity) of automatic cells?
  a. Slope of phase 4
  b. Unidirectional block
  c. Threshold potential
  d. Resting membrane potential

ANSWER: b. Unidirectional block. The automatic pacemaker cells fire when they reach a threshold voltage. Three things shown in the diagram affect the time a cell takes to reach firing threshold:
1. Discharge threshold (dotted line) can change
2. Slope of phase 4 (Ca++ leakage) can change
3. Lower resting potential forces the cell to take
    longer to reach threshold

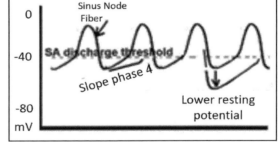

See: Berne & Levy, chapter on "Electrical Activity in the Heart."

5. Concerning the ion transfer across myocardial cell membranes, throughout systole (QT interval):
  a. Sodium seeps in
  b. Sodium rushes in
  c. Potassium leaks out
  d. Potassium seeps in

ANSWER: c. Potassium leaks out. Throughout systole the K+ ions slowly exit and Ca++ ions slowly enter. The positive ions pass each other making the voltage change to approximate zero during this phase 2 plateau period. After the Ca stops seeping in, phase 3 or repolarization is due to K continuing to leak out of the cell. These slow currents follow the rapid in-rushing of sodium during rapid depolarization. See: Fogoros, chapter on "The Cardiac Electrical System."

6. What part of the ventricular action potential is the resting membrane potential?
   a. Phase 1
   b. Phase 2
   c. Phase 3
   d. Phase 4
   e. Phase 5

ANSWER: d. Phase 4 is the resting membrane potential. This is the period that the cell remains in until it is stimulated by an external electrical stimulus (Typically, an adjacent cell). This phase of the action potential is associated with diastole of the ventricles. It is the flat or slowly rising final phase. In ventricular muscle tissue, the resting membrane potential rises until it reaches a threshold, where it automatically fires. This resulting slow heart rate is the intrinsic ventricular rate of 20-40 bpm which serves as a backup, should the higher pacemakers fail. This diagram shows the action potential phases and the ion channels. Note, there is no phase 5, just an additional phase 0 for rapid depolarization. See: www.ncbi.nlm.nih.gov/bookshelf/

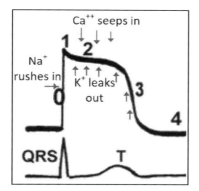 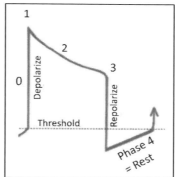

7. What is the trans-membrane potential when a purkinje cell is in the resting state? It is _____ and _____.

   a. Polarized, negatively charged inside
   b. Polarized, positively charged inside
   c. Depolarized, negatively charged inside
   d. Depolarized, has relatively NO charge inside

ANSWER: a. Polarized, negatively charged inside. In the resting state the cell is charged up like a battery. It is negatively charged inside to -90 mV. The ion pumps have repolarized it with more + ions outside the cell (Na & Ca) making the inside of the cell (K) relatively negative. This repolarizing phase #3 is the refractory period of the cell. Ventricular repolarization corresponds to the T wave on the ECG. Atrial repolarization is small and buried in the QRS complex. All cardiac muscle cells are like this, although some cardiac cells do not have such a square shaped action potential or so low a resting voltage. E.g., SA & AV nodes have a slow upstroke, a sinusoidal shape and repolarize to -60 mV.

Fogoros says, "Once a cell is depolarized, it cannot be depolarized again until the ionic fluxes that occur during depolarization are reversed. The process of getting the ions back to where they started is called repolarization. The repolarization of the cardiac cell roughly corresponds to phases 1 through 3 (i.e., the width) of the action potential...The action potential we have been using as a model is a typical Purkinje fiber action potential.... The action potential that differs most radically from the Purkinje fiber model are found in the SA node and AV node." See: Fogoros chapter on The Cardiac Electrical System

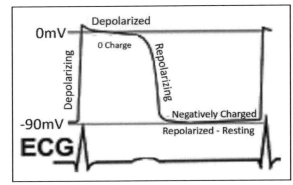

8. **Compared to myocardial cells, SA node cells are prone to a faster _____ because of their steeper phase _____.**
   a. **Rhythmicity, 3**
   b. **Automaticity, 4**
   c. **Depolarization, 3**
   d. **Depolarization, 4**

ANSWER: b. Automaticity, 4. The "slow cells" are found in the SA node, natural pacemaker regions, and AV node "junctional areas." These are the main areas which can act as automatic pacemakers in the heart. Although slow to depolarize in phase "0", their inherent automatic rate is much faster than myocardial cells. The "slow cells" are faster during phase 4 diastolic depolarization. Thus, the sinus node normally sets the pace. It reaches itself excitation threshold and emits a new impulse before either the AV node or the Purkinje fibers can. Note the flatter phase "4" slope of myocardial cell shown. See: Berne & Levy, chapter on "Electrical Activity of the Heart."

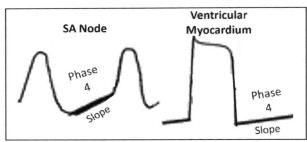

9. **What ion rushes across the myocardial cell membrane during phase 0 of the action potential?**
   a. **Sodium seeps in**
   b. **Sodium rushes in**
   c. **Potassium leaks out**
   d. **Potassium seeps in**

ANSWER: b. Sodium rushes in during phase zero which is the time of the ECG QRS complex. This is termed a fast current, because it happens quickly as the cell wall suddenly becomes permeable to the Na^+ ion. Cardiac muscle cells are different from purkinje and automatic tissues in that their rapid upstroke (phase 0) is due to Na^+ rushing in through the fast channel. Automatic cells don't have this rapid channel; and their phase zero is a slow upstroke. The slope of phase zero also influences conduction velocity. E.g., Nodal tissue has slow upstroke and slow conduction velocity.
See: Fogoros, chapter on " The Cardiac Electrical System."

10. SA and AV node depolarization (action potential upstroke) comes through the:
   a. Na^+ **fast channel**
   b. Na^+ **slow channel**
   c. Ca^{++} **fast channel**
   d. Ca^{++} **slow channel**

ANSWER: d. Ca^{++} slow channel. SA and AV nodal cells are termed slow cells because they are slow to depolarize, repolarize, and conduct. These automatic cells are different from cardiac muscle cells in that they have NO FAST Na^+ channels. The sodium channels are termed "fast channels" and the calcium channels are termed "slow channels" node action potential because of their depolarization rate. Fogoros says, "the SA and AV nodes are thought to be dependent entirely upon the slow calcium channel for depolarization." Cardiac muscle cells are different in that their rapid upstroke (phase 0) is due to Na^+ rushing in through the fast channel.
See: Fogoros, chapter on "The Cardiac Electrical System."

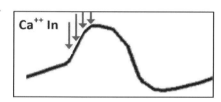

11. Match the shape and speed of each action potential phase in the box with its effect on myocardial cells.
   1. **Phase 0 (upstroke)**   a. **Refractory period**
   2. **Phase 1-2-3 (plateau & repolarization)**   b. **Automatic rate**
   3. **Phase 4 (diastolic depolarization)**   c. **Propagation velocity**

CORRECTLY MATCHED ANSWERS ARE:
Phase 0, Rapid depolarization rate determines the conduction or propagation velocity of that tissue. The Purkinje tissue shown will conduct rapidly. Antiarrhythmic drugs such as lidocaine and procainamide effect only this fast channel.

Phase 1-2-3 includes the overshoot, plateau, and repolarization phases. During this time the heart is refractory and cannot contract, even if stimulated. Because CA+ ions enter then, Calcium channel blockers lengthen this refractory period.

Phase 4, diastolic depolarization, or resting phase determines the automatic heart rate of that tissue. The more rapid the slope of phase 4, the faster the heart rate of that tissue. This

Purkinje tissue will fire at a slow rate (junctional escape), because of the slowly rising phase 4. Myocardial cells have an even slower escape rate.

Fogoros says, "The shape of the action potential determines the conduction velocity, refractory period, and automaticity of cardiac tissue." See: Fogoros, chapter on "The Cardiac Electrical System" and Braunwald, chapter on Genesis of Arrhythmias.

12. What cardiac tissue has the fastest electrical conduction velocity?
   a. **SA node**
   b. **Atrial muscle**
   c. **AV node**
   d. **Purkinje fibers**
   e. **Ventricular muscle**

ANSWER: d. Purkinje fibers. Purkinje fibers rapidly conduct the electrical signal to the ventricles 2-3 m/sec. That is a factor of 20 times faster than the other cardiac tissues, thus the normally narrow QRS complex. By comparison, the node and muscle fibers conduct slowly 0.1 - 0.5 m/sec. (Broad QRS). See: Braunwald chapter on Arrhythmias, Sudden death, and Syncope.

13. The ERP of ventricular tissue most closely correlates with its:
   a. **Absolute Refractory Period**
   b. **Functional Refractory Period**
   c. **Relative Refractory Period**
   d. **Ending of phase 3 action potential**

ANSWER: a. Absolute Refractory Period. "The ERP is the period after depolarization during which the cell cannot be depolarized again. When introducing a premature impulse, that impulse will fail to propagate through tissue that is refractory.... In general, the ERP occurs sometime during the 1st third of phase 3 of the action potential." ERP is what we measure in the EP lab. Relative or functional ERP occurs after the absolute refractory period; this is a period where larger pacing spikes may still cause depolarization albeit a weakened and slowed one. See: Fogoros, chapter on "Principles of the EP Study"

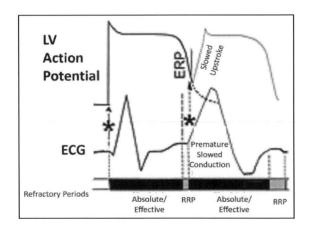

14. From the timing of the action potentials labeled, match the cardiac tissue it represents.
   a. SA nodal tissue
   b. AV nodal tissue
   c. Purkinje tissue
   d. Atrial muscle
   e. Ventricular muscle

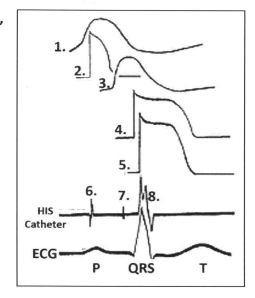

CORRECTLY MATCHED ANSWERS ARE:

1. SA node Slow cell, pacemaker of the heart. A relatively steep phase 4 will bring the cell to firing threshold before the other cells shown. SA nodal cells normally have the fastest intrinsic heart rate.
2. Atrial muscle fast cell, timed to coincide with atrial contraction on His bundle electrogram (HBE) and ECG.
3. AV node slow cell depolarization follows atrial depolarization. It fires between atrial contraction and purkinje depolarization. Because of its slow depolarization AV nodal cells conduct slowly. This causes the normal conduction delay at the AV node. The slowly rising phase 4 allows junctional tissue to develop an automatic escape rate of 40-60/min in the lower area of the AV junction, when needed.
4. Purkinje fast cell follows AV node depolarization, and rapidly conducts the depolarization wave to the ventricular muscle cells.
5. Ventricular muscle fast cell follows the purkinje depolarization.
6. "A" wave due to atrial contraction seen on the His bundle electrogram. It coincides with ECG "P" wave and atrial action potential phase 0.
7. "H" wave of His depolarization seen on the His bundle electrogram. It falls between the AV node depolarization and purkinje cell depolarization.
8. "V" wave of ventricular depolarization seen on the His bundle electrogram. This coincides with the ventricular action potential, phase 0, and the beginning of the ECG QRS complex. See: Braunwald, chapter on Genesis of Arrhythmias.

15. The plateau (phase 2) of the ventricular action potential occurs on the surface ECG during the _____ and during mechanical _____:
   a. QRS complex, systole
   b. QRS complex, diastole
   c. QT interval, systole
   d. QT interval, diastole

ANSWER: c. QT interval, systole. The QRS occurs during phase 0, but phase 2 plateau happens in QT interval. This is the period of mechanical systole, where the arterial pressure is generated. See: diagram

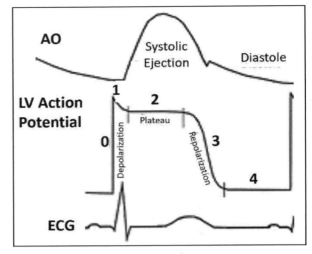

16. What ionic flows occur across the cardiac muscle cell membrane during the plateau (phase 2) of the action potential?
   a. Ca^{++} exits, NA$^+$ exits
   b. Ca^{++} exits, NA$^+$ enters
   c. Ca^{++} enters, K$^+$ exits
   d. Ca^{++} enters, K$^+$ enters

ANSWER: c. Ca^{++} enters, K$^+$ exits throughout systole, the K$^+$ ions slowly exit and Ca^{++} ions slowly enter the cell. The positive Na$^+$ ions pass each other making their contribution negligible during this phase 2 plateau period. These slow currents follow the rapid in-rushing of sodium during rapid depolarization. There are too many of these ionic currents (I) and gates to memorize. We only emphasize the most important ionic flows. Some are shown in this diagram FYI. See: Fogoros, chapter on The Cardiac Electrical System.

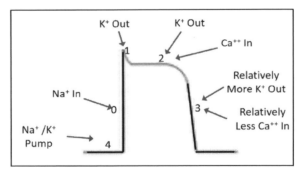

17. What ionic flows occur across the cardiac muscle cell membrane during the resting phase (phase 4) of the action potential?
   a. Ca^{++} exits, NA$^+$ exits
   b. Ca^{++} exits, NA$^+$ enters
   c. Ca^{++} enters, K$^+$ exits
   d. Ca^{++} enters, K$^+$ enters

ANSWER: d. Ca^{++} exits, K$^+$ enters. Throughout diastole the K$^+$ ions slowly reenter and Ca^{++} ions slowly exit. This is just the opposite of what happens in systole. This resting phase recharges the cell membrane (like recharging a battery to -90 mV). The Na-K pump and Na-Ca pump restore ionic balance, putting back the main ions that moved in systole, Ca and K. This is often depicted in diagrams as rotating paddle wheels on the cell wall, where the wheels push certain ions out and pulls other in. Note the Na ions balance each other out. These pumps use the most energy (ATP) in the cell. Like charging a battery up, the cell is storing energy for when it is released in systole. See: Fogoros, chapter on "The Cardiac Electrical System."

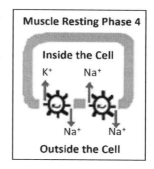

18. Which two cardiac tissues have a slow phase 0 action potential and thus a slow conduction velocity?
   a. **Atrial muscle & ventricular muscle**
   b. **Atrial muscle & SA node**
   c. **AV node & ventricular muscle**
   d. **SA node & AV node**

ANSWER: d. SA node & AV node. Both depolarize slowly from the slow Calcium channel, and both are sinusoidal in shape. It is this slow upstroke and velocity in the AV node that causes the normal AV delay. As opposed to this, latent pacemaker cells in the AV junction, Purkinje and cardiac muscle cells have a rapid phase 0 upstroke due to rapid Na+ influx. This allows rapid conduction through the specialized conduction system and bundle branches. See: Fogoros, chapter on The Cardiac Electrical System.

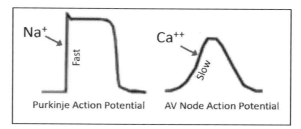

19. What is the response of cardiac tissues paced during the relative refractory period (RRP)? Compared to fully repolarized cells, stimulation in the RRP _____.
   a. **Requires higher mA but create a weaker contraction**
   b. **Requires higher mA & create a stronger contraction**
   c. **Will respond at lower mA, but may induce arrhythmia**
   d. **Will respond at lower mA, and will not induce arrhythmia**

ANSWER: a. Require higher mA but creates a weaker contraction. Since currently the tissue is partially refractory, it requires a larger than normal stimulus, and it results in a smaller than normal response. Consider how a PVC propagates slowly and does not fully contract the ventricle. The RRP is also the vulnerable period for starting arrhythmias; so, answer c is partially correct. See: diagram modified from Fogoros.

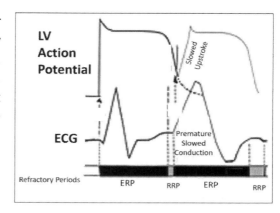

Fogoros says, "The relative refractory period (RRP) requires the introduction of a new concept. Recovery from refractoriness turns out to be a gradual process instead of an instantaneous one. As shown, the end of the ERP occurs during phase 3, before a cell is fully depolarized (that is, before phase 4 begins). If a cardiac cell is stimulated after the end of the ERP but before the cell is fully repolarized, the resulting action potential has a slower upstroke (phase 0) and therefore propagates at a slower conduction velocity. The period from the end of the ERP to the beginning of phase 4 is called the RRP. Formally the RRP of a tissue is the longest coupling interval for which a premature impulse result in slowed conduction through that tissue. At the end of the RRP, the tissue is fully recovered." See: Fogoros, chapter on Principles of the EP study

21. **Which of the following is the heart's normal conduction sequence to the His bundle?**
   a. **SA node, RA atrial muscle, LA muscle, AV node**
   b. **SA node, LA atrial muscle, RA muscle, Purkinje fibers, AV node**
   c. **AV node, Atrial muscle, SA node**
   d. **AV node, Bachman's bundle, Atrial muscle, SA node**

ANSWER: a. SA node, RA atrial muscle, LA muscle, AV node. The SA node normally initiates right atrial contraction. The impulse then travels through three specialized atrial conduction fibers to the AV node, and through Bachman's Bundle across the atrial septum into the LA. The RA contracts first, then the LA. As the RA completes its contraction the impulse enters the AV node where it is delayed allowing ventricular filling. See: Braunwald, chapter on Electrocardiography. also, Todd, Vol. II, Chapter on ECG.

22. **What is the primary ion exiting the cell during phase 3 of a ventricular myocardial cell?**
   a. **Chloride**
   b. **Sodium**
   c. **Calcium**
   d. **Potassium**

ANSWER: d. Potassium. Substrate maps are commonly utilized in the LA during PVI (pulmonary vein isolation) for AF. This will access the tissue health with higher voltages representing healthier tissue and lower voltages being more diseased or scar. This method is also commonly utilized in VT ablations to demarcate areas of scar. There are other uses for substrate maps as well such as identifying a low voltage bridge for slow pathway ablations and even to help identify and "healthier" channels within an area of scar that map participate in a reentrant tachycardia (atypical AFL / ischemic VT).

Impulse Formation, Filters, & Mechanisms:

1. Which is NOT a requirement to sustain a reentry circuit?
   a. Two parallel pathways connected proximally and distally
   b. One pathway is an isthmus between two conductive areas
   c. One pathway conducts slower than the other
   d. One pathway has a longer refractory period

ANSWER: b. One pathway is an isthmus between two conductive areas - NOT. Notice, "conductive" instead of "nonconductive" boundary areas. In atrial flutter the cavotricuspid isthmus is between the nonconductive TV and the nonconductive IVC. The term "isthmus" means a narrow strip of land. This area is easiest to ablate in typical AFL because it is the narrowest part of the macro-reentry circuit.

Fogoros says, Reentry requires that the following criteria be met:
   1. Two roughly parallel conducting pathways must be connected proximally and distally by conducting tissue, thus forming a potential electrical circuit.
   2. One of the pathways must have a refractory period that is substantially longer than the refractory period of the other pathway.
   3. The pathway with the shorter refractory period must conduct electrical impulses more slowly than the other pathway.

"If all these seemingly implausible prerequisites are met, reentry can be initiated when an appropriately timed premature impulse is introduced to the circuit…. A continually circulating impulse is established, spinning around and around the reentry loop. All that remains for this reentrant impulse to usurp the rhythm of the heart is for this reentrant impulse to exit from the circuit at some part during each lap and thereby depolarize the myocardium outside the loop." See: Fogoros

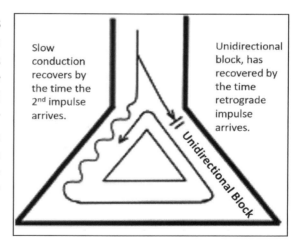

Slow conduction recovers by the time the 2nd impulse arrives.

Unidirectional block, has recovered by the time retrograde impulse arrives.

Unidirectional Block

2. What causes fractionated electrograms?
   a. Colliding depolarization wave fronts
   b. Triggered depolarization (EAD or DADs)
   c. Nonuniform anisotropy (Zigzag conduction)
   d. Rapid repolarization (phase 4 Automaticity)

ANSWER: c. Nonuniform anisotropy (Zigzag conduction). Anisotropy is the property where conduction is nonuniform, as opposed to isotropy, which is normal concentric conduction in all directions. The diagram shows how conduction must zigzag around scar tissue creating low voltage fractionated signals.

Issa says: "In normal ventricular myocardium, conduction in the direction parallel to the long axis of the myocardial fiber bundles is approximately three times more rapid than that in the transverse direction.... Change in the characteristics of anisotropic propagation at the macroscopic scale from uniform to nonuniform strongly predisposes to reentrant arrhythmias. Nonuniform anisotropy has been defined as tight electrical coupling between cells in the longitudinal direction but uncoupling to the lateral gap junctional connections. Therefore, there is disruption of the smooth transverse pattern of conduction characteristic of uniform anisotropy, which results in a markedly irregular sequence or zigzag conduction, producing the fractionated extracellular electrograms." See Issa, chapter on Mechanisms of Cardiac Arrhythmias

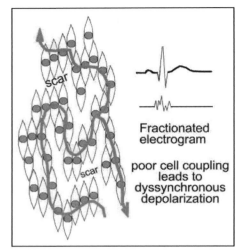

Fractionated electrogram

poor cell coupling leads to dyssynchronous depolarization

3. **The pause after rapid atrial pacing ceases is termed:**
   a. **Pacer induced aberrancy**
   b. **Ashman phenomenon**
   c. **Overdrive suppression**
   d. **Pacemaker induced refractoriness**

ANSWER: c. Overdrive suppression. Fogoros says, "The pause induced in an automatic focus by a temporarily overdriving pacemaker is called overdrive suppression." The focus or tissue becomes fatigued by the fast rate and takes some time to recover. See: Fogoros chapter on Principles of the Electrophysiology Study

4. **Most arrhythmias in the EP lab are caused which mechanism?**
   a. **Vagal response**
   b. **Automaticity**
   c. **Triggered**
   d. **Reentry**

ANSWER: d. Reentry. Purves says, "Many, if not most of the clinically important tachycardias are reentrant tachycardias.... The classic reentrant tachycardia requires two potential pathways of conduction that can be dissociated. Tachycardia is initiated by an ectopic beat that blocks in one zone and "reenters" via the other zone to initiate a "circus" or circular movement." We seldom see automatic or triggered arrhythmias in the EP lab, because they are not easily inducible and are rare. See, Purves, chapter on Common Clinical Tachycardias

5. Triggered arrhythmias are often associated with digitalis toxicity or elevated interventricular Ca⁺⁺ levels. What mechanism causes triggered arrhythmias?
   a. **Automaticity in ventricular tissue**
   b. **Automaticity in atrial tissue**
   c. **After-depolarization**
   d. **Reentry**

ANSWER: c. After-depolarization. Triggered beats are always coupled to a preceding action potential (as are reentry beats). But these are not a circus movement of an impulse. Triggered beats are a spontaneous depolarization somehow coupled to the preceding action potential through abnormal Ca⁺⁺ channel activity.

There are two types of triggered beats: EADs and DADs. Early after-depolarizations (EADs) occur early at the end phase 2 or in early phase 3. Delayed Afterdepolarizations (DADs) occur late in phase 3 or early phase 4. Issa says, "Digitalis causes DAD-dependent triggered arrhythmias by inhibiting the Na+-K+ exchange pump.... DAD-related triggered activity is thought to be a mechanism for tachyarrhythmia associated with MI, reperfusion injury, right ventricular outflow tract (RVOT) VT and some atrial tachyarrhythmias. DADs are more likely to occur with fast spontaneous or paced rates, or with increased premature beats. In general, triggered activity is influenced markedly by overdrive pacing." See: Issa, chapter on "Mechanisms of Cardiac Arrhythmias"

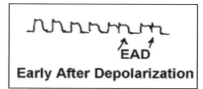

6. The arrhythmogenic triggered activity shown at #1 is _____, and an associated arrhythmia is _____.
   a. **DAD, torsades de pointes**
   b. **DAD, RVOT VT**
   c. **EAD, torsades de pointes**
   d. **EAD, RVOT VT**

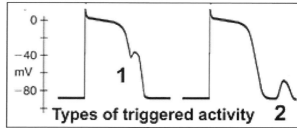

ANSWER: c. EAD, torsades de pointes, caused by Ca⁺⁺ overload in the myoplasm and sarcoplasmic reticulum. Early after-depolarizations (EADs) occur with abnormal depolarization during phase 2 or phase 3. Image #2 is a DAD, delayed afterdepolarization in phase 4.

Issa says, "A fundamental condition that underlies the development of EADs is action potential prolongation, which is manifest on the surface electrocardiogram (ECG) by QT prolongation. Hypokalemia, hypomagnesemia, bradycardia, and drugs can predispose to the formation of EADs.... EAD-mediated triggered activity likely underlies initiation of the characteristic polymorphic VT, torsades de pointes, seen in patients with congenital and acquired forms of long-QT syndrome."

#2: shows a delayed afterdepolarization (DAD). These occur in the resting phase four. Issa says, "DAD- related triggered activity is thought to be a mechanism for tachyarrhythmia associated with MI, reperfusion injury, right ventricular outflow tract (RVOT) VT and some atrial tachyarrhythmias. DADs are more likely to occur with fast spontaneous or paced rates, or with increased premature beats. DADs usually occur under a variety of conditions in which Ca^{++} overload develops in the myoplasm and sarcoplasmic reticulum." See: Issa chapter on EP Mechanisms of Cardiac Arrhythmias

7. In this diagram, a hexapolar electrode catheter tip is positioned at a source of myocardial activation (depolarization). Match the electrode combination with its expected EGM recording.

1. **Unipolar**
2. **Bipolar 5-6**
3. **Bipolar 3-4**
4. **Bipolar 1-2**

a. **Broad QS wave**
b. **Midway bipolar signal**
c. **Earliest bipolar signal**
d. **Last bipolar signal**

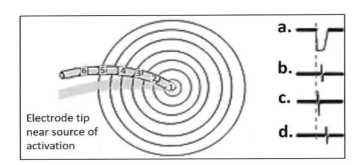

ANSWERS:
1. Unipolar = a. Broad QS wave
2. Bipolar 5-6 = d. Last bipolar signal
3. Bipolar 3-4 = b. Midway bipolar signal
4. Bipolar 1-2 = c. Earliest bipolar signal.

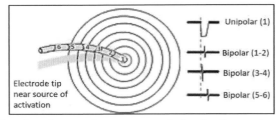

The unipolar electrode records the entire depolarization from the center of the bullseye to its edge. The depolarization moves entirely AWAY from the positive terminal. So, it is a deep & broad QS much like a V1 recording of LBBB. We also see deep Q waves on the surface ECG when an electrode is over an area of infarct, where the initial ventricular depolarization moves AWAY from the dead area.

The bipolar recordings only show local activity as the wave of depolarization passes beneath them, first the distal electrodes (1-2), then the middle electrodes (3-4), and finally the proximal electrodes (5-6). If the bipolar recordings are stacked from distal to proximal and are correctly stacked up on the recorder, the signal shifts to the right and later in time, as the wave passes under them. This is much like recording a retrograde A wave from an orthodromic LV accessory pathway as it moves eccentrically from the LA to the RA. See Issa, chapter on "Mapping & Navigation"

8. In this diagram, a hexapolar electrode catheter body is positioned across a source of myocardial activation as shown. Match the electrode combination with its expected EGM recording.

1. Unipolar
2. Bipolar 5-6
3. Bipolar 3-4
4. Bipolar 1-2

a. Midway low voltage bipolar signal
b. Earliest bipolar
c. Midway high voltage bipolar signal
d. Broad RS wave

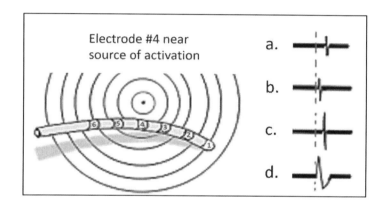

CORRECTLY MATCHED ANSWERS ARE:
1. Unipolar = d. Broad RS wave
2. Bipolar 5-6 =a. Midway low voltage bipolar signal
3. Bipolar 3-4 = b. Earliest bipolar signal
4. Bipolar 1-2 = c. Midway high voltage bipolar signal

The unipolar electrode records the entire depolarization including the far field signal. The depolarization wave moves initially towards the unipolar electrode, passes under it, and moves away as the wave leaves the outer ring of the bullseye. So, it initially shows an upright R complex coming towards and finally a deep S wave moving away.

The bipolar recordings only show local activity as the wave of depolarization passes beneath them, first the middle electrodes (3-4), the distal and proximal electrode pairs are about equal distance away from the center, so they each show the depolarization at the same time. However, the distal tip electrode (1-2) shows a higher voltage because they are in contact with the myocardium. If the bipolar recordings are stacked from distal to proximal and correctly positioned on the recorder, the signal diverges from the middle electrode pairs and moves both distal and proximal, right and left at the same time. Learn to read relative activation times especially on CS catheters. See Issa, chapter on Mapping & Navigation

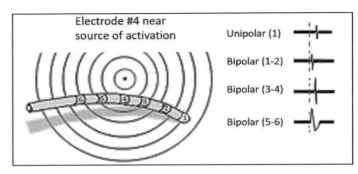

9. Surface ECG leads are usually filtered at:
   a. **0.1 to 100 Hz**
   b. **1 to 100 Hz**
   c. **30 to 300 Hz**
   d. **50 to 500 Hz**

ANSWER: a. 0.1 to 100 Hz. Reducing the high-pass filter to 0.1 Hz means T waves and ST changes will be accurately measured. One problem with such a low setting is baseline drift. "The surface ECG is usually filtered at 0.1 to 100.0 Hz. The bulk of the energy is in the 0.1- to 20.0-Hz range. Because of interference from alternating current (AC), muscle twitches, and similar relatively high-frequency interference, it is sometimes necessary to record the surface ECG over a lower frequency range (reduce the low pass filter) or to use notch filters (which filter out 60 Hz noise)." See: Issa, chapter on EP Testing

10. Normal EGM filter settings for bipolar EP catheters are:
   a. **0.1 to 100 Hz**
   b. **3 to 300 Hz**
   c. **30-300 Hz**
   d. **100-500 Hz**

ANSWER: c. 30-300 Hz. Issa says, "To acquire true local electrical activity, a bipolar electrogram with an interelectrode distance less than 1 cm is preferable. Smaller interelectrode distances record increasingly local events. In normal homogeneous tissue, the initial peak of a filtered (30 to 300 or more Hz) bipolar recording coincides with depolarization beneath the recording electrode" See: Issa, chapter on EP Testing

11. If large T waves on an electrogram interfere with A or V wave recognition you should:
   a. **Lower the high-pass filter**
   b. **Raise the high-pass filter**
   c. **Lower the low-pass filter**
   d. **Raise the low-pass filter**

ANSWER: b. Raise the high-pass filter. The high-pass filter removes lower frequencies by passing frequencies higher than the filter setting. The higher you set the high pass filter frequency, the less baseline drift and the waveforms become more biphasic. Far-field waves and slow T waves may be filtered out from bipolar electrodes at a high-pass filter setting of 30 Hz. Unipolar electrodes may use a high-pass filter setting of 1-2 Hz. Surface ECG settings set the high-pass filter even lower, at 0.5 Hz because you want to see ST-depression and T waves.

The low pass filter removes high frequencies by passing frequencies lower than the filter setting. The lower the low-pass filter setting the less sharp the V wave becomes. High frequency EMI and muscle tremor will be filtered out.

Electrogram recordings use band-pass filters, for both high and low-pass filters. A common setting is 30 Hz for the high-pass filter and 300 Hz for the low-pass filter. This graph shows how pacemaker sensing amplifiers discriminate between discriminating T waves from P waves, and R waves from muscle potentials. Only frequencies in the gray U area are sensed. See: http://www.theeplab.com

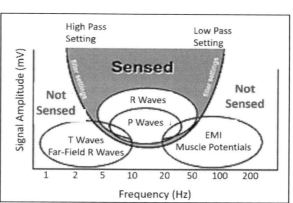

12. When filtering an EGM, a low pass filter setting of 500 Hz means:
   a. **Signals over 500 mV will be clipped**
   b. **Signals under 500 mV will be clipped**
   c. **Frequencies <500 Hz will be eliminated**
   d. **Frequencies >500 Hz will be eliminated**

ANSWER: d. Frequencies >500 Hz will be eliminated. Issa says, "Defining a band of frequencies to record, such as setting the high-pass filter to 30 Hz and the low-pass filter to 500 Hz, defines a band of frequencies from 30 to 500 Hz that are not attenuated (i.e., band pass filtering). A notch filter is a special case of band pass filtering, with specific attenuation of frequencies at 50 or 60 Hz to reduce electrical noise

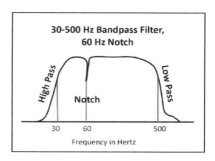

introduced by the frequency of common AC current." Note in the diagram how the low pass end of the filter is really on the high end. It only passes frequencies lower than 500 Hz. See: Issa, chapter on EP Testing

13. Band pass filtering like 30-500 Hz is used on bipolar EGMs to:
   a. **Amplify minute signals and improve signal-to-noise ratio**
   b. **Amplify minute signals and remove 60-cycle noise**
   c. **Eliminate far-field signals and improve signal-to-noise ratio**
   d. **Eliminate far-field signals and remove 60-cycle noise**

ANSWER: c. Eliminate far-field signals and improve signal-to-noise ratio. In the diagram note how much clearer the His signal is in the bipolar tracing, but the unipolar shows direction of current flow throughout depolarization.

Defining a band of frequencies to record, such as setting the high-pass filter to 30 Hz and the low-pass filter to 500 Hz, defines a band of frequencies from 30 to 500 Hz that are not attenuated (i.e., band pass filtering).

Issa says, "Intracardiac electrograms are usually filtered to eliminate far-field noise, ... Because the far-field signal is similar at each instant in time, it is largely subtracted out, leaving the local signal. Therefore, compared with unipolar recordings, bipolar recordings provide an improved signal-to-noise ratio, and high-frequency components are more accurately seen." See: Issa, chapter on EP Testing

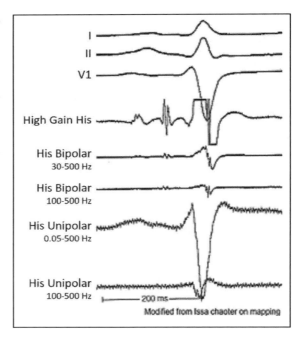

14. When a mapping catheter is guided to the site of origin of a focal tachycardia its distal bipolar EGM records the earliest intrinsic presystolic deflection. To confirm this as the focus, switch your mapping catheter to ___ and look for a___.
   a. **Unipolar (filter settings of 0.05 - 300 Hz), negative QS deflection**
   b. **Unipolar (filter settings of 30 - 300 Hz), positive QR or R deflection**
   c. **Bipolar (filter settings of 0.05 - 300 Hz), negative QS deflection**
   d. **Bipolar (filter settings of 30 - 300 Hz), positive QR or R deflection**

ANSWER: a. Unipolar (filter settings of 0.05 - 300 Hz), negative QS deflection. These are termed "unfiltered" since they are the same frequency cutoffs used in surface ECGs.

Issa says, "Once the site with the earliest bipolar signal is identified, the unipolar signal from the distal ablation electrode should be used to supplement bipolar mapping. The unfiltered (0.05 to 300 Hz) unipolar signal morphology should show a monophasic QS complex with a rapid negative deflection if the site was at the origin of impulse formation.... a QS complex should not be the only mapping finding used to guide ablation. Successful ablation is unusual, however, at sites with an RS complex on the unipolar electrode, because these are generally distant from the focus.... The presence of ST elevation on the unipolar recording and the ability to capture the site with unipolar pacing are used to indicate good electrode contact."
See: Issa, Cardiac Arrhythmology and Electrophysiology, Companion to Braunwald, Heart Disease, chapter on Arrhythmia

Signals & Measurements:

1. Which of the following is the normal conduction sequence after an electrical impulse has traveled through the AV node?
   a. **Bundle branches, Bachmann's bundle, purkinje fibers**
   b. **Bundle branches, bundle of His, purkinje fibers**
   c. **Bundle of His, bundle branches, purkinje fibers**
   d. **Purkinje fibers, His bundle, AV junction**

ANSWER: c. Bundle of His, bundle branches, purkinje fibers. The sequence is:
1. SA node
2. Inter-atrial tracts (Bachmann's bundle & coronary sinus)
3. AV node
AN = Transitional tissue between Atria and AV node. N = Mid AV nodal tissue (most of the AV time delay occurs in these upper 2 regions of the AV node) NH = region where nodal fibers gradually merge with bundle of His tissue. His = the upper portion of ventricular conduction tissue
   4. Bundle of His
   5. Right and Left Bundle branches (Left has 2 fascicles, ant. & Post.)
   6. Purkinje System - to myocardium
See: Conduction branches in heart- after Rushmer fig. 3-9

2. Closely spaced bipolar cardiac electrodes record local _____.
   a. **Depolarization only (phase 0)**
   b. **Depolarization only (phase 1)**
   c. **Depolarization and repolarization (phase 0 and 3)**
   d. **Depolarization and repolarization (phase 1 and 4)**

ANSWER: a. Depolarization only (phase 0). Closely spaced bipolar leads only measure depolarization phase 0 activity of the local cardiac tissue in the immediate vicinity of the catheter's electrodes. Repolarization (T waves) are too low a frequency and are filtered out of most bipolar leads. The surface ECG measures the sum of all electrical energy both depolarization and repolarization for the entire heart. With the low frequency cutoff below 1 Hz, surface leads can even measure ST elevation during phase 2, but bipolar leads cannot. See: Issa, chapter on EP Testing

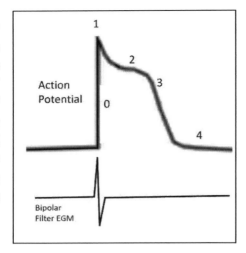

3. Which catheter would display five bipolar CS channels (standard setup)?
   a. **Quadripolar**
   b. **Hexapolar**
   c. **Decapolar**
   d. **Duodecapolar**

ANSWER: c. Decapolar. Deca means ten. Ten electrodes record five electrogram channels with the standard setup. Steinberg says, "The CS electrode catheter should have as many closely spaced electrodes as possible to visualize how atrial depolarization moves through the left atrium, also to localize left sided bypass tracks." See: Steinberg, chapter on The EP Lab

4. The MOST common catheter positions for performing an initial diagnostic EP study are:
   a. **HRA, LRA, CS, RVA**
   b. **CS, LRA, HIS, HRA**
   c. **LRA, RIJ, CS, RVOT**
   d. **HRA, HIS, RVA, CS**

ANSWER: d. HRA, HIS, RVA, CS. Watson says, "The catheters are generally placed in four sites. The atrial catheter is placed in the high right atrium (HRA) and records electrical activity in and around the sinus node. The His bundle catheter is placed across the tricuspid valve and records the His bundle electrogram (HBE). It also allows recording of low atrial and ventricular activity, which allows for evaluation of AV conduction. The ventricular catheter is placed in the right ventricular apex (RVA) and allows electrical activity to be recorded from the base of the right ventricle. The CS catheter, whether placed from above or below, records both atrial and ventricular activity from the base of the left atrium close to the atrioventricular (AV) groove. The CS catheter also allows for retrograde atrial activation sequence determination (EGMs). See: Watson, chapter on, Electrophysiology. See: Underhill, chapter on "Cardiac Electrophysiology." also, Todd, Vol. II, Chapter on "ECG."

5. This fluoroscopy image shows four catheters positioned for a diagnostic EP study. Match each catheter with its normal EGM.

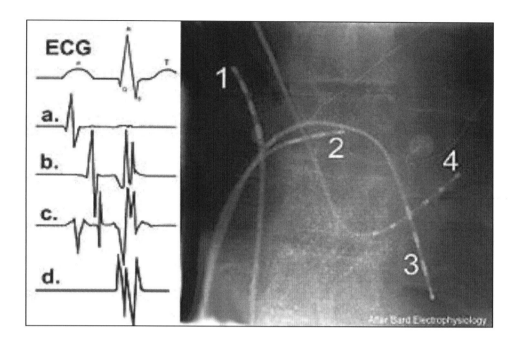

CORRECTLY MATCHED ANSWERS ARE:

1. a. In the high RA (HRA) large A waves are recorded. The closer the electrodes are to the SA node the earlier the A wave is recorded.

2. c. As an electrode passes through the tricuspid valve near the HIS bundle, His (H) is seen between the A and V waves. The His is recorded as the wave of depolarization passes through the AV node and passes down the common AV bundle.

3.b. The coronary sinus catheter is in the AV groove where it can sense both atrial and ventricular depolarization. This catheter is shown coming in from the SVC and neck, which makes CS access easier. Usually, femoral vein access is used.

4.d. In the ventricle only large V waves are usually recorded. The atrial complex is usually too low in magnitude to be sensed in the ventricular apex.

ELECTROGRAMS

HRA = Large A, & small V near SA node

HIS Bundle= Large A, H, & V through tricuspid valve

CS: = Large A & small V In left AV groove

RV apex: = Large V only

Note that the electrodes in a chamber generally record large voltage electrograms only from that chamber.

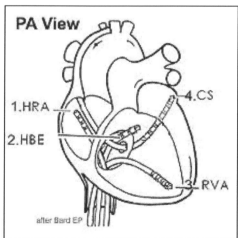

Those between chambers (HIS & CS) record voltage signals from both chambers (a & v waves). See: Kern, chapter on "Electrophysiology."

6. Identify the wave labeled #3.
    a. **A wave**
    b. **H wave**
    c. **V wave**
    d. **P wave**

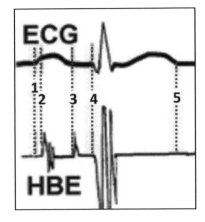

ANSWER: b. H wave (His). The His bundle depolarization is recorded from the electrode catheter across the tricuspid valve near the AV node. Note that it is not seen on the surface ECG.

WAVEFORMS SHOWN:
- P wave origin from surface ECG, global atrial activation
- A wave on HBE, due to low RA depolarization. H wave on HBE, due to His bundle depolarization (not seen on surface ECG).
- V wave from HBE, due to ventricular depolarization (correlates to QRS on surface ECG)
- End of surface T wave - no associated HBE waveform
- Note that the PR interval is composed of 3 segments: PA, AH, & HV.

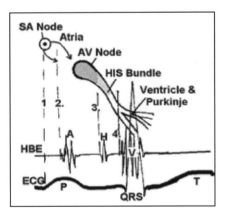

See: Underhill, chapter on Electrocardiography.

7. Identify the interval measured between #2 & #3 on this His bundle electrogram?
    a. **PA or IACT interval**
    b. **AH interval**
    c. **PH interval**
    d. **HV interval**
    e. **QT interval**

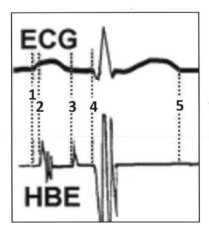

ANSWER: b. 2-3. AH: beginning of the A to onset of the earliest ventricular deflection which is most commonly seen on the surface ECG.

The AH interval is the longest of the supraventricular HBE intervals, and it is important because it may "jump" even longer in patients with dual AV node physiology and AVNRT.

Other intervals are:
- 1-2. PA or IACT: P wave to A wave time. also called Intra-Atrial Conduction Time (IACT)
- 2-3. AH
- 3-4. HV: Time from H to beginning of the earliest ventricular activation. Prolonged HV is termed infra-hisian block, which is more severe than supra-hisian block.
- Note that the PR interval is composed of 3 segments: PA, AH, and HV. See: Underhill, chapter on ECG

8. A HIS bundle electrogram has the following measurements: AH interval = 160 ms, HV interval = 40 ms, QRS duration = 180 ms. Which diagnosis is most likely?
   a. **Infra-Hisian block 1st degree heart block**
   b. **Supra-Hisian 1st degree heart block**
   c. **Supra-Hisian block WPW**
   d. **Infra-Hisian block WPW**

ANSWER: b. Supra-Hisian 1st degree heart block. Normal AH intervals vary from 60-140 ms and HV intervals from 30-55 ms. Note that the PR interval adds to 220 ms. Normally the His spike is closer to the V but not that close. Thus, the AH conduction time is prolonged indicating a delay between the SA node and the His bundle. This is termed supra-hisian block and is associated with 1st degree heart block. Infra-Hisian block is more severe and may require a pacemaker. See: HIS bundle Electrogram Kern, chapter on EP

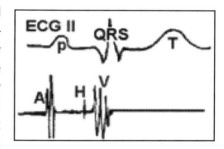

9. In measuring EGMs, the earliest recorded atrial activation is almost always taken from the ___ while the earliest recorded ventricular activation is almost always taken from the ___.
   a. **Surface P wave, surface QRS complex**
   b. **Surface P wave, RVa electrogram**
   c. **HRA electrogram, surface QRS complex**
   d. **HRA electrogram, RVa electrogram**

ANSWER: a. Surface P wave, surface QRS complex. Murgatroyd says, "As with the AH interval, the timing of the His electrogram is taken from its onset. The earliest recorded ventricular activation is almost always the beginning of the surface QRS complex." See, Murgatroyd, chapter on Basic EP Study

10. When you see V waves on the RA electrode it is termed:
   a. **Retrograde conduction**
   b. **Antidromic conduction**
   c. **Ventricular artifact**
   d. **Far-field sensing**

ANSWER: d. Far-field sensing. Normally the atria are electrically isolated from the ventricle, and V waves cannot normally be sensed. However, large QRS complexes may occasionally be sensed in the atrial appendage termed Far Field R waves (FFRW). This is termed far field sensing.

The Medical Dictionary says: "Far-field sensing is an intrinsic electrical signal, visible on an EGM, which originates from myocardial cells distant to the measuring electrode, often from a different cardiac chamber. "

11. Your patient is brought into the EP lab for an SVT ablation. Four catheters were placed. Based on this EGM, where is the catheter at the arrow located?
   a. **HRA**
   b. **His Bundle**
   c. **CS**
   d. **RVA**

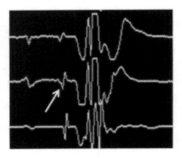

ANSWER: b. His Bundle. Typical catheter placement includes: HRA, His Bundle, CS, and RVA. Depending on what type of procedure is being performed, not all these catheters may be used. Many times, on smaller patients, the number of catheters is reduced by eliminating the HRA or using a dual-purpose catheter such as one catheter that has electrodes for both the His and the RV.

According to Fogoros "Catheters are placed in strategic locations within the heart for two essential tasks: recording the heart's electrical signals and pacing. Electrode catheters consist of insulated wires; at the distal tip of the catheter each wire is attached to an electrode, which is exposed to the intracardiac surface. At the proximal end of the catheter, each wire is attached to a plug, which can be connected to an external device" See: Fogoros chapter, Principles of the Electrophysiology Study

12. Identify the waveform at the arrow in the EGM?
   a. **Fractionated electrogram**
   b. **A**
   c. **V**
   d. **H**

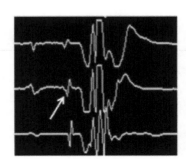

ANSWER: d. H. Murgatroyd says, "The His bundle electrogram is seen between atrial and ventricular electrograms. Direct recording of AV nodal activation is not possible in clinical practice, but the His bundle catheter indicates the timing of impulses entering and leaving the AV node via the adjacent atrial tissue and the His bundle, or vice versa." See. Murgatroyd, chapter on The Basic Electrophysiology Study.

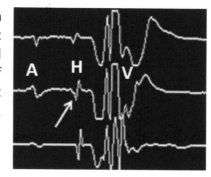

13. What is the waveform that is pointed out in the example?
  a. Fractionated Electrogram
  b. H
  c. A
  d. V

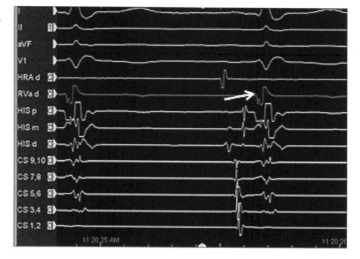

ANSWER: d. V. The RVa catheter shows only the ventricular signal because it is too far away to see the atrial activity. The atrial myocardium is much thinner than the ventricle, so there is less myocardial recruitment. The V lines up with the QRS on the surface ECG.

The HRA catheter shows only the atrial signal. It is too far away to see the His or RV. The His catheter shows the A as it enters the AV node, the His as it exits the node, and the V from the RV. This example shows the A on the HRA lined up with the A on the His catheter. Here HIS d has the best A, and HIS p shows the best H.

The CS catheter shows both the atrial and ventricular signal because the CS runs in the AV groove (in between the atrium and ventricle). The proximal CS (9,10) is located at the CS ostium in the RA and the distal (CS 1,2) on the left lateral side of the LA.

According to Murgatroyd, the HRA catheter is typically a quadripolar catheter located on the lateral wall, near the superior vena cava / right atrial junction. The RVa catheter

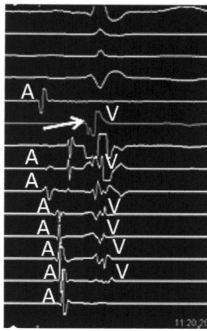

is also quadripolar and may need to be adjusted to achieve satisfactory sensing and pacing. A range of multipolar catheters are available for coronary sinus recording. Anatomic variation requires some flexibility of approach. For CS access, it is usually easiest entering the heart via the superior vena cava, after subclavian or jugular venipuncture, but the femoral approach is usually successful if a steerable catheter is used. See. Murgatroyd chapter on The Basic Electrophysiology Study.

14. What is the circled wave?
   a. Cannon wave
   b. P wave
   c. T wave
   d. U wave

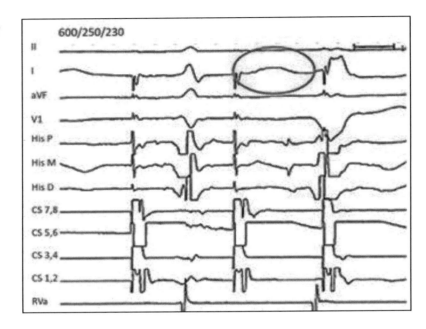

ANSWER: c. T wave. The pacing spike is at the beginning of the T wave by coincidence. Surface leads are not filtered to eliminate all low frequencies (T waves) like EGMs are. The QT interval is the same as in the 1st beat. If it was a P wave the previous pacer spike would be followed by another P wave.

15. What is the large ECG waveform at the arrow?
   a. Fractionated electrogram
   b. ST segment
   c. V wave
   d. QRS

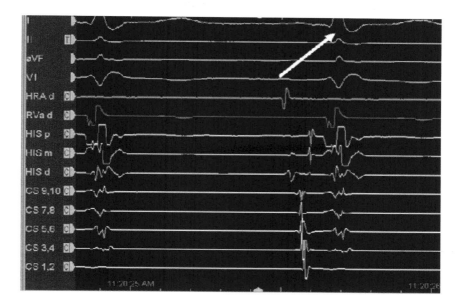

ANSWER: d. QRS. The surface ECG does not display any of the intracardiac signals. The only signals observed are the P, QRS, and T wave. This allows measurement of the PR interval, QT interval and ST segment.

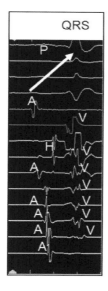

The intracardiac electrogram is essentially an ECG recorded from within the heart. The major difference between a body surface ECG and an intracardiac electrogram is that the surface ECG gives a summation of the electrical activity of the entire heart, whereas the intracardiac electrogram records only the electrical activity of a localized area of the heart. Also, the intracardiac signals have low frequency components filtered out, so you don't normally see T waves.

16. What is the waveform at the arrow in this EGM?
   a. A wave
   b. H wave
   c. V wave
   d. QRS

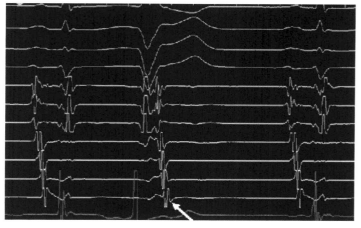

ANSWER: a. A wave following a PVC. PVCs are premature ventricular contractions (PVC), or extrasystoles, are a relatively common event where the heartbeat is initiated by the heart ventricles rather than by the sinoatrial node, the normal heartbeat initiator. The electrical events of the heart detected by the electrocardiogram allow a PVC to be easily distinguished from a normal heartbeat. A PVC may be perceived as a "skipped beat" or felt as palpitations in the chest. In a normal heartbeat, the ventricles contract after the atria have helped to fill them by contracting; in this way the ventricles can pump a maximized amount of blood both to the lungs and to the rest of the body. In a PVC, the ventricles contract first, with insufficient filling. However, single beat PVC arrhythmias do not usually pose a danger and can be asymptomatic in healthy individuals.

Labels will not always be provided on the EGM, so familiarize yourself with the waveforms and catheter placement first. The second beat is a PVC. Note the large early V in the bottom RV tracing. Here the V comes first and then a retrograde A. VA conduction goes the opposite direction from AV conduction, retrograde up the AV node. The 1st and 3rd beats are sinus, so you see the A, H, V waves from high to low.

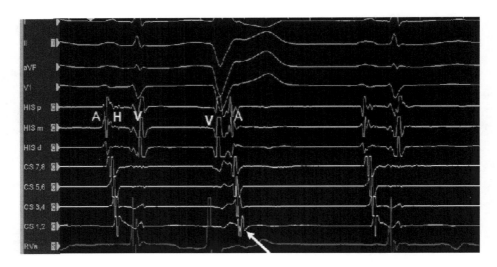

17. What is the waveform pointed to?
   a. A wave
   b. H wave
   c. V wave
   d. QRS

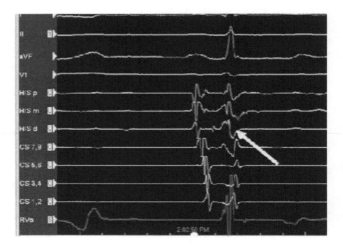

ANSWER: c. V wave. This appears to be a sinus beat, so the final waveform would be the V. Notice how it lines up with the surface ECG QRS complex. The second beat is also sinus. The third beat is a junctional beat because the H deflection is first with the A and V following simultaneously. Note the absence of a P wave on the surface ECG.

Murgatroyd teaches that the baseline intervals should be measured during sinus rhythm, if possible, if not the rhythm should be stated. This would be a good place for measurements. The patient appears to be in sinus rhythm as noted by the surface ECG and the atrial, His, and ventricular deflections on the His catheter. All impulses look concentric from high (SA node) to low (ventricle) and right side of the heart to the left. The third beat would not be used for measurements since it originates from the junction. (No A or A buried in QRS).

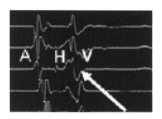

18. **In the EGM, what type of conduction happens in the third (last) complex shown?**
    a. **Sinus beat**
    b. **PAC**
    c. **PVC**
    d. **PJC**

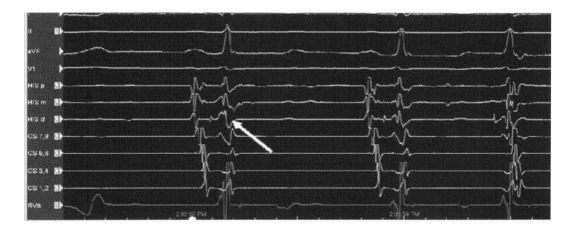

ANSWER: d. PJC, junctional premature contraction. The third beat above is a junctional beat because the H deflection is first with the V and A following simultaneously. It is premature and the surface P follows the QRS.

Chapter 4
Procedural Foundation

1. Sterilization, Aseptic Technique, Bloodborne Pathogens (pg. 149)
2. IVs & Access (pg. 165)
3. CIED Access (pg. 174)
4. Transseptal Access (pg. 176)
5. Epicardial Access (pg. 194)
6. Temporary Pacemakers & BLS/ACLS (pg. 197)

EP Essentials LLC

Sterilization, Aseptic Technique, Bloodborne Pathogens:

1. Match the meaning of the term to its number below.

1. **Disinfect**	a. **Destroys all microorganisms**
2. **Bacteriostatic**	b. **Inhibits or stops grown of bacteria**
3. **Bactericidal**	c. **Kills bacteria**
4. **Antiseptic**	d. **Destroy most pathogens on living tissue**
5. **Sterilize**	e. **Destroy most pathogens on instruments, unsafe for living tissue**
6. **Aseptic**	f. **Destroy all pathogens**

CORRECTLY MATCHED ANSWERS ARE:
    TERM = MEANING
1. Disinfect = e. Destroy most pathogens on instruments. Un-safe for living tissues
2. Bacteriostatic = b. Inhibits or stops growth of bacteria (-static = hold steady)
3. Bactericidal = c. Kills bacteria (-cidal = kill)
4. Antiseptic = d. Destroy most pathogens on living tissue, safe to use on skin
5. Sterilize = a. Destroys all microorganisms
6. Aseptic= f. Destroys all pathogens (-sepsis = infection)

See: Burton, Chapter on "Control of Microbial Growth."

2. Match the agent to the aseptic function it performs listed below
  a. **Penicillin, Amoxicillin**
  b. **Clorox, Glutaraldehyde (Cidex)**
  c. **Hexachloraphene, Benzalkonium chloride (Zephiran)**
  d. **Alcohol (70%), Povidone-iodine**
  e. **Autoclave, ETO Gas**

  1. **Disinfect**
  2. **Bacteriostatic**
  3. **Bactericidal**
  4. **Antiseptic**
  5. **Sterilize**

CORRECTLY MATCHED ANSWERS ARE: AGENT- CLASS- FUNCTION

Clorox, Glutaraldehyde (Cidex) = Disinfect = destroy most pathogens on instruments, unsafe for living tissues

Hexachlorophene, Benzalkonium chloride (Zephiran) = Bacteriostatic = inhibits or stops growth of bacteria. Often put in soap to inhibit growth of skin flora for several hours.

Penicillin, and other antibiotics = Bacteriocidal = kills bacteria but not virus in vivo.

Alcohol (70%), Povidone-iodine =Antiseptic = destroy most pathogens on living tissue, safe to use on skin

Autoclave, ETO Gas =Sterilize = destroys ALL microorganisms if certain precautions are taken (Time, Temp, packing, circulation...).

See: Burton, Chapter on "Control of Microbial Growth."

3. Bacteria that CANNOT live in the presence of AIR are known as:
  a. **Aerobes**
  b. **Anaerobes**
  c. **Mesophiles**
  d. **Bacteriophiles**

ANSWER: b. Anaerobes can live only in the absence of air; oxygen is poisonous to these germs. Pathogens such as tetanus and botulism are anaerobic bacteria. The opposite type of germs are "aerobes" such as TB, cholera, and diphtheria that require oxygen and thrive in the lungs.

See: Gruendemann & Meeker, Chapter on "Principles and procedures of asepsis."

4. The most complete, practical, efficient, and inexpensive method to sterilize metal instruments involves:
  a. **Chemicals**
  b. **Dry heat**
  c. **Steam heat**
  d. **Ethylene Oxide Gas**

ANSWER: c. Steam heat. Burton says, "Heat is the most practical, efficient, and inexpensive method of disinfection and sterilization of objects that can withstand high temperatures. Because of these advantages, it is the means most frequently employed." ETO gas sterilization is effective, but it is more expensive and takes a long time. Gruendemann says, "Any item that can be steam sterilized should never be gas sterilized."

In a rush, metal instruments may be "flash" sterilized with dry heat. Burton says, "Heat applied in the presence of moisture, such as boiling, or steaming, is more effective than dry heat because moist heat causes the proteins to coagulate... Moist heat is faster than dry heat, and can be done at lower temperatures..." The effectiveness of dry heat depends on how deeply the heat penetrates. So, the items to be "baked" must be arranged so the warm air circulates freely among them. See: Burton, Chapter on "Control of Microbial Growth."

5. **Effective sterilization by autoclave depends on adequate:**
    a. **Temperature and pressure**
    b. **Temperature and time**
    c. **Time and pressure**
    d. **Time and concentration**

ANSWER: b. Temperature and time. Adequate autoclave sterilization requires a minimum of 120 degrees C for 20 minutes. An autoclave is a pressure cooker with pressures of 15 psi. The circulating pressurized steam increases the temperature above regular boiling point. The Autoclave Time and temperature cycles are recorded on a graph to document the adequacy of the cycle.

Resistant microorganisms such as spores and viruses may survive autoclaving if they are hidden inside blood or tissue due to the insulation provided by the surrounding material. Thus, pay careful attention to packaging and quality control. See: Burton, Chapter on "Control of Microbial Growth."

6. **What is the most common vector for the spread of infection within the hospital?**
    a. **Insects and parasites**
    b. **Coughing (air borne)**
    c. **Failure to wash hands**
    d. **Soiled linen and instruments**

ANSWER: c. Failure to wash hands. Torres says, "Microbes are mostly spread from one person to another by human hands. It follows that the best means of preventing the spread of microorganisms is handwashing...even if gloves have been worn.... Any exposed breaks in your skin must be covered by a waterproof protective covering." Hepatitis B virus can live for over a week in dried blood. It can easily be picked up by your hands and spread.
See: Torres, Chapter on "Infection Control."

7. Shelf life is the length of time a sterilized pack may be considered sterile. What is the shelf life of a single cloth wrapped pack?
   a. **Not sterile**
   b. **21-30 days**
   c. **6 months - 1 year**
   d. **Indefinitely**

ANSWER: a. Not sterile
SHELF LIFE:

- Single cloth wrapping = Not sterile. Can only be sterilized if double wrapped inappropriate cloth.

- Double cloth wrapping = 21-30 days

- Single-layer heat sealed plastic wrapping = 6 months - 1 year

- Sealed envelopes encased in sealed plastic wrapping are sterile indefinitely if not damaged, stored incorrectly, or managed roughly. Shelf life is more event dependent than time dependent. Things that must be considered in determining "shelf-life" are type and number of layers of packaging, imperviousness of cover, package handling, and conditions of storage.

See: Gruendemann & Meeker, Chapter on "Principles and procedures of asepsis."

8. A sterilized item dropped on the floor is considered sterile only if it has not been damaged and is:
   a. **Used immediately**
   b. **Enclosed in impervious material (plastic)**
   c. **Wrapped in three or more layers of woven cloth**
   d. **Fell in a surgically clean area**

ANSWER: b. Enclosed in impervious material (plastic). Such airtight packaging prevents entry of dust and moisture, but only if the integrity of the packaging is maintained. Dropped cloth-wrapped items should no longer be considered sterile. See: Allmers, Review for Surgical Tech. Exam, chapter on "Fundamentals"

9. How should a circulator open the first flap of cloth-wrapped sterile packs? First place the sterile pack on the back table, pull off the sterile indicator tape then:
   a. **Move first flap towards you (over front of table)**
   b. **Move first flap away from you (over the top of the pack)**
   c. **Move the right flap over the right side of the table**
   d. **Grasp both flaps and spread them right and left over both sides of the table.**

ANSWER: b. Move first flap AWAY from you (over the top of the pack). This prevents you from touching the open sterile field because it is away from you. Finally, the near flap is opened TOWARDS you as you back away, preventing contamination. This sequence is opposite to that used by a sterile person opening a pack. See: Burton, Chapter on "Control of Microbial Growth

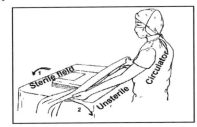

10. How should a sterile scrub assistant open a sterile pack? Open the first flap ___ you and the last flap ___ you.
    a. **Towards, Away**
    b. **Towards, Towards**
    c. **Away, Towards**
    d. **Away, Away**

ANSWER: a. Towards, away. This establishes a sterile field between you and the pack so you can protect the sterile pack and your gown from contamination. The final sterile flap is moved AWAY from you over the top of the pack as shown.
See: Gruendemann & Meeker, Chapter on "Principles and procedures of asepsis."

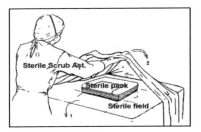

11. How should the skin be prepped with each povidone-iodine sponge prior to an electrophysiology study?
    a. **Soaked overnight with a soaked sponge, then scrubbed briskly back and forth**
    b. **Shaved the day before, then scrubbed in the same direction as the hair grows**
    c. **Begin at the outside and scrub in, in a spiraling manner towards the puncture site**
    d. **Begin at the inside and scrub away from the puncture site in a spiraling manner**

ANSWER: d. Begin at the inside and scrub away from the puncture site in a spiraling manner. Discard the used sponge. A soiled sponge is never brought back to the central area of puncture site. The general rule is "proceed from clean to dirty." Repeat prep using soaked gauze. Discard the used sponge forceps as contaminated. See: Gruendemann & Meeker, Chapter on "Principles and procedures of asepsis."

13. You are setting up the sterile table for an EP study. The patient is brought in and put on the table. The Physician then calls and cancels the procedure. What should you do with the sterile table that is set up in the room?
    a. **Leave it open and save it for the next case, immediately to follow.**
    b. **Tear it down and discard all disposable items. Start a new table for next case.**
    c. **Cover it with a sterile cloth drape. It is considered sterile for only 6 hours**
    d. **Discard all solutions and cover it with a sterile plastic drape. It is considered sterile for 12 hours.**

ANSWER: b. Tear it down and start completely over for the next case. Surgery encyclopedia says, "The environment contains potential hazards that may spread pathogens through movement, touch, or proximity... restrict traffic in the operating room. Sterile packages or fields are opened or created as close as possible to time of actual use." The safety of the next patient entering the room is the most important. If you can cover the dry table before the patient enters the room, it may be saved and used in the next case.

See: http://www.surgeryencyclopedia.com/A-Ce/Aseptic-Technique.html

14. You are scrubbed-in on a pacemaker implant procedure when you contaminate your right glove. The circulator should help you by:
   a. **Helping you re-gown and re-gloving using the closed technique**
   b. **Helping you re-gown and re-gloving using the open technique**
   c. **Pulling off your right glove, and open a new pair for you**
   d. **Pulling off both your gloves, and open a new pair for you**

ANSWER: c. Have the circulator pull off your right glove and open a new pair for you. You can use your sterile left hand to don the right glove using either the open or closed technique. You need not replace the left glove or re-gown unless they were contaminated.

See: Allmers, Review for Surgical Tech. Exam, chapter on "Fundamentals"

15. When performing a surgical scrub, how high should you scrub up your arm?
   a. **Scrub to the mid-forearm**
   b. **Scrub to two inches below the elbow**
   c. **Scrub to the elbow**
   d. **Scrub to two inches above the elbow**

ANSWER: d. Two inches above the elbow. The surgical scrub should include the hands, wrists, forearms, elbows, antecubital fossa up to two inches above the elbow.

See: Allmers, Review for Surgical Tech. Exam, chapter on "Fundamentals"

16. When pouring a sterile solution from a screw top bottle onto a sterile field:
   a. **Open, pour only once, then discard left-over solution**
   b. **Once opened, solutions may be poured again from same bottle, but only on the same case**
   c. **Use sterile procedure to pour again during same case if sterile cap is replaced between uses**
   d. **Use sterile procedure to pour as many times as you wish if sterile cap is replaced between uses.**

ANSWER: a. Open, pour only once, then discard left-over solution. After a sterile bottle is opened, the contents must be used or discarded. The cap cannot be replaced without contamination of the pouring edges. The edges of anything that encloses sterile contents are considered unsterile. See: Allmers, Review for Surgical Tech. Exam, chapter on "Fundamentals"

17. **The opening in a single use sterile femoral drape sheet is called a:**
    a. **Lumen**
    b. **Window**
    c. **Foramen**
    d. **Access site**
    e. **Fenestration**

ANSWER: e. A fenestrated drape has a round or slit-like opening in the center. "Single use/disposable drapes are composed of nonwoven natural and synthetic materials ... These fabrics include a fluid-proof polyethylene film laminated between the fabric layers at strategic locations of the drape, usually around the drape fenestration..." From: Essential of Perioperative Nursing," chapter on Aseptic Practices, by Cynthia Spry, Jonas and Bartlett Publishers

18. **Draped sterile tables are considered sterile on the top:**
    a. **And sides if the scrub person watches the table**
    b. **And sides, down to one inch from the bottom edge**
    c. **And patient's side only**
    d. **Top only - not any sides**

ANSWER: d. On the top surface only, not any sides. A sterile table is considered sterile only on the top. The edges and sides extending below the table level are not considered sterile. See: Allmers, Review for Surgical Tech. Exam, chapter on "Fundamentals"

19. **All the following statements regarding sterility are true EXCEPT:**
    a. **Wrapper edges are unsterile**
    b. **Instruments or sutures hanging over the table edge are discarded**
    c. **Sterile persons pass each other back-to-back**
    d. **A sterile person faces a nonsterile person when passing**

ANSWER: d. A sterile person faces a nonsterile person when passing - is incorrect. A sterile person turns his back to a nonsterile person or area when passing. This is to protect the scrub assistant's sterile frontal area.

See: Allmers, Review for Surgical Tech. Exam, chapter on "Fundamentals"

20. All the following rules of surgical asepsis are correct EXCEPT:
   a. **When in doubt about the sterility of an item, consider it unsterile**
   b. **The front and back of a wrap-around gown is considered sterile**
   c. **The sides of sterile tables are considered unsterile**
   d. **Instruments used in contact with the skin such as sponge forceps are discarded and not reused**

ANSWER: b. The front and back of a wrap-around gown is considered sterile - WRONG! Because they cannot be carefully watched, the backs of gowns are considered contaminated. They are only considered sterile in the front, from the waist (table) level, and only from two inches below the elbow down to the gloves.
TRUE: When in doubt about the sterility of an item, consider it unsterile. For the patient's safety, anyone who sees a break in aseptic technique should immediately mention it to the person in charge.
FALSE: The front and back of a wrap-around gown is considered sterile. For this reason, arms should not be crossed and tucked under the gown, sterile areas armpit
TRUE: The sides of sterile tables are considered unsterile. Only the top surface of the table is sterile. A sterile person rolling a sterile table should hold it by the top surface only, not the sides. 4. TRUE: Instruments used in contact with the skin such as sponge forceps are discarded and not reused. Sponge sticks should NOT be put back among the other sterile instruments. Remove them from your sterile field. They touched the patient's skin.
See: Gruendemann, Chapter on "Principles... of asepsis

21. When using alcohol-based hand rubs prior to gowning and gloving for an electrophysiology study, all the following are true EXCEPT:
   a. **Apply to both hands and forearms**
   b. **Rub in the alcohol-based product until dry**
   c. **Hands must be cleaned, washed, and dried first**
   d. **Alcohol rubs are less effective than traditional scrub-brush methods**
   e. **Nails and subungual areas of both hands must be cleaned with a nail file**
   f. **first**

ANSWER: d. Rubs are less effective than traditional scrub brush methods – is incorrect. Spry, says, "Alcohol based hand rub products have been shown to save time and reduce costs, are more effective than products used in the traditional scrub method, and because of added emollients are gentle to the hands...The procedure should include the following:
   • Hands and forearms are washed with soap and running water.

- The nails and subungual areas of both hands are cleaned with a nail file.
- Hands and forearms are rinsed and thoroughly dried with a clean towel.
- Hands and forearms are rubbed until dry.
- An FDA approved antiseptic rub is used.
- The manufacturer's instructions must be followed.

From: Essential of Perioperative Nursing," chapter on Aseptic Practices, by Cynthia Spry, Jonas and Bartlett Publishers

22. Match the gloving method labeled in the box with its description below.

1. **Self-gowning, closed**
2. **Self-gowning, open**
3. **another individual**

a. **Gown sleeves are used to manage gloves**
b. **First glove is grasped by bare hand inside of cuff**
c. **Glove is stretched open with both hands**

CORRECTLY MATCHED GLOVING METHODS ARE:

1.a. SELF-GOWNING CLOSED METHOD   = In this method your hands are surrounded "closed in" and protected by the gown sleeve that is used to manage the gloves. Left glove is placed palm down on your left sleeve as shown. Grasp the cuff of the glove through the gown with our left hand. With your right hand protected by the sleeve, grasp the top of the glove, and stretch it over your left hand. Insert your left hand into the glove through the gown sleeve.

2.b. SELF-GOWNING OPEN METHOD = In this method your hands are unprotected and are "open" to the air. The first glove is grasped by your bare hand inside of the cuff. Grasp the left glove cuff with your right hand. Insert left hand into glove. Pick up the right glove with cuff as shown. Insert right hand into glove. Roll back cuffs over sleeves.

3.c. GLOVING ANOTHER INDIVIDUAL = Glove is stretched open with both hands. After one individual has gowned and gloved herself, she grasps the preferred glove by the cuff, as shown. The second individual inserts his hand into an opened glove. Be able to match all above answers. See: Gruendemann & Meeker, Chapter on "Principles and procedures of asepsis."

23. You are gowned and gloved. The operating physician has just scrubbed and enters the lab looking at you. All the following statements are true regarding gowning them EXCEPT:

    a. **Open the hand towel and lay it on the physician's hand**

    b. **Place the folded gown into the hands of the physician.**

    c. **Keep your hands outside of the gown under a protective cuff**

    d. **Open the gown and hold it so the physician can insert their dry hands into the sleeves**

ANSWER b. Place the folded gown into the dry hands of the physician - is incorrect. Before managing a gown, grasp it at the neckband and hold it up to let the lower parts unfold. While keeping your hands protected on the outside of the gown, open it, and hold it by its outside shoulders so the Dr. can insert his hands into the sleeves. Do all this while protecting yourself from contamination. The physician must dry his hands before donning his sterile gown. See: Allmers, Review for Surgical Tech. Exam, chapter on "Fundamentals"

24. Your electrophysiologist requests preoperative hair removal from both groins of your patient. To minimize surgical site infections, remove the patients groin hair with a/an:

    a. **Disposable razor**

    b. **Straight razor**

    c. **Electric clipper**

    d. **Depilatory cream**

ANSWER: c. Electric clipper reduces the chance of infection and is recommended by CDC infection control guidelines. Dross says, "shaving damages the skin and increases the risk of infection. The source pathogens for most nosocomial infections are skin-dwelling microorganisms. Razor shaving increases the risk of infection by creating micro abrasions in the skin that allow skin-dwelling microorganisms to collect and multiply. These organisms may then migrate into the incision site and may also collect on catheters or sheaths that must remain in place for a period following the procedure. The longer a catheter or sheath is in place, the higher the risk for catheter-associated infection."

"In contrast to shaving, clipping hair using a rechargeable electric trimmer with a disposable head does not damage the skin and is associated with lower infection rates. In a prospective study that compared infection rates among 1,980 surgical patients whose hair was either shaved or clipped pre-operatively, patients who were clipped had a statistically significantly lower infection rate than patients who were shaved (p = 0.024)"

"Hair should be removed as close to the time of surgery as possible and in an area away from the sterile field (in the pre-catheterization holding area, for example) to prevent loose hair clippings from dispersing onto sterile surfaces and causing contamination. A rechargeable electric clipper with a disposable head or one that can be removed and disinfected should be used."

Depilatory cream use is safer than shaving with a razor, but it has separate problems of causing allergy and skin irritation. Cutdown procedures also have a higher incidence of local infections than percutaneous. In addition to hair removal, make sure the implant site is free from adhesive residue left over from ECG patches. See: Dave Droll, RT(R)(T)(CV), RCIS in http://www.cathlabdigest.com/article/4614

25. What tissue layers are sutured when a pacemaker pocket is closed?
   a. **Peritoneum & fascia**
   b. **Epidermis, dermis & fascia**
   c. **Pleura, dermis & epidermis**
   d. **Epidermis, dermis & peritoneum**

ANSWER: b. Epidermis, dermis & fascia. Most physicians want two or three rows of suture to close the three layers of tissue. "The epidermis and dermis are tightly adhered and clinically indistinguishable, and together constitute the skin. Dermal approximation provides the strength and alignment of skin closure. The subcutaneous layer is comprised of adipose tissue. Nerve fibers, blood vessels, and hair follicles are located here. Although this layer provides little strength to repair, sutures placed in the subcutaneous layer may decrease the tension of the wound and improve the cosmetic result. The deep fascial layer is intermixed with muscle and occasionally requires repair in deep lacerations." See: Dermabond.com and Ethicon manual

Ellenbogen says, "The pocket is closed in layers using 2-0 to 4-0 resorbable suture. Care must be taken to avoid piercing the lead with the suture needle. The skin edges may be approximated with skin sutures, resorbable subcuticular sutures or surgical stables. A sterile dressing is then applied."

The Kuder article says, "Good suturing technique should eliminate dead space in subcutaneous tissues, minimize tension that causes wound separation. This shows a running horizontal mattress suture to close the deep tissue."

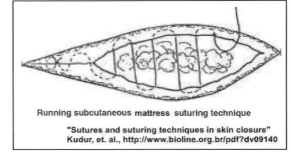

Running subcutaneous mattress suturing technique

"Sutures and suturing techniques in skin closure" Kudur, et. al., http://www.bioline.org.br/pdf?dv09140

"Running subcutaneous suture: It is initiated by placing a single subcutaneous suture with the knot tied towards the wound surface. Then, it is looped through the subcutaneous tissue by passing through the opposite sides of the wound. It is tied at the distal aspect of the wound, with the terminal end of the suture to the previous loop placed on the opposing side of the wound." See: "Sutures and suturing techniques in skin closure" Kudur, et. al., http://www.bioline.org.br/pdf?dv09140

Some labs close two layers and then add a thin layer of Dermabond glue on top, in place of a third layer.

26. All these below are true and help reduce PPI infection EXCEPT:
   a. **The best prep. is povidone-iodine**
   b. **The best wound dressings contain silver**
   c. **Administer antiseptic one hour before PPI**
   d. **Compulsive attention to sterile technique**

ANSWER: a. The best prep. is povidone-iodine - incorrect. It is chlorhexidine-alcohol. These are AHA, Recommendations for Antimicrobial Prophylaxis at the Time of CIED (Cardiovascular Implantable Electronic Devices) Placement 2010.

"Preoperative antiseptic preparation of the skin of the surgical site should be done.... Preoperative skin cleansing with chlorhexidine-alcohol is superior to povidone-iodine, ... Intraprocedurally, compulsive attention to sterile technique is mandatory.... Prevention of CIED infection can be addressed before, during, and after device implantation. Before device implantation, it is important to ensure that patients do not   Pacer Pocket infection and have clinical signs of infection. A parenterally administered antibiotic is recommended one hour before the procedure. Data ... strongly supports the administration of antibiotic prophylaxis for CIED implantation. Most experts continue to advocate a first-generation cephalosporin, such as cefazolin, for use as prophylaxis." (Or Gentamicin)

http://circ.ahajournals.org/content/121/3/458.full ...."It has been known for years that silver has antimicrobial properties. Arglaes (Medline Industries, Inc., Mundelein, IL) dressings use silver antimicrobial technology and are designed to prevent SSIs [Surgical Site Infections]. The dressings are transparent, designed for wound care and were the first antimicrobial, sustained-release dressings on Wire infection/vegetation the market. Arglaes provides a continuous and controlled release of silver ions, which function as an antibacterial agent. The ionic silver creates an environment that is hostile to bacteria and fungi, yet non-cytotoxic (e.g., will not harm healthy tissue), and the sustained-activity ionic silver maintains full efficacy for up to 7 days."

http://www.innovationsincrm.com/cardiac-rhythm-management/2010/october/25-prevention-of-bacterial-infections-cied

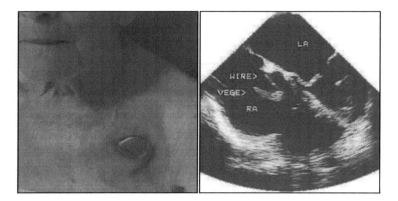

Our experts also suggest the following to decrease PPI infection rate:
- Antibiotic given within an hour of implant
- Only essential staff in the room
- No entering or leaving the room after the table is open
- Decrease talking
- No going under the drapes after the chest is prepped
- Irrigate the pocket before placing the device (after lead insertion)
- The MD double gloves and changes the outer pair before touching the device, and only the physician touches the actual device.
- Develop a very comprehensive patient education program.
- Change our suture to Ethicon VPC which is bacterial resistant. (The beginning of most infections can be traced to the suture line)
- Cover the surgical site with the Arglais Film or Pad Dressing which is a 7-day dressing impregnated with silver ion and is breathable.

Above suggested by: Jim Combs RCSA, RCIS, RCES, EMTP, Rockford Memorial Hospital

27. What does this symbol with three broken semicircles stand for?

   a. **Poison**
   b. **Fire danger**
   c. **Biohazard**
   d. **Radiation hazard**

ANSWER: c. Biohazard. OSHA says: "Labeling: The standard requires that fluorescent orange or orange-red warning labels be attached to containers of regulated waste, to refrigerators and freezers containing blood and other potentially infectious materials, and to other containers used to store, transport, or ship blood or other potentially infectious materials" Used on "sharps" containers and "biohazard bags." See: OSHA Regulations on Blood borne Pathogens

28. Which body fluid is LEAST likely to transmit HIV to a health care worker?
   a. Semen
   b. Blood
   c. Pericardial fluid
   d. Saliva

ANSWER: d. Saliva. The CDC says: "HIV has been isolated from blood, semen, saliva, tears, urine, vaginal secretions, cerebrospinal fluid, breast milk, and amniotic fluid, but only blood and blood products, semen, vaginal secretions, and possibly breast milk, have been directly linked to transmission of HIV. Contact with fluids such as saliva and tears have not been shown to result in infection. Although other fluids have not been shown to transmit infection, all body fluids and tissues should be regarded as potentially contaminated by HBV or HIV and treated as though they were infectious...." HIV may also be transmitted by sexual contact, including semen. See: Dept Labor/Dept Health & Humans Services, Joint advisory Notice, "Protection against occupational exposure to HBV and HIV"

29. How may a health care worker develop hepatitis B viral infections without being exposed to HBV infected patients?
   a. Tattooing or ear piercing
   b. Inhalation of aerosolized nasal secretions
   c. Ingestion of contaminated food or drinking water
   d. Direct contact with dried blood on environmental surfaces

ANSWER: d. Contact with Dried blood on environmental surfaces. Such secondary infection is the main reason all blood spills and spatters must be cleaned up and disinfected and why it is so important to wash your hands frequently. The CDC says, "Although percutaneous injuries are among the most efficient modes of HBV transmission, these exposures probably account for only a minority of HBV infections among health care professionals (HCP). In several investigations of nosocomial hepatitis B outbreaks, most infected health care professionals could not recall an overt percutaneous injury, although in some studies, up to one third of infected HCP recalled caring for a patient who was HBsAg- positive. In addition, HBV has been demonstrated to survive in dried blood at room temperature on environmental surfaces for at least 1 week. Thus, HBV infections that occur in health care professionals with no history of nonoccupational exposure or occupational percutaneous injury might have resulted from direct or indirect blood or body fluid exposures that inoculated HBV into cutaneous scratches, abrasions, burns, other lesions, or on mucosal surfaces..., There is no evidence that HBV or HIV can be transmitted via food, drinking water, or airborne aerosols." There is evidence that HBV can also be transmitted by unprotected sex. See: Dept Labor/Dept Health & Humans Services, Joint advisory Notice, "Protection against occupational exposure to HBV and HIV"

30. For which viruses currently are there NO immunizing vaccines?
   a. **HIV and HBV**
   b. **HIV and HCV**
   c. **HAV and HBV**
   d. **HAV and HCV**

ANSWER: b. HIV and HCV have NO immunizing vaccines as of year 2010. These are the Human Immunodeficiency Virus and the Hepatitis C Virus. Unfortunately, both viruses can be spread by blood or body fluids from infected individuals. See: www.immunize.org

31. When a patient acquires a new infection in the hospital where he is a patient, it is termed:
   a. **A local infection**
   b. **An enteric infection**
   c. **A primary infection**
   d. **A nosocomial infection**

ANSWER: d. A nosocomial infection. Any infection acquired in a health agency is called a nosocomial infection. This is one of the main reasons to get patients out of the hospital as early as possible. An enteric infection is spread by feces containing the causative organism. A local infection, such as an abscess, is limited to the body's tissues and remains there. A primary infection is one that occurs before a subsequent infection develops. See: Lippincott's State Board Review for NCLEX-PN

32. Eyewear, goggles, and/ or face-shields need to be worn only:
   a. **On invasive procedures (where blood may spatter)**
   b. **On interventional procedures (not diagnostic cases)**
   c. **On cases who are in isolation (with blood borne pathogens)**
   d. **On positive HIV or HBV cases (with end stage disease)**

ANSWER: a. On invasive procedures (where blood may spatter) during vascular access. Health care workers need to wear protective barriers on all cases where blood or body fluids may splash. That includes all invasive procedures. You can best protect yourself by shielding your eyes, nose, and mouth mucus membranes from blood spatter; and by wearing gloves whenever touching any patient's body fluids. OSHA says: "Masks in combination with eye protection devices, such as goggles or glasses with solid side shields, or chin-length face shields, shall be worn whenever splashes, spray, spatter, or droplets of blood or other

potentially infectious materials may be generated and eye, nose, or mouth contamination can be reasonably anticipated."
See: OSHA Regulations on Blood borne Pathogens

33. While doing an invasive procedure on a patient, if you get a splash of their blood in your eye you should immediately:
   a. **Report the incident, Test the patient for blood-borne-disease,**
   b. **Chance of blood-borne infection is negligible**
   c. **Take a shower and rinse eyes while blinking for 5-10 minutes**
   d. **Rinse the eye with soap and water for 2-3 minutes**
   e. **Rinse the eye with water or saline for 15 minutes**

ANSWER: e. Rinse the eye with water or saline for 15 minutes.
"After exposure to the eyes, flush the eyes immediately for at least 15 minutes. That is according to OSHA. Use either water or sterile saline. If exposure occurred at work or school, one should contact the occupational hazard nurse asap. All institutions should have this. If it occurred in a private setting, and there is a worry of a transmissible disease, a doctor should be involved to check for hepatitis B, HIV or whatever else is suspected in both the person who got splashed and the patient."

34. You are instructed to transport a patient to the EP lab for an ICD implant. He is on an IV, a portable ECG monitor and a temporary pacemaker. His history includes type 2 diabetes, MRSA, and pneumonia. He has no droplet precautions.
The transporter should:
   a. **Transport with all attached devices. No contact precautions.**
   b. **Put a mask on the patient. Transport with all attached devices. No contact precautions.**
   c. **Put on gown and gloves when you enter his room and remove them when you leave the room. Then wash your hands. Bring along a pair of unopened gloves.**
   d. **Put a mask on the patient. Put on your gown, gloves, and mask when you enter his room and wear them during transport. Remove them after transport. Wash your hands.**

ANSWER: c. Put on gown, gloves, and mask when you enter the room, and remove them when you leave the room. Then wash your hands. Bring along a pair of unopened gloves.
Medscape says, "When transporting an MRSA patient, a chief concern is avoiding actions that require the nurse or other attendant to touch the patient and then possibly contaminate environmental surfaces (door handles, elevator buttons, etc.). If a single caregiver is transporting the patient, gown and gloves are worn until the patient is on the stretcher or wheelchair, and then gloves are removed, and hands are washed. This caregiver then

transports the patient without having any direct patient contact. A mask is required only if the patient is on droplet precautions as recommended by the CDC."

If it is anticipated that the patient might require some hands-on intervention during transport, you should bring along a pair of gloves. Another approach is to have two individuals transport the patient. One wears a gown and gloves and is responsible for touching the patient, if needed, during transport. The other individual, without gloves, manages the doors and elevator buttons.

Multidrug-Resistant Organisms such as methicillin-resistant Staphylococcus aureus (MRSA) and vancomycin-resistant Enterococcus (VRE) are a severe problem in hospitals. "Individuals who become colonized with MRSA tend to remain colonized for months or even years. It is important to realize that individuals colonized with MRSA can serve as reservoirs for MRSA and transmit the bacteria to others, just as those infected with MRSA. Therefore, hospitals choose to assume that patients who were formerly colonized with MRSA are likely to still be colonized with MRSA. E.g., 'Once an MRSA patient, always an MRSA patient' (unless cultures prove otherwise.) Their medical records are flagged so that contact precautions can immediately be resumed if these patients return to the hospital. Colonization refers to the presence of microorganisms in or on a host with growth and multiplication, but without tissue invasion or damage. Colonized patients are also known as asymptomatic carriers."

See: http://www.medscape.com/viewarticle/546221

IVs & Access:

1. **When placing an IV prior to permanent pacer implant it is most important to consider:**
   a. **Site of implant**
   b. **Type of pacemaker**
   c. **Expected medications**
   d. **Vein size and tortuosity**

ANSWER: a. Site of implant: Right or Left Side. Most implants are made to the patient's nondominant side. Right-handed patients get left side implants and left arm IVs. Since the PPI leads are normally inserted into the left subclavian vein, use that side for IV access.

Having the IV on the same side allows you to perform a venogram to highlight stenosis or tortuosity in the left subclavian venous system. The BP cuff will then be placed on the opposite (usually right) arm. Only thoracic veins are used for PPI, and arm veins are the usual IV route. Ellenbogen says about the site of implant, "Most often the left side is chosen because most patients are right-handed and there is a less acute angle between the left subclavian and the innominate vein than exists on the right side. "Ellenbogen, Chapter on "Techniques of pacemaker implantation and removal"

2. **In general, when selecting an IV site in the arm at the beginning of a case start with the:**
   a. **Largest vein available**
   b. **Vein closest to the heart**
   c. **Most medial site**
   d. **Most peripheral (distal) site**

ANSWER d. Most peripheral (distal) site. Intermed says, "Generally IVs are started at the most peripheral site that is available and appropriate for the situation. This allows cannulation of a more proximal site if your initial attempt fails. If you puncture a proximal vein first, and then try to start an IV distal to that site, the fluid may leak from the injured proximal vessel. The preferred site in the emergency department is the veins of the forearm, followed by the median cubital vein that crosses the antecubital fossa.... In circumstances in which no peripheral IV access is possible a central IV can be started.
[subclavian, IJ...]" See: http://intermed.med.uottawa.ca/procedures/iv/

3. **A patient comes to your lab with an IV started in his hand with KVO (or TKO) orders. The patient complains that the site hurts. The hand looks swollen and red. Your first action should be to:**
   a. **Remove the IV**
   b. **Turn off the IV**
   c. **Lower the IV bag below the patient's chest level**
   d. **Flush the IV needle with a syringe of saline**

ANSWER: b. Turn off the IV to stop the infiltration. This is so common an occurrence that everyone in the lab should be aware of how to stop it. Large black and blue marks can result. It may look like a hematoma - except softer. Once the infiltration is stopped, then the IV will have to be replaced. KVO is abbreviation for "Keep Vein Open." TKO is abbreviation for "To Keep Open." See: Lewis, Lippincott's State Board Review for NCLEX-PN.

4. **Care of an IV is different from the care of an IA (arterial) line in that IVs:**
   a. **Require pressurized flush bags**
   b. **Require a continuous heparinized saline drip**
   c. **Safely allow injection of small air bubbles**
   d. **Are inserted by the Seldinger technique**

ANSWER: c. Safely allow injection of small air bubbles. Air bubbles are not usually a problem in IVs or catheters on the right side of the heart. Small air bubbles will be effectively filtered out by the lungs, then slowly absorbed. It may take a hundred ccs of air to cause a critical pulmonary embolism. This is NOT true on the left side where air emboli lodge in peripheral capillaries and obstruct critical flow, leading to tissue infarction or the "bends." Even so, technologists should get in the habit of keeping bubbles out of all catheter lines. This is more critical when IVs are connected to transseptal sheaths, in which air bubbles may cross to the left side of the heart and the brain.

IV lines can be dripped continuously with a gravity drip. Arterial pressure will "back up" gravity IV because arterial pressure is so great. Pressure bags are necessary in arterial lines. See: Grossman, chapter on "Cardiac Ventriculography."

5. A patient has a hematoma on her right groin. Your EP physician chooses the left femoral approach for an arterial line for monitoring pressure during ablation. In his first puncture attempt he accidentally punctured the left femoral vein. He withdraws the needle and holds pressure for three minutes. His next LFA puncture attempt should be _____ to the last puncture site.
   a. 1 cm medial
   b. 2 cm medial
   c. 1 cm lateral
   d. 2 cm lateral

ANSWER: c. 1 cm lateral to vein. Remember NAV (or NAVL) is for the right groin. For the left groin it would be reversed to - VAN. So, he should stick 1 cm to the right of (lateral to) the original venipuncture site. NAVL stands for: NERVE - ARTERY VEIN - (LIGAMENT). The femoral vein is about 1 cm medial to the femoral artery. See: Kern, "Arterial & Venous Access."

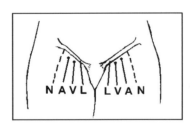

6. Match the neck venous access site to its number in the diagram.
   a. **Subclavian vein**
   b. **Innominate vein**
   c. **Internal Jugular**
   d. **External Jugular**

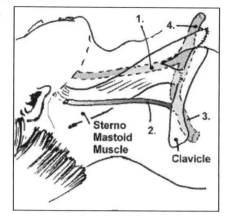

BE ABLE TO MATCH ALL ANSWERS BELOW TO PICTURE:
VENOUS ACCESS:
   1. c. Internal Jugular: in the triangle of sternomastoid muscle insertions
   2. d. External Jugular: on surface sternomastoid muscle
   3. a. Subclavian: inferior and beneath clavicle
   4. b. Innominate or brachiocephalic vein flows into the SVC.

See: ACLS chapter on Vascular access.

7. How should the patient's head be positioned for right internal Jugular Vein Access?
   a. **Looking straight ahead (up)**
   b. **Turned 5-10 degrees to left**
   c. **Turned 30 degrees to left**
   d. **Turned 45-60 degrees to left**

ANSWER: c. Turned 30 degrees to left. Kerns says, "To identify landmarks, the operator instructs the patient to lie supine without a pillow under the head and, in the case of the right internal jugular, with the head turned 30 degrees to the left. Patients with low venous pressures may be placed in the Trendelenburg (head down) position." See: Kern, chapter on Arterial and Venous Access,

8. You plan to perform an AF ablation on a patient who has had multiple catheterizations and has a scarred groin. You have a 0.035 guidewire in the RFV, but you are having trouble advancing the 6F - 11 cm long sheath into the vein.
   a. **Predilate the site with an angioplasty balloon**
   b. **Use scalpel and hemostat to enlarge the puncture site**
   c. **Use a series of dilators to predilate the entry site**
   d. **Use a 6F sheath that is braid reinforced**
   e. **Force the 6F dilator and sheath through the scar tissue with a rotating motion**

ANSWER: c. Use a series of dilators to predilate the entry site. Use 4, 5, & 6 French dilators to enlarge the puncture site. Remember sheaths outside diameters are larger than the inside diameter. Schneider says: "When planning sheath placement through a difficult entry site (e.g., a scarred groin or a previously placed bypass graft), a series of vascular dilators should be used to predilate the entry site. This eases placement and helps prevent a buckle at the tip of the sheath that can damage the arteriotomy site and unnecessarily enlarge it." Although rotating the sheath helps, forcing the sheath through may damage the tip of the sheath and the vessel wall. Using a scalpel and hemostat helps enlarge the skin wound, but not the scarred vein. See: Schneider, chapter on "Access for Endovascular Therapy" P 190

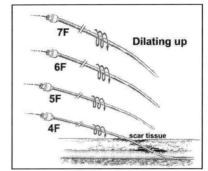

9. Percutaneous catheter insertion using a needle, guide wire, and finally a catheter (Or sheath) over the guide wire, is known as the:
   a. **Arterial technique**
   b. **Cournand technique**
   c. **Seldinger technique**
   d. **Judkins technique**
   e. **Sones technique**

ANSWER: c. Seldinger technique. Seldinger was a European radiologist who developed this popular insertion method. It has made possible all the catheter/wire combinations we use today, including Angioplasty. The sequence of a Seldinger insertion is:

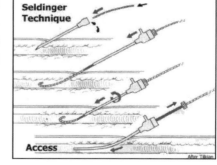

   1. Needle insertion into a vessel
   2. Insertion of a wire through the needle
   3. Removal of the needle over the wire
   4. Insertion of the catheter (or sheath) over the wire

See: Grossman, Chapter on Percutaneous Approach.

10. When performing an arterial puncture, you can best tell when the needle tip is within the artery by the:
   a. **Color of the blood (red)**
   b. **Presence of pulsatile blood**
   c. **Depth of puncture**
   d. **Up and down dancing of the needle**

ANSWER: b. Presence of pulsatile blood. You can't always tell by the color of the blood. Lung disease, shunts, and low CO are associated with dark arterial blood. High pulsatile pressure is the best clue that it is arterial blood. With normal arterial blood pressure, blood will squirt out an 18 g. needle. Wear your mask and goggles to protect your mucus membranes from accidental blood exposure.

In venous sticks, blood will drip out. When making a venous stick, operators commonly attach a small syringe half full of saline. They hold negative pressure when inserting the needle. Upon entering the vein blood will instantly flash into the syringe. Venous pressure is normally low and negative pressure on the syringe is often necessary to know you are in. See: Kern, "Arterial & Venous Access."

11. Arterial monitoring lines are commonly used during transseptal procedures. They should be connected to a continuous flush device which at 300 mmHg infusion pressure will deliver approximately:
   a. **1-2 ml flush/min**
   b. **5-10 ml flush/min**
   c. **3-8 ml flush/hour**
   d. **20-40 ml flush/hour**

ANSWER c. 3-8 ml flush/hour. These continuous flush devices have made extended hemodynamic monitoring possible. At this low flow rate catheters can be kept open while simultaneously measuring pressure through the transducer. The pressure increase due to this slow infusion is negligible in most catheters. Squeezing the device gives a rapid infusion for filling the transducer or flushing the system after drawing blood.
See: Daily, Bedside Hemodynamic Monitoring, chapter on Arterial Pressure Monitoring.

12. Which type of PPI access is most associated with pneumothorax?
   a. **Percutaneous subclavian stick**
   b. **Percutaneous Internal jugular stick**
   c. **Cephalic vein cutdown**
   d. **Jugular vein cutdown**

ANSWER: a. Percutaneous subclavian stick. Ellenbogen says: "Pacing leads may be introduced through a venotomy in an exposed vein (cephalic, jugular, iliofemoral), or venous access may be achieved using the Seldinger technique. The subclavian puncture poses the risk of injury to nearby structures, including the artery, lung, thoracic duct and nerves, and is sometimes the most hazardous part of the implantation procedure." See: Ellenbogen chapter on Techniques of PPI

Cohen says, "The pacemaker implantation procedure is associated with several complications. First, venous access complications may result in a pneumothorax (collapse of the lung) This complication is seen only in percutaneous subclavian access (sticks), and is not seen with a cephalic vein cutdown approach (in which the actual vessel is exposed and a nick is made in the vessel for lead entry) Pneumothorax requires treatment if more than one-third of the lung has collapsed or if the patient is symptomatic with a drop in oxygen saturation or is complaining of chest discomfort." See: Cohen, chapter on Permanent Pacemaker

13. Bleeding under the skin from a vascular catheterization site is termed a/an:
   a. **Hemopoiesis**
   b. **Hematoma**
   c. **Phlebotomy**
   d. **Extravasation**

ANSWER: b. Hematoma. Know all these terms described below.
- HEMOPOIESIS: Production and development of blood cells (in the bone marrow) Suffix: - poiesis = formation
- HEMATOMA: A swelling, or mass of blood confined to a tissue space and caused by a break (needle hole) in a blood vessel, most common in arteries due to higher pressure.
- PHLEBOTOMY: Opening a vein to withdraw blood
- EXTRAVASATION: The escape of fluid into a surrounding space (like an IV needle that comes out of the vein, flooding the tissues)

See: Taber's Medical Dictionary.

14. On which IV access site is hemostasis most difficult to achieve?
   a. **Femoral vein**
   b. **Subclavian vein**
   c. **Internal jugular vein**
   d. **External jugular vein**

ANSWER: b. Subclavian veins must be entered blindly beneath the clavicle. Holding pressure beneath the clavicular bone is almost impossible. Johnsrude says, "On removal of the catheter, secure hemostasis by firm infraclavicular pressure at the site where the catheter enters the vein." Venous extravasation hematoma into the thorax is a possible complication. See: Johnsrude, Chapter on "Catheterization Techniques."

15. You are doing a 4-catheter right heart SVT study done from both RFV and IJ approaches. For optimal stability, the _____ catheter should be placed first and then once it is in position _____.

    a. CS, sutured down

    b. CS, Connect it to the stimulator

    c. RV, sutured down

    d. RV, Connect it to the stimulator

ANSWER: a. CS, sutured down. Issa says, "If used, the CS catheter should be placed first, because its positioning can be impeded by the presence of other catheters. It is also recommended that the CS catheter sheath be sutured to the skin to prevent displacement of the catheter during the EP study." This is only necessary if using the IJ approach. Some labs put the RV catheter in first and connect it to the stimulator in case emergency pacing is needed. See: Issa, chapter on "EP Testing"

16. Which EP catheter is most easily positioned when inserted from an upper extremity or neck vein?

    a. CS

    b. HRA

    c. RV Apex

    d. RV Outflow

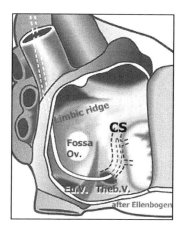

ANSWER: a. CS catheter from the neck. Fogoros says: "Catheters are inserted from the upper extremities.... when positioning of the catheter is easier (such as in coronary sinus catheterization)." Note the flap of tissue anterior to the IVC (Eustachian valve). The Eustachian and Thebesian valves are a barrier when entering the CS from the IVC, but not from the SVC. See: Fogoros chapter on Principles of the Electrophysiology Study "A femoral, internal jugular, or subclavian vein may be used. It is easier to cannulate the CS using the right internal jugular or left subclavian vein versus the femoral vein because the CS valve is oriented anterosuperior and, when prominent, can prevent easy access to the CS from the femoral venous approach." See Issa, chapter on "Catheterization Techniques"

17. What is the most reliable landmark for femoral arterial access?

    a. Pubic Symphysis

    b. Inguinal Crease

    c. Femoral Head

    d. Femoral Pulse

ANSWER: d. Femoral Pulse. "The inguinal crease is frequently used as a landmark, based on the belief that the level of the inguinal crease is closely related to the inguinal ligament. However, the distance between the inguinal crease and the inguinal ligament is highly variable, ranging from 0 to 11 cm, and the bifurcation of the CFA is above the inguinal crease in 75.6% of patients.9 Another frequently used landmark, the maximal femoral pulse, is over the CFA in 92.7% of limbs, and the CFA is projected over the medial aspect of the femoral head in 77.9% of limbs. This indicates that the level of the strongest femoral pulse is a more reliable means of localizing the CFA than the level of the inguinal crease. Therefore, although popular, the use of the inguinal skin crease should be considered an unreliable guide for CFA puncture." Optimal technique for common femoral artery access. (n.d.). Retrieved May 08, 2021, from https://evtoday.com/articles/2013-jan/optimal-technique-for-common-femoral-artery-access

18. The following is an example of an arterial line blood pressure recorded during the procedure. What is recommended?
   a. **Reposition the arterial line**
   b. **Give an IV fluid bolus**
   c. **Aspirate / Flush the transducer**
   d. **Replace the transducer**

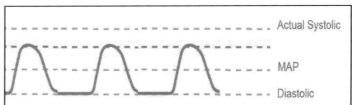

ANSWER: c. Aspirate / Flush the transducer. This is an example of an over-damped waveform. "A waveform that is damped will appear small in amplitude and flattened. The dicrotic notch will be hard to visualize and appreciate. Additionally, the systolic pressure will be poorly reflected, causing it to be reported lower than it actually is. Conversely, the diastolic blood pressure will be over-estimated, and will be reported higher than it actually is. There are a number of causes of an over-damped waveform. Tiny air bubbles in the tubing, a clot at the tip of the catheter, tubing that is "too" stiff or kinked and / or a catheter that is positioned against the wall of the blood vessel. Remember that air is easily compressible and will almost always cause an over-damped waveform. An over-damped waveform is a relatively common occurrence and can be fairly easy to correct."

CIED Access:

1. During a permanent pacemaker subclavian stick, your patient develops SOB, coughing and the chest film shown. The physician will increase O2 administration and:
   a. Insert a chest tube
   b. Anticoagulate the patient
   c. Perform a pericardiocentesis
   d. Attempt to aspirate air through a PA catheter

ANSWER: a. Insert a chest tube. Note, the dark triangle in the lower left lung indicates air in the lung, with a sloping line demonstrating the air-lung interface of the partially deflated lung. This large pneumothorax will severely limit the left lung expansion and oxygenation. Ellenbogen says, "Pneumothorax is often asymptomatic and discovered on the routine post-procedure chest radiograph. Rarely it may be the cause of severe respiratory distress intraprocedurally. Pleuritic pain, cough (especially if productive of blood-tinged sputum) and difficulty breathing suggest the diagnosis.... Respiratory symptoms arising during the procedure should prompt assessment of pulse, blood pressure, oximetry, and blood gas analysis. Fluoroscopic examination of both lung fields should also be performed."

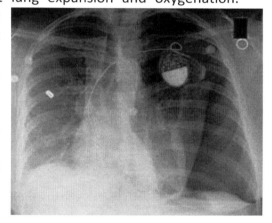

"Treatment of pneumothorax depends on its severity and associated symptoms. Respiratory distress during the procedure may necessitate the urgent/emergency insertion of a chest tube.... if its extent is >10% a chest tube should be considered. If a small pneumothorax does not resolve or enlarge on serial radiographs, evacuation [chest tube] is indicated. Inspiration of 100% oxygen by facemask may help resolve a small pneumothorax. "See: Ellenbogen chapter on "Techniques of Pacemaker implantation and Removal"

2. During subclavian puncture and sheath insertion what is an immediate sign of air embolism?
   a. A hissing sound
   b. Patient makes a "snoring" sound
   c. Cyanosis and/or drop in BP
   d. Chest pain or coughing up bloody sputum

ANSWER: a. A hissing sound. Ellenbogen says, "Air embolism can occur when a central vein is accessed by a sheath, regardless of the technique used to introduce it. This complication may be signaled by a hiss of air sucked into the sheath by negative intrathoracic pressure and may occur suddenly when a heavily sedated, snoring patient deeply inspires at a time when control over the sheath's orifice is not adequate." See: Ellenbogen chapter on "Techniques of Pacemaker implantation and Removal"

3. In a pacemaker implant, to reduce risk of pneumothorax and air embolism prior to making your subclavian puncture:
   a. **Do an antecubital venogram**
   b. **Check chest film for anomalies**
   c. **Relax the patient and teach him to Valsalva**
   d. **Place the patient in reverse Trendelenburg position**

ANSWER: a. Do an antecubital venogram. By injecting contrast into the antecubital IV, you can visualize the route of the subclavian vein, compare it to the clavicle on fluoro, and more accurately make your subclavian vein puncture. The best position to reduce air embolism is the Trendelenburg head-down position (not reverse Trendelenburg) because it increased venous pressure in the thorax.

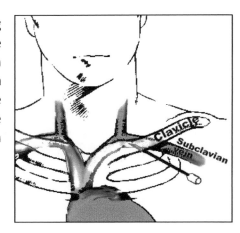

4. To avoid pneumothorax during subclavian PPI procedure it is the most important to:
   a. **Elevate the patient's head**
   b. **Reverse Trendelenburg position**
   c. **Use sheaths with hemostatic valves**
   d. **Have the patient take a deep breath**
   e. **Use large bore Seldinger needle**

ANSWER: c. Use sheaths with hemostatic valves. Ellenbogen says, "The most important of these [precautions against air embolism] is routine use of valved sheaths." Other preventative measures listed by Ellenbogen include use small sheaths, pinch or occlude neck of sheath when appropriate, using sheaths with hemostatic valves, increase CVP by hydrating well, Trendelenburg position, cautioning the patient against deep inspiration and to Valsalva when the sheath is open. See: Ellenbogen chapter on "Techniques of Pacemaker implantation and Removal"

5. To reduce the risk of air embolism during PPI, it is important to be sure your patient is well hydrated because:

    a. **Higher CVP makes it easier to feel venous pulse**

    b. **Increased blood volume increases preload and BP**

    c. **Increased blood volume minimizes effect of blood loss**

    d. **Higher CVP reduces negative pressure on inspiration**

ANSWER: d. Higher CVP reduces negative pressure on inspiration.

Higher venous pressure makes less of a pressure gradient between intrathoracic pressure and atmospheric air pressure, so air is less likely to be sucked in during deep inspiration when the thoracic pressure drops. Intrathoracic pressure is always negative and gets more negative during deep inspiration. This negative pressure is transmitted to the intrathoracic vessels. The Trendelenburg position (elevated legs) also raises CVP and helps prevent air embolism during subclavian stick.

Gul and Kayrak say "Three obligatory conditions need to coexist for pulmonary air embolism to occur: (1) there must be a source of gas/air; (2) a direct access to the venous system; and (3) a pressure gradient between the source of gas/air and the venous system. It can be prevented through operator care and using introducers with hemostatic valves. The diagnosis is obvious because it is heralded by a hissing sound as the air is sucked in and with the fluoroscopic confirmation that follows" Enes Elvin Gul and Mehmet Kayrak http://cdn.intechopen.com/pdfs/13786/InTechCommon_pacemaker_problems_lead_an d_pocket_complications.pdf

Transseptal Access:

1. Match the transseptal catheterization equipment in the diagram with its name.

    a. **Mullins sheath**

    b. **Brockenbrough needle**

    c. **Brockenbrough catheter**

    d. **Bing stylet**

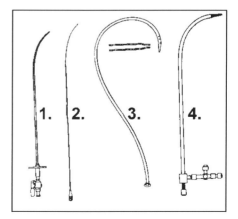

ANSWER: a. Mullins sheath and dilator

BROCKENBROUGH NEEDLE: is a 70 cm long curved 18-gauge needle (21 gauge at tip). This is the instrument that punctures the atrial septum as it is advanced through the RA catheter. It has a needle flange (hilt) with a pointed end showing the direction of the curve. It has a built-in one-way stopcock.

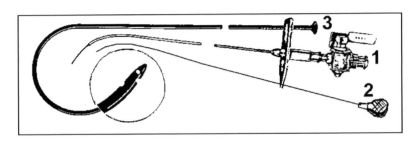

BING STYLET: is a curved blunt obturator slightly longer than the needle to safely pass the long Brockenbrough needle up the catheter without catching on the catheter wall. This blunt stylet is withdrawn just before the atrial puncture is made.

BROCKENBROUGH CATHETER: is a rigid Teflon 70 cm. tapered tip catheter to allow percutaneous entry and smooth passage through the atrial septum. It has an end hole and 6 side-holes for angiography. The bend shape is circular with radii of 2.0, 2.5 and 3.0 cm. The tapered hub must be attached to a flare adapter once the puncture is done.

MULLINS SHEATH: This is a long Teflon sheath that can be advanced with its introducer catheter over the needle across the fossa ovalis and into the LA. It is usually used to introduce other catheters into the LA such as a special pigtail or valvuloplasty catheter. These sheaths are also used in Mitral valvuloplasty catheter introduction.

MULLINS DILATOR (CATHETER): Like the Brockenbrough catheter but with less curve. It is designed specifically to introduce and extend beyond the Mullins sheath. See: Grossman, chapter on "Percutaneous Approach (& Transseptal Cath)"

2. The sharp and curved guidewire that may be used to puncture the septum in transseptal catheterization is:
  a. **TransWire**
  b. **Wholey Wire**
  c. **SafeSept guidewire**
  d. **Movable core J wire**

ANSWER: c. SafeSept guidewire made by Pressure Products Inc. It is a 135 cm .014-inch nitinol wire designed for transseptal puncture. As soon as it punctures the septum curls into an atraumatic J shape. Then the standard needle, dilator, and sheath are advanced into the LA as shown. The company says it requires much less force than puncturing with a transseptal needle. They say "there is virtually no possibility of aortic or pericardial perforation.... After the transseptal dilator has "tented" the fossa ovalis, effortless advancement of the SafeSept tip perforates the membranous fossa. Unsupported by the needle and dilator, the tip of the wire assumes a 'J' shape, rendering it incapable of further tissue penetration." See: http://www.pressure-products.com

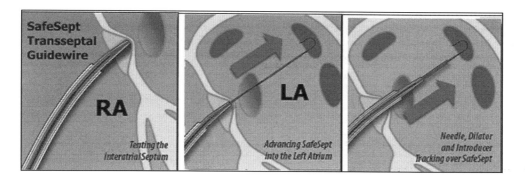

3. The new RF powered transseptal needle that may be used to puncture a fibrotic or aneurysmal atrial septum has:
- **a. An irrigated tip RF electrode**
- **b. A mounted ICE transducer**
- **c. Side holes for pressure & contrast**
- **d. A leading atraumatic J guide wire**

ANSWER: c. Side holes for pressure and contrast. This is the Baylis NRG RF Transseptal Needle. Baylis Co. Says it, "Predictably crosses all types of septa, can cross an aneurysmal septum in a controlled manner, can effectively cross a fibrotic septum, minimizes the danger of skiving and scraping, compatible with standard sheaths / dilators." You may watch a video at www.baylismedicalcanada.com

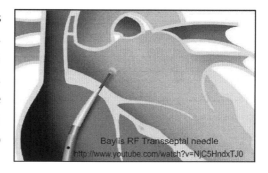

4. Which procedure below requires transseptal access?
- **a. Right-Lateral Accessory Pathway Ablation**
- **b. Pulmonary Vein Isolation**
- **c. RVOT PVC Ablation**
- **d. LVOT PVC Ablation**

ANSWER: b. Pulmonary Vein Isolation. Pulmonary vein isolation, or PVI, is an ablation procedure used to treat atrial fibrillation. The pulmonary veins are located on the posterior aspect of the left atrium; therefore, the LA must be accessed.

A right-lateral accessory pathway is located within the right atrium. If the pathway is in the left atrium (i.e., left-lateral) then transseptal access is most likely utilized. However, some physicians will ablate these pathways from the ventricular aspect utilizing a retrograde approach.

RVOT PVCs are located on the right side of the heart, so left heart access is not required. If the PVC is in the LVOT, the physician will typically utilize retrograde access. This is when the arterial system is accessed, and the catheter is advanced from the femoral artery to the aorta and then the ventricle. This manner also allows for easier mapping of the aortic cusps if needed. LVOT ablations may be performed utilizing transseptal access, but retrograde is the standard approach.

5. What is the most common cause of aborted transseptal puncture?
   a. **Failure to localize the fossa ovalis**
   b. **Aneurysmal fossa ovalis**
   c. **Scarred fossa ovalis**
   d. **None of the above**

ANSWER: a. Failure to localize the fossa ovalis. "Identification of fossa ovalis and of surrounding anatomies is the most crucial step of TSP. Failure to localize the FO is the single most common cause of aborted TSP (transseptal puncture). Traditionally, fluoroscopic images have been utilized in the localization of FO. However, various other aids are commonly employed to maximize fluoroscopic localization of TSP site and decrease untoward complication."
Sharma, et al, Transseptal Puncture: Devices, Techniques, and Considerations for Specific Interventions. Current Cardiology Reports, 2019.

6. During a transseptal puncture, a pigtail catheter may be placed in the aortic root to prevent:
   a. **Puncture of the posterior wall**
   b. **Puncture of the aorta**
   c. **Puncture of the SVC**
   d. **Clot introduction**

ANSWER: b. Puncture of the aorta. The aorta is located anterior to the fossa ovalis. Some physicians will utilize a pigtail catheter within the aorta to help with visualization on x-ray even with or without contrast injection. The catheter is used as an anatomical marker. Intracardiac echo (ICE) may be utilized to visualize to be sure the needle is not projecting towards the aorta. ICE may also be used to detect clots within the heart before attempting the transseptal puncture.

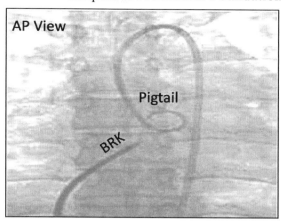

"Alternatively, a diagnostic electrophysiology catheter can be used to mark the bundle of His which is positioned close to the aortic root or the coronary sinus ostium, which lies in the same vertical plane as the aortic root when viewed in the right anterior oblique projection." Sharma, et al, Transseptal Puncture: Devices, Techniques, and Considerations for Specific Interventions. Current Cardiology Reports, 2019.

7. The transseptal sheath, dilator, and needle assembly should be pointed at the _____ position and then withdrawn from the SVC to the fossa ovalis.
   a. 2 o'clock
   b. 4 o'clock
   c. 8 o'clock
   d. 10 o'clock

ANSWER: b. 4 o'clock. The long sheath is inserted into the SVC and then the guidewire is replaced with the transseptal needle. Some physicians will have a continuous flush on the needle, a syringe or a stopcock for pressure monitoring, and contrast injection. "The entire assembly is then rotated posteriorly with the arrow of the needle pointing to approximately the 4 o'clock position and then withdrawn towards the patient's feet." The arrow on the hub of the needle and the side port of the transseptal sheath are on the same side as the direction of the curve such as in the following image.

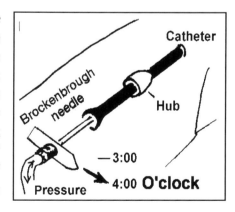

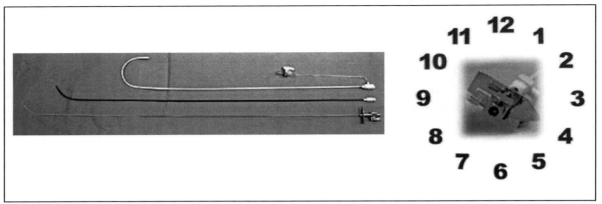

Sharma, et al, Transseptal Puncture: Devices, Techniques, and Considerations for Specific Interventions. Current Cardiology Reports, 2019.

8. All the following may increase the risk of perforation during the transseptal puncture except _____.
   a. **Aneurysmal Septum**
   b. **Dilated Aortic Root**
   c. **Small Atria**
   d. **Patent PFO**

ANSWER: d. Patent PFO. Each of the other answers may increase the risk of perforation during a transseptal puncture. Other factors that increase the risk include either an elastic or fibrosed septum, the presence of a septal occlude device, large atria, and thoracic spine deformities. The use of special puncture needles and other modalities may be utilized to help prevent complications in these patients. Sharma, et al, Transseptal Puncture: Devices, Techniques, and Considerations for Specific Interventions. Current Cardiology Reports, 2019.

9. During transseptal access, what decreases the need for additional pressure to push the needle through the septum?
   a. **Use of a Steerable transseptal needle**
   b. **Electrocautery applied to needle**
   c. **Long support sheath**
   d. **ICE imaging**

ANSWER: b. Electrocautery applied to needle. "A brief application of electrocautery to the standard needle tip has been used successfully for difficult TSP. With the application of cautery to the needle, the need for additional pressure when pushing the needle through the septum is typically avoided minimizing the risk of sudden lurching and perforating posterior part of the left atrial wall. McWilliams et al. reported over 350 double transseptal punctures using electrocautery without major complications in 2009. Since then, several reports have demonstrated the safety and efficacy of electrocautery for TSP with difficult septal anatomy. Much cheaper than other special needles, electrocautery can also be used as a bailout procedure when conventional methods fail to gain transseptal access in 3 or > 3 attempts." Sharma, et al, Transseptal Puncture: Devices, Techniques, and Considerations for Specific Interventions. Current Cardiology Reports, 2019.

10. What anatomic anomaly may be observed in patients with long-standing mitral valve disease?
   a. **Posteriorly located fossa ovalis**
   b. **Superiorly located fossa ovalis**
   c. **Anteriorly located fossa ovalis**
   d. **Inferiorly located fossa ovalis**

ANSWER: d. Inferiorly located fossa ovalis. With an inferiorly located fossa on a patient undergoing percutaneous mitral valve repair, a modification of the technique may be performed. "Within the FO, a posterosuperior location is preferred to allow for a more tangential approach to the mitral valve to facilitate device delivery. The largest experience of percutaneous mitral valve repair is with MitraClip which requires the introduction of a 22-F device via septal puncture." Sharma, et al, Transseptal Puncture: Devices, Techniques, and Considerations for Specific Interventions. Current Cardiology Reports, 2019.

11. This Teflon catheter and stainless-steel curved needle are used to puncture the:
   a. **Ventricular Septum**
   b. **Ductus Arteriosus**
   c. **Fossa Ovalis**
   d. **AV ring**

ANSWER c. Fossa Ovalis. The Brockenbrough (BRK) transseptal set shown is for atrial transseptal puncture. Puncture is made through the fossa ovalis, the thinnest part of the atrial septum. See: Grossman, chapter on "Percutaneous Approach."

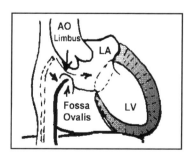

12. A patient has a mechanical aortic valve prosthesis. Here access to the LV is most safely made by:
- a. **Retrograde aortic catheterization (Brachial approach)**
- b. **Retrograde aortic catheterization (Femoral approach)**
- c. **Apical LV puncture (direct transthoracic)**
- d. **Antegrade left heart catheterization (Transseptal)**

ANSWER d. Transseptal LHC. Tilting disc valves are unsafe to cross retrograde. They may pinch and trap a catheter. The catheter may pass through the back side of the disk forcing it open. The problem occurs when the catheter is withdrawn. It may catch the disk and become trapped. Dr. Grossman recommends the transseptal method in these instances. The Complication rate is 3-4% even in experienced hands. See: Grossman, chapter on "Percutaneous Approach."

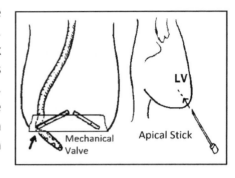

13. When a Mullins sheath is used in transseptal heart catheterization, after successful transseptal puncture the sheath tip should:
- a. **Be advanced into the LV over the dilator, after the dilator has been successfully positioned in the LV**
- b. **Be advanced into the LA with the dilator**
- c. **Remain in the femoral artery**
- d. **Remain in the RA**

ANSWER b. Be advanced into the LA with the dilator. The long Mullin sheath should be advanced into the LA along with the dilator (catheter). This is done over the transseptal needle once it has been successfully placed in the LA. Correct positioning of the transseptal needle in the LA must be established by pressure, oximetry, and/or contrast injection. Then the transseptal needle is "pinned or fixed" to the patient, while the dilator and sheath are advanced as a unit across the septum.

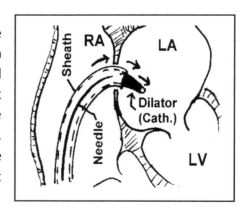

This is an "antegrade" passage following blood flow up the IVC - puncture across the atrial septum - into LA - across the mitral valve - and into the LV.
See: Pepine, Chapter on "Review of General Cath Techniques."

14. In performing transseptal catheterization all the following may be used EXCEPT:
   a. **Brockenbrough needle**
   b. **Mullins sheath**
   c. **ICE guidance**
   d. **Multipurpose catheter**

ANSWER: d. Multipurpose catheter is not used. "The technique for transseptal catheterization using the Mullins sheath...Once the sheath is in the left atrium, the needle and dilator are withdrawn, and the sheath is flushed carefully." Intracardiac Echo (ICE) may be used to guide the needle during inter-atrial puncture. See: Grossman, chapter on "Percutaneous Approach"

15. What gauge is the long needle used for transseptal catheterization?
   a. **16 tapering to 18 gauge**
   b. **18 tapering to 21 gauge**
   c. **20 tapering to 22 gauge**
   d. **22 and 70 cm long**

ANSWER: b. 18-gauge diameter which tapers to 21 gauge at the curved tip. The standard femoral Brockenbrough transseptal needle is 70 cm long. See: Grossman, chapter on "Percutaneous Approach"

16. What percentage of normal individuals have a "probe patent" atrial septum. In these individuals the transseptal catheter can be pushed into the LA without needle puncture across the atrial septum?
   a. **None, only in patients with ASDs**
   b. **10-20%**
   c. **30-50%**
   d. **60-75%**

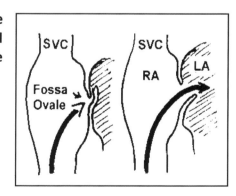

ANSWER b. In 10-20% of normal individuals the transseptal catheter can be pushed across the fossa ovalis, without making a needle puncture. Remember that this "trap door" normally closes

at birth due to higher LA pressure. In some individuals it just does not seal shut. Slight pressure on the fossa with the catheter may allow its easy passage into LA. Why use needle puncture if you don't have to?
See: Grossman, Cardiac Cath., Angiogram., and Interventions, Chapter on "Percutaneous Approach." and Kern, Chapter "Special Techniques." and Pepine, Chapter on "Review of General Cath Techniques."

17. An important anatomic landmark for transseptal puncture is the bulge of the ascending Aorta in the atrial septum just superior to the fossa ovalis. The transseptal catheter is pulled down, over this ridge, then jumps rightward into the fossa ovalis where the puncture is made. What is the name of this atrial septal ridge?
   a. **Eustachian ridge**
   b. **Coronary sinus ridge (ledge)**
   c. **Aortoseptal groove (tunnel)**
   d. **Limbus (Limbic Ledge)**

ANSWER: d. The Limbus, Limbic ridge or ledge is formed by the Aortic root bulging into the atrial septum. It is just above the fossa ovalis where you need to puncture. When withdrawing the needle/catheter from SVC (shown as a dotted catheter) the needle "trips" over the limbic ridge before "falling" into the depression of the fossa ovalis. In Aortic Stenosis the root may be dilated and displace the fossa ovalis antero-superiorly.

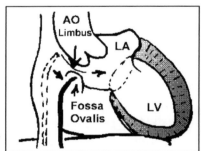

See: Grossman, Cardiac Cath., Angio., and Chapter on "Percutaneous Approach." and Clugston, CATHET. AND CV DIAGNOSIS, 26, 1992, "Transseptal Cath. Update 1992."

18. Following unsuccessful transseptal puncture how should the femoral catheter and needle be repositioned for another puncture?
   a. **Retract the needle into the catheter, reposition the catheter tip in the SVC.**
   b. **Retract the needle into the catheter, reposition the catheter tip in mid RA.**
   c. **Remove the needle from the catheter, use a guidewire to reposition the catheter tip in the SVC.**
   d. **Remove the needle from the catheter, use a guidewire to reposition the catheter tip in the mid RA.**

ANSWER: c. Remove the needle. It is dangerous to torque the catheter in the RA with the sharp needle inside in the PA view. Replace it with a guide wire. Advance the wire and catheter into the SVC. Replace the wire with the needle protected by the catheter. Slide the catheter tip down the medial wall of the SVC, into the RA, over the limbic ridge (AO) and into the fossa ovalis. Only then should the needle be exposed.

Grossman says, "One should never attempt to reposition the catheter-needle combination in the SVC in any other way, since perforation of the RA or atrial appendage is a distinct possibility during such maneuvers." See: Grossman, Cardiac Cath., Angio., and Interventions, Chapter on "Percutaneous Approach."

19. The most common way to access the LA for AF ablation procedures utilizes all the following EXCEPT:
   a. **Brockenbrough catheter**
   b. **Right femoral artery access**
   c. **Full patient heparinization**
   d. **Pressure monitoring through transseptal needle**

ANSWER: b. Right femoral artery access – No, right femoral vein access is needed. Transseptal catheterization is the only practical way to access the left heart without going retrograde up the aorta.

Most labs heparinize only after crossing the septum and not before, for fear of bleeding from the transseptal puncture. Other labs heparinize before crossing the septum because studies have shown thrombus can develop on sheaths and needles before the puncture and be injected into the left heart. E.g., this ICE image shows thrombus at tip of transseptal sheath in tented fossa ovalis prior to puncture. Bruce says, "Early administration of intravenous heparin, specifically before transseptal puncture, decreases the incidence of left atrial thrombi." See: "Early heparinization decreases the incidence of left thrombus on transseptal sheath atrial thrombi detected by intracardiac echocardiography during radiofrequency ablation for atrial fibrillation," by Bruce, in JOURNAL OF INTERVENTIONAL CARDIAC ELECTROPHYSIOLOGY (2008)

20. All the following may be used to document crossing the IA septum with the transseptal needle EXCEPT:
   a. **LA pressure waveform**
   b. **Pass a 0.014 guide wire into PV**
   c. **Contrast injection seen in LA**
   d. **Confirm LA Electrogram**
   e. **Oxygen saturation**
   f. **Agitated saline injection on ICE**

ANSWER: d. Confirm LA Electrogram. All these methods would verify crossing the septum, but pressure waveforms are used most. If you accidentally enter the aorta, you will know immediately by the high pressure. (Don't just pull out of the AO; it will leak and cause tamponade. Take the patient to OR with the needle in place.)

"It is important to recognize that merely recording LA electrograms does not confirm intracavitary catheter location because an LA recording can be obtained from the epicardial surface [you may have punctured into the pericardial space] .... After passage through the fossa ovalis and before advancing the dilator and sheath, an intraatrial position of the needle tip within the LA, rather than the ascending aorta or posteriorly into the pericardial space, needs to be confirmed. Recording an LA pressure waveform from the needle tip confirms an intraatrial location. An arterial pressure waveform indicates intraaortic position of the needle. Absence of a pressure wave recording can indicate needle passage into the pericardial space or sliding up and not puncturing through the atrial septum. A second method is injection of contrast through the needle to assess the position of the needle tip. Alternatively, passing a 0.014-inch floppy guidewire through the Brockenbrough needle into a PV helps verify that needle tip position is within the LA. If the guidewire cannot be advanced beyond the cardiac silhouette or if it follows the path of the aorta, contrast should be injected to assess the position of the Brockenbrough needle before advancing the transseptal dilator..." See Issa, chapter on "EP testing"

21. When ICE is used to confirm the location of the transseptal needle prior to puncture you look for "tenting." What is tenting?
   a. **V shaped indentation in fossa**
   b. **Curved position of the fossa like a reversed C**
   c. **Burst of echo contrast (bubbles) in fossa Ovale**
   d. **Opening the flap into the LA (septum secundum)**

ANSWER: a. V shaped indentation, like a >. A "tent" is the shape a canvas makes when pushed up with a pole, like a >. This is like the indentation the transseptal needle makes as you push it lightly into the thin fossa. Then as you advance the needle the taught fossa pops and collapses as you make the "stick." Medical dictionary says, 'tenting' can also be the symmetrical 'peaking' of T waves.

Issa says, "The sheath, dilator, and needle assembly is introduced into the RA and the dilator tip is positioned against the fossa ovalis, as described earlier. Before advancing the Brockenbrough needle, continuous ICE imaging should direct further adjustments in the dilator tip position until ICE confirms the tip is in intimate contact with the middle of the fossa, confirms proper lateral movement of the dilator toward the fossa, and excludes inadvertent superior displacement toward the muscular septum and aortic valve. With further advancement of the dilator, ICE demonstrates tenting of the fossa. If the distance from the tented fossa to the LA free wall is small, minor adjustments in the dilator tip position can be made to maximize the space. The Brockenbrough needle is then advanced. With successful transseptal puncture, a palpable "pop" is felt, and collapse of the tented fossa is observed. The advancement of the needle is then immediately stopped. With no change in position of the Brockenbrough needle, the transseptal dilator and sheath are advanced over the guidewire into the LA," See: Issa, chapter on "EP testing"

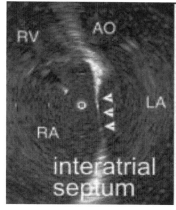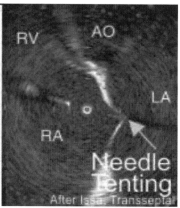

22. How many movements or "drops" are felt on the transseptal needle when pulling the needle assembly back from the SVC to the final position on the fossa ovalis?
   a. 1
   b. 2
   c. 3
   d. 4

ANSWER: b. 2. "As the assembly is withdrawn, two distinct movements are appreciated. The first one is felt when the assembly enters the right atrium (from SVC, over the aortic knob into the RA and onto the intra-atrial septum) and the second one is appreciated when assembly falls onto FO from the thicker muscular intra-atrial septum. A monophasic pressure waveform confirms the contact between the catheter tip and FO. Verification of the position within the FO can be achieved by ensuring the catheter is inferior and posterior to the pigtail catheter in the right anterior oblique position. In a left oblique view, the catheter tip should be directed posteriorly. Additionally, injection of the contrast through the needle may be used to demonstrate the tenting on the fossa ovalis."

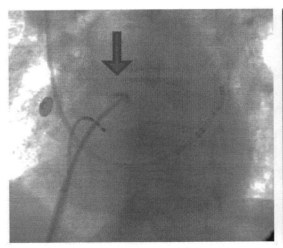 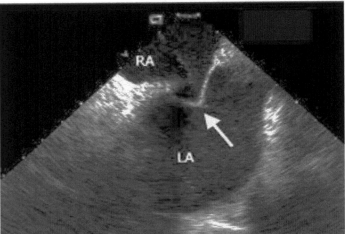

Tenting is shown with the arrow when injecting contrast through the needle in the first image and with intracardiac echo in the second.

Sharma, et al, Transseptal Puncture: Devices, Techniques, and Considerations for Specific Interventions. Current Cardiology Reports, 2019

23. Transseptal heart catheterization is performed only from the _____ entry site.
    a. **Right Femoral Arterial**
    b. **Right Femoral Venous**
    c. **Left Femoral Arterial**
    d. **Left Femoral Venous**

ANSWER b. Right femoral vein is the only standard vascular entry for transseptal heart cath. Other venous entry sites may distort the needle position. This is an "antegrade" passage up the IVC, puncture across the atrial septum, into LA, across the mitral valve, and into the LV.

Grossman says, "Classically, trans-septal catheterization is performed only from the right femoral vein.... With the advent of percutaneous mitral valvuloplasty and antegrade aortic valvuloplasty using the Inoue balloon, as well as the availability of improved equipment, trans-septal catheterization has again become a common procedure." See: Grossman, Cardiac Cath., Angiogram., and Interventions, Chapter on "Percutaneous Approach."

24. Transseptal heart catheterization utilizes all the following EXCEPT:
    a. **Pressure monitoring through transseptal needle**
    b. **Right femoral vein puncture**
    c. **Brockenbrough catheter**
    d. **Patient heparinization**

ANSWER b. Full patient heparinization is contraindicated for transseptal catheterization. Transseptal puncture should be done without heparin due to the possibility of accidental Aortic puncture and tamponade. See: Grossman, chapter on "Percutaneous Approach."

25. Your patient comes to the EP lab for pulmonary vein isolation for treatment of atrial fibrillation. How much heparin should the patient receive at the beginning of the case?
a. 1000-2000 units of heparin IV
b. 3000-5000 units of heparin IV
c. 10,000 units of heparin IV
d. No Heparin

ANSWER d. No heparin is given initially. Heparin is withheld until the transseptal catheter is correctly positioned in the LA or LV.
See: Grossman, Chapter on "Percutaneous Approach"

26. During Mr. Jones transseptal heart catheterization several unsuccessful transseptal needle advances were made. Now Mr. Jones becomes confused and lethargic. His BP is 80/40 mmHg. and falling. RA pressure is 18 mmHg. The heart rate is 105 in sinus rhythm. The therapy is:
a. IV Dopamine and Nitroprusside
b. Fluid administration and IV Atropine
c. IV Epinephrine and having Mr. Jones cough
d. Emergency valve surgery
e. Pericardiocentesis

ANSWER e. Pericardiocentesis. Pericardial tamponade is a serious complication of transseptal heart catheterization. Unsuccessful transseptal attempts may puncture the aorta or pericardial space allowing bleeding into the pericardium. This bleeding (tamponade) compresses the heart so that it cannot fill properly.

Cardiac tamponade may be a fatal complication if not recognized and promptly treated with Pericardiocentesis. Here a needle and then a small catheter are placed within the pericardium, and the fluid is drawn off. This simple lifesaving maneuver usually relieves the constriction immediately and establishes normal hemodynamics.

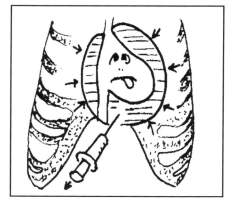

Grossman says, "Classically, transseptal catheterization is performed only from the right femoral vein.... With the advent of percutaneous mitral valvuloplasty and antegrade aortic valvuloplasty using the Inoue balloon, as well as the availability of improved equipment, trans-septal catheterization has again become a common procedure." See: Grossman, chapter on "Percutaneous Approach"

1. Your patient with AF has a CHADS2 score of 1. During transseptal puncture you did not need to use the transseptal needle to enter the LA. With a probe-patent fossa ovalis, you should further evaluate the patient for:
   a. **Nothing, unless symptomatic**
   b. **R-L shunt during cough**
   c. **L-R shunt during inhalation**
   d. **Endocarditis and vegetation**

ANSWER: a. Nothing, unless symptomatic. Probe patency is common and can only be entered from the right side. It is not usually a problem unless there have been signs of cryptogenic (unexplained) stroke or TIA.

- Braunwald says, "A probe-patent foramen ovale that allows access to the left atrium is present in 20% to 30% of adult patients. It can be entered by use of a multipurpose catheter with the tip directed medially and slightly posterior...."
- "The foramen ovale, which allows blood flow across the atrial septum in utero, normally closes shortly after birth as pulmonary blood flow increases and the flap-like septum primum is forced against the septum secundum. However, in approximately 25% of adults, closure of the foramen ovale is not complete. "
- "The presence of a patent foramen ovale (PFO) has been implicated in paradoxical embolism, cryptogenic stroke, arterial gas embolism in decompression illness, high-altitude pulmonary edema, and migraine."
- "Several lines of evidence suggest a role in the pathogenesis of cryptogenic stroke, including documented instances of paradoxical embolism of venous thrombi into the arterial system, a higher-than-expected incidence of PFO in stroke patients with otherwise unexplained stroke or who are young, and a lower-than-expected incidence of recurrent stroke after PFO closure. Factors that appear to increase the risk of paradoxical embolism include the presence of a large trans atrial shunt at rest, a mobile atrial septal aneurysm, and elevated right atrial pressures. Several lines of evidence also suggest a role in the pathogenesis of migraine, particularly in patients with aura. These include a high incidence of PFO in migraine sufferers, a reduction in migraine frequency and severity following PFO closure for stroke, and anecdotal reports of marked benefit."

- "Although patients with atrial septal defects (ASDs) often remain asymptomatic until early adulthood, they may present at any age with exertional dyspnea, fatigue, right ventricular failure, pulmonary hypertension, atrial arrhythmias, or paradoxical embolism. The functional significance of an ASD is primarily determined by the presence of right atrial or ventricular enlargement in the presence of an echocardiographic defect diameter larger than 10 mm or documentation of an elevated left-to-right shunt ratio (Qp/Qs > 1.5:1), determined from oxygen saturation at the time of catheterization." "The most common device used for percutaneous closure is the Amplatzer ASD atrial septal occluder, consisting of two self-expanding nitinol disks, with each containing embedded synthetic fabric patches and joined by a central waist. A device with a waist diameter slightly larger than the defect is selected to be occlusive and to center the device.

Amplatzer Nitinol PFO Closure Device

- The procedural approach to percutaneous ASD closure is like that for PFO closure." See Braunwald chapter on Cardiac Catheterization and Percutaneous Therapies for Structural Disease in Adults.

2. During transseptal cardiac catheterization you are monitoring Brockenbrough needle pressure on 40 mmHg scale. The EP physician advances the needle, and you note the waveform shown. Match each waveform to its needle location.

  a. **Myocardial wall**
  b. **Pericardium**
  c. **Aorta**
  d. **LA**

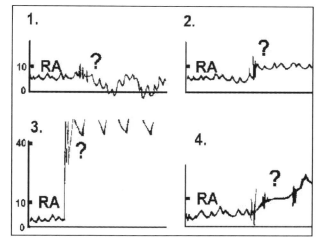

CORRECTLY MATCHED ANSWERS:

1. b. PERICARDIUM. As the needle crosses into the pericardium the pressure drops suddenly because of negative pleural pressure. This can lead to potential complication of tamponade. When the small needle tip is withdrawn it usually heals over. Do not advance the catheter. That just widens the hole, and tamponade is more likely.

2. d. LA: That is what you want. LA pressure is 5-12 mmHg. with "A" and "V" waves. This can be checked by drawing a small blood sample (it should be bright red) or by a contrast test injection through the needle.

3. c. AORTA: Aortic pressure is off the screen. This pressure monitoring is essential to see inadvertent aortic puncture. When the small needle tip is withdrawn it usually heals over. Do not advance the catheter if the needle is in the aorta. That just widens the hole, and tamponade is likely. If bleeding does occur the Brockenbrough catheter can be used to plug the puncture site while the patient is taken to surgery. Pericardiocentesis in the lab may be lifesaving.

4. a. MYOCARDIUM: THIS pressure appears damped because it is intra-myocardial, within atrial or aortic tissue. Small test injections (done by hand) may stain the myocardium, mark it, and make it more visible. With this, if the needle is found to be in the free it should be withdrawn. Advance only if it is within the in the interatrial septum or LA. See: Grossman, Chapter on "Percutaneous Approach."

3. In a transseptal procedure a Brockenbrough catheter and stainless-steel curved needle are used to puncture the:
    a. **Ligamentum Arteriosum**
    b. **Ductus Arteriosus**
    c. **Foramen Ovale**
    d. **Fossa Ovalis**

ANSWER: d. Fossa Ovalis. The Brockenbrough transseptal set shown above is for atrial transseptal puncture. Puncture is made through the fossa ovalis, the thinnest part of the atrial septum. This is where the Foramen Ovale was in the fetus. See: Grossman, chapter on "Percutaneous Approach."

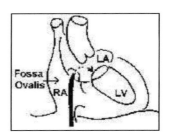

4. During the Brockenbrough transseptal catheterization several important measurements must be made between the needle flange and the catheter hub. The measurement labeled at #1 on the diagram is critical because it sets the tip of the_____ at the tip of the Brockenbrough catheter.
    a. **Brockenbrough Needle**
    b. **Mullins Sheath**
    c. **Blunt Stylet**
    d. **Guidewire**

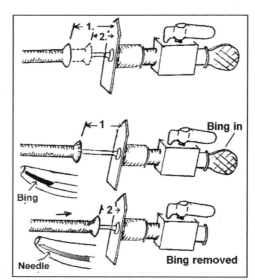

ANSWER: c. Blunt Stylet. This is a critical measurement because the operator must know exactly when the tip of the stylet exits the catheter to prevent damage to atrial structures. It may not be seen on fluoroscope. See: Grossman, Cardiac Cath., Angio., and Interventions, Chapter on "Percutaneous Approach."

Epicardial Access:

1. This area is commonly utilized for epicardial access for VT ablation.
  a. **Transseptal via RFV**
  b. **Rt. Supraclavicular**
  c. **Radial artery**
  d. **Subxiphoid**

ANSWER: d. Subxiphoid. The subxiphoid area is inferior to the xiphoid process and is a typical site for percutaneous epicardial access. Endocardial VT ablation is performed by accessing the LV via either a retrograde approach (most common) or through a transseptal atrial puncture and then advancing the catheter through the mitral valve into the LV.

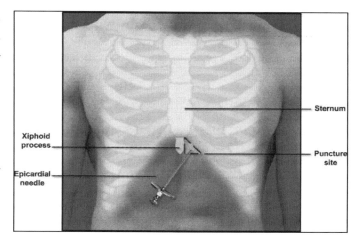

2. For EP procedures which type of vascular access is most challenging in patients that have had open-heart surgery?
  a. **Femoral artery and/or vein**
  b. **Subclavian vein**
  c. **Transseptal**
  d. **Epicardial**

ANSWER: d. Epicardial. After open-heart surgery, there may be adhesions within the pericardial space and other disturbances of the pericardial anatomy.

To obtain epicardial access: "A 2-mm left para-xiphoid space incision is made after application of local anesthesia. A blunt-tipped epidural needle is directed toward the cardiac silhouette under fluoroscopic guidance. As the needle penetrates through the fibrous pericardium, a palpable "give" is appreciated and a puff of contrast demonstrates layering within the pericardial space. A guidewire is advanced into the pericardial space, and RAO/LAO views are used to confirm guidewire position before advancing a sheath over the wire." Ebrille, et al, Successful Percutaneous Epicardial Access in Challenging Scenarios. Pacing and Clinical Electrophysiology, 2014

3. Which three of these complications are most associated with cases utilizing epicardial access?

    a. Subcutaneous Emphysema

    b. Coronary Vascular Injury

    c. RV Pseudoaneurysm

    d. Hepatic Puncture

    e. TIA or Stroke

ANSWER: b, c, & d. Coronary Vascular Injury, RV Pseudoaneurysm, and Hepatic Puncture. May be seen with epicardial access, albeit rare complications. Other rare complications include RV-to-Abdomen fistula and profound coronary arterial vasospasm.

Koruth, et al, Unusual Complications of Percutaneous Epicardial Access and Epicardial Mapping and Ablation of Cardiac Arrhythmias. Circulation: Arrhythmia and Electrophysiology. 2011

4. This is the most common complication of epicardial access and mapping.

    a. Cardiac tamponade

    b. Aortic puncture

    c. LV puncture

    d. Pericarditis

ANSWER: d. Pericarditis. Pericarditis and inadvertent right ventricular puncture are common complications. Other complications, displayed in the following images, include persistent intra-myocardial staining suggesting intra-myocardial hematoma (A), RV perforation and dilator placement in RV (B), and hepatic trauma (C - angiogram of hepatic vein shown).

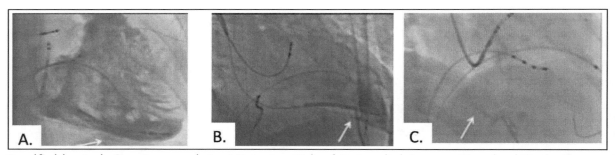

Bradfield, et al, Our Approach to Minimize Risk of Epicardial Access: Standard Techniques with the Addition of Electroanatomic Mapping Guidance. Journal of Cardiovascular Electrophysiology, 2012

5. After epicardial access is attempted, what is the next step to assure appropriate pericardial access?

    a. Insertion of the mapping catheter

    b. Pericardial pressure recording

    c. Pericardiogram

    d. O2 saturation

ANSWER: c. Pericardiogram. This contrast image of the pericardial space will not only demonstrate the correct location but also help determine the presence of pericardial adhesions. To perform, a J-wire is first positioned most often then followed by a soft dilator (4F). An injection of 5-10 cc of contrast is delivered and if access is appropriate then the dilator is exchanged for a larger sheath.

Here is an RAO projection with pericardiogram showing multiple adhesions along the anterior right ventricle.

Bradfield, et al, Our Approach to Minimize Risk of Epicardial Access: Standard Techniques with the Addition of Electroanatomic Mapping Guidance. Journal of Cardiovascular Electrophysiology, 2012

Temporary Pacemakers:

1. Before using a temporary pacer put in a new:
   a. 2.8-volt alkaline battery
   b. 2.8-volt Lithium battery
   c. 9-volt alkaline battery
   d. 9-volt Lithium battery

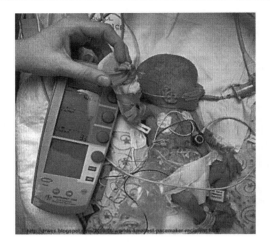

ANSWER: c. 9-volt alkaline battery. Watson says, "Batteries that are used to power pacemakers must be reliable and long lasting. Temporary pacers are typically powered by 9 V batteries. [The rectangular type used in home smoke detectors.] In temporary generators, batteries are usually changed before instituting pacing and at regularly scheduled intervals.... Permanent pulse generators are typically powered by a 2.8 V lithium iodine battery."
See: Watson chapter on "Cardiac Pacing"

2. Which of the following is NOT an electrical safety rule when using temporary endocardial VVI pacing?
   a. Wear rubber gloves when handling pacer wires
   b. Do not touch electrical equipment and the pacing wires simultaneously
   c. Discharge any static electricity onto a grounded metal surface prior to touching the patient
   d. Cover exposed electrode connections with sterile saline soaked 4x4s

ANSWER: d. Cover exposed electrode connections with saline soaked 4x4s - is incorrect. This would "short out" the pacer and prevent pacing. Watson says, "Electrical safety is a major concern for this patient population, as the pacing lead provides a direct route for current flow to the heart tissue. Pacing leads must always be protected from any potential source of electrical current whether environmental or equipment related. Nurses caring for patients should ensure proper maintenance and grounding of equipment. In addition, they should discharge any potential static electricity on a metal surface prior to contact with patients. Rubber gloves should be worn when handling pacing leads (wires) and exposed pacing wires should also be protected with insulating material (i.e., a rubber glove). Contact between two pacing wires should be avoided. Nurses should not simultaneously touch electrical equipment and pacing wires. A recent study suggests that policies for electrical safety may not be adequate in many facilities." See: Watson, Chapter on Cardiac pacing

3. Compared to the permanent pacemaker, the temporary pacer has:
   a. **Constant voltage and generates up to 20 volts**
   b. **Constant voltage and generates up to 5 volts**
   c. **Constant current and generates up to 20 volts**
   d. **Constant current and generates up to 5 volts**

ANSWER: c. Constant current and generates up to 20 volts. Temporary pacers use a 9.5 v alkaline battery whose voltage can be doubled to almost 20 volts. That's a big pacer spike. Temporary pacers use a method to generate their pacer spikes different than permanent pacers. They generate a constant current spike, whereas permanent pacers use a constant voltage spike.
See: Moses, Chapter on Electrophysiology of Pacing

4. When connecting a bipolar pacing lead to the PSA or pulse generator the distal electrode should be connected to the _____ terminal.
   a. **Black active negative**
   b. **Black active positive**
   c. **Red indifferent negative**
   d. **Red indifferent positive**

ANSWER: a. Black active negative. Watson says, "Care should be taken to ensure that the connections are made correctly. On a bipolar lead, the distal electrode is active (negative) and the proximal (ring electrode) is indifferent (positive).
A mnemonic for remembering this is:
R.I.P. (Red Indifferent Positive)
B.A.N. (Black Active Negative)

If connections are reversed the stimulation threshold may be significantly higher. In addition, anodal (positive) stimulation can induce ventricular fibrillation even at subthreshold outputs."
See: Watson, Chapter on Cardiac pacing

5. What will this dual chamber temporary pacer do when you press the "emergency/async." button shown?
   a. **All sensing and pacing stops**
   b. **Pace Ventricle only, at max output rate 72 bpm**
   c. **Pace both chambers fixed rate at maximum output at minimum sensitivity and rate 60 bpm**
   d. **Pace both chambers fixed rate at maximum output at current rate**

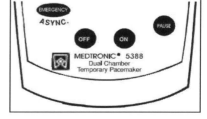

ANSWER: d. Pace fixed rate at max A & V outputs at current rate. So, if the current paced rate is 72, fixed rate (asynchronous) pacing will begin on both A and V channels at maximum output (10 mA). This is needed if for some reason the patient goes bradycardic, and you suspect the pacer settings are incorrect. This is default pacing at maximum output which is sure to pace healthy myocardium if the electrodes are in their proper chambers, even if they are not touching myocardium. But beware of asynchronous pacing as it fires blindly and may fire into a T wave resulting in a ventricular arrhythmia. See: Medtronic.com

6. Which acute myocardial infarction patient is in most serious need of a prophylactic temporary RV pacemaker?
   a. **Inferior MI with Mobitz I AV block**
   b. **Inferior MI with bundle branch block**
   c. **Anterior MI with Mobitz I AV block**
   d. **Anterior MI with bundle branch block**

ANSWER: d. Anterior MI with bundle branch block. Moses says about anterior MI: "AV block with patients with acute anterior MI is usually a more serious matter than that with inferior MI....Selective block of a portion of the infranodal conduction system often precedes complete AV block and should be considered a warning signal . . . injury to the infranodal conduction system is a marker for widespread necrosis." He recommends temporary pacing in patients with acute anterior MI with LBBB, RBBB, or bifascicular block (any 2 of the 3 conduction bundles). Since the RCA usually supplies the AV node, this may result in some degree of temporary heart I block. But the heart rate is usually adequate, and it responds well to atropine. Mobitz I AV block seldom requires a pacer. See: Moses, Chapter on Indication for Pacing

7. Your patient recovering from an MI, is asleep in NSR. The ECG monitor alarms with VF. You rush into the patient's room and while checking the patient you discover that the ECG lead has become disconnected. This is an example of applying what ACLS concept?
   a. **"CABD - Chain of survival"**
   b. **"Consider the simplest things first"**
   c. **"Treat the cause not the condition"**
   d. **"Treat the patient not the arrhythmia"**

ANSWER: d. "Treat the patient not the arrhythmia." Muscle tremor and disconnected leads may mimic VF. Unless you check the patient (the ABCs/CABs) you could accidentally defibrillate a sleeping man. Don't rely on the ECG to make a complete diagnosis. ACLS current says. "Human nature pushes providers to focus on specific resuscitation challenges: get the IV started, insert the tracheal tube, identify the arrhythmia, remember the right medication to use. These actions are the means to the end. Emergency care providers must constantly aim for an overall view of every resuscitative effort.... The ACLS approach uses the primary and secondary CABD surveys in combination with the algorithms. This will keep you centered on the most important acts of resuscitation." See: AHA, ACLS Provider Manual, chapter on "Human Dimension of CPR, ACLS..."

8. People who experience arrest in VF most often need a defibrillator. People who experience cardiac arrest in asystole or PEA most often need _____.
   a. **Medication**
   b. **A diagnosis**
   c. **A pacemaker (TCP)**
   d. **Cardioversion (synchronized)**

ANSWER: b. Diagnosis. The ACLS current manual says: "Emergency personnel must quickly identify medical conditions that led to the cardiac arrest. People who experience arrest in VF need a defibrillator, people who experience arrest in asystole or pulseless electrical activity need a diagnosis. Once rescuers identify a diagnosis, they must start appropriate therapy quickly. VF is a unique condition in sudden cardiac arrest where a single intervention can completely reverse an otherwise lethal arrhythmia. Fortunately, VF is observed frequently in sudden cardiac arrest."

For the non-VF rhythms, however, there is often no single specific therapy. To reverse asystole and pulseless electrical activity, you need to reverse the cause of the collapse. These causes include electrolyte abnormalities, toxicological problems, hypovolemia, anaphylaxis, cardiac tamponade, pulmonary embolism, and pneumothorax." Remember the mnemonic for the 5h and 5t reversible causes (Hypovolemia, Hypoxia, Hydrogen Ion (acidosis), Hypo-/hyperkalemia, Hypothermia   Tension pneumothorax, Tamponade-cardiac, Toxins, Thrombosis – pulmonary, Thrombosis - coronary).
See: AHA, ACLS Provider Manual, chapter on "Final, Take-Home ACLS concepts."

8. In ACLS what does the concept "Time is muscle" refer to?
   a. **The critical three minutes until brain death begins**
   b. **Thrombolysis must begin within two hours of MI symptoms**
   c. **Arrhythmias deteriorate over time (PVCs-VT-VF-asystole)**
   d. **Survival decreases with each minute of poor blood flow oxygenation**

ANSWER: d. Survival decreases with each minute of poor blood flow and poor oxygenation. ACLS current guidelines say: "Time Is Critical A short time interval from collapse to care decides patient outcomes."

"The probability of patient survival decreases rapidly with every passing minute of poor blood flow and poor oxygenation. Some interventions (... CPR is the best example) slow the rate of decline in the probability of survival. Other interventions, such as opening an obstructed airway or defibrillating VF, can restore a beating heart within seconds; this changes the probability of survival dramatically. Never forget the clock: the longer it takes to restore the heartbeat, the lower the chances of successful resuscitation."
See: AHA, ACLS Provider Manual, chapter on "Final, Take-Home ACLS concepts."

9. When administering IV medications during CPR:
   a. **D5W is the preferred IV solution for use in cardiac arrest**
   b. **Use of central venous lines with 12 to 14-inch length are preferred**
   c. **IV drugs given by bolus should be followed by a 20cc bolus of fluid and elevation of the extremity**
   d. **IV sites of first choice should be external jugular or subclavian**

ANSWER: c. IV drugs given by bolus should be followed by a 20cc bolus of fluid. However, during arrest, bolus drugs are not quickly transported to the heart. To speed this up, follow all bolus

medications with at least 20 mL of IV saline or LR (Lactate Ringers, not D5W) to flush the drug into the central circulation unless the patient is hypoglycemic. The preferred IV sites are peripheral veins in the arm or leg. These sites are easily compressed to achieve hemostasis. Central venous lines via the neck are good but are too close to the CPR and ventilation to access easily. D5W is not recommended during resuscitation unless the patient is hypoglycemic.
See: AHA, ACLS Provider Manual, chapter on "Advanced ACLS Skills"

10. During cardiac arrest administer _____ every 3-5 minutes to vasoconstrict and optimize CO and BP for defibrillation.
   a. **Lidocaine**
   b. **Amiodarone**
   c. **Dobutamine**
   d. **Epinephrine**

ANSWER: d. Epinephrine is recommended for all types of cardiac arrest. It is a strong vasoconstrictor that increases BP. It also increases myocardial and cerebral blood flow and enhances defibrillation.
Dobutamine is a synthetic catecholamine used to increase cardiac contractility in CHF. Lidocaine and amiodarone are antiarrhythmics which don't optimize for defibrillation. They are intended to affect the VF rhythm itself. See: AHA, ACLS Provider Manual, chapter on "VF/Pulseless VT"

11. The first medication given to all ACLS patients should be:
   a. **Nitroglycerine**
   b. **Morphine**
   c. **Aspirin**
   d. **Oxygen**

ANSWER: d. Oxygen. Note that the CABD's should always be done first. The B (breathing) includes providing ventilation and oxygen to all ACLS patients where it is available. Aspirin is important too, but it may be given at any time and only to suspected ischemic chest pain patients. The secondary CABD's include IV and administration of medications. The ACLS Manual says: "Oxygen is always appropriate for patients with acute cardiac disease or pulmonary distress.... During cardiopulmonary emergencies use supplemental oxygen as soon as it is available.... In patients with acute MI, supplemental oxygen reduces both magnitude and extent of ST-segment changes on the ECG." See: AHA, ACLS Provider Manual, chapter on "VF/Pulseless VT"

Chapter 5
Radiology

EP Essentials LLC

Radiology:

1. Radiographic film badges usually report radiation dosage in this type of unit:
   a. **Milli-REM**
   b. **Milli-RAD**
   c. **Milli-Roentgens**
   d. **Milli-Curies**

ANSWER: a. Milli-REM. Personnel monitoring devices like film badges are analyzed in REMs (roentgen equivalent in man). This is the unit of occupational exposure. A safe dose is below 100 mrem per month. Anything over this should be investigated. See: Bushong, chapter on "Concepts of Radiation"

2. All EP lab staff wear radiation film badges. What alternate units can be used to measure radiation exposure by EP lab personnel?
   a. **Rad or Gray**
   b. **Rad or Sievert**
   c. **Rem or Gray**
   d. **Rem or Sievert**

ANSWER: d. Rem or Sievert. Rem is the roentgen equivalent in man is the traditional unit of radiation dose equivalent. It is the product of the absorbed dose in rads and a weighting factor, which accounts for the effectiveness of the radiation to cause biological damage. A rem is a large amount of radiation, so the millirem (mrem), which is one thousandth of a rem, is used on medical radiation badges. Bushong says, "rem is the unit of dose equivalent to occupation exposure. It is used to express the quantity of radiation received by radiation workers... in the SI system the rem x 0.01 = Sievert (Sv)."

"The rad is the unit of radiation absorbed dose. Biologic effects usually are related to the rad, and therefore the rad is the unit most often used when describing the radiation quantity received by a patient.... Rad x 0.01 = Grays (Gy)" Note that both the new units, Sv and Gy are 100 times larger than the older and smaller units, rem, and rad. See, Bushong, chapter on 'Concepts of Radiation'

3. For safety purposes the maximum Occupational Dose Limit (ODL) of whole body X-radiation that radiologic personnel are allowed to accumulate IN ANY ONE YEAR period is:
   a. **0.5 Rem/yr.**
   b. **2.5 Rem/yr.**
   c. **5.0 Rem/yr.**
   d. **10.0 Rem/yr.**

ANSWER: c. 5.0 Rem/yr. This Occupational Dose Limit (ODL) was previously termed the MPD (Maximum Permissible Dose). NCRP = National Council of Radiation Protection and Measurements recommends a maximum accumulation of 5 Rem (5000 mrem) in a one-year period. More than this, and you may be asked to stay out of X-ray for a year. The two important dose limits to remember are an accumulated dose limit of 1 Rem per year of age, or 5 Rems in any one year (see next question). Occupational dose limits are:

Pregnant Worker	0.5 REM/gestation period
Cumulated Dose Lifetime (DDE)	1 REM/year of age
Deep Dose Equivalent (DDE)	5 REM/year
Lens of Eye Dose Equivalent (EDE)	15 REM/year
Shallow Dose Equivalent (SDE)	50 REM/year

Although these are the absolute maximum limits most states require notification and corrective actions when a worker's dose limit reaches 1/10th of any of these maximum numbers. See: Johnson, et. all, Review of Radiation Safety in the Cardiac Catheterization Laboratory." in Catheterization and Cardiovascular Diagnosis 1992.

4. For EP Lab staff the safest level of X-ray radiation exposure is:
   a. **<5 MSv/year**
   b. **<5 Rem/year**
   c. **There is NO safe level**
   d. **Current levels of fluoroscopy in industry are safe**

ANSWER: c. There is NO safe level. Although, < 5 Rem/year or 3 Rem in a 3-month period are correct answers, the best answer is "There is NO perfectly safe level."

Braunwald says, "The main guiding principle of x-ray exposure is ALARA (as low as reasonably achievable). This implies that no level of radiation is completely safe to patients or providers....The basic principles of minimizing radiation exposure include minimizing fluoroscopic beam time for fluoroscopy, using beam collimation, positioning the x-ray source and image reception optimally, using the least magnification possible, changing the radiographic projection in long procedures to minimize entrance port skin exposure, recording the estimated patient dose, and selecting equipment with dose reduction features including low fluoroscopy mode." See: Braunwald, chapter on Cardiac Cath

Braunwald says, "Stochastic effects are related to probability and not proportional to dose, although the likelihood of an effect is related to dose. Examples of this effect include neoplasms [cancers] and genetic defects. The estimated dose range for cardiac catheterization is 1 to 10 milli Sievert (mSv), which is the equivalent of 2 to 3 years of natural background radiation. The typical dose is 3 to 5 mSv" See: Braunwald chapter on "Technical Aspects of Cardiac Catheterization "

5. The greatest radiation hazard to EP lab scrub assistant personnel comes from:
   a. **Remnant radiation**
   b. **Primary beam radiation**
   c. **Scattered X-radiation**
   d. **Radiation penetrating tube housing**

ANSWER: c. Scattered X-Radiation. Unless you have your hands in the x-ray field during fluoroscopy (like a cardiologist moving catheters) most of the radiation you get is scattered from the patient. Also, there is a small amount of radiation leakage from the x-ray tube. Some x-ray photons deflect off the denser body tissues, like the heart and blood vessels, and exit the patient in all directions. During procedures lead aprons should be worn by everyone in the procedure room. Remnant radiation is what exits the patient body to expose the image intensifier. See: Kern, chapter on "Angiographic Data."

6. In the EP lab, scatter radiation most harmful to staff comes from the:
   a. **Lead shielding**
   b. **Fluoroscope screen**
   c. **X-ray tube**
   d. **Patient**

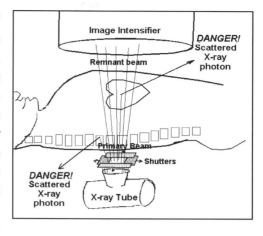

ANSWER: d. Patient. Imagine the patient "glowing" when he/she is being x-rayed. Their "glow" is a secondary scatter radiation that can expose you. Bushong says, "The scattering object can be considered as a new source of radiation. During both radiography and fluoroscopy, the patient is the single most important scattering object." Kern says, "Scatter from this beam (primary beam) exposes all subjects to radiation in a dose geometrically inverse to the distance from the source. Radiation scatter is increased when the angle of the tube is set obliquely. Acrylic shields and table-mounted lead aprons should be used to reduce the amount of scatter." See: Kern, chapter on "Angiographic Data."

7. What is the likelihood of any adverse radiation effects on EP lab personnel whose dose is kept below recommended guidelines?
    a. Zero
    b. Remote
    c. Probable
    d. Inevitable

ANSWER: b. Remote. Although your likelihood of radiation effects is remote, you must not become complacent about radiation safety. It could lead to accidental overexposure. It has been estimated that 1% of all leukemia cases in the general population results from diagnostic radiography. Bushong says, "Radiology is now considered a completely safe occupation. . . Current studies suggest that even the low doses of x-radiation employed in routine diagnostic procedures may result in a small incidence of latent harmful effects. It is also well established that the human fetus is highly sensitive to x-radiation early in pregnancy. This sensitivity decreases as the age of the fetus increases. . .. At radiation doses below the MPD, neither somatic nor genetic responses should occur. At doses at the level of the MPD, the risk is not zero, but it is small and consistent with the risks associated with other occupations and reasonable in light of the benefits derived. "See: Bushong, chapter on "Concepts of Radiation"

8. When EP lab personnel wear one film badge, it should be worn:
    a. On the collar outside the lead apron
    b. On the waist outside the lead apron
    c. On the waist inside the lead apron
    d. On the finger whenever scrubbed in

ANSWER: a. On the collar outside the lead apron.

Bushong says: "If the technologist participates in fluoroscopy and wears a protective apron, as recommended, then the personnel monitor should be positioned on the collar above the protective apron. . .. It has been shown that during fluoroscopy, when a protective apron is worn, exposure to the collar region is 10 to 20 times greater than that to the trunk of the body beneath the protective apron. So, if the personnel monitor is worn beneath the protective apron, it will record a falsely low exposure and will not indicate what could be hazardous exposure to unprotected body parts." See: Bushong, chapter on "Radiation Protection Procedures"

9. Current recommendations are for all EP lab operators (electrophysiologist) to wear two film badges located, one on the collar _____ and one on the ___.
   a. **inside the lead apron, belt inside the lead apron**
   b. **inside the lead apron, belt outside the lead apron**
   c. **outside the lead apron, belt inside the lead apron**
   d. **outside the lead apron, belt outside the lead apron**

ANSWER: c. One on collar outside the lead apron and one on the belt inside the lead apron. These should both face outward, toward the radiation source. Baim and Grossman say, "If a single "collar" badge is worn, it should be worn on the left shirt collar outside the lead apron, to give a maximal view of head and neck exposure. Current recommendations also call for a second "waist" badge, which is worn on the operator's belt just beneath the lead apron." Note that this same recommendation also applies to pregnant staff members. See: Baim and Grossman, chapter on "Angiography...")."

10. Leaded eyeglasses are primarily designed to protect you from:
   a. **Laser and Ultraviolet radiation**
   b. **Eye cancer**
   c. **Retinal damage**
   d. **Cataract formation**

ANSWER: d. Cataract formation. Kern says, "It has been known that a single x-ray exposure of 200 R can produce cataract formation in humans. Eyeglasses made of 0.5 to 0.75-mm lead-equivalent glass should be worn by personnel exposed to radiation daily. Plastic lenses offer no eye protection from radiation."
See: Kern, chapter on "Introduction to the Cath Lab."

11. EP lab personnel are at increased risk of radiation induced cancer. The organs most susceptible to radiation induced cancer include all the following EXCEPT: (Which is NOT associated with cancer)
   a. Bone marrow (leukemia)
   b. Female breast (breast cancer)
   c. Thyroid (Thyroid cancer)
   d. Eyes (cataracts)

ANSWER: d. Eyes (cataracts). The eyes are at increased risk of developing cataracts and protective leaded glass should be worn by all exposed personnel. However, cataracts are not carcinogenic pathology. Baim and Grossman say, "The issue of stochastic risks (carcinogenesis) is clearly also of concern for catheterization personnel. The organs most sensitive to radiation-induced cancer are the bone marrow, female breast, and the thyroid." See: Baim and Grossman, chapter on "Angiography...")."

12. A lead apron should be equivalent to _____ mm of lead, which will filter out _____% of the x-rays
   a. 0.5 mm, 40%
   b. 0.5 mm, 80%
   c. 1.0 mm, 40%
   d. 1.0 mm, 80%

ANSWER: b. 0.5 mm, 80%. Kern says, "Lead aprons should contain 0.5-mm thick lead lining. . .. lead aprons (preferably wraparound): >=0.5 mm thickness provides 80% protection." One advantage of a wraparound lead apron is that where it crosses in front doubles the protection where you need it most.
See: Kern, chapter on "Introduction to the Catheterization Laboratory."

13. Skin burns from high dose X-radiation:
   a. May take a year to evolve and heal
   b. Are clinically like thermal burns
   c. May show up in low doses of x-radiation (<1 Gy)
   d. May not show up with high doses of x-radiation (>10 Gy)

ANSWER: a. May take a year to evolve and heal. Bushong says, "After a single dose of 3 to 10 Gy an initial mild erythema may occur within the first or second day. This first wave of erythema then subsides, only to be followed by a second wave that reaches maximum intensity in about 2 weeks. At higher doses, this second wave of erythema is followed by moist desquamation, which in turn may lead to dry desquamation. These skin effects follow a nonlinear, threshold radiation-induced relationship.... Small doses of x-radiation do not cause erythema. Extremely high doses of radiation cause erythema in all persons so irradiated." This may take months to years to heal. Note the picture showing the time progression of an x-radiation burn from a PCI. This patient received over 20 Gy of radiation. See: Bushong, chapter on "X-Ray Tube"

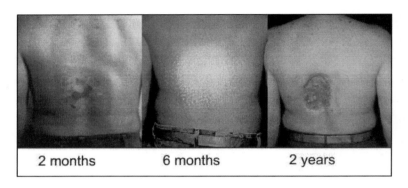

| 2 months | 6 months | 2 years |

14. Which of the following radiographic views will produce the highest X-ray exposure to staff working on the right side of the patient?
   a. PA Cranial
   b. PA Caudal
   c. RAO
   d. LAO

ANSWER: d. LAO. Grossman says, "Scatter radiation is greatest where the operator is in close proximity to the beam entry point." This is because scatter radiation bounces from the area of the patient nearest the Xray tube. In the LAO and Left Lateral views, the x-ray tube is on the patient's right side, next to the operator and scrub tech. Shield yourself with lead. See: Grossman chapter on "Cineangiographic Imaging"

15. The modern device that replaces the image intensifier tube and converts x-rays into visible light is the:
   a. X-ray grid
   b. Cine camera
   c. Photo-receiver
   d. Flat panel detector

ANSWER: d. Flat panel detector. The flat panel x-ray detector is replacing the image intensifier in EP labs. It uses charge coupled devices or photodiodes to directly convert the phosphor light into electrons with no intervening intensifier tube or optics. Flat panel X-ray images are based on solid-state integrated circuit (IC) technology, similar in many ways to the imaging chips used in commercial digital cameras. The light generated by the scintillator is absorbed by the photodiodes in the array, creating electrons which are stored on the capacitance of the photodiode itself then converted into a digital pixel. See: http://www.varian.com

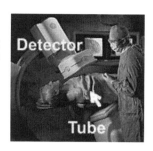

16. Label the component of the x-ray tube labeled #1 in the diagram.
   a. **Anode (rotating)**
   b. **Focusing cup**
   c. **Target**
   d. **Filament**

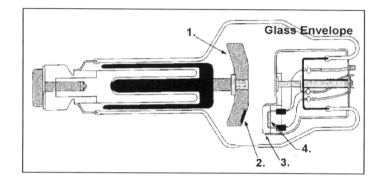

ANSWER: a. Anode (rotating). The large rotating disc has one spot on it where the electron beam is focused. This is the target where x-rays are generated. The Cathode is the right-hand negative side, with a heated filament. Thermionic emission generates a cloud of electrons which are focused with the focusing cup towards the target on the anode.
ALL ANSWERS BELOW:
   1. Anode
   2. Target
   3. Focusing cup
   4. Filament
See: Bushong, chapter on "The X-ray Machine.

17. Electromagnetic radiation may interact with matter in diverse ways.

1. **Attenuation**	a. **When an energy beam completely disappears in tissue**
2. **Absorption**	
3. **Scatter**	b. **Reduction in beam energy as it passes through tissue**
4. **Reflection**	c. **Photons emerging from tissue interaction change direction (refraction)**
	d. **Turning back of a ray that does not penetrate the tissue, like light reflecting from a mirrored surface.**

CORRECT ANSWERS:

1. Attenuation: b. Reduction in beam energy as it passes through tissue

2. Absorption: a. When an energy beam completely disappears (is absorbed) in tissue

3. Scatter: c. Photons emerging from tissue interaction change direction - also termed refraction

4. Reflection: d. Turning back of a ray that does not penetrate the tissue, like light reflecting from a mirrored surface.

Note that when x-rays are absorbed or scattered by their interaction with matter, they remove electrons from that atom. This ionization process is the mechanism of biological damage. See: Bushong, chapter on "X-ray interaction with matter"

18. Your x-ray tube has two focal spots: a 1.2 mm focal-spot and a 0.6 mm focal-spot. The smaller focal spot (0.6 mm) is most used on _____ EP cases, because it _____ image resolution.
   a. **Pediatric, Improves**
   b. **Adult, Improves**
   c. **All, Improves**
   d. **Adult, Reduces**
   e. **Pediatric, Reduces**

ANSWER: a. Pediatric, Improves. Although the smaller focal spot provides better resolution for children, it may overheat on long cases. Thus, the small focal spot tube is usually only used for pediatric cases - not adult. Baim and Grossman say, "Two focal spots are included in most catheterization laboratory x-ray tubes. . .. Whereas the small focal spot (usually 0.6 mm) more closely resembles a "point source" and thus provides potentially better geometric sharpness, the small focal spot in most x-ray tubes is quite limited in terms of its power handling capacity (35 kW). This forces the automatic exposure control to resort to a low mA-high kV technique, which provides adequate film blackening only at the expense of poor image contrast. The small focal spot thus usually is used only for fluoroscopy or cineangiography in pediatric patients. Routine cineangiography in adult patients, particularly when performed in extreme angulation, are better performed using the larger (usually 1.0 mm) focal spot." See: Baim and Grossman, chapter on "Angiography...")."

19. The degree of blackness on an area of X-ray film is termed its:
   a. **Resolution**
   b. **Radiolucency**
   c. **Contrast**
   d. **Density**

ANSWER: d. Density. The degree of blackness on a film is termed radiographic density. It is chiefly regulated by mA - the quantity of x-ray photons created at the tube target in one cine pulse. The more x-ray photons exposing a section of film, the blacker the film will be. See: Bushong, chapter on "Concepts of Radiation"

20. What happens when you take your foot off the fluoroscopic foot pedal?
   a. The production of primary and scattered radiation immediately stops.
   b. The amount of radiation from the source decays with a half-life of 1-2 minutes
   c. A lead shutter immediately blocks the X-ray beam to prevent the emission of primary radiation.
   d. Low levels of radiation continue to be generated to keep the tube up to temperature

ANSWER: a. The production of primary and scattered radiation immediately stops because the electron filament and cathode (mA) shut off. Since X-rays travel at the speed of light and cannot be stored, shutdown is immediate. See: Bushong, chapter on "X-Ray Tube"

21. Which of the following will increase the patient's x-ray exposure? (Select all that apply)
   a. Increasing the frame rate
   b. Using collimators
   c. Steep angulation
   d. Raising the table

ANSWERS: a. increasing the frame rate & c. steep angulation. We want to minimize the patient's x-ray exposure. This may be done by decreasing the frame rate, using collimators, avoiding steep angulation, and raising the table bringing the patient closer to the II and farther from the x-ray source. This will decrease the patient's skin dose.

22. What is the frame rate setting that would lead to the lowest dosage to the operator?
   a. 30 FPS
   b. 7.5 FPS
   c. 10 FPS
   d. 15 FPS

ANSWER: b. 7.5 FPS. "The old standard was 30 frames per second (FPS), and today it is usually 15 FPS. Most operators can lower this to 10 FPS without a major impact on the imaging. Others reduce their rate to 7.5 FPS, which may take some getting used to because images can appear jerkier, but it results in big dose savings." 14 ways to reduce radiation exposure in the cath lab. (2021, May 05).
Retrieved May 08, 2021, from https://www.dicardiology.com/content/blogs/14-ways-reduce-radiation-exposure-cath-lab

Xray Views:

1. How should you orient yourself to angulated angiographic views?
Align yourself as if you are looking _____.
   a. From the x-ray tube
   b. Through the image intensifier
   c. From the feet of the patient
   d. Superior to the patient

ANSWER: b. As if looking through the image intensifier/flat plate detector. For example, if you shoot an LAO caudal view (Left Anterior Caudal). This angiogram is a short axis view and viewed as if you were at the apex of the heart looking down the LV "barrel as shown." In LAO caudal the Image intensifier (I.I.) is positioned above the LV apex, left oblique (Left side of chest) and caudally (towards the foot). It is as if the I.I. were a "tube" you look through into the heart. What you see through the "tube" is what the angiogram shows. See: Baim and Grossman, chapter on "Coronary Arteriography."

Viewing through I.I.

2. What is the best x-ray position to image the His and RV catheters when initially passing the catheters across the tricuspid valve?
   a. LAO
   b. RAO
   c. PA
   d. Lateral

ANSWER: b. RAO. Moulton says, "RAO view is used primarily to position RAA, His, and RV catheters. LAO view is used primarily to position CS and Halo catheters." Note in the diagram how the His and RV catheters point towards you and are foreshortened in the LAO view. But the RV and His catheter tips are more clearly seen from the side and point to the right. Issa says, "During cannulation of the CS from the IVC approach [femoral], the tip of the catheter is first placed into the RV, using the RAO view, and flexed downward toward the RV inferior wall. Subsequently, the catheter is withdrawn until it lies at the inferoseptal aspect of the tricuspid annulus."

"Using the LAO or RAO view, the catheter is then withdrawn gently with clockwise rotation until the tip of the catheter drops into the CS ostium. Afterward, the catheter is advanced into the CS concomitantly with gradual release of the catheter curve. Alternatively, the tip of the catheter is directed toward the posterolateral RA wall and advanced with a tight curve to form a loop in the RA, using the LAO fluoroscopy view, with the tip directed toward the inferomedial RA. The tip is then advanced with gentle up-down, right-left manipulation using the LAO and RAO fluoroscopy views to cannulate the CS." See Issa, chapter on "Catheterization Techniques" and Moulton "Electrophysiology Review Course"

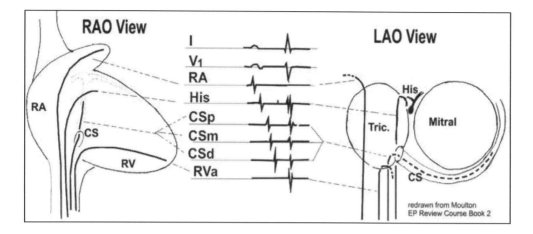

3. What is the best x-ray view to see the entire anterior RV (or ventricular septal wall) as perpendicular to the x-ray beam.
   a. PA
   b. RAO
   c. LAO
   d. Lateral

ANSWER: b. RAO. The RAO view shows the long axis of the ventricles, and separates the atria from the ventricles, as shown in this diagram with overlapping atria (RA & LA) on the left and overlapping ventricles (RV & LV) on the right.

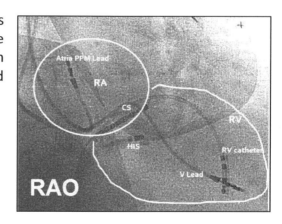

4. Knowing which veins are most likely to be used during a CRT procedure, what is usually the best view to image the CS during a balloon inflation venogram?
   a. PA
   b. Lateral
   c. RAO
   d. LAO

ANSWER: d. LAO. The CS should be imaged in both RAO and LAO views, but since the CS curves around the left AV junction, it is best seen in the LAO view where it is circular, as shown. LAO will best show the ostium and the needed posterolateral veins. Also, in an EP study the LAO view is usually used to place the CS catheter as it is directed towards the left shoulder. In the diagram note the posterior cardiac vein which will usually be the best for LV pacing.

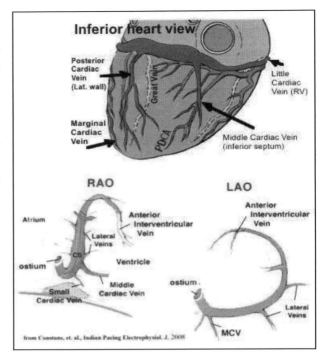

5. From the RAO and LAO views shown, where is the ABL catheter located?
   a. RA
   b. RV
   c. LA
   d. LV
   e. CS

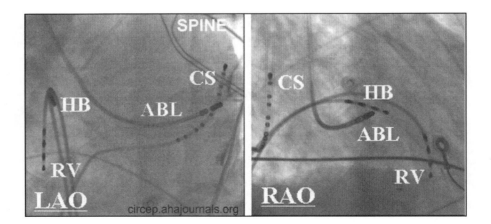

ANSWER: d. LV. Since the HB catheter defines the septum in LAO, the ABL catheter must be on the left side of the heart. Since the CS catheter defines the AV ring in the RAO, the ABL catheter must be in a ventricular chamber. Put the two together: left side of heart + ventricular chamber = LV. It takes information from both views to determine where a catheter tip lies. See, Yamada, et, al., CIRCEP, June 2012, Electrocardiographic and Electrophysiological Characteristics in Idiopathic Ventricular Arrhythmias Originating from the Papillary Muscles in the Left Ventricle

6. This patient was being studied in the EP lab for suspected accessory pathway. Evaluate the biplane images labeled A & B. Match each numbered catheter on the x-ray with its location in the heart and its name?

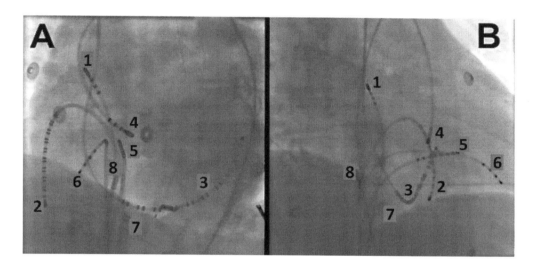

    a. RA, ICE catheter
    b. HIS, octapolar
    c. Aortic, RF ablation catheter
    d. CS, duodecapolar
    e. Crista Terminalis, Halo catheter
    f. RV, quadripolar
    g. Sheath, transseptal (empty)
    h. RA, RF ablation catheter

CORRECTLY MATCHED ANSWERS ARE:

1. h. RA, RF ablation catheter	5. b. HIS, octapolar
2. e. Crista Terminalis, Halo catheter	6. f. RV, quadripolar
3. d. CS, duodecapolar catheter	7. g. Sheath, transseptal (empty)
4. c. Aortic, RF ablation catheter	8. a. RA, ICE catheter

Image A is LAO because the apex is pointing at you and the spine is at the right of the image. The CS catheter makes a distinctive crescent around the mitral ring. Image B is RAO because the apex is pointing to your right and the spine is at the left of the image.

7. When positioned correctly in the LAO view, which catheter normally points straight at you?
   a. HRA
   b. CS
   c. RV
   d. His

ANSWER: d. His in RAO normally points directly at the viewer. Asirvatham says, "The His bundle catheter is used to define the septum in the LAO view. Notably, the His bundle is almost always located in the septum at the level of the annulus anteriorly. Since the His bundle electrogram is unique [H wave], if a catheter shows this characteristic electrocardiographically, then it is located at the His bundle region, and the LAO view can be adjusted to make the His bundle catheter seem to look straight at the examiner, thus defining the septum."

In the LAO, x-ray image focus is on the His catheter (HB). Since it points straight at the viewer everything to the right of it must be on the left side of the heart. Also note that the CS catheter crosses the spine in this view, so it is moving to the left side of the heart.

In the RAO view, focus is on the CS catheter, as it defines the AV ring; so, everything to the right of the CS must be ventricle (either RV or LV). Use these two criteria to deduce which chamber a catheter is in - LAO for right or left sided, RAO for atrial or ventricular. See, Asirvatham, Mayo Clinic EP Manual, chapter on Introduction to EP Manual

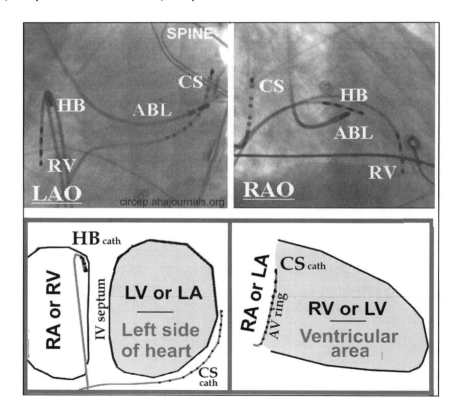

8. Match the PPM access approach to its X-ray below.
   a. **Cephalic**
   b. **IJ**
   c. **Subclavian**
   d. **Epicardial**

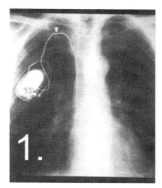 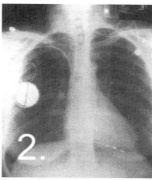 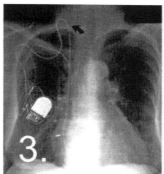 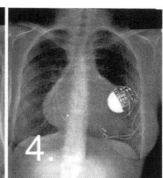

CORRECTLY MATCHED ANSWERS ARE:
#1. c. Subclavian stick (below clavicle)
#2. a. Cephalic and Axillary vein from the arm.
#3. b. Internal Jugular coming in from the neck.
#4. d. Epicardial RV lead, subclavian RA lead.
Venous access for the pacemaker leads depends on where the easiest and safest stick can be made. The pacemaker is usually placed subcutaneously near this access site. Ellenbogen, chapter on "Techniques of Pacemaker Implantation..."

9. From the EP catheters shown, what is this X-ray view?
   a. **AP**
   b. **RAO**
   c. **LAO**
   d. **Lateral**

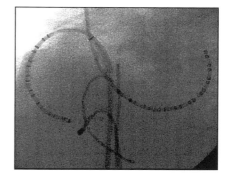

ANSWER: c. LAO. The two duodecapolar catheters outline the RA & LA, respectively. The CS catheter is in the left AV groove. The 30-degree LAO looks down the barrel of the ventricle. RAO nicely separates the right heart from the left, but the atria and ventricles overlap. That is why it is essential to use a combination of views.

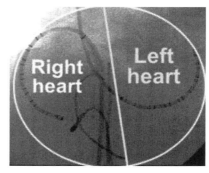

10. From the EP catheters shown, what is this X-ray view?

    a. AP
    b. RAO
    c. LAO
    d. Lateral

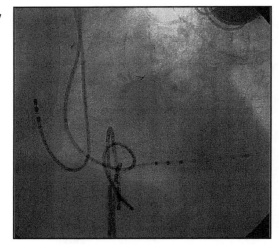

ANSWER: c. LAO. A good hint here is the fact that the CS catheter reaches to the left side of the patient's heart in the AV groove. The HRA catheter is going towards his right. The RV catheter will be coming straight at you. You can barely make out the backbone on your right and ribs descending to the left = LAO.

11. Match the position of each of the EP electrodes with its number on the PA chest film.

    a. HRA
    b. His
    c. CS
    d. RV

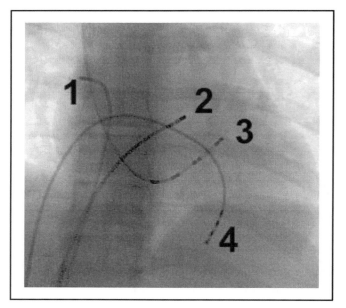

CORRECTLY MATCHED ANSWERS:
1.a. HRA catheter near junction of lateral RA with SVC
2.b. His catheter position through medial tricuspid valve
3.c. CS catheter position near location of Circumflex
4.d. RV catheter position, Apex of RV See: Murgatroyd, chapter on Patient Instrumentation

12. What is this X-ray view?
    a. AP
    b. RAO
    c. LAO
    d. Lateral

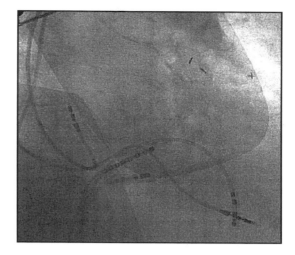

ANSWER: b. RAO. Note the apex of the heart is to your right outlined in white. RAO shows what is the atrium and what is the ventricle, but you cannot tell what is left or right sided.

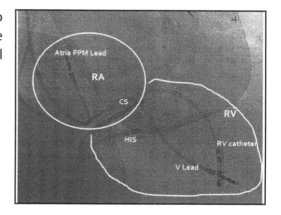

13. What type of device is seen in this PA & lateral chest X-ray?
    a. Biventricular ICD
    b. Dual Chamber PPM with Septal RV placement
    c. Dual Chamber ICD with RVOT placement
    d. Dual Chamber ICD with RV apex placement

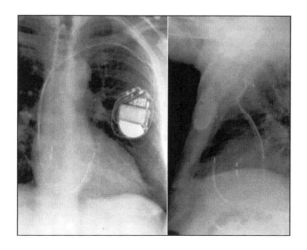

ANSWER: c. Dual Chamber ICD with RVOT placement. Notice the size of the device, it is larger than a PPM. Also, you can tell it is an ICD due to the atrial defibrillation coils on the RV lead. The tips of the electrodes are for pacing, the coils, and can be used for defibrillation. No third lead is observed in the CS, which rules out BiV ICD. The ventricular lead clearly does not reach to the apex but is positioned in the RV outflow track.

14. Mr. Jones had this chest film and venogram. He has:
   a. **Transposition of great vessels**
   b. **Persistent superior vena cava**
   c. **Situs Inversus**
   d. **Dextrocardia**

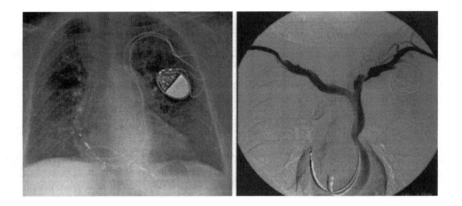

ANSWER: b. Persistent SVC. This is an anomaly of venous drainage, where the SVC drains into the coronary sinus. The venogram shows the pacing leads entering the left subclavian vein and coursing from the SVC into the CS and then through the CS ostium, into the RA and RV.

15. This is a PA chest film, and enlargement of the pacemaker image. What is observed in this X-ray?
   a. **Lead Fracture**
   b. **RV perforation**
   c. **Pneumothorax**
   d. **Atrial Lead dislodgement**

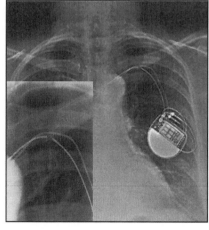

ANSWER: a. Lead Fracture. Note the break shown in the wire on the x-ray. One lead is not functioning, hopefully the atrial lead. If the RV lead breaks there will be no ventricular pacing.

16. What is abnormal about this x-ray?
   a. **Right-sided ICD**
   b. **Dextrocardia**
   c. **Persistent SVC**
   d. **X-ray is flipped**

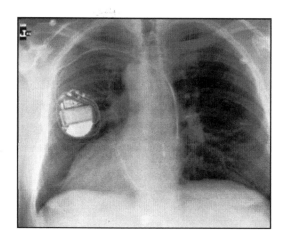

ANSWER: d. X-ray flipped horizontally. The LV apex is on the wrong side. Also, the pacemaker, usually on the patient's left, is on the wrong side. The atrial and ventricular leads are also on the wrong side. Even the letter "L" in the upper left is backwards. This is the same Xray as shows earlier, only reversed.

17. From this X-ray, what type of ablation is being performed?
   a. **Atrial Flutter**
   b. **Slow pathway**
   c. **AVRT**
   d. **Atrial Tach**

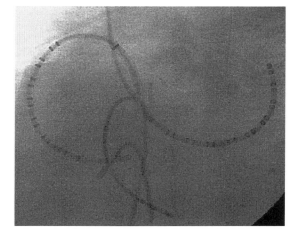

ANSWER: a. Atrial Flutter. Notice the two duodecapolar catheters, one in RA and one in CS. The large tip ablation catheter is located at the cavotricuspid isthmus for ablation of atrial flutter.

Fogoros says, "atrial flutter is an arrhythmia that often can be readily ablated....in typical atrial flutter, the flutter wave must pass through a narrow isthmus defined by the inferior vena cava and the tricuspid annulus...if a linear lesion (ablation) can be made, extending from the tricuspid annulus to the opening of the inferior vena cava, the electrical blockade of the necessary isthmus can be created....Successful ablation can be achieved acutely in over 90% of patients who have typical atrial flutter." Note in the diagram how the burn interrupts the reentry loop. See: Fogoros, chapter on "Transcatheter Ablation"

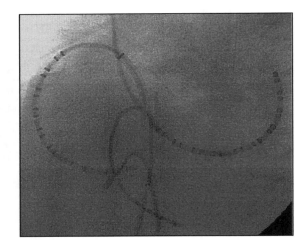

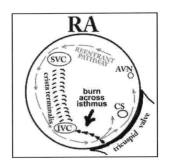

18. This X-ray followed a PPM replacement. What type of device is implanted?
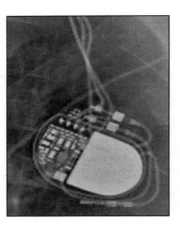
   a. Bipolar Biventricular PPM
   b. Bipolar dual chamber PPM
   c. Dual Chamber ICD
   d. Unipolar dual chamber PPM

ANSWER: b. Bipolar dual chamber permanent pacemaker. There are three wires, but one is unplugged because it had failed and was left in place, abandoned, and capped. It is a dual chamber bipolar pacer with two poles on each active lead. Note the bipolar header with two connectors on each catheter, one for each of the bipoles.

19. During permanent pacemaker lead insertion through a central venous catheter, a bouncing shadow is seen in the center of the cardiac silhouette as shown. What is depicted at the arrow?
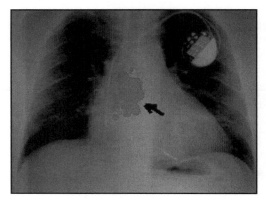
   a. Air in RA
   b. X-ray quantum mottle
   c. Thrombus on electrode
   d. Epicardial defibrillator patch

ANSWER: a. Air in RA. "Air embolism is more commonly seen with central venous catheters; however, it may also occur with peripheral catheters. If air is introduced into the vascular system, it may accumulate and cause complications such as blockage of the right side of the vascular system (i.e., venous) leading to outflow obstruction of the right ventricle and pulmonary arteries. Symptoms include impaired gas exchange, hypotension, and circulatory collapse. Obstruction of the coronary or cerebral arteries by air can lead to myocardial infarction and acute stroke, respectively."

"While it is classically taught that 5 ml / kg of air is needed to produce an "air lock" of the right ventricle and pulmonary artery, circulatory collapse has been reported with as little as 20cc of air. Should significant air embolization occur, the patient should be placed in a left lateral recumbent position to trap the air in the right atrium. Available interventions include aspiration via a central venous catheter, hyperbaric treatment, and in severe cases, thoracotomy."

To prevent air embolism, all tubing should be flushed prior to utilization, all connections must be tight, and fluid bags should not be allowed to completely empty before replacement, and the patient's legs elevated to increase RA pressure. See: http://emprocedures.com/peripheralIV/complications.htm

20. Based on the X-ray and electrogram tracing, what type of ablation is being performed?
   a. **AVNRT**
   b. **Transseptal AVRT**
   c. **Retrograde AV node**
   d. **RVOT VT**

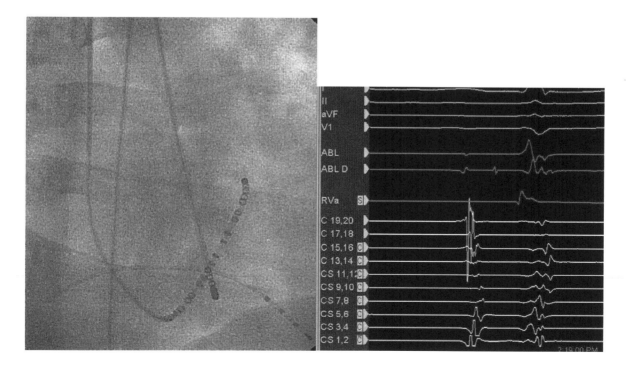

ANSWER: c. Retrograde AV node. First, notice the His spike on the ablation catheter. Second notice that the ablation catheter is not coming in from the same place that the RV catheter is. The RV catheter is coming up from the IVC, whereas you can see the ablation catheter coming up from the AO and through the AO valve. The catheter is clearly not going across the septum.

This is referred to as the Retrograde approach. For AV node ablations you need a good His signal. Most of the time this is accomplished on the Rt side of the heart, but in a few cases after extensive mapping and/or ablation the physician may have to ablate from the Lt side. In AVNRT, you do not want to see the His. This means that you may damage the fast pathway rather than the slow which would lead to CHB.

21. **This obese patient 74-year-old patient had a 7-year-old dual chamber ppm. She came to the EP lab for a generator change out. When interrogating the device, the atrial lead was programmed at a high output of 5V. With that information and this X-ray, we decided to add a new A lead. Check the conditions below that could have necessitated the high output on the A lead?**

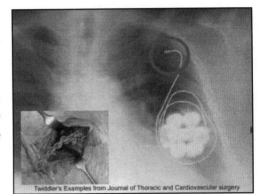
Twiddler's Examples from Journal of Thoracic and Cardiovascular surgery

   a. **Generator not sutured to chest wall**
   b. **Twiddler's syndrome**
   c. **Lead dislodgement due to excessive patient movement**
   d. **Battery depletion**
   e. **Pacemaker syndrome**

ANSWER: a, b, & c. Although any of these may cause the device to revert to high output pacing, this patient's cause was slightly different. This was an obese patient with a large chest, the device was sutured to the chest wall, but with the lack of muscle tone the suture did not hold. When the patient would stand, the weight of her chest would pull the device down and the leads out. On Twiddler's syndrome, you will see the lead coiled around the generator or twisted.

22. When starting an EPS with the four standard catheters, our EGMs do not look quite right. From the EGM and X-ray what is wrong?
   a. Catheter fell out of CS
   b. RV catheter not in the RV
   c. HRA needs to be advanced
   d. His catheter not over His bundle

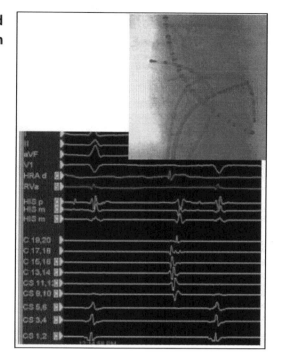

ANSWER: a. Catheter fell out of CS. Notice that the CS catheter never crosses to the left side of the heart. This CS catheter was inserted from the IJ which is a standard approach for many physicians. However, all these catheters are clearly still on the right side of the heart. Follow your instincts.

Remember that the CS catheter runs in between the LA and LV; therefore, you should see an A and V signal on every CS channel when the catheter is appropriately positioned.

This CS catheter only has an atrial deflection on CS 19,20 to CS 9,10 and only a V signal on the distal (closer to the tip) electrodes. This catheter fell out of the CS and is lying partly in the RA and partly in the RV.

23. What type of device is shown on this Lateral X-ray?
   a. ICD
   b. CRT
   c. CRT-D
   d. Dual chamber pacemaker

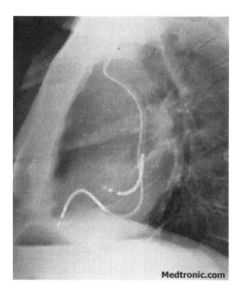

ANSWER: a. ICD. There are two leads: atrial and ventricular. They have defibrillation coils on the body of each electrode and pacing electrodes on the tip. ICD devices can function as a dual chamber pacemaker as well as perform ATP, cardioversion, and defibrillation. Shocks can be delivered/vectored between the two coils, or between the coil and the can (device). A CRT device would have three electrodes: atrial, RV and LV

24. What devices are shown in this X-ray?
  a. HeartMate II LVAD, CRT
  b. HeartMate II LVAD, CRT-D
  c. Impella LVAD, CRT
  d. Impella LVAD, CRT-D
  e. Transseptal sheath, CRT
  f. Transseptal sheath, CRT-D

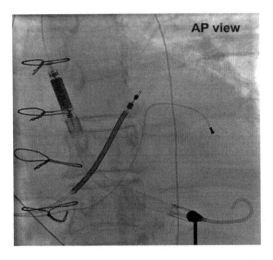

ANSWER: d. Impella LVAD, CRT-D (Cardiac Resynchronization Device - with defibrillator). The large coil is the inlet tube for the Impella LVAD. The rotary pump can pump 2.5 L/min into the AO across the aortic valve. The smaller coil is the RV defibrillator coil. There is an RA defibrillation coil not seen on the Xray. The third electrode with a large tip is lodged in a coronary vein and is used to stimulate the LV and resynchronize ventricular contraction.

25. This patient is two weeks post MI. From this X-ray, what external device does this patient have?
  a. Telemetry device
  b. LV assist device
  c. Subcutaneous ICD
  d. Wearable defibrillator
  e. Transcutaneous pacemaker

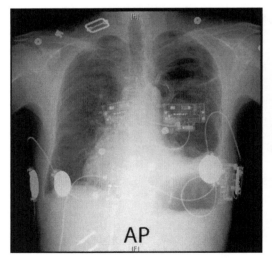

ANSWER: d. Wearable defibrillator. This Zoll Life Vest senses the patient's ECG and will notify the patient if it is a shockable rhythm, then secrete gel onto the electrodes and deliver a shock like an AED. Recommended to STEMI patients with LV dysfunction for 30-90 days post MI (when most SCD occurs), or until an ICD is implanted. It may also be used on patients who have had their ICD explanted due to infection and are waiting for their infection to resolve.

The device features three defibrillation electrode pads and four sensing electrodes held close to the body by an elastic belt; it can deliver up to five 150-J shocks. Note this patient has an enlarged heart.

This Xray comes from Dr. Wes's blog   http://drwes.blogspot.com/(lifevest) (alarms on Lifeless) Also See: http://www.lifevest.zoll.com/medical-professionals/

26. What are the two main detrimental effects of long-term pacing in patients with devices like that shown in this X-ray? (Select best two answers)
   a. **Atrial fibrillation**
   b. **Reduced LVEF**
   c. **Pacemaker syndrome**
   d. **Ventricular Tachycardia**
   e. **RV myocardial infarction**
   f. **Reduced LV end systolic size**
   g. **Reduced atrial filling pressure**
   h. **Electrode erosion & pericardial tamponade**

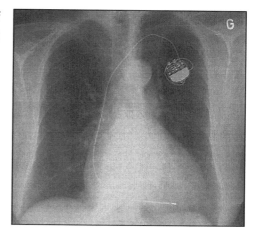

ANSWERS: a. Atrial fibrillation and b. Reduced LVEF(CHF). Ellenbogen says: "analyses from MOST have reported an association between a high percentage of right ventricular (RV) apical pacing and worse clinical outcomes, including an increased risk for AF and heart failure hospitalization. This raises concern that the beneficial effects of maintaining AV synchrony may have been mitigated by the deleterious effects of RV apical pacing."

The ill effects of RV pacing may occur when the ventricle is paced more than 40% of the time, and are due to ventricular dyssynchrony, mitral regurgitation, reduced LVEF, and increased filling pressures. Many of these ill effects were improved with algorithms designed to minimize unnecessary ventricular pacing and AAI mode. It should be noted that no large clinical trials have yet demonstrated that any of the other RV pacing sites are better than the traditional RV apical site. See: Ellenbogen chapter on "Pacing for Sinus Node Disease"

27. What type of pacemaker and leads are shown on this X-ray?
   a. **DDD & abandoned lead**
   b. **DDD & double unipolar leads**
   c. **VDD & abandoned lead**
   d. **VDD & double unipolar leads**
   e. **Double image due to motion artifact**

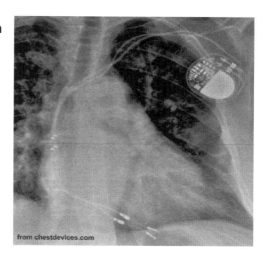

ANSWER: c. VDD & abandoned lead. The bipolar lead does not contact the RA wall and so cannot pace the atrium effectively, but it can sense atrial activity. Thus, the second letter is a D. Note the upper lead is not connected to the header. Defective leads are not usually extracted unless infected. Extraction is a risky procedure. ChestDevices.com says, "The single-lead VDD unit senses atrial and ventricular activity, but paces only in the ventricle. These pacemakers are implanted in patients with high degree atrioventricular block and normal sinus node function. The unit incorporates a bipolar atrial sensing which is a full-ring dipole with a closed dipole spacing. Compared with DDD systems, implantation and fluoroscopy times are significantly shortened." See: ChestDevices.com

28. What type of implanted device is shown on this X-ray?
   a. **Leadless ICD**
   b. **Leadless VVI pacemaker**
   c. **Implantable insulin pump**
   d. **Implantable loop ECG recorder**

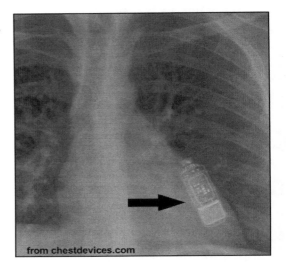

from chestdevices.com

ANSWER: d. Implantable loop ECG recorder. This is an insertable cardiac monitor. There are even smaller injectable versions available. The implantable loop recorder is used to diagnose patients with recurrent unexplained episodes of syncope or palpitation, but also for long-term monitoring of rarely occurring arrhythmias. See: ChestDevices.com

29. Two years after VVI pacemaker implantation this patient's pacemaker consistently fails to capture the ventricle. Resistance readings on the lead are 200 ohms. This condition shown on the X-ray is termed:
   a. **Lead fracture**
   b. **Lead dislodgement**
   c. **Loose header connection**
   d. **Subclavian crush**

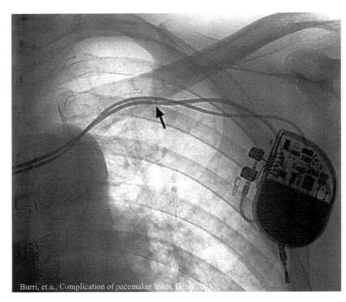

Burri, et.a., Complication of pacemaker leads, Heart 2009

ANSWER: d. Subclavian crush phenomenon. Ellenbogen says about PPI subclavian vein vascular access, "the extreme medial position results in a tight fit, subjecting the lead to compressive forces and causing binding between the first rib and the clavicle. Occasionally, this binding can even crush the lead, now called the subclavian crush phenomenon.... Autopsy data demonstrated generation of significantly higher pressure when leads were inserted in the clavicular angle than with a more lateral puncture. ... lead damage is caused by soft tissue entrapment by the subclavius muscle rather than the bony contact. This soft tissue entrapment causes a static load on the lead at that point, and repeated flexure around the point of entrapment may be responsible for the damage."

This patient's x-ray shows a depression in the ventricular lead that may expose the lead conductor causing a low resistance reading (current can short circuit) and loss of pacing. There is also and abandoned lead shown behind the pacer can. See Ellenbogen, chapter on Permanent Pacemaker & ICD implantation. See: Medtronic.com

Chapter 6
Equipment

EP Essentials LLC

Equipment

1. **Which diagnostic EP electrodes increase mapping resolution?**
   a. **Irrigated Electrodes**
   b. **Smaller Electrodes**
   c. **Larger Electrodes**
   d. **Deflectable tips**

ANSWER: b. Smaller Electrodes. Electrodes have become progressively smaller and more closely spaced in effort to reduce the sampled tissue size and increase the mapping resolution (the tissue area represented by each bipolar EGM). Notice the difference in the example below with a signal acquired with a diagnostic catheter vs. an 8mm ablation catheter. The signal from the ablation catheter appears stretched and low amplitude making it difficult to observe small fractionated electrograms. See: Barkagan, et al, A novel

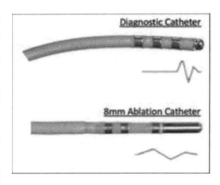

multielectrode catheter for high-density ventricular mapping: electrogram characterization and utility for scar mapping. EP Europace, 2020

2. **Most cardiac catheters cannot be reused. After being used in a patient, what type of "single use devices" may be resterilized by third party reprocessing companies and then reused on other patients?**
   a. **Irrigated ablation catheters**
   b. **Polyurethane (PU) catheters**
   c. **Teflon sheaths or guiding catheters**
   d. **Diagnostic EP catheter**

ANSWER: d. Diagnostic EP catheters. With current concerns over blood transmitted diseases, the only catheters now commonly reused are the diagnostic EP pacing and sensing electrodes. This is a controversial medico-legal issue because catheter manufacturers place

"For Single Use Only" disclaimers on all catheters. Doubtless, this is to protect them from legal repercussions.

Since they have no lumen (technically not a catheter) EP catheters are much easier to inspect, clean and sterilize. The FDA requires that each item reprocessed and resterilized be tracked, forms submitted, and strict quality control procedures followed. Equipment that is approved for reprocessing reuse includes: EP diagnostic catheters, EP cables, and femoral compression devices. Resterilization is usually only allowed a maximum of six times before a catheter must be discarded (catheter dependent).

Of course, most equipment that has NOT been used (i.e., expired or accidentally opened) CAN be resterilized and reprocessed. If any tubular catheter is used on a patient or otherwise contaminated with blood, then they can NOT be reprocessed or reused. See: www.sterilmed.com/rg-devices.shtml

3. What French size is a catheter with an outer diameter of 2.66 mm?
   a. **5 F**
   b. **6 F**
   c. **7 F**
   d. **8 F**

ANSWER: d. 8 F. The way to remember this is that a 6F catheter is 2 mm in diameter. Other sizes are proportional. See: Tilkian and Daily, chapter on "Tools for Catheterization."

4. The outside diameter of a 5.5 F catheter is:
   a. **1.5 mm**
   b. **1.66 mm**
   c. **1.83 mm**
   d. **2.00 mm**
   e. **2.17 mm**

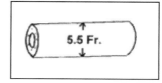

ANSWER: c. 1.83 mm. This can be solved using a ratio method or remember the fact that each French size is 1/3 of a mm.

5F = 1.66 mm and 6F = 2 mm, so halfway between 5 and 6F would be halfway between 1.66 and 2.0 mm, or 1.83 mm. As wall thickness diminishes, lumen diameters increase. Similarly, you can multiply the French size by 0.33 to get the mm diameter. 5.5 x 0.33=1.82 mm. See: Tilkian and Daily, chapter on Tools for Catheterization.

5. Match the EP catheters in the diagram with their name.
   a. **Halo/Crista**
   b. **Damato**
   c. **Josephson**
   d. **Lasso / Circular**
   e. **Multipurpose**
   f. **Cournand**

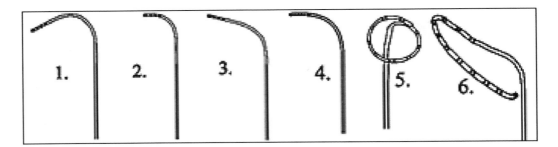

CORRECTLY MATCHED ANSWERS BELOW:
1. Damato
2. Josephson
3. Multipurpose
4. Cournand
5. Lasso / Circular mapping catheter
6. Halo / Crista

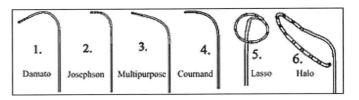

The Damato and Cournand are quadripolar with four electrodes. A decapolar catheter has ten electrodes. Duodecapolar is twice ten or twenty electrodes.

Electrodes on EP catheters are paired to record bipolar signals, especially noticeable on this halo or Crista catheter image. The closer the electrodes the more precisely localizes a cardiac signal. If there are four electrodes total, then there are two pairs. The distal tip is connected to the negative recording pole, as in pacemaker electrodes. One pair will correspond to one line on the EGM. For example, the Halo/Crista catheter has 20 electrodes and results in ten lines, or channels, on the recording system.

The fifth catheter is the Lasso. This is a circular mapping catheter designed to be placed in a pulmonary vein for an atrial fibrillation procedure.

The sixth catheter is the Halo/Crista designed for RA recording of atrial flutter. (Angels have Halo's and wings that flutter). Different companies have similar catheters with different names. See: Boston Scientific & Biosense Webster catalogs

6. Which of the following are true about the circular mapping type catheter show, such as a Spiral or Lasso catheter? (Select 2 answers)
   a. Will admit a 0.014" guidewire
   b. Only approved for use in LA
   c. Rotate the shaft clockwise only
   d. Tension wire maintains the circular loop
   e. Springy Tin alloy maintains circular shape
   f. Should be straightened when crossing an AV valve
   g. Used mainly on AFL cases

ANSWERS: b. Only approved for use in LA. c. Rotate the shaft clockwise only. Instructions specify clockwise only. There is a lawsuit pending where an EP fellow rotated one counterclockwise and got it entangled in and damaged the mitral chordae tendinea. It can act like a corkscrew when rotated incorrectly. It was designed to map around the inside of a pulmonary vein in patients with AF - not AFL. They should not be placed across an AV valve. See: http://www.thehastingscenter.org/Bioethicsforum

The springiness and memory come from the Lasso's Nitinol alloy that is preformed and set into the circular shape at the time of manufacture. It is composed of Nitinol, a nickel titanium alloy (not tin) with excellent shape memory and super-elasticity. The term Nitinol comes from the 1st two letters in Nickel and the 1st two letters in Titanium - Ni-ti-nol.

The circular mapping catheter can be straightened by placing it in a sheath and it springs back to the circular shape when extended out of the sheath tip. Some of these have a variable radius to allow the circle radius to be shortened and to spring open in a pulmonary vein to establish good physical and electrical contact. Different loop sizes are available. Prior to insertion or withdrawal, the loop should be fully relaxed (handle grip rotated fully to the left) See: http://www.biosensewebster.com/lassonav.php

7. What mapping catheter uses 64 electrodes on eight self-expanding splines as shown on the x-ray?
a. Basket catheter
b. Egg beater catheter
c. Stereotaxis catheter
d. Non-contact multiple electrode array balloon

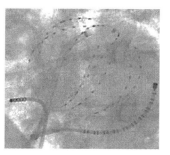

ANSWER: a. Basket catheter. "The mapping catheter consists of an open lumen catheter shaft with a collapsible, basket shaped, distal end. Currently basket catheters consist of eight equidistant metallic arms, providing a total of 64 unipolar or 32 bipolar electrodes capable of simultaneously recording electrograms from a cardiac chamber. The catheters are constructed of a super elastic material to allow passive deployment of the catheter and optimize endocardial contact. The size of the basket catheter used depends on the dimensions of the chamber to be mapped, requiring antecedent evaluation (usually by echocardiogram) to ensure proper size selection. The collapsed catheters are introduced percutaneously into the appropriate chamber where they are expanded." See: Clinical Experience

"Percutaneous endocardial mapping with multi-electrode basket shaped catheter has been shown to be feasible and safe in patients with ventricular tachycardia (VT) in coronary disease. Fragmented early endocardial activation—suggesting a zone of slow conduction that may be a suitable ablation target—is frequently demonstrated. However, the relatively large inter-electrode spacing in available catheters has prevented high resolution reconstruction of the reentrant circuit in many patients." Boston Scientific advertises their Constellation full contact mapping catheter for use in the RA although it has apparently also been used safely in the ventricle. See: http://www.ncbi.nlm.nih.gov/pmc/articles/PMC1767151/ Heart, June 2002, P. Friedman

8. **What would a lead like this be used for?**
   a. **PV ablation**
   b. **CS recording**
   c. **RA appendage pacing**
   d. **Biventricular LV pacing**

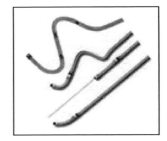

ANSWER: d. Biventricular LV pacing. "Some leads have multiple electrodes that can be used individually or in combinations. Most [LV] lead designs rely on passive wedging the lead tip into the target vein for fixation. Reversible self-retaining cants, S- or pigtail-shaped curves, and deployable retention lobes can increase the effective diameter of smaller leads for mechanical stability without degrading maneuverability, but they may be difficult or impossible to extract." See: Zipes, chapter on CRT

9. **These steerable catheters with handles and large platinum tips are designed for:**
   a. **High-density voltage mapping**
   b. **Diagnostic electrophysiology**
   c. **Radiofrequency ablation**
   d. **Cryoablation**

ANSWER: c. Radiofrequency ablation. These catheters use a large metal tip to concentrate RF energy at an endocardial conduction pathway. They are steerable. Tightening the handle causes the tip to curl up and put pressure on the area to be ablated.

Kern says, "In addition to the standard catheters, special steerable tip catheters have been designed to facilitate mapping and ablation procedures. They are constructed with a large platinum tip (4 to 8 mm), which can produce adequate lesion size in the endocardial surface. An energy source is also necessary. In radiofrequency energy ablations a generator capable of delivering a continuous unmodulated sine wave at approximately 500 kHz is standard. These generators also continuously monitor energy output and catheter impedance. The circuit is completed by a large indifferent skin electrode usually positioned in the infrascapular (beneath the scapula) region of the patient's back." RF ablation creates a thermal lesion to destroy abnormal reentrant circuits that cause supraventricular or ventricular tachycardia."

When removing a deflectable ablation catheter, make sure that it is in a neutral position by releasing the curve and tension on the deflection wires, so it won't damage the endocardium or vein. If the patient has an implanted device, withdraw catheters carefully under fluoro, so as not to disturb the implanted leads. See: Kern chapter on "Electrophysiology Studies and Ablation Techniques"

10. What type of catheter is this?
   a. **Irrigated tip RF ablation**
   b. **Irrigated tip cryoablation**
   c. **Multiple side hole CS angiography**
   d. **Multiple side hole mapping catheter**

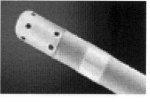

ANSWER: a. Irrigated tip RF ablation. Josephson says, "Apart from new designs in handles, one of the major developments in recent years has been the ability to cool the catheter tip while ablating. This reduces dissipation of heat into the blood, enabling more efficient energy delivery to the tissue, potentially with lower power settings. The most common design involves a series of holes in the catheter tip through which saline is irrigated during ablation (so called 'irrigated tip' catheters)" See: Radiofrequency ablation of cardiac arrhythmias: past, present, and future by J.P. Josephson
Current ablation systems allow for temperature monitoring and temperature control; valuable tools during radiofrequency ablation procedures as they provide important

information regarding the adequacy of tissue heating, minimize the development of coagulum, and maximize the lesion size. Newer technical modifications, such as a larger distal electrode and saline cooling of this electrode, have helped to minimize impedance rises and allow creation of larger and deeper lesions." http://qjmed.oxfordjournals.org/content/105/4/303.full

11. Stereotaxis catheters:
a. **Have magnets in the tip**
b. **Generate an ultrasound wave at the tip**
c. **Measure electrical impedance at the tip**
d. **Generate a low voltage 5.7 kHz signal at the tip**

ANSWER: a. Have magnets in the tip. "The [stereotaxis] catheters have small magnets embedded near their tips. These small magnets respond to changes in the magnetic field around the patient causing the catheter to change direction and move. The magnetic field can be controlled precisely by two large magnets on each side of the patient. These larger magnets move around the patient three dimensionally making subtle changes in the magnetic field allowing for very precise manipulation of the catheter inside the patient." See: http://www.coastalcard.net/Ehrlich.pdf

12. Match the outside diameter of the catheterization with how it is usually measured:

a. **Diagnostic catheter OD**	1. **Inches**	
b. **Inflated Balloon catheter OD**	2. **mm.**	
c. **Needle OD (Outside diameter)**	3. **French**	
d. **Guidewire**	4. **Gauge**	

CORRECTLY MATCHED ANSWERS:
a. Diagnostic catheter OD: French. 1 Fr. = 0.33 mm = .013 in.
- One French size equals 1/3 (0.33) of a mm or .013 inches. The outside diameter (OD) of cath equipment is traditionally measured using four different scales.

b. Balloon diameter: mm 1 mm = .0394 inches
c. Needle OD in gauge.   18 gauge = .050 in. (nonlinear system)
d. Guidewire OD in thousandth of inches.035 inch = 0.89 mm

We mix the English, French, metric, and gauge measuring systems. This tradition of mixing systems makes it difficult to convert between the systems. It becomes especially confusing when attempting to pass one system through another, as in PCI. See: Co. literature and Tilkian, chapter on "Tools for Catheterization."

13. What is the minimum size of the sheath that will just allow passage of a 7 French catheter?

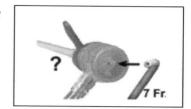

 a. 7 F
 b. 8 F
 c. .038"
 d. .045"

ANSWER: a. 7 French. Sheaths are numbered by the size of a catheter they will admit. E.g., A 6 French sheath will admit a 6F catheter of 2.0 mm outside diameter (OD). A very small clearance (.05-.1 mm) is allowed between the sheath ID and the catheter OD. The sheath will have an Inside Diameter (ID) of approximately 2.1 (0.1 mm of play) but an OD of 2.33 mm (7.5 French). Note: OD= Outside Diameter; ID = Inside Diameter. See: Co. catalog.

14. Arterial sheaths on heparinized patients should be meticulously flushed immediately after insertion and _____.

 a. Every 1-2 minutes thereafter
 b. Whenever the ACT falls below 120 seconds
 c. Aspirated and flushed after each catheter is removed.
 d. Flush continuously with continuous flow device infusing flush at 10-20 ml/min

ANSWER: c. Aspirated and flushed after each catheter is removed. Kern says, "The sheath should be aspirated and flushed after each catheter is removed." Whenever you remove a catheter, the sheath can strip off thrombus adherent to the catheter wall. By aspirating you remove any thrombus remaining in the sheath. Discard this bloody fluid. Then flush with heparinized saline to clear blood from the sheath. It heparinizes and lubricates the sheath for the next catheter insertion.

A sheath can clot if blood is allowed to stagnate in it. Periodic flushing is recommended every 5 minutes or more frequently if clots are seen in the aspirant.
Grossman recommends a continuous flow device at 30 ml/hour [0.5 ml/min] on the arterial sheath. He recommends power flushing with this device with heparinized saline after any new catheter is introduced or removed. Some labs use continuous flow devices on all sheaths.

15. In general, what is the LONGEST AMOUNT OF TIME (in a non-heparinized patient) a standard diagnostic guide wire should be used in the body before it is removed and carefully wiped with a heparinized gauze?

 a. 3 min
 b. 10 min
 c. 20 min
 d. No limit

ANSWER: a. 3 min. Kern recommends that diagnostic guide wires be removed and wiped every 3 minutes to reduce the chance of clot formation on the wire. This is especially recommended in non-heparinized patients, and in critical procedures, like crossing stenotic aortic valves in AS. In AS the wire is in a critical area (Ascending AO) and is heavily manipulated for long periods. Some labs start a stopwatch to time the wire manipulation time for three minutes before removing and wiping it with a heparinized gauze. However, smaller diameter coated PTCA tracking wires are left in for much longer periods with few complications. See: Kern, chapter on Hemodynamic Data.

16. Which guidewire has a nitinol spring steel core in a polyurethane jacket with a special coating that becomes slippery (lubricous) when wet?
   a. **Hydrophilic glidewire**
   b. **Cook BH coated wires**
   c. **Hydrophobic (Silicone) coated wires**
   d. **Teflon (PTFE) coated wires**

ANSWER: a. Hydrophilic Glidewire. The Terumo hydrophilic glide-wire wire is covered with a tungsten impregnated Polyurethane plastic. Then it is coated with a hydrophilic polymer. (Hydrophilic means it attracts and absorbs water.) Instead of a wire coil this wire's body derives from one strand of a tapered springy Nickel-steel alloy. It has excellent memory, torquability, and is less traumatic due to its smooth surface.

The Glidewire may be so "slimy" that the operator may be unable to manipulate it. A damp sponge, pin-vise or turning tool may provide a better grip. It needs to be stored moist in its hoop. The Glidewire is available in various lengths, diameters, bends, core tapers, core stiffness and with a gold tip. Many companies now use these materials. See: Co. product literature.

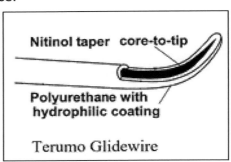

17. Which guidewire is the most kink-resistant?
   a. **Braided stainless steel wires**
   b. **Coiled stainless steel wires**
   c. **Hypo-tube and safety ribbon wires**
   d. **Nitinol core-to-tip wires**

ANSWER: d. Nitinol core-to-tip wires. This wire uses very springy steel throughout, from proximal to distal tip. Freed says, "Guidewires with nitinol cores are virtually kink resistant, while those with stainless steel cores are more susceptible to kinking." Once a guidewire becomes kinked it can hang-up on the catheter hub and lose its 1 to 1 torque response. It should be replaced. Stainless steel coiled and hypo-tube wires kink easily. See: Freed, Chapter on PTCA Equipment

18. To avoid damage to a plastic coated glidewire, be careful to NEVER:
   a. Use it with a single wall needle
   b. Use it once it is kinked
   c. Pull it back through a needle
   d. Torque it excessively

ANSWER: c. Pulling back through the needle. Never pull back these plastic wires through a needle that can sever them or shave off pieces of plastic, as they are likely to catch in the needle's sharp beveled edge. They may be advanced though the needle, then the needle removed. Only then the Glidewire can be manipulated back and forth. Davies says: "However, a hydrophilic guidewire may not be appropriate for initial introduction because its coating may be sheared off by the end of the metallic needle if the wire is retracted (even partially). It is safer to initiate the intervention with a standard steerable, soft-tip metallic guidewire and then, following sheath introduction, exchange if for a Glidewire..." See: Davies & Brophy, Vascular Surgery, Chapter on "Endovascular Approaches and Techniques" Published by Springer, 2005"

19. In most nitinol-tipped guide wires:
   a. The tip curve is fixed and cannot be changed
   b. The tip curve can be shaped by the operator before placement
   c. The hydrophobic coating repels water
   d. The hydrophobic coating increases torque control

ANSWER: a. The tip curve is fixed and cannot be changed. Davis says, "Many wires have a preformed curve or angle, and if the core is made of nitinol (an elastic nickel-titanium alloy with memory), this cannot be changed. This (core-to-tip design) gives more torque control and makes the wire very steerable." You may select a Glidewire with a bend in the tip; you just can't change that bend. Many special wires have malleable tips that can be shaped by the operator. The Terumo coating is hydrophilic (draws in water), not hydrophobic (repels water). Remember a "phobia" is something you fear and push away. See: Davies & Brophy, VASCULAR Surgery, Chapter on "Endovascular Approaches and Techniques" Published by Springer, 2005

20. The unique feature of the SafeSept guidewire for transseptal puncture is:
   a. Laser-tip guidewire
   b. RF-tip straight guidewire
   c. Floppy-tipped guidewire
   d. Sharp-tipped J guidewire

ANSWER: d. Sharp-tipped J guidewire. This unique guidewire makes the transseptal puncture easily because of its sharp stylet guidewire. Once through the septum it folds into an atraumatic J-curve. The dilator and catheter may then be advanced into the LA over this wire. EP Digest says, "To improve the success and safety of the TSP [Transeptal Puncture], a specially designed 0.014-inch diameter nitinol guidewire (SafeSept™ transseptal guidewire, Pressure Products Inc., San Pedro, CA) has been produced to facilitate safe access to the left atrium. The guidewire is introduced through a standard transseptal apparatus allowing probing of the interatrial septum. During TSP, the wire is supported within the dilator, giving the sharpened tip of the wire column support, and allowing it to cross the fossa, even if the fossa is thickened or fibrotic. Once across the fossa it is no longer supported and bends on itself, rendering the tip completely atraumatic and reducing the risk of perforating adjacent structures. When advanced into the pulmonary vein, the curved shape and floppiness of the wire tip will again not allow tissue damage."

SafeSept transseptal guidewire
from Pressure Products Inc.

See: EP Lab Digest Sept 2009, Initial Clinical "Experience of Transseptal Punctures Performed Using the SafeSept™ Transseptal Guidewire", by Wadehra & Chow Other new transseptal equipment (with video demonstrations) include:

SoloPath Expandable transseptal Introducer, Onset Medical Corp.

Baylis NRG RF Transseptal Needle that burns through the septum. See: Simulated transseptal training video.

http://simbionix.com/simulators/angio-mentor/library-of-modules/transseptal-punctur e/

One reviewer says, "When doing transseptal cases, we've run into the situation a few times where the septum is either very thick or very "springy" and we've been unable to puncture it successfully. When this happens, we drop a cautery pen on the sterile field and touch it to the transseptal needle outside the body, therefore burning through the septum at the needle tip. No fancy or expensive piece of equipment needed!" Shelly Haddox, RT R, Arkansas Heart Hospital at little Rock

21. What are the standard equipment sizes of micro puncture introducer sets.
   a. **18-gauge needle, .035-inch wire**
   b. **18-gauge needle, .018-inch wire**
   c. **21-gauge needle, .024-inch wire**
   d. **21-gauge needle, .018-inch wire**

ANSWER: d. 21-gauge needle, .018-inch wire. Company literature says, "The micro puncture introducer set is used for placement of .035 or .038-inch diameter wire guide wires into the Vascular system when a small 21-gauge needle stick is desired.

After initial access and placement of the .018-inch diameter Torq-Flex (40 cm long) wire guide, the coaxial catheter pair is introduced. Removal of the inner dilator and wire guide facilitates placement of the .035 or .038-inch diameter wire guide through the outer catheter."

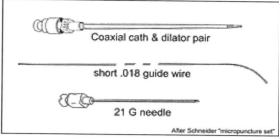

Once the micro puncture coaxial catheter is placed a larger guidewire and dilator/sheath may be put in. Introducer sets are available for 4, 5, 6 & 7 F catheters. It is most used in pediatric cases and known peripheral artery disease. There is purported to be a reduction in bleeding complications with the smaller needle puncture and smaller catheter. It is placed like any sheath, except the size of the instruments (needle, wire & sheath) are smaller. See: www.cookmedical.com Co. literature and Schneider, chapter on "Percutaneous Vascular Access".

22. When entering a "dry" pericardial space from the subxiphoid approach, it is best to use:
   a. **Single wall needle, bevel up**
   b. **Smart needle (Doppler), bevel down**
   c. **Seldinger needle with pointed stylus**
   d. **Tuohy needle with bevel pointing up**

ANSWER: d. Tuohy needle with bevel pointing up. A Tuohy needle is a hollow hypodermic needle, very slightly curved at the end, suitable for inserting epidural or pericardiocentesis catheters. It does not have a knife-like cutting tip and is less likely to puncture the endocardium or coronary arteries. It was originally designed for epidural puncture to prevent nerve damage. Video at: http://www.nejm.org/doi/full/10.1056/NEJMvcm0907841

Tuohy needle

23. What type of diagnostic guidewire is recommended for torturous atherosclerotic vessels on older individuals? It is also recommended when passing a wire through a previously placed stent. (Select two answers)
   a. **Straight stiff-tip guidewire**
   b. **"J" guidewire**
   c. **Benston guidewire**
   d. **Support guidewire**

ANSWER: b. & c. "J" guidewire and Benston guidewire. Tortuous "twisty" arteries are often difficult to pass with a guidewire. The tip of a straight wire may hang up in pockets of the tortuous aorta and on atherosclerotic lesions or flaps. J guides often pass easily as the "shoulder" of the guide seeks the center of the vessel. It is safer because the "J" deforms easily when pushed, and because of the atraumatic shape it is less likely to knock off plaque or cause arrhythmia in the heart.

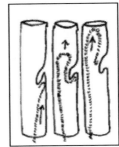

Schneider says: "J-tip guidewires are useful for passage through an occlusion or a previously stented arterial segment. The curved J tip is less likely to pass through the struts of a stent or create a false passage."

On young patients with normal vessels straight guide- with long floppy tips may work satisfactorily. The operator can "tractor" a straight floppy tip guidewire like the Benston around lesions by advancing the body of the wire. Its shoulder will loop over the lesion, like treads on a tank move over an obstruction. See: Schneider, chapter on Guidewire - Catheter Skills

24. When making a vascular puncture with a front/single wall needle how should it be inserted into the skin?

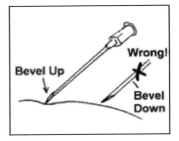

    a. **Bevel up**
    b. **Bevel down**
    c. **Holding onto the syringe**
    d. **With the sharp stylus fully advanced**

ANSWER: a. Bevel up. With the beveled part of the needle up, you can see the lumen of the needle and the sharp point is down, touching the skin. This allows the needle to dive down into the tissue. See: Grossman and Johnsrude, chapter on Equipment.

25. Before catheters, needles and sheaths are inserted into the patient they should be _____ .

    a. **Flushed with pure heparin (1000 USP units/cc)**
    b. **Flushed with heparinized flush**
    c. **Flushed with sterile saline**
    d. **Flushed with sterile contrast**
    e. **Left dry**

ANSWER: b. Flushed with heparinized "flush." Flush within catheters helps prevent air embolization and thrombosis. It also checks the equipment for defects and leaks. See: Grossman, chapter on Percutaneous Approach.

26. Which type of guidewire is 260-300 cm long?
   a. Interventional balloon tracking guidewire
   b. Transseptal guide wire
   c. Exchange guide wires
   d. Safety guide wires

ANSWER: c. Exchange guidewires. These are three times as long (260 - 300 cm) as a diagnostic catheter (100 cm). This length simplifies catheter exchange but complicates handling. They are especially helpful in tortuous anatomy, where wire position may be difficult to achieve. The long wire is threaded down a positioned catheter. The catheter is removed, leaving the wire in place. A new catheter is threaded over the exchange wire which then tracks back to the original catheter tip position. It is like leaving a railroad "track" to slide different trains (catheters) along. Standard 145 cm diagnostic guidewires are not long enough for this. See: Pepine, chapter on Equipment.

27. Match each part of an introducer sheath set with its name.
   a. Guidewire, short
   b. Sheath
   c. Dilator
   d. Seldinger needle

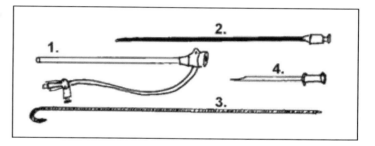

MATCHED ANSWERS ARE:

1: SHEATH: The Teflon sleeve that admits the dilator and catheter. Most sheaths have a hemostasis valve proximal to the sidearm. They are made of slits in a rubber diaphragm or several layers of rubber. A good hemostasis valve prevents bleed-back through the proximal end of the sheath during catheter exchange. You can insert and remove catheters without bleeding back through the sheath.

2: DILATOR: The short section of tapered catheter that expands the vessel puncture site. The taper makes the transitions between guide-wire OD size and sheath ID size. The dilator is the same French size as the largest catheter you can introduce through the sheath. A 6F sheath can introduce a 6F catheter.

3. Guidewire SHORT: These short .035-inch OD guides are used only for inserting the sheath. They extend through the dilator but are too short to be used with a catheter.

5. SELDINGER NEEDLE: The 18T needle used for wire insertion by the Seldinger method See: Grossman, chapter on "Percutaneous Approach."

28. To make the initial incision through the subcutaneous tissue for an ICD implant, most catheterizing physicians use a _____.
a. **#10 scalpel blade**
b. **#11 scalpel blade**
c. **#12 scalpel blade**
d. **#15 scalpel blade**

ANSWER: a. #10 scalpel blade.

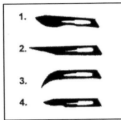

1. #10 BLADE: A large, curved blade for surgery.
2. #11 BLADE: The pointed blade used for the stab wound.
3. #12 BLADE: A hooked "eagle beak" shaped point for fine slicing
4. #15 BLADE: A small, curved blade used for making skin incisions as in cutdown procedures.

29. Which needle size would be SMALLEST and least traumatic to inject local subcutaneous anesthetic beneath the skin before deep infiltration with xylocaine and arterial puncture?
a. **16 gauge**
b. **25 gauge**
c. **0.025 inch**
d. **0.038 inch**

ANSWER: b. 25 gauge. These diameter needles are the smallest we usually use in the EP lab (.020"). 16 gauge is about the largest we ever use (.065"). The larger the gauge the smaller the needle diameter. Note this is an INVERSE relation. Stubs developed the "Stubs" gauging system for electrical wire that is still used commercially for wire and metal tubing. See: Tilkian, chapter on Tools for Catheterization.

30. Match the following surgical instruments to the correct name.
    a. Metzenbaum Scissors
    b. Army Navy Retractor
    c. Senn Retractor
    d. Needle Holder
    e. Debakey Forceps
    f. Weitlaner Retractor
    g. Adson Pickups
    h. Hemostat
    i. Right Angle Forceps
    j. Mayo Scissors

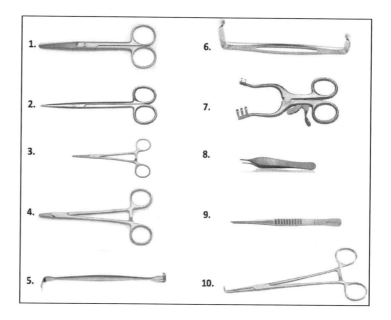

ANSWERS: 1. j, 2. A, 3.h, 4.d, 5.c, 6.b, 7.f, 8.g, 9.e, 10.i

Chapter 7
Pre-Procedure & Lab Values

1. Proper Body Mechanics & Patient Transport (pg. 247)
2. Medical – Legal (pg. 250)
3. Patient Setup & Pre-Procedural (pg. 259)
4. Lab Values (pg. 269)

EP Essentials LLC

Proper Body Mechanics & Patient Transport

1. To avoid injury to yourself use your strongest muscles while lifting and positioning patients. A cardiovascular specialist should use the strongest muscles in his/her body, which are in the:
    a. **Upper extremities**
    b. **Lower extremities**
    c. **Core lumbar spinal areas**
    d. **Core thoracic spinal areas**

ANSWER: b. Lower extremities. The strongest muscles are in the legs or lower extremities. The smaller back muscles frequently are injured because excess strain is placed on them. Besides the legs, your biceps arm muscles are also strong. Both should be used in conjunction with good posture when lifting. Flexing the legs slightly makes the legs a shock absorber and increases balance.
See: Torres, chapter on Basic Patient Care in Diagnostic Imaging."

2. A major safety guideline to a person transferring a premedicated patient from a bed onto a gurney is:
    a. **Transfer patients slowly**
    b. **Wear protective gloves and mask**
    c. **Get adequate assistance**
    d. **Use a heavy sheet to pull him over**

ANSWER: c. Get adequate assistance. Torres says: "A patient must never be moved without adequate help; to do so may cause injury to the patient or the RT [Health Care Provider]." Don't try to do it alone unless the patient is conscious and can move himself over. If the patient has been premedicated four assistants will be needed, two on each side to assist in pulling the patient with the supporting sheet.

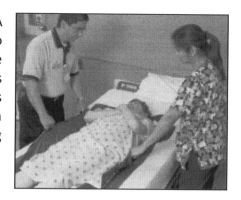

After a new device is put in, it is important to prevent the patient from using their arms to assist in the move. If they try to help, they could dislodge the new lead.
See: http://www.safety.duke.edu/Ergonomics/Documents/AmbFallsPrevention.pdf

3. How should wheelchair footrests be positioned when moving the patient to or from the wheelchair?
   a. **Moved aside**
   b. **Parallel to the floor**
   c. **Beneath the patient's feet**
   d. **Above the patient's feet**

ANSWER: a. Moved aside or removed so the patient won't trip over them. In addition, when moving a patient into or out of a wheelchair the big wheels must be locked to prevent its rolling.

See: Torres, chapter on Basic Patient Care in Diagnostic Imaging

4. What is the best method to move an ambulatory patient from a wheelchair onto a bed or gurney? After lifting the wheelchair foot rests you should assist the patient by standing:
   a. **With three other assistants alongside the wheelchair to lift him onto the table with a draw sheet**
   b. **Between the patient and the cath. table, one arm on the table and one to help the patient**
   c. **With your foot between the patient's feet, and the other close to the cath. table, knees bent**
   d. **With both your feet between the patient's feet, knees locked**

ANSWER: c. With your foot between the patient's feet, and the other close to the cath. table, knees bent. This is a body mechanics question, to make sure the patient is well supported and that you don't hurt your back as you assist him. Of course, you never want to lock your knees. Remain bent to absorb the patient's weight should he fall. One foot should be between the patient's feet to provide direct lifting support from that leg. See: Torres, chapter on "Basic Patient Care in Diagnostic Imaging"

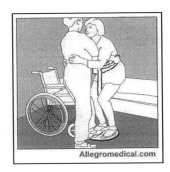

5. All the following are important when moving a patient from the bed to a wheelchair EXCEPT?
   a. **Get adequate assistance**
   b. **Elevate the head of the bed first**
   c. **Lower the bed to the level of the wheelchair**
   d. **Have the patient swing his legs over the side of the bed**
   e. **As you support the patient, twist at your waist while moving him onto the wheelchair**

ANSWER: e. As you support the patient, twist at the waist moving him onto the wheelchair - NO. "To get started lower the patient's bed as far as it will go and raise the head. Support the patient's head and knees. Lift and rotate the patient to a sitting position with their legs hanging over the edge of the bed. At this point some patients will be able to stand and get to the wheelchair on their own.
- To prevent back injury to you (the care giver), bend at the hips and knees, not at the waist, as you prepare to lift someone; then straighten at the hips and knees as you lift.
- Keep a wide base of support by spreading your feet apart. If you're transferring someone from one place to another, stagger your feet in a walking position, and shift your weight from front to back as you lift, while keeping the person as close to you as possible.
- To avoid back injury: When turning, pivot on your feet or move them. Don't twist at the waist. See: http://www.als-mda.org/publications/everydaylifeals/ch7/

6. A patient is to be transported to the EP lab for an ICD implant. He is on an IV, a portable ECG monitor and a temporary pacemaker. His history includes type 2 diabetes, MRSA, and pneumonia. He has no droplet precautions. The transporter should:
   a. **Transport with all attached devices. No contact precautions.**
   b. **Put a mask on the patient. Transport with all attached devices. No contact precautions.**
   c. **Put on gown and gloves when you enter his room and remove them when you leave the room. Then wash your hands. Bring along a pair of unopened gloves.**
   d. **Put a mask on the patient. Put on your gown, gloves, and mask when you enter his room and wear them during transport. Remove them after transport. Wash your hands.**

ANSWER: c. Put on gown, gloves, and mask when you enter the room, and remove them when you leave the room. Then wash your hands. Bring along a pair of unopened gloves in case you need to adjust the IV or touch the patient during transport.

Stokowski says: "When transporting an MRSA patient, a chief concern is avoiding actions that require the nurse or other attendant to touch the patient and then possibly contaminate environmental surfaces (door handles, elevator buttons, etc.). If a single caregiver is transporting the patient, gown and gloves are worn until the patient is on the stretcher or wheelchair, and then gloves are removed, and hands are washed. This caregiver then transports the patient without having any direct patient contact. A mask is required only if the patient is on droplet precautions as recommended by the CDC."

If it is anticipated that the patient might require some hands-on intervention during transport, you should bring along a pair of gloves. Another approach is to have two individuals transport the patient. One wears a gown and gloves and is responsible for touching the patient, if needed, during transport. The other individual, without gloves, manages the doors and elevator buttons.

Multidrug-Resistant Organisms such as methicillin-resistant Staphylococcus aureus (MRSA) and vancomycin-resistant Enterococcus (VRE) are a serious problem in hospitals. "Individuals who become colonized with MRSA tend to remain colonized for months or even years. It is important to realize that individuals colonized with MRSA can serve as reservoirs for MRSA and transmit the bacteria to others, just as those infected with MRSA. Therefore, many hospitals choose to assume that patients who were formerly colonized with MRSA are likely to still be colonized with MRSA. E.g., 'Once an MRSA patient, always an MRSA patient' (unless cultures prove otherwise.) Their medical records are flagged so that contact precautions can immediately be resumed if these patients return to the hospital. Colonization refers to the presence of microorganisms in or on a host with growth and multiplication, but without tissue invasion or damage. Colonized patients are also known as asymptomatic carriers." See: Stokowski, "Questions about MRSA..." http://www.medscape.com/viewarticle/546221

Medical - Legal:

1. Prior to doing an EP study the physician should evaluate and explain the risk to the patient. The patients with the highest risk are: (select three below)
  a. **Critical AS & HOCM**
  b. **Low Ejection Fraction**
  c. **Chronic type 1 diabetes**
  d. **Chronic atrial fibrillation**
  e. **Electrolyte abnormalities**
  f. **Multifocal ventricular arrhythmias**
  g. **Left Main or three vessel coronary disease**

ANSWER: a. Critical AS & HOCM, b. Low Ejection Fraction and g. Left Main or three vessel coronary disease. Issa says "Preprocedural Evaluation. Patients with critical aortic stenosis, severe hypertrophic cardiomyopathy, left main or severe three vessel coronary artery disease, or decompensated heart failure are at an elevated risk of complication. Induction of sustained tachyarrhythmias in these patients can cause severe deterioration. Heart failure, myocardial ischemia, and electrolyte abnormalities should be treated and adequately controlled before any invasive EP testing is undertaken." See: chapter on Electrophysiological Testing, by Issa, Miller and Zipes

2. When a case starts, the physician reviews the game plan for the procedure with the patient and the staff. This is termed:
   a. **Time-out**
   b. **Case-review**
   c. **Case-preview**
   d. **Full disclosure**
   e. **Patient-consent**

ANSWER: a. Time out. Cohen says, "The Joint Commission on Accreditation for Hospital Organizations also demands that a "time-out" be performed prior to the procedure. This is where the physician greets the patient with the staff present and reviews exactly what the game plan is for the procedure." See: Cohen, chapter on Preoperative Checklist

3. According to the Joint Commission, a pre-cath "time-out" should do all the following EXCEPT: (Select two incorrect answers.)
   a. **Confirm correct patient identity**
   b. **Confirm availability of special equipment**
   c. **Agreement on the procedure to be done**
   d. **Include the major team members in the case**
   e. **Identify the intended side and site of incision or insertion**
   f. **Confirm that correct premedication has been administered**

ANSWER: d. & f. Include the major team members in the case- NO. It must involve the entire cath team present on the case. f. Correct premedication is not one of the essential items in a time-out. Time-out is: "active communication among all members of the surgical/procedure team, consistently initiated by a designated member of the team, conducted in a "fail-safe" mode, i.e., the procedure is not started until any questions or concerns are resolved." "Time out? the surgical pause that counts," AORN Journal, Dec 2004 by Nancy Charlton NPSG.01.02.01 Chapter: National Patient Safety Goals: "The final verification process involves the entire team, uses active communication, and includes the following:
   • Correct patient identity
   • Correct side and site

- Agreement on the procedure to be done
- Correct patient position

Availability of appropriate documents, correct implants, and any special equipment- Involves the entire operative team in the time out using active communication. See: http://www.anesthesiapatientsafety.com/pdfs/Wrong_Site_Poster.pdf

4. Prior to any cardiac invasive procedure, the ultimate responsibility for obtaining informed consent lies with the:
a. **Assigned risk manager**
b. **The operating physician (Electrophysiologist)**
c. **Circulating nurse assigned to the case**
d. **Patient's primary care referring physician**

ANSWER: b. The operating physician (Electrophysiologist). The ultimate responsibility for obtaining permission is the operating physician's, usually the operating cardiologist. The EP lab staff are responsible for checking that the consent form is on the chart, properly signed, and that the information on the form is correct. Some PAs & CRNPs also may gain consent. See: Allmers, Review for Surgical Tech. Exam, chapter on "Fundamentals"

5. According to the Joint Commission what is the minimum number of patient identifiers that should be checked before you proceed with a case? (e.g., Name band, birthday, SS#, ask patient his name, medical record #, etc.)
a. **2**
b. **3**
c. **4**
d. **5**

ANSWER: a. 2 patient identifiers are required before proceeding with an invasive procedure. The Joint Commission says, "Acceptable identifiers may be the individual's name, an assigned identification number, telephone number, or other person-specific identifier. Electronic identification technology coding, such as bar coding or RFID, that includes two or more person-specific identifiers (not room number) will comply with this requirement....The two identifiers may be in the same location, such as a wristband....the two patient/client/resident-specific identifiers must be directly associated with the individual and the same two identifiers must be directly associated with the medications, blood products, specimen containers (such as on an attached label), other treatments or procedures." See: http://www.jointcommission.org/AccreditationPrograms/LongTermCare/Standards/09 _FAQs/NPSG/Patient ID/NPSG.01.01.0/Two Patient Identifiers.

6. Which federal agency creates regulations to protect patients' rights?
   a. HIPAA
   b. FDA
   c. OSHA
   d. Joint Commission

ANSWER: a. HIPAA. The "Health Insurance Portability and Accountability Act" (HIPAA) of 1996.... address the security and privacy of health data. The standards are meant to improve the efficiency and effectiveness of the nation's health care system by encouraging the widespread use of electronic data interchange in the U.S. health care system....and the security and privacy of health data" See: http://en.wikipedia.org HIPPA

7. A cardiologist does a TEE on your PVI patient. He leaves the room, and your EP physician arrives to do the case. Joint Commission standards require that:
   a. Each physician must be board certified and approved by hospital policy
   b. The cardiologist reports his findings to the EP physician before leaving
   c. The "Time-out" only needs to be done with the operating EP physician.
   d. A new "Time-out" needs to be done with the arrival of each physician

ANSWER d. A new "Time-out" needs to be done with the arrival of each physician Joint Commission Universal Protocols say about Performing a time-out:
   - The procedure is not started until all questions or concerns are resolved.
   - Conduct a time-out immediately before starting the invasive procedure or making the incision.
   - A designated member of the team starts the time-out.
   - The time-out is standardized.
   - The time-out involves the immediate members of the procedure team: the individual performing the procedure, anesthesia providers, circulating nurse, operating room technician, and other active participants who will be participating in the procedure from the beginning.
   - All relevant members of the procedure team actively communicate during the time-out.
   - During the time-out, the team members agree, at a minimum, on the following:
     - Correct patient identity
     - Correct site
     - Procedure to be done
   - When the same patient has two or more procedures: If the person performing the procedure changes, another time-out needs to be performed before starting each procedure.

- Document the completion of the time-out. The organization determines the amount and type of documentation.
- The access site does not need to be marked for bilateral structures

See: "Speak Up" poster from Joint Commission
www.jointcommission.org/assets/1/18/UP_Poster.pdf"

7. A lack of demonstrated care or skill, which is unreasonable or imprudent from a medical professional is termed:
   a. Assault
   b. Abandonment
   c. Negligence
   d. Battery

ANSWER: c. Negligence is legally defined as the omission to do something which a reasonable and prudent person would do or doing something which a reasonable and prudent person would not do. For example, a circulating nurse who fails to establish a patient's identity prior to an invasive procedure is negligent. See: Medical Dictionary

8. A legal obligation that holds each individual responsible for his or her own actions, is termed:
   a. Legal duty
   b. Liability
   c. Tort law
   d. Malpractice

ANSWER: b. Liability holds each individual responsible for his or her own acts. If our actions cause injury, loss, or damage to a patient, we are liable. Liability means we are legally bound, answerable, and responsible to our patients. Patients or family members may institute civil actions against any person who does not fully meet their obligations to protect the patient from injury and provide the best care possible. See: Medical Dictionary

9. Criteria that identify, measures, monitors, and evaluates patient care come from:
   a. OSHA regulations
   b. Medicare guidelines
   c. Automated information systems
   d. Quality assurance programs

ANSWER: d. Quality assurance programs establish criteria, identify, measure, monitor, and evaluate patient care. Such programs are often mandated by Joint commission (JCAHO). This agency sets the standards for optimal care, patient safety and continuity of patient care in medical facilities. Occupational Safety and Health Administration (OSHA) is a US federal agency that regulates workplace safety and health, not patient safety. See: Allmers, chapter on "Fundamentals"

10. Most invasive malpractice claims could be avoided by simply:
a. **Thinking before you act**
b. **Obtaining properly informed consent**
c. **Clearer handwriting in the medical record**
d. **Better communication with the patient**

ANSWER: d. Better communication with the patient. All these are important. But Dr. Kern says: "Medical malpractice actions are frequently initiated as a result of unresolved anger and frustration on the part of the patient.... The best advice in this area is to try always to keep lines of communication open between the provider (Dr., nurse, technologist) and the patient. Remember to take the time to let your patient know that he or she is important to you."
See: Kern, chapter on "Documentation in the Cardiac Catheterization Laboratory"

11. Patient's rights include all the following EXCEPT:
a. **Refusal of treatment**
b. **Continuity of care**
c. **Possession their original medical images**
d. **Confidentiality of his medical records**

ANSWER: c. The right to possess their medical images. The American Hospital Association identifies twelve key areas in their "Patient's Bill of Rights." These rights do not include the right to possess their medical images. Although most physicians will freely give image copies to patients, patients are not qualified to interpret them, and the originals remain in the medical record as property of the hospital or laboratory. See: Appleton & Lange's Review for the Radiographic Examination, chapter on "Patient Care

12. To ensure the correct patient is being operated on, when a patient is brought to the EP lab you should check all the following EXCEPT:
a. **Check ID band**
b. **Check their name**
c. **Ask patient date of birth**
d. **Ask patient the site of the procedure**
e. **Check responses against the consent form**

Ensuring Correct Procedures

A Helping Hand to Ensure Correct Procedures

Give yourself a helping hand.

... making things safer for our patients

Step 1: Consent Form
Consent form must include:
- Patient's full name
- Procedure site
- Name of procedure
- Reason for procedure

Step 2: Mark Site
The procedure site must be marked by a physician or other privileged provider who is a member of the operating team
Do not mark non-procedure sites

Step 3: Patient Identification
Staff will ask the patient to STATE (not confirm):
- Their full name
- SSN or date of birth
- Site for the procedure
- Check responses against the marked site, ID band, consent form

Step 4: "Time Out"
Prior to the beginning of a procedure, verbally confirm through a "time out":
- Presence of the correct patient
- Marking of the correct site
- Procedure to be performed
- Availability of the correct implant (if applicable)

Step 5: Imaging Data
If imaging data is used to confirm the site, verify the images are correct and properly labeled

---

ANSWER: b. Checking their name alone is not adequate. They must STATE their full name. You are supposed to have the patient state their full name, not just say, "Are you John Doe?" See: Joint Commission

13. To be legally valid, what is the LATEST that the patient should sign the informed consent form?
- a. Before administration of preoperative antiplatelet agents (such as Plavix)
- b. Before administration of conscious sedation (such as Versed)
- c. Before any invasive incisions or percutaneous punctures are made
- d. Before any interventions are made (ICD, ablation...)

ANSWER: b. Before administration of conscious sedation (such as Versed). Consent forms must be signed before the administration of sedative medications. This is to ensure that the patient fully understands and is informed about the procedure and the risks involved. If the patient's mind is clouded by preoperative medications such as Demerol or sedatives such as Versed, the consent is not legally valid. See: Allmers, Review for Surgical Tech. Exam, chapter on "Fundamentals"

14. The intent of informed consent for EP procedures is to:
   a. **Authorize all routine hospital procedures**
   b. **Protect patient from high-risk procedures**
   c. **Protect the operating physician and the hospital from claims of an unauthorized operation**
   d. **Authorize the physician to withhold lifesaving measures as he deems appropriate**

ANSWER: c. Protects the operating physician and the hospital from claims of an unauthorized operation. An informed consent (operative permit) protects the operating physician and the hospital from claims of an unauthorized operation. A general consent authorizes the physician and staff to render treatment and perform procedures which are routine duties normally conducted at the hospital. It also protects the patient from procedures they have not been informed about. The physician cannot perform different procedures or withhold lifesaving measures unless the patient has approved it. See: Allmers, Review for Surgical Tech. Exam, chapter on "Fundamentals

15. All the following are true regarding informed consent for an electrophysiology study EXCEPT:
   a. **Discussion should cover alternative treatments**
   b. **Only considered legal for 2-3 days from date of signature**
   c. **Consent must be obtained before patient receives sedation**
   d. **If not obtained, the patient has the right to sue for malpractice**

ANSWER: b. Only considered legal for 2-3 days from date of signature - NO. "Legally, informed consent is valid for a reasonable period. Per Joint Commission, this reasonable period consists of 30 days. In cases where treatments are planned, such as chemotherapy, consent may be obtained for the treatments to be provided up to 6 months in advance. If informed consent is not obtained, the patient has the right to sue for medical malpractice.... The legal requirement to obtain informed consent rests with the attending (or operating) physician.... Informed consent should include discussion of the following:
   • Diagnosis
   • Purpose of proposed treatment / procedure
   • Risks and benefits of proposed treatment / procedure

- Alternatives to proposed treatment / procedure
- Risks of not receiving treatment / procedure

Consent is not required for treatment in life-saving emergencies." See: http://www.med-ed.virginia.edu/courses/rad/consent/

16. When charting in the medical record it is most important to write:
   a. Write legibly with pencil or fountain pen
   b. Generalizations like "Mr. Jones appears lethargic"
   c. Routine safety measures like "Bed rail secured in up position"
   d. Care you are planning like "Will send patient to Xray in AM"

ANSWER: c. Routine safety measures like "Bed rail secured in up position." Kern says: "Information in the medical record should reflect only accurate facts regarding the particular patient. Avoid generalizations and speculating by charting only what you see, hear, feel, and smell. Do not use words such as inadvertently, unfortunately, appears, resembles, and the like.... Chart after the delivery of care, not before. Never make an entry in anticipation of something to be done...The chart note should identify precautionary or protective measures that have been taken for the safety of the patient, including the use of side rails and restraints." Charting should always be done with a permanent ink pen, although especially runny ink may smear.
See: Kern, chapter on "Documentation in the Cardiac Catheterization Laboratory"

17. The electrophysiologist gives the nurse a verbal telephone order to administer a medication to her patient "stat." She should:
   a. Immediately give the medication.
   b. Tell him telephone orders cannot be accepted.
   c. Write the order down, then read it back to the physician for approval.
   d. Restate the order in your own words to the physician, then write it down.

ANSWER: c. Write the order down, then read it back to the physician for approval. When verbal and telephone orders are issued, they must be written and read back to the physician. The physician then becomes responsible for the order that is to be treated as any other physician order and conducted by the appropriate hospital personnel.
The health care worker receiving the verbal order shall transcribe the order onto the medical record and Physician Order Sheet, identifying the order as a verbal order and the name of the provider who issued it. The health care worker will then sign the Physician Order Sheet." See: http://www.utmb.edu/Policies_And_Procedures/Clinical/PNP_005077

Patient Setup & Pre-Procedural:

1. Prior to an EP procedure where you expect to ablate a patients AV node place twelve standard ECG leads, defibrillation patches and:
   a. **3D mapping patches**
   b. **An esophageal temperature probe**
   c. **Transcutaneous pacing pads**
   d. **An indifferent skin electrode pad**

ANSWER: d. An indifferent skin electrode pad. This provides a return current path for the ablation current. Burns can occur around the edges if they are not large, and the moist conductive gel does not make good skin contact. When using an 8 mm tip ablation catheter, two grounding (indifferent) pads are recommended. Murgatroyd says: "an indifferent skin electrode plate is placed [on the back] if ablation is intended." See: Murgatroyd, chapter on Patient Preparation

2. Prior to a surgical implant in the OR how should the implant site be marked?
   a. **Prep the left clavicular area, unless otherwise directed**
   b. **Prep the nondominant clavicular area (right-handed patients have left sided implants)**
   c. **Surgeon must initial the site in ink before the case starts**
   d. **Nurse must mark the site after checking the verification checklist**

ANSWER: c. Surgeon must initial the site in ink before the case starts. Some EP labs use the same stringent requirements as the operating room and require the operating physician to mark the site with his signature. See below:
"Joint Commission Goals for Reducing Wrong-site, Wrong-patient, Wrong-procedure 1. A Surgical Site Verification Checklist will be used for every surgical procedure performed in the Main Operating Room
Two patient identifiers will be used to correctly identify each patient and will be documented on the Surgical Verification Checklist.
Surgeries involving extremities, laterality (right vs. left), multiple structures (fingers, toes), or levels (spine) of the body are required to have surgical site markings by the surgeon with documentation on the Surgical Site Verification Checklist. The surgeon's initials will be used as the surgical site marking. The initials should be over or as close as possible to the incision site and must be visible after the patient has been draped. The following exemptions to site markings apply:
   • Interventional cases for which the catheter/instrument insertion site is not predetermined.
   • The patient refuses surgical site markings....

To the extent possible, the patient (or legally designated representative) will be involved in the surgical site verification process. The patient should be awake and aware if possible.

The Surgical Site Verification checklist must be completed in its entirety. Each person completing any portion of the checklist must initial that portion of the list.

An incomplete checklist will result in postponement of the surgical encounter until the documentation is completed.

Any discrepancy noted during the verification process will result in an immediate halt to the surgical encounter until the discrepancy can be resolved by all members of the surgical team. After the patient is draped and immediately before the incision or start of the procedure, final confirmation of correct patient, correct side and site, correct procedure, patient position, and the availability of correct implants, special equipment or other specific requirements is verbally confirmed by the physician, anesthesia, RN circulator, and technologists. Many labs have both sides prepped, unless one side is unusable, such as with a port or venous occlusion. Also, some labs paste the patient's name somewhere readily accessible (like on his hat), so you don't have to continually undrape the arm and risk contamination. See: Joint Commission

3. While setting up for an ICD implant on a shy young girl, she says she is worried about how it will affect her lifestyle. As an experienced EP professional your most appropriate response would be to:
   a. **Tell her about other young patients with ICDs**
   b. **Explain the types of morbidity associated with an ICD**
   c. **Tell her about what it feels like when an ICD goes off**
   d. **Listen attentively and empathetically but don't express your opinion**
   e. **Suggest that she discuss it with the Dr. on the case when he arrives**

ANSWER: a. Tell her about other young patients with ICDs and how their lives were positively affected, is an appropriate response to a girl. Scaring her with morbidity and describing the feeling of the ICD shock do not ANSWER: the question she asks. How will this change my life? Don't just rely on the physician to impart his experience. Your experience may be more valid, and what she needs to hear. It is of course wise to also discuss this with the Dr. after he arrives.

Watson says: "When a patient asks about a given procedure and its expected outcomes, staff are duty-bound to disclose an appropriate degree of information. The question that follows, then, is "what is appropriate?" Simply put, that is the job of the professional to determine.... Does this patient want facts and figures, and if those facts and figures are presented, will it provide a comforting atmosphere or will it increase fear? Ultimately, members of the CCL team have a duty to the patient first, society second and colleagues third." See Watson, chapter on Ethical considerations

4. An alert older male patient has an ICD that has recently discharged many times. In the EP physician's office, he asks to have it turned off because the frequent shocks are too painful. The MD explains his objection and offers to improve the ICD programming but is uncomfortable turning it off because it is lifesaving. The patient still insists it be turned off. The MD finally writes a written order for you (his office nurse) to program it to "off" status. You should:

    a. Turn it off. The patient has the final authority to decide.
    b. Try to change the patient's mind. Tell him "We cannot do that legally."
    c. Refuse to turn it off. Only the patient's physician should turn it off.
    d. Object to turning it off, as it is a form of illegal euthanasia

ANSWER: a. Turn it off. The patient has the final authority to decide. Commonly it is the company representative or the physicians nurse that presses the "off" button, but only with written physician orders to legally cover themselves.

The HRS consensus statement presents several key points on managements of CIEDs (Cardiac Implanted Electronic Device): HRS says:

- A patient with decision-making capacity has the legal right to refuse or request the withdrawal of any medical treatment or intervention, regardless of whether he or she is terminally ill, and regardless of whether the treatment prolongs life and its withdrawal results in death.

- Legally and ethically, conducting a request to withdraw life-sustaining treatment is neither physician-assisted suicide nor euthanasia.

- The right to refuse or request the withdrawal of a treatment is a personal right of the patient and does not depend on the characteristics of the treatment involved (i.e., CIEDs).

- A clinician cannot be compelled to conduct an ethically- and legally permissible procedure (i.e., CIED deactivation) that he or she personally views as in conflict with his/her personal values. In these circumstances, the clinician cannot abandon the patient but should involve a colleague who is willing to carry out the procedure.

See: http://www.hrsonline.org/News/Press-Releases/2010/05/Expert-Consensus-Statementon Management-of-CIEDS#ixzz3VdnF1rlw

5. Your alert patient states that he is having a defibrillator implant, but the consent form is for a pacemaker. What should you do?

    a. Contact the implanting MD
    b. Check the chart for diagnosis
    c. Set up for what the patient stated
    d. Set up for what is state on the consent form

ANSWER: a. Contact the implanting MD. Only he knows what procedure he scheduled for this patient. It is possible this patient is scheduled for CRT-D, which is a biventricular pacemaker with an ICD combination – as opposed to a simple pacer only. The physician may need to update the consent form. Reference: Ellenbogen, chapter on "Cardiac Resynchronization Therapy"

6. When preparing a patient for an irrigated ablation procedure expected to last over 4 hours:
   a. **Put in a Foley catheter**
   b. **Use general anesthesia**
   c. **Use TEE or ICE instead of fluoroscopy**
   d. **Place the patient on a cycling air-mattress**

ANSWER: a. Put in a Foley catheter. Issa says, "Urinary Problems. Urinary retention can occur during lengthy EP procedures, particularly if combined with sedation, fluid administration, and tachycardia related diuresis. When such a situation is anticipated, it is useful to insert a Foley catheter before the procedure." Patients who need to urinate frequently, get large IV doses, or receive irrigated tip ablation may also require a Foley catheter.
See: chapter on Electrophysiological Testing, by Isa, Miller and Zipes

7. Patients with diabetes or renal insufficiency are at risk for contrast-induced renal failure or nephropathy (CIN). This risk is reduced by starting the patient on ___ the night before.
   a. **Low dose dopamine**
   b. **Ca-channel blockers**
   c. **D5W drip**
   d. **0.45 % NaCl**

ANSWER: d. 0.45 normal saline drip starting the night before cath will hydrate the patient and keep the kidneys flowing. But the best prevention of NIC is to limit the amount of low osmolar contrast during the case. Grossman says, "The main defense against contrast induced nephropathy is limitation of total contrast volume to 3 mL/kg. ... limit views and multiple contrast "puffs" during interventional wire and device placement.... Adequate pre-hydration is also critically important ...Hydration with half normal saline for 12 hours before and after the contrast procedure provided the best protection against creatinine rise...." Other drugs such as Fenoldopam, Lasix, Mannitol, Dopamine, Sodium Bicarbonate, etc. have not proven as helpful. See: Grossman, chapter on "Complications of Cardiac Catheterization"

8. A patient with AF is scheduled for PVI; he is NPH-insulin dependent. What specific precautions should be taken?
   a. Avoid the use of ionic, high osmolar contrast media
   b. Avoid reversing heparin with protamine
   c. Premedicate the patient with Benadryl and steroids
   d. Premedicate the patient with atropine and epinephrine

ANSWER: b. Avoid reversing heparin with protamine. NPH-insulin is "Neutral Protamine Hagedorn Insulin." These individuals may have increased sensitivity to Protamine. Up to 25% of these individuals may have a major anaphylactic type of allergic response. Protamine should be avoided in these individuals. Protamine is made from fish products and fish sensitive individuals should also avoid Protamine.
Other reactions patients have to Protamine are:
- Back and flank pain (minor reaction)
- Flushing with peripheral vasodilation and hypotension (minor reaction)
- Facial flushing and vasomotor collapse which may be fatal (major reaction)

In addition, insulin dependent individuals who are instructed to fast overnight (NPO after midnight) may experience hypoglycemia with normal insulin use. These individuals are recommended to use 50% of their normal insulin dosage in the AM. See: Kern, Chapter on "Intro. to Cath. Lab."

9. In the weeks prior to doing an EP study on a patient in persistent AF or AFL, it is safest to (select two below).
   a. Remove the patient from Warfarin
   b. Do a TEE to rule out atrial clots
   c. Anticoagulate the patient with Warfarin
   d. Do a stress test to rule out coronary artery disease
   e. Do a cardiac catheterization to rule out coronary artery disease

ANSWER: b & c. Do a TEE to rule out atrial clots and b. Anticoagulate the patient with Warfarin Issa says, "Anticoagulation for 4 weeks before the procedure, transesophageal echocardiography (to exclude the presence of intracardiac thrombus), or both is required before studying patients who have persistent atrial fibrillation (AF) or atrial flutter (AFL).... The ACC and AHA have strongly recommended the outpatients without a contraindication to warfarin who have been in AF for more than 48 hours should receive 3 to 4 weeks of warfarin prior to and after cardioversion.

The rationale for anticoagulation prior to cardioversion is that more than 85% of LA thrombi resolve after 4 weeks of warfarin therapy. An alternative approach that eliminates the need for prolonged anticoagulation prior to cardioversion, particularly in low-risk patients who would benefit from earlier cardioversion, is the use of transesophageal echocardiography (TEE) guided cardioversion. Cardioversion is performed if TEE excludes the presence of intracardiac clots. Anticoagulation after cardioversion, however, is still necessary."

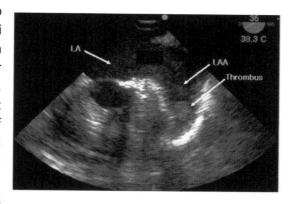

See: chapters on Electrophysiological Testing and Atrial Fibrillation, by Issa, Miller and Zipes

10. Patients coming to the EP lab for CRT who have had a previous allergic reaction to contrast media should:
   a. Have their case deferred due to unacceptable risk
   b. Receive non-iodinated contrast only
   c. Receive reduced volume contrast injections and DSA procedures
   d. Be premedicated with atropine, valium, and epinephrine
   e. Be premedicated with steroid and antihistamine

ANSWER: e. Be premedicated with Steroid and Antihistamine. For patients with a history of contrast allergy, Dr. Kern recommends Steroid and Antihistamine premedication along with the standard premed-cocktail. He recommends:
   • Prednisone (60 mg the night before and 60 mg pre-cath)
   • Diphenhydramine (Benadryl - 50 mg pre-cath)

These medications reduce the incidence of allergic reactions even among those extensive allergic histories.

Patients may have just as severe a reaction with a small volume contrast injection as a large volume load. That is why contrast test doses have NEVER been a helpful screening method. All contrast contains Iodine as the radiopaque metal. Patients with acid reflux may pe premedicated with Pepcid. See: Kern, Chapter on "Intro. to Cath. Lab."

11. A patient with a prosthetic Mitral valve needs a right heart EP study. He takes Coumadin daily and has had no clotting problems.
   a. Maintain the normal coumadin therapy & administer vitamin K prior to EP study
   b. Maintain the patient's normal coumadin therapy and administer fresh frozen plasma prior to EP study
   c. Discontinue coumadin 48 hrs. prior to procedure until INR < 1.8
   d. Wean patient from coumadin 1 week prior to procedure, and replace with heparin drip to keep INR around 2.0

ANSWER: c. Discontinue Coumadin 48 hrs. prior to procedure and let it drift down until INR < 1.5 to 1.8. However, it depends on how critical the oral anticoagulation is to the patient. If the patient is in great danger of clotting his valve, Dr. Grossman says it is OK to stop Coumadin and switch to heparin drip or LMWH (enoxaparin), two days prior to cath, because heparin is easier to reverse than Coumadin. He states that if the patient MUST be kept on Coumadin or if it is an emergency DO NOT REVERSE COUMADIN WITH ITS ANTIDOTE VITAMIN K. IV vitamin K occasionally induces a hyper-coagulable state, which is what you don't need. In emergencies Grossman recommends using Fresh Frozen Plasma (FFP) which contains many clotting factors, including platelets, to counteract the Coumadin. A study in "Heart Rhythm" concluded "While the results were not statistically significant, there was a trend toward reduced complications in patients randomized to warfarin continuation [verses bridging with heparin or warfarin interruption]. This strategy should be considered in patients undergoing PPM or ICD implantation."
See: Grossman, Chapter on "Complications..."chapter #1, Contraindications

12. An average sized woman is scheduled for Atrial Flutter ablation using an irrigated RF catheter. Before the case starts you insert a Foley catheter but get no urine back-flow. After inserting it fully with no flow your next step should be to:
   a. **Fully inflate the balloon**
   b. **Take it out and re-insert again**
   c. **Take it out and try again with a new catheter**
   d. **Apply suction to the catheter while slightly pulling back**

ANSWER: c. Take it out and try again with a new catheter. You should get urine back once you enter the bladder. If you do not, you may be in the vaginal canal which is considered nonsterile. In this case you have a contaminated catheter and need to remove and discard it and start again with a new one. Do not fully inflate the balloon, as it may cause damage to the ureter. Reported RN experience.

13. When a patient arrives in your lab with a Foley catheter bag, it is important to:
   a. **Place the drainage bag above the level of the bladder**
   b. **Place the drainage bag below the level of the bladder**
   c. **Clamp the Foley catheter for the time of the study**
   d. **Not touch the tubing or bag**

ANSWER: b. Place the Foley drainage bag below the level of the bladder so it can properly drain by gravity. See: Appleton & Lange's Review for the Radiographic Examination, chapter on "Patient Care"

14. A Foley retention catheter is positioned in the _____ and the balloon is inflated with _____.

    a. Intestine, air

    b. Intestine, saline

    c. Bladder, air

    d. Bladder, saline

ANSWER: d. Urinary bladder, saline or other fluid. A Foley retention catheter drains urine from the bladder into a collection bag. It is retained in place with a rubber balloon at the tip which is inflated with fluid.
See: Mosby's Comprehensive Review of Nursing for NCLEX-RN, Chapter on "Urinary systems"

15. A patient in acute pulmonary edema should be positioned in a:

    a. Prone position

    b. Sitting up Fowler's position

    c. Trendelenburg position

    d. Right or left lateral position

ANSWER: b. Sitting up Fowler's position to facilitate breathing and decrease venous return. A patient with dyspnea is usually uncomfortable in a lying supine position (orthopnea). This is because reclining increases venous fluid pooling (preload) in the lungs which increases edema in CHF patients. They breathe easier sitting up, in either a semi-sitting (mid- Fowler's) position 30 degrees, sitting (high- Fowler's) position 45 degrees or reverse Trendelenburg position (body tilted head up). See: Medical Dictionary

16. During electrophysiology study, a patient with congestive heart failure in the EP lab becomes extremely short of breath. The physician orders furosemide (Lasix) 40 mg given IV. The physician will follow up this order by ordering a/an:

    a. Foley catheter

    b. Fogarty catheter

    c. Multipurpose catheter

    d. Additional IV line for the furosemide infusion

ANSWER: a. Foley catheter. The usual initial dose of furosemide is 20 mg to 40 mg given as a single dose, injected intramuscularly or intravenously. The intravenous dose should be given slowly (1 to 2 minutes). Ordinarily a prompt diuresis ensues. A Foley catheter will prevent you having to give the patient a urinal or a bedpan every few minutes. See: Mosby's Comprehensive Review of Nursing for NCLEX-RN, Chapter on "Urinary systems"

17. Grossman and Peterson state that the key factor in reducing complication rates during invasive procedures is the:
   a. Speed of doing the case
   b. Experience of the operating physician
   c. Systemic Heparinization of the patient
   d. Meticulous attention to details of technique

ANSWER d. Meticulous attention to details. Grossman mentions this "meticulous attention to details" several times in his section of preventing complications. The other Distractors (experience, heparin, and speed) are all helpful, but are included in the correct answer.
See: Grossman, Chapter on "Complications..." Peterson, Chapter on "Basic Techniques and Complications."

18. You inserted an IV catheter and started a dopamine drip on a patient 30 minutes ago. Now the patient is complaining of coldness and swelling at the IV site.
   a. What should you do FIRST?
   b. Stop the IV and attempt to aspirate
   c. Stop the IV and apply pressure to the swollen area
   d. Open the IV to see if it flows freely
   e. Lower the IV bag below the level of the heart to see if you get blood or fluid coming back

ANSWER: a. Stop the IV and attempt to aspirate. Hadaway says, "Extravasation occurs when a peripheral catheter erodes through the vessel wall at a second point, when increased venous pressure causes leakage around the original venipuncture site, or when a needle pulls out of the vein. Signs and symptoms of extravasation include edema and changes in the site's appearance and temperature, such as swelling, blanching, and coolness.

The patient may complain of pain or a feeling of tightness around the site. Antibiotics, electrolytes, or vasopressors cause severe tissue injury or destruction when they extravasate.... If extravasation occurs... Immediately stop the infusion and disconnect the tubing as close to the catheter hub as possible. Attach a syringe to the hub and attempt to aspirate the remaining drug from the catheter.... If aspiration was unsuccessful, remove the catheter without placing pressure on the site. Elevate the affected arm. ...For most extravasations, you'll apply ice for 20 minutes at least four times a day for 24 to 48 hours." Consider injecting an antidote to the infused drug if necessary. See: online: "Preventing and managing peripheral extravasation" Nursing, May 2004 by Hadaway, Lynn C

19. Your patient is noncompliant in taking his medications for systemic hypertension. He should be taught that a common complication of uncontrolled hypertension is:
   a. Arterial calcification
   b. Cerebral hemorrhage
   c. Congestive Heart Failure
   d. Pulmonary fibrosis with pulmonary hypertension

ANSWER: b. Cerebral hemorrhage leading to stroke. Hemorrhaging and occlusion of blood vessels in the body are common complications of uncontrolled hypertension. This complication can occur in the brain (stroke), the eyes, the heart (myocardial infarction) and the kidneys. It is our professional duty to educate such patients and alert them to the risks of not taking their medication. See: Lippincott's State Board Review for NCLEX-PN.

20. Your patient is told that he has a poor prognosis, but says he believes there is some mistake. According to Dr. Elisabeth Kubler- Ross, this patient is most probably in what grief stage?
   a. Anger
   b. Denial
   c. Bargaining
   d. Depression

ANSWER: b. Denial. "When a terminally ill person states that there must be a mistake or that he is being confused with someone else, he is most probably denying his impending death. These five stages of grief are described by Dr. Elisabeth Kubler- Ross:

- Denial & disbelief: "What! There must be some mistake "
- Anger: "Why me?"
- Bargaining: "If I'm healed, I promise to..."
- Depression: "Woe, is me!"
- Acceptance: "OK. They will be done."

See: Lippincott's State Board Review for NCLEX-PN.

Lab Values:

1. Match the normal blood chemistry ranges to its electrolyte.
   a. 95-105 mEq/L
   b. 135-145 mEq/L
   c. 0.8-1.0 mg/L
   d. 1.5-2.1 mEq/L
   e. 3.5-4.5 mEq/L

   1. Sodium
   2. Potassium
   3. Chloride
   4. Total Calcium
   5. Magnesium

BE ABLE TO CORRECTLY MATCH ALL ANSWERS BELOW:
BLOOD CHEMISTRIES: Normal Value
   • SODIUM: 135-145 mEq/L
   • POTASSIUM (K+): 3.5-4.5 mEq/L
   • CHLORIDE: 95-105 mEq/L
   • TOTAL CALCIUM: 0.8-1.0 mg/L
   • MAGNESIUM: 1.5-2.1 mEq/L
See: Underhill, chapter on "Laboratory Tests" also, Todd, Vol II, Chapter on "Cath Protocol and Preparation"

2. Going into an EP procedure, the patient should have normal lab values. Match the following electrolyte and lab results with their normal value.
   a. >80,000 cells/ micro-L
   b. 3.5 – 5.5 mEq/L
   c. <1.5 ratio
   d. <12,000 cells/micro-L

   1. K
   2. Platelets
   3. INR
   4. WBC

ANSWERS MATCHED BELOW:
   • K: 3.5 - 5.5 mEq/L, Potassium electrolyte
   • Platelets> 80,000 or (150,000 - 400,000 cells/ micro-L)
   • INR: < 1.5 International Normalized Ratio (PT time ratio)
   • WBC: <12,000 cells/micro-L (or 4,500 - 12,000 white blood cells) Leucocytes

See: Cohen, chapter on Preoperative Checklist and Tilkian, Clinical Implications of Lab Tests

3. Which electrolyte imbalance exacerbates digitalis (Digoxin) toxicity?
   a. Hypokalemia
   b. Hyperkalemia
   c. Hypocalcemia
   d. Metabolic alkalosis

ANSWER: a. Hypokalemia is associated with the diuretics commonly given with digitalis, resulting in lower potassium levels that makes dig. toxicity more likely. Dig may be given as an antiarrhythmic, to slow AV conduction, or to strengthen cardiac contraction in CHF. Opie says, "Diuretics may induce hypokalemia which sensitizes the heart to digoxin toxicity and shuts off the tubular secretion of digoxin when the plasma potassium falls below 2 to 3 mEq/L."

Digitalis which contains cardiac glycosides (sugars) is extracted from the foxglove plant. Digoxin increases intracellular calcium which gives a positive inotropic (contractility) effect. For this reason, it is used to increase contractility in CHF patients. Digoxin also has a vagal effect on the parasympathetic nervous system, and as such may be used to slow the ventricular rate during atrial fibrillation. Dig. Toxicity is also seen with low Magnesium levels. Tip: when you see two opposite answers (hyper & hypokalemia) one of them is likely to be correct. See: Opie, chapter on "Digitalis..." EP Anatomy

4. To reduce the incidence of renal failure in angiography non-ionic or low osmolar contrast agents are recommended in patients with:
   a. **Elevated blood creatinine levels and/or elevated BUN levels.**
   b. **Reduced blood creatinine levels and/or reduced BUN levels.**
   c. **Elevated blood sodium levels and/or elevated potassium levels.**
   d. **Reduced blood sodium levels and/or reduced potassium levels.**

ANSWER: a. Elevated blood creatinine and/or elevated BUN (Blood Urea Nitrogen). These are waste products that are normally cleared by the kidneys. Since the kidney is the only organ that can eliminate contrast from the body, efficient kidney function is essential for angiographic patients to be able to excrete the contrast.

Normal creatinine levels are 0.6-1.2 mg/100 ml. So, many labs use 1.2 as the top end of normal (Old high limit was 1.5) and use low-osmolar contrast above this level. However, Grossman states that his lab switches to low-osmolar or non-ionic contrast in renal insufficiency patients when the creatinine exceeds 2.0. He also recommends its use for internal mammary angiography and in patients with a history of prior allergic contrast reactions. Normal BUN is < 25 mg/dl. However, Grossman states that too high is > 40 mg/dl. See: Grossman, Chapter on "Complications..."

5. To prevent excessive bleeding from the puncture site, PVI patients should come to the lab with a blood Prothrombin Time (PT) time: (Note > is greater than)
   a. **< 5 sec PT time**
   b. **< 18 sec PT time**
   c. **> 18 sec PT time**
   d. **> 50 sec PT time**

ANSWER: b. < 18 sec. PT time. Grossman recommends a PT time < (less than) 18 seconds long. Normal PT time is 12-15 sec. This assures that heparinization can be optimized during the case and that it can be reversed with protamine if necessary. It facilitates hemostasis at the end of the case. Pressure holding time will not be excessive and hematomas will be minimized. Mayo clinic suggests 10-14 is a normal range for PT. See: Grossman, Chapter on "Complications..."

6. CVA and TIA can best be prevented during and immediately after AF ablation by:
   a. **Keeping the INR => 2.0**
   b. **Keeping the INR => 3.0**
   c. **Keeping the ACT => 150**
   d. **Keeping the ACT => 300**

ANSWER d. Keeping the ACT > 300 with full Heparin anticoagulation. The INR is only for Warfarin anticoagulation monitoring. CVA (cerebral vascular accident) is a stroke or cerebral thrombosis. TIA (transient ischemic attack) is a small temporary stroke. Both involve thrombi to the brain.

Issa says, "Meticulous attention to sheath management, including constant infusion of heparinized saline and air filters; minimizing char formation during lesion creation by regulating power delivery to prevent abrupt impedance rise; and using ICE for early detection of intracardiac thrombi and accelerated bubble formation consistent with endocardial tissue disruption with RF application. Administration of large doses of protamine on completion of the ablation procedure to reverse heparin abruptly may promote thrombogenesis and warrant further evaluation to confirm its safety.... Thromboembolic events typically occur within 24 hours of the ablation procedure, with the high-risk period extending for the first 2 weeks following ablation."

"Once vascular access is achieved, intravenous heparin (bolus of 100 U/kg, then infusion of 10 U/kg/hr.) is administered. During the initial experience with AF ablation, anticoagulation with heparin was delayed until after LA access had been achieved because of fear of complications with transseptal puncture. Later, it became evident that such a strategy can allow thrombus formation on sheaths, catheters, and in the RA before transseptal puncture, and these thrombi could potentially travel to the LA. More recently, experienced operators have favored complete heparinization after vascular access, and clearly before transseptal puncture, especially when intracardiac echocardiography (ICE) is used to guide transseptal puncture. Even in patients fully anticoagulated with warfarin therapy at the time of ablation, it is still recommended to administer intravenous heparin during the ablation procedure."

"The activated clotting time (ACT) should be checked at 10- to 15-minute intervals until therapeutic anticoagulation is achieved and then at 30-minute intervals during the procedure, and the heparin dose is adjusted accordingly. The lower level of anticoagulation should be maintained at an ACT of at least 300 to 350 seconds throughout the period of mapping and ablation in the LA. If significant LA enlargement or spontaneous echo contrast is observed, targeting a higher ACT level (350 to 400 seconds) is more appropriate.

7. What is the clotting test used to measure the effect of warfarin?
   a. PT
   b. ACT
   c. INR
   d. PTT

ANSWER: a. PT. Prothrombin time (PT) — The clotting test used to measure the effect of warfarin is the prothrombin time International Normalized Ratio (INR) — The INR is a way of expressing the PT in a standardized way by comparing it to a reference value; this ensures that results obtained by different laboratories in different facilities can be compared reliably. Prothrombin Time (PT) measures the integrity of the extrinsic system as well as factors common to both systems and Partial Thromboplastin Time (PTT), which measures the integrity of the intrinsic system and the common components.
Blood Laboratory: Hemostasis: PT and PTT tests. (n.d.). Retrieved May 17, 2021, from https://www.medicine.mcgill.ca/physio/vlab/bloodlab/pt_ptt.htm

8. How often does the Hemochron point of care testing for ACTs need to be quality control tested?
   a. Every 8 hours (during patient care)
   b. Every 24 hours (during patient care)
   c. Once a week
   d. Once a month

ANSWER: a. Every 8 hours (during patient care). According to pointofcare.net: "Handling and Storage: Whole Blood controls are stable until the marked expiration date when stored at 4-8°C. Room temperature storage is possible for non-punctured vials; room temperature dating is to a maximum of seven weeks but must never exceed the marked expiration date. Note: If kept refrigerated, allow all quality control and coagulation test vials and/or test tubes to first reach room temperature and then stabilize for at least 20 minutes before use. This may take up to 60 minutes. Frequency: If Electronic QCs are not used, two levels of quality control (normal and abnormal) must be performed every 8-hour shift that patient testing occurs. Controls should also be run after any maintenance procedures and whenever the patient's values do not match the expected results. It is the responsibility of the personnel performing the patient testing to perform quality control. If Electronic QCs are used, two levels of whole blood QC are used to validate each box of ACT test tubes. Once a box is validated for use, print or affix a "VERIFIED" label on the outside of the box."

9. What core body temperature is when the patient is considered to be hypothermia? (The highest temperature that is considered to be hypothermia)
   a. 34° C
   b. 35° C
   c. 36° C
   d. 37° C

ANSWER: b. 35° C. "Hypothermia is a medical emergency that occurs when your body loses heat faster than it can produce heat, causing a dangerously low body temperature. Normal body temperature is around 98.6 F (37 C). Hypothermia occurs as your body temperature falls below 95 F (35 C)." Hypothermia has been shown to cause various cardiac arrhythmias including QT prolongations, and bradycardia due to the decrease in oxygen demands in response to lower temperatures. Hypothermia. (2020, April 18). Retrieved April 26, 2021, from https://www.mayoclinic.org/diseases-conditions/hypothermia/symptoms-causes/syc-20352682

10. What is an appropriate ACT level for performing an LAA closure?
   a. **300 to 400 seconds**
   b. **<100 seconds**
   c. **100 to 200 seconds**
   d. **>400 seconds**
   e. **200 to 300 seconds**

ANSWER: e. 200 to 300 seconds. "During the procedure, the Watchman-approved labeling recommends patients receive heparin to achieve a minimum activated clotting time (ACT) of 200 to 300 seconds. During the PROTECT AF trial, heparin was administered as a bolus to achieve an ACT > 250 seconds, and if the procedure time exceeded 60 minutes, an additional bolus of heparin was given to maintain an ACT > 250 seconds.6 The study utilized a bolus rather than continuous infusion due to the short duration of the procedure." Emerging options for anticoagulation IN LAA Closure. (n.d.). Retrieved April 27, 2021, from https://citoday.com/articles/2017-july-aug/emerging-options-for-anticoagulation-in-laa-closure

Chapter 8
<u>Baseline Testing</u>

EP Essentials LLC

Pacing Terminology

Incremental Pacing (decremental): Pacing at a constant cycle length slightly shorter than the patient's spontaneous rhythm then decreasing cycle length (or increasing pacing rate) by small steps.

Burst Pacing: Pacing at a fixed cycle length

Pace Mapping: A mapping technique designed to help locate the tachycardia focus by pacing at different endocardial sites and comparing the characteristics / morphology of the paced beat to the reference beat. The reference beat is an ECG recorded during clinical tachycardia.

Entrainment Mapping: Pacing at a cycle length slightly shorter than the tachycardia. If the post pacing interval is short, then the catheter is in the reentry circuit. A variation of pace mapping.

Ventricular Overdrive Pacing (Morady Maneuver or Ventricular Entrainment): This is different than entrainment mapping. It is a pacing maneuver used to differentiate Atrial tachycardia from AVNRT and AVRT.

Extrastimulus Testing: Drive train of typically eight beats followed by 1, 2, or 3 premature beats. (S1, S1, S1.... S2, S3)

ATP: Anti Tachycardia Pacing: Pacing the heart faster than its intrinsic rate. In the case of VT, we try to try to break the tachycardia before it progresses to ventricular fibrillation. ATP is only effective if the underlying rhythm is ventricular tachycardia but is never used for ventricular fibrillation.

See: Murgatroyd, Handbook of Cardiac Electrophysiology

Stimulation Basics & Measurements

1. In measuring the HV interval, the earliest ventricular activation is usually seen on the:
   a. **CS channels**
   b. **RV apex channels**
   c. **Surface QRS**
   d. **RV outflow channels**

ANSWER: c. Surface QRS. Murgatroyd says: "The HV interval is measured between the His bundle electrogram and the earliest recorded ventricular activation. As with the AV interval, the timing of the His electrogram is taken from its onset. The earliest recorded ventricular activation is always the beginning of the surface QRS complex. An HV interval of 35-55 ms is considered normal."
See: Murgatroyd, Chapter on The Basic Electrophysiology Study

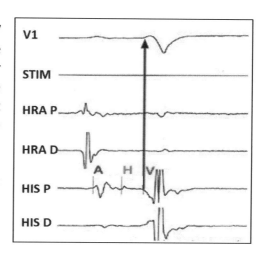

2. The AH interval measures _____ and is measured from the ___ to the beginning to the beginning of the H on the His bundle catheter.
   a. **AV node conduction time, early A wave on the His bundle catheter**
   b. **AV node conduction time, early A on the HRA catheter**
   c. **Atrial conduction time, early A wave on the His bundle catheter**
   d. **Atrial conduction time, early A on the HRA catheter**

ANSWER: a. AV node conduction time, early A wave on the His bundle catheter.
Murgatroyd says, "The AH interval is the time taken for the cardiac impulse to travel over the AV node and is measured from the electrograms recorded by the His bundle catheter. The AH interval is measured between the atrial electrogram recorded by his bundle catheter and the beginning of the His electrogram itself." See: Murgatroyd, Chapter on The Basic Electrophysiology Study

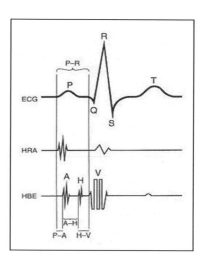

3. Match the normal values for each EP measurement shown.
1. AH interval   **a. 250-400 ms**
2. HV interval   **b. 180-290 ms (ventricular)**
3. AERP   **c. 35-55 ms**
4. AVNERP   **d. 180-330 ms (atrial)**
5. VERP   **e. 50-120 ms**

CORRECTLY MATCHED ANSWERS:
1. AH Interval: e. 50 – 120 ms
2. HV Interval: c. 35 – 55 ms
3. AERP: 180 – 330 ms (atrial)
4. AVNERP: 250 – 400 ms
5. VERP: 180 – 290 ms (ventricular)

See: Fogoros chapter on EP Testing for Bradyarrhythmias or Murgatroyd table of normal measurements

4. Match the following measurements with the numbers that make it up on this electrogram:
1. BCL   **a. #1**
2. AH   **b. #4**
3. HV   **c. #2 + 3**
4. IACT   **d. #1 + 2 + 3 + 4 + 5 + 6**

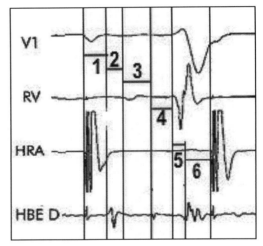

CORRECTLY MATCHED ANSWERS BELOW:
1. BCL: d. #1 + 2 + 3 + 4 + 5 + 6
2. AH: c. #2 + 3
3. HV: b. #4
4. IACT: a. #1

Fogoros says: "BCL (Basic cycle length) is the interval between successive A waves (measured from the RA catheter); ... IACT (intra-atrial conduction time) is the interval from the SA node to the AV node and is measured from the beginning of the P wave on the surface ECG to the A deflection on the His bundle electrogram ....The conduction interval from the

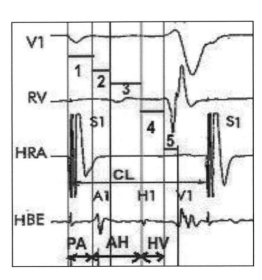

beginning of the A deflection to the beginning of the H deflection (the AH interval) represents the conduction time through the AV node (normally 50-120 ms)....The interval from the beginning of the H deflection to the beginning of the V deflection (the HV interval) represents the conduction time through the His-Purkinje system (normally 35-55 ms). Disease in the AV node will often produce prolongation of the AH interval, whereas disease in the distal conduction system produces a prolongation of the HV interval. " See: Fogoros chapter on Principles of the EP Study

5. On this electrogram, measure the CL, PA, AH and HV intervals.
   a. **Cycle length =** _____ **ms**
   b. **PA interval =** _____ **ms**
   c. **AH interval =** _____ **ms**
   d. **HV interval =** _____ **ms**

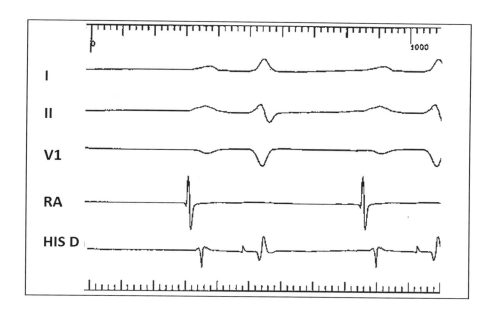

CORRECT ANSWERS:
- Cycle length = 544 ms
- PA or IACT interval = 46 ms
- AH interval = 128 ms
- HV interval= 43 ms

Note That these measurements are all within normal ranges - as listed below. The IBHRE CEPS exam provides movable cursors on the screen, while the RCES does not. In this case use the laminated paper Pearson VUE gives you; hold that up to the screen and mark the measured distance with the pen provided. Then to make ms

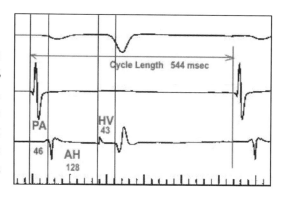

measurements, move that to the time scale on the EGM. See: Fogoros chapter on Principles of the Electrophysiology Study

6. Programmed stimulation normally consists of two types of paced beats. (Select two)
   a. **Extrastimuli**
   b. **DDDR pacing**
   c. **Biventricular pacing**
   d. **Incremental pacing**
   e. **Ramp pacing**

ANSWER: a. Extrastimuli and d. Incremental pacing. Fogoros says, "Programmed stimulation consists of two general types of pacing: incremental and extrastimulus pacing." These are the bursts of fixed rate pacing (Incremental pacing S1) usually followed by a single premature extrastimuli S2. Even more premature beats may be added on, termed S3 & S4.
See: Fogoros chapter on Principles of the Electrophysiology Study

7. A pulse train with a fixed cycle length is termed:
   a. **Incremental (Burst) pacing**
   b. **Decremental pacing**
   c. **Synchronous pacing**
   d. **Asynchronous pacing**

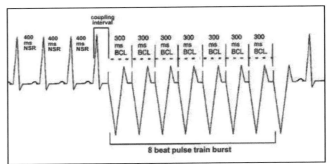

ANSWER: a. Incremental pacing. Fogoros says: "Incremental pacing (or burst pacing) consists of introducing a train of paced impulses at a fixed cycle length. The incremental train may last for a few beats or for several minutes." These are the bursts of fixed rate pacing (Incremental pacing S1). See: Fogoros chapter on Principles of the Electrophysiology Study

8. In EP the first extrastimuli after a pulse drive train is labeled a/an:
   a. **S1**
   b. **S2**
   c. **PVC**
   d. **Extrasystole**

ANSWER: b. S2. Fogoros says: "The extrastimulus technique consists of introducing one or more premature impulses, each at its own specific coupling interval. The extrastimuli are introduced synchronously either from an intrinsic cardiac impulse or following a short train of incrementally paced impulses (traditionally eight beats). The term S1 (stimulus 1) is used for the incrementally paced impulses or the intrinsic beat from which the first extrastimulus is timed; S2 is used for the first programmed extrastimulus; S3 for the second programmed extrastimulus, etc. This nomenclature (in which, for instance the number 2 is attached to the first extrastimulus) causes a lot of confusion among the uninitiated."

The upper diagram shows a ventricular pulse train (S1) followed by ventricular contractions (V1) and after 8 beats the extrastimulus S2. The lower diagram shows an atrial pulse train (S1) followed by atrial contractions (A1). After 8 beat pulse train the extrastimulus S2 causes an atrial contraction (A2). Then normal sinus rhythm resumes.
See: Fogoros chapter on Principles of the Electrophysiology Study

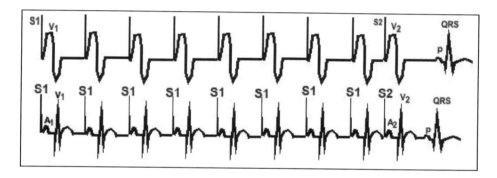

9. When using the auto-decrement feature on the EP stimulator, what does a pause of 2000 ms indicate?
   a. **30 bpm backup pacing**
   b. **2000 ms pause after intrinsic beat**
   c. **Two-second delay between drive trains**
   d. **Decrement down to 2000 ms drive train.**

ANSWER: c. Two-second delay between drive trains. Claris, Bloom, and MicroPace all have this feature in which the stimulator will automatically pace and decrement in between drive trains. This will decrease at whatever interval you program, such as decrementing the S2 by 20 ms on every drive. The pause refers to the interval in between consecutive drives, or a rest period. In this example, after each run (drive train with programmed number of extra stimulus beats) the stimulator will wait 2000 ms or 2 seconds to allow the tissue to recover before pacing again.

10. What does the channel on the bottom of the screen marked S1 and a pacing artifact represent (seen at the arrow)?
  a. Sensing
  b. Stim
  c. Signal Test #1
  d. System Test #1

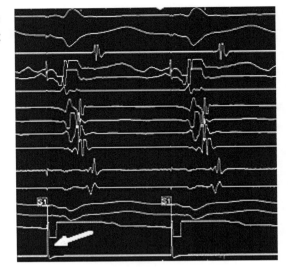

ANSWER: b. Stim, from the stimulator output. Not all physicians want the stim channel displayed. All this channel shows is that we are straight pacing the heart. You can see this by the S1, S1, S1, S1, S1. There is no S2 on this screen which would be an extrastimulus. Remember, this only shows that the catheter is sending out an impulse, not whether the impulse was conducted.

11. What information will the stim channel display?
  a. Capture
  b. Chamber paced
  c. Burst pacing or extrastimuli
  d. Stimulation threshold
  e. Stimulus duration

ANSWER: c. Burst pacing or extrastimuli. Using the stim channel you are unable to determine capture, what chamber is paced, or whether block occurs. Some physicians and/or EP personnel like this channel displayed to show that they are sending out an impulse. The patient's response to that impulse must be evaluated by the ECG and other EGMs.

12. To perform LV pacing during a standard EP study, pacing typically occurs via _____.
  a. RV electrodes placed at the RV septum
  b. His distal electrodes – Max output
  c. Proximal CS electrodes
  d. Distal CS electrodes

ANSWER: b. Distal CS electrodes. If the LV needs to be paced during a standard EP study, it is often achieved via the distal electrodes of the CS catheter. If capture is not obtained, the distal tip of the CS catheter may be advanced down various CS branches (as in CRT) and reattempt pacing. The CS catheter travels in the CS on the posterior aspect of the heart in-between the left atrium and ventricle. Therefore, pacing of the LV may be achieved without obtaining left-heart access.

13. Looking at this EGM, pacing is performed via which catheter?
   a. **High Right Atrium**
   b. **His Bundle**
   c. **Right Ventricle**
   d. **CS**

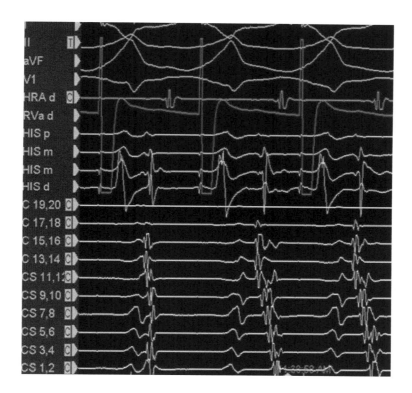

ANSWER: c. RV. Always familiarize yourself with the EGM first.
Arrangement in this example:

- First 4 lines are surface ECGs
- 5th from the top is the HRA (Showing only an atrial deflection)
- 6th is the RVa (showing only ventricular depolarization)
- 7th-10th is the His (showing A, H, and V deflections)
- Distal 10 electrode pairs are in the CS (showing atrial and ventricular deflections).

There is a large pacing artifact on RVa and the wide QRS complex. Don't forget to use your surface ECG. Mark E Josephson teaches, "Look on the outside of the heart first." Likewise,

Murgatroyd teaches us to, "Proceed from the general to the specific. Analyze the surface ECG recordings before looking at the intracardiacs."

In beats #2 and #3 the CS and His catheter shows the V first and the A second.
The HRA only shows A waves, and no pacer spikes. As shown on the diagram below in the LAO projection, the Mitral valve is on the left side of the heart and the Tricuspid on the right. The CS catheter wraps around the Mitral valve (left side of the heart). The similar catheter on the Rt is for a different use that will be described in future chapters. The first electrode pairs (CS 1,2) are on the distal end of the catheter on the far-left lateral side of the heart in the AV groove. The most proximal electrode pair (CS 19,20) is at the CS ostium which originates on the right side. CS catheters come in various electrode configurations, some with 8, 10, or 20 electrodes.

In the lower diagram, the ventricular signal starts with RV pacing and moves eccentrically from distal to proximal along the CS catheter (lower arrow). Then the atrial signal on the His and proximal CS EGMs finally spread to the HRA and the LA (activated last in upper arrow). This is normal (concentric) atrial activation. Study what is normal, then the abnormal will "pop" out at you.

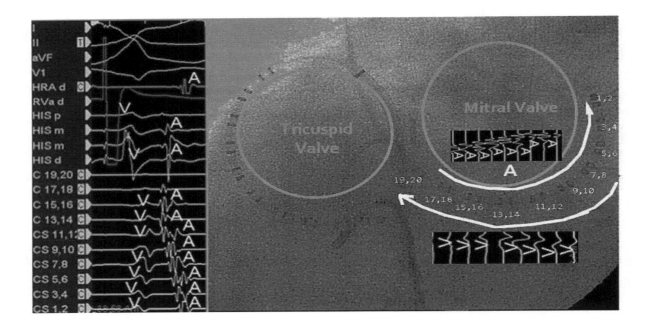

14. At the start of an electrophysiology study the physician may pace the heart from several different areas for baseline measurements. What catheter is being paced in this example?

 a. **High Right Atrium**
 b. **His Bundle**
 c. **Right Ventricle**
 d. **Coronary Sinus**

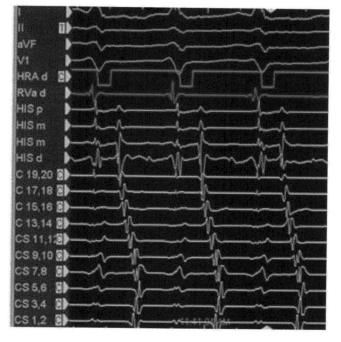

ANSWER: a. High RA. As we just learned, always look at the surface ECG before diving into the intracardiac EGMs. In this example the QRS is very narrow. Ventricular pacing would have a wide QRS complex.

Notice the pacing artifact on the HRA catheter. The wave of depolarization starts in the HRA, His, proximal CS, distal CS, then the RV. This is normal (concentric) activation, right to left and high to low. Notice how all the CS electrograms are labeled in pairs (CS 1,2 CS 3,4… from distal to proximal). Likewise, in the HRA, RVa, and His, they are not labeled as electrode pairs. This is called a bipolar recording configuration. The intracardiac electrogram records the electrical activity between two sets of electrodes (electrode pair). The deflection recorded from the electrode catheter represents depolarization of the cardiac tissue in the immediate vicinity of the catheter's electrodes.

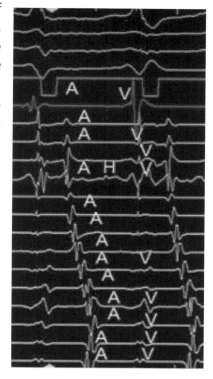

Therefore, the intracardiac electrogram gives precise, localized data on the heart's electrical impulse. (See Fogoros chapter 4, Principles of the Electrophysiology Study). The pacing artifact here is the downstroke on the HRA. It appears to line up with the QRS complex which may be misleading. The HRA is being paced very early, so if the ECG was run at 25mm/sec sweep speed rather than 200, a pacer spike and a bump (P wave) on the T wave would be noticed.

15. This example shows pacing from which catheter?
   a. HRA
   b. HIS
   c. CS
   d. RVa

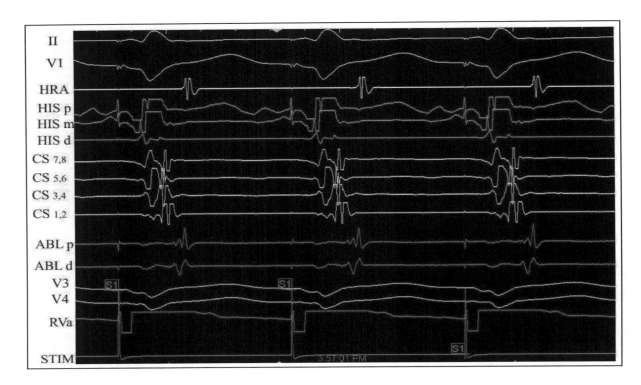

ANSWER: d. RVa. By observing the surface ECG, one can tell by the wide complex QRS and the pacing spike that pacing is occurring on the RVa channel.

Many physicians choose to start their electrophysiology study with ventricular pacing if looking for an SVT. If starting with atrial pacing, you may induce SVT and not be able to complete the entire diagnostic study causing one to miss valuable information and jump to conclusions. Although some SVT can be induced with ventricular pacing; it is not as common. Likewise, if the patient is in the lab for a VT study, pace the atrium first for a complete study.

16. In the previous EGM, the bottom line is the Stim. What information does the Stim contain?
   a. Pacing output
   b. Capture
   c. Stimulation Protocol
   d. Pacing Voltage

ANSWER: a. Pacing output. This is the stim channel. All it shows is that the patient is being paced. It does not show whether there is capture. Here it shows S1, S1, S1, S1.... which is straight fixed-rate pacing (burst pacing). If it was extrastimulus testing, you would also see an S2 after the S1s. This is termed incremental pacing, which overdrives the spontaneous rhythm (pacing faster than the patient's intrinsic rate). This allows the observation and measurement of impulse conduction and tissue refractoriness during steady-state conditions, and the recovery of normal function after the cessation of pacing. Note in the EGM that the A follows V indicating retrograde VA conduction. See. Murgatroyd chapter on The Basic Electrophysiology Study

17. What chamber is being paced on this EGM?
   a. **HRA**
   b. **HIS**
   c. **CS**
   d. **RVa**

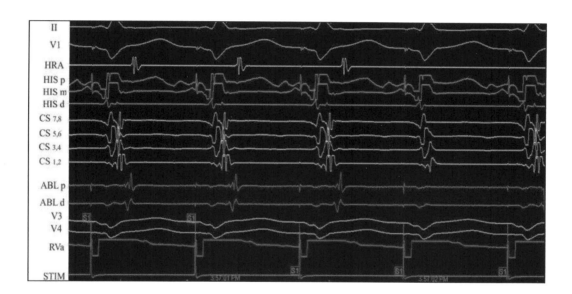

ANSWER: d. RVa. Notice the pacing spike (stim) occurs at the same time as the RVa which also shows paced morphology (broad QRS with LBBB pattern). One can clearly see that none of the other channels depolarize at the same time as the pacing spike. There is ventricular capture throughout the EGM. The stim impulses (S1, S1, S1....) line up with the pacing spike throughout the EGM and ECG.

We determine capture by observing that every pacing spike on the surface ECG is followed by a ventricular depolarization. This is seen on all the channels. Notice that pacing spike on the RVa channel (15th line) lines up exactly with the stim channel.

If there were no capture the surface ECG would be narrow (unless baseline wide complex) and would not immediately follow the pacing spike. This would also show on the RVa channel by just a pacing spike but no following waveform. The 3rd beat shows VA block.

18. The EGM shows catheters placed in the His, CS, and RV apex. What catheter is being paced?
   a. Ablation catheter
   b. CS
   c. HRA
   d. RV

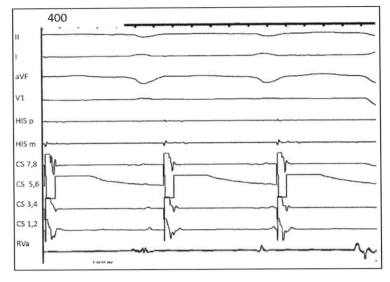

ANSWER: b. CS. Note the large pacing artifact on the CS, which captures the low RA at the ostium of the CS. The His catheter is not in a very reliable location, with little signal for us to use. Adjusting this catheter may help the physician determine the type and/or location of any induced tachycardia. There is a wide QRS complex on the surface ECG which may make you think ventricular pacing. But the patient may be experiencing a rate-related bundle branch block or have an underlying BBB which would be noted on the baseline 12-lead ECG. Clearly, we are not pacing the RVa because the RV channel has no pacing spike before the small V deflection. Typically, there will be a large ventricular signal on the RVa channel.

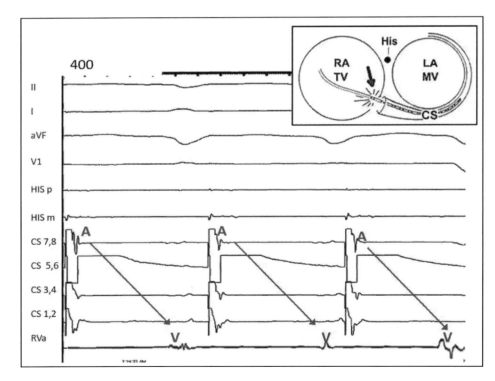

19. Which patient below has normal electrogram measurements in milliseconds?

a.	AA 673,	QRS 105,	QT 401,	AH 73,	HV 48
b.	AA 673,	QRS 401,	QT 105,	AH 48,	HV 73
c.	AA 673,	QRS 105,	QT 401,	AH 130,	HV 25
d.	AA 673,	QRS 86,	QT 401,	AH 73,	HV 105

ANSWER: a. Normal Measurements:

- AA – Total Cycle length
- QRS - <100 ms normal
- QT - approximately 400 ms
- AH – 55-125 ms
- HV – 35-55 ms

Sinus Node Testing

1. To evaluate SA node automaticity in the EP lab we perform:
   a. **SNRT or CSNRT measurements**
   b. **Atrial ERP or RRP measurements**
   c. **AV conduction mapping**
   d. **Atrial conduction mapping**

ANSWER: a. SNRT or CSNRT measurements. Fogoros says: "the electrophysiology study can be used to assess the automaticity of the SA node. The measurement
designed to do this is the sinus node recovery time (SNRT).... two indices are commonly used to relate SNRT to the BCL. The first is the corrected sinus node recovery time (CSNRT), which is calculated by subtracting the cycle length of the patient's sinus rhythm in ms from the SNRT. Thus: CSNRT = SNRT - BCL

The upper normal value of CSNRT is usually considered to be 525 ms.... The second index commonly used for assessing SA nodal function is the ratio of SNRT to the BCL (SNRT/BCL) x 100%) A ratio of greater than 16% is usually considered abnormal." See: Fogoros chapter on Principles of the Electrophysiology Study

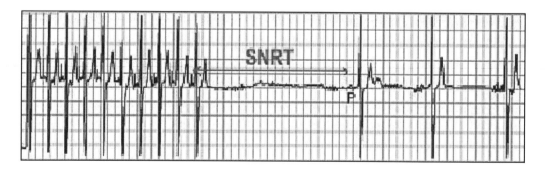

2. An EP test indicative of severe sinus node dysfunction is:
   a. Atrial FRP > 200 ms
   b. AERP   < 200 ms
   c. CSNRT > 525 ms
   d. CSNRT < 525 ms

ANSWER: c. CSNRT >525 ms is abnormal. CSNRT = SNRT – BCL. The upper normal value of CSNRT is usually considered to be 525 ms. See: Fogoros chapter on EP Testing for Bradyarrhythmias

3. What EP pacing maneuver is used to measure SNRT?
   a. Overdrive suppression
   b. Programmed stimulation
   c. Parahisian pacing
   d. Evaluating antegrade AV conduction

ANSWER: a. Overdrive suppression. Fogoros says: "Measurement of the SNRT is based on the phenomenon of overdrive suppression, which is the pause induced in an automatic focus by a temporarily overdriving pacemaker. With an electrode in the high right atrium near the SA node, pacing is initiated at a rate slightly faster than the basic sinus rate. Pacing is continued at a constant rate for at least 30 seconds and then is abruptly stopped. The recovery interval (The interval from the last paced atrial complex to the first spontaneous SA node depolarization) represents the degree of overdrive suppression induced by pacing." The SA node becomes fatigued by the fast rate and takes some time to recover - Sinus Node Recovery Time. See: Fogoros chapter on Principles of the Electrophysiology Study

4. The technique to measure the SA node conduction time (SACT) uses:
   a. Isuprel to increase the sinus rate
   b. A High RA extrastimuli to reset the sinus node
   c. A 30 second HRA pulse train, just faster than the sinus rate
   d. The conduction time between high RA and low RA electrodes

ANSWER: b. A High RA extrastimuli to reset the sinus node. Murgatroyd says, "The technique (measuring SACT) depends on resetting the sinus node with single extrastimuli delivered to the high right atrium.... sinoatrial conduction time (SACT) is intended to detect delayed conduction between sinus node and adjacent atrial tissue." See: Murgatroyd, Chapter on, The Basic Electrophysiology Study

6. A patient's sinus node recovery time was measured at 1175 ms, sinus cycle length 930 ms, QRS duration 86 ms, and HV of 52. What is the CSNRT?
    a. 1.26 sec
    b. 1089 ms
    c. 245 ms
    d. 1037 ms

ANSWER: c. 245 ms.
CSNRT (corrected sinus node recovery time) is SNRT – BCL = 1175-930= 245.
SNRT considered normal <1500 ms and CSNRT <550

7. The SNRT evaluates sinus node automaticity. CSNRT is "corrected". What is the upper limit of normal for the CSNRT?
    a. 525-550 ms
    b. 600-700 ms
    c. 725-800 ms
    d. 1000 ms or longer

ANSWER: a. 525-550 ms depending on author. Fogoros says, "A conservative upper limit of 'normal' for the SNRT, above which most experts would agree that the SA node dysfunction is present, is 1500 ms.... the corrected sinus node recovery time (CSNRT), which is calculated simply by subtracting the patients BCL from the SNRT. Thus: CSNRT = SNRT - BCL. By convention, the upper limit of 'normal' for the CSNRT is 525 ms. In other words, the SNRT should be no more than 525 ms longer than the BCL"
Murgatroyd lists 550 ms as the high limit of normal CSNRT. See: Fogoros or Murgatroyd chapters on SA Node.

8. SACT measurement is used to evaluate a patient for:
    a. SA node exit block
    b. Dual AV pathways
    c. SA node automaticity
    d. Retrograde SA node conduction
    e. Sick Sinus Syndrome

ANSWER: a. SA node exit block is evaluated by the SACT (Sino Atrial Conduction Time). Fogoros says: "Prolonged SACT's are thought to indicate a propensity for SA nodal exit block (in which impulses are formed normally within the SA node but do not penetrate through the perinodal tissue to the atrial myocardium.) ..... Although SNRT assesses SA nodal automaticity (its intrinsic ability to continue firing), the measurement of sinoatrial conduction time (SACT)

was developed to assess SA conduction (the time it takes to conduct that impulse to the atrium). If the SA node fires normally, but it is blocked getting out of the node area, that is SA node exit block."
See: Fogoros chapter on EP Testing for Bradyarrhythmias

9. The SACT (Sino Atrial Conduction Time) is calculated by the formula:
   a. **(SNRT - BCL)**
   b. **(SNRT - BCL) / 2**
   c. **(Return interval - BCL)**
   d. **(Return interval - BCL) /2**

ANSWER: d. (Return interval - BCL) / 2. Fogoros says: "To measure SACT, an electrode is placed in the high right atrium near the SA node and atrial pacing is used to depolarize and thus reset the SA node. The subsequent return interval (the time from the last paced atrial depolarization to the first spontaneous SA nodal depolarization) is assumed to reflect the sum of the time it takes for the paced impulse to penetrate into the SA node (at which time it resets the SA node), plus the basic sinus cycle length, plus the time it takes for the subsequent spontaneous beat to penetrate out of the SA node. Assuming the time of penetration into and out of the node are equivalent, then:
Return interval = BCL + 2 SACT.... A normal SACT is considered to be 50 to 125 ms."
See: Fogoros chapter on EP Testing for Bradyarrhythmias

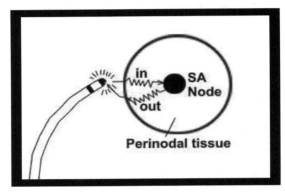

10. SNRT and CSNRT should be measured at several cycle lengths. In the measurements below what CSNRT should be reported?
   a. **CL 600 ms, SNRT 1100, CSNRT 500**
   b. **CL 500 ms, SNRT 1010, CSRNT 510**
   c. **CL 450 ms, SNRT 970, CSNRT 520**
   d. **CL 400, SNRT 930, CSNRT 530**
   e. **CL 350, SNRT 870, CSNRT 520**

ANSWER d. 530. The upper limit of normal is 525 ms. Here 530 is the highest number and the only CSNRT outside of the normal range. Fogoros says: "the electrophysiology study can be used to assess the automaticity of the SA node. The measurement designed to do this is the sinus node recovery time (SNRT).... two indices are commonly used to relate SNRT to the

Basic Cycle Length (BCL). The first is the corrected sinus node recovery time (CSNRT), which is calculated by subtracting the cycle length of the patient's sinus rhythm in ms from the SNRT. CSNRT = SNRT − BCL

The upper normal value of CSNRT is usually considered to be 525 ms.... The second index commonly used for assessing SA nodal function is the ratio of SNRT to the BCL (SNRT/BCL) x 100%) A ratio of greater than 16-% is usually considered abnormal."
See: Fogoros chapter on Principles of the Electrophysiology Study

Block & ERP:

1. In this EGM, decremental pacing in the third beat results in: (select two answers)
   a. **VA Block**
   b. **AV Block**
   c. **PVC**
   d. **Sinus P**
   e. **Ventricular Fusion**
   f. **Atrial Fusion**

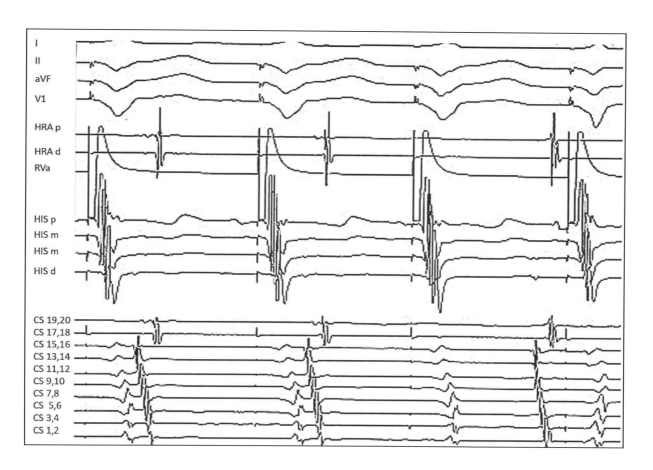

ANSWER: a. VA Block & e. Ventricular Fusion. Note pacing from the RVa catheter spikes resulting in a wide QRS on the surface V1 lead.

All CS channels have V's followed by A's. On the third paced beat there is a V with a much-delayed A to follow and a slightly different morphology So, the retrograde A must have been blocked. Wherever the last A comes from we see it first in CD 15-16 near the CS ostium. This last A passes the AV node partially depolarizing the ventricle, making the fourth QRS is a narrower beat on the surface leads indicating a fusion of antegrade and retrograde V activation. The two impulses meet coming from each direction. This causes a QRS that is neither as wide as a ventricular paced beat nor as narrow as a normal sinus QRS complex. It is a "fusion" of the two.

2. This was recorded on a 27-year-old brought to the EP lab for a wide complex tachycardia. Pacing is occurring from CS 7,8. What happens on the third beat?
   a. **AV Block**
   b. **VA Block**
   c. **LBBB**
   d. **RBBB**

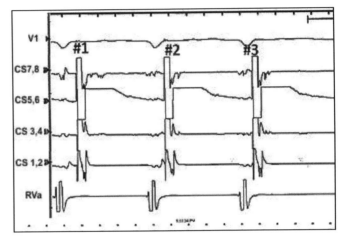

ANSWER: a. AV Block. Note the A and V deflections on the CS 7,8 channels. Pacing is from the proximal CS in the atrium. Since the CS catheter is in the AV groove it records both chambers. There is a clear ventricular signal on the RVa channel followed by CS pacing. Note the long AV interval and lengthening of the AV interval until block occurs – Wenckebach. This decremental property of the AVN (AV block or AVNERP) is a normal finding. Everyone's AV node will block at one point. This helps prevent rapid depolarization of the ventricles in the case of a rapid atrial rate. E.g., If a patient were to go into atrial fibrillation, if the AV node conducted every beat down to the ventricle, then the patient could accelerate into ventricular tachycardia/fibrillation. An atrial rate of 200 or so would be too fast for the ventricles to effectively pump.

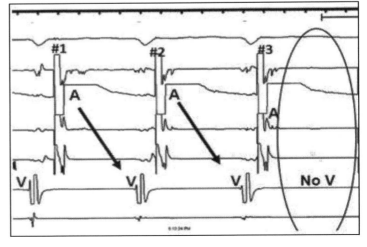

3. At the start of the procedure on this 65-year-old male, what happens on the fourth beat during incremental pacing?

   a. Mobitz I heart block
   b. Mobitz II heart block
   c. VA block
   d. AV block

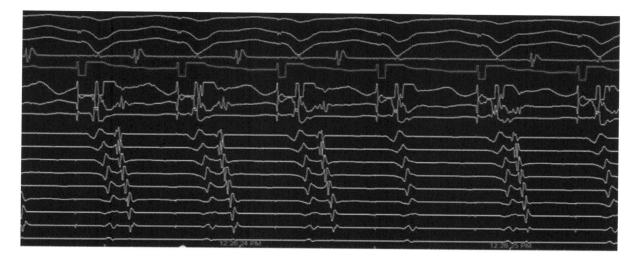

ANSWER: c. VA Block. Ventricular Pacing is occurring. Notice the pacing spike on the RVa channel, and in front of every QRS complex, there is a wide appearance (LBBB) morphology, and ventricular signals on the His and CS channel; therefore, capture is occurring. Note the fourth beat is missing the A on the HRA, His, and CS channel.

    This example shows retrograde conduction over the AV node or VA conduction from the ventricles to the atrium. It is not usually obvious to what extent decremental (delayed) VA conduction is due to delay in the His-Purkinje system, and to what extent it is due to delay in the AV node. However, in some cases a retrograde His electrogram can be used. Most often the His is buried in the V during ventricular pacing (such as in this example), but sometimes one may see a prolongation in the VH interval. In retrograde conduction during incremental ventricular pacing, block usually occurs in the AV node (HA interval prolongation). See: Murgatroyd's chapter on the Basic Electrophysiology Study.

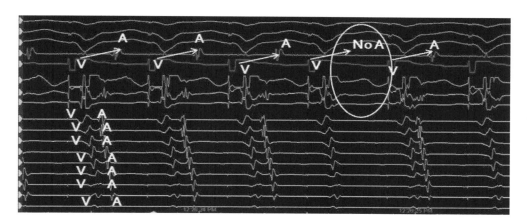

4. During post ablation testing with incremental pacing, the following EGM shows:
   a. **RVOT VT (RV outflow tract ventricular tachycardia)**
   b. **Jump w/ Echo**
   c. **AV Block**
   d. **VA Block**

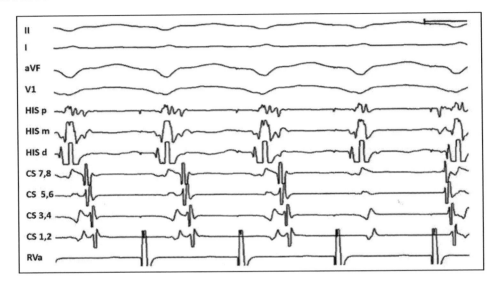

ANSWER: d. VA block. We are capturing the V as noted by the pacing spike on the RVa catheter and the wide QRS complex. We have 1:1 VA conduction up to the 3rd ventricular paced beat which does not conduct to the atrium. Lengthening is not always noticed before block occurs. The arrows drawn below clarify direction of conduction and block like a ladder diagram. Note on the CS there are two signals; the first is the V the second is the A.

According to Murgatroyd, "Ventricular pacing provides an opportunity to evaluate retrograde conduction over the His-Purkinje system and the AV node, and to detect the presence of accessory pathways. Stimulation is conventionally performed at the right ventricular apex, from where impulses rapidly invade the His-Purkinje system via the distal right bundle branch. If stimulation is performed at another location, activation may take longer to travel to the AV node, and allowance must be made for this in analyzing measurements. "See: Murgatroyd, chapter on "Basic Electrophysiology Study"

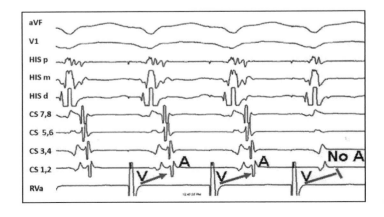

5. While performing incremental atrial pacing on this 14-year-old patient this unlabeled EGM was recorded. You should note:

    a. AV Block second degree type I

    b. AV Block second degree type 2

    c. VA Block

    d. CHB

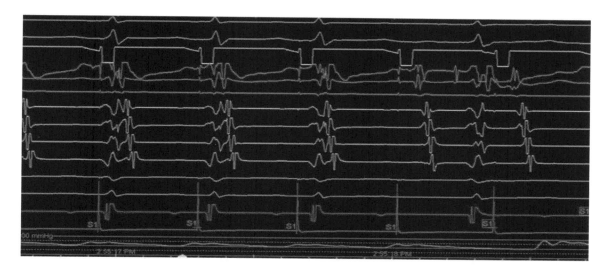

ANSWER: a. AV block second degree type I, Wenckebach. This MD is pacing off the HRA... notice the pacing artifact, the atrial waveform, and a narrow QRS. The S1 Stim on the bottom just shows pacing, not capture. Notice the block occurs in the AV node. You may notice the AV interval get progressively longer until block... this shows the decremental properties of the AV node, unlike accessory pathways which do not decrement. They conduct all or none. This is a different catheter set up than the previous examples based on physician preference. This MD also uses an arterial pressure line on the bottom. An arterial pressure waveform is nice to have since some patients do not tolerate rapid pacing. There is about 200 ms delay from V to arterial pulse.

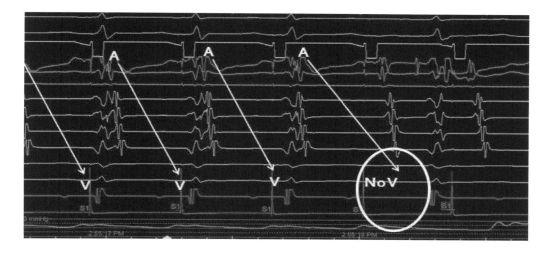

6. In this EGM, what occurs during incremental pacing?

   a. **AERP**
   b. **AV Wenckebach**
   c. **VERP**
   d. **VA Block**

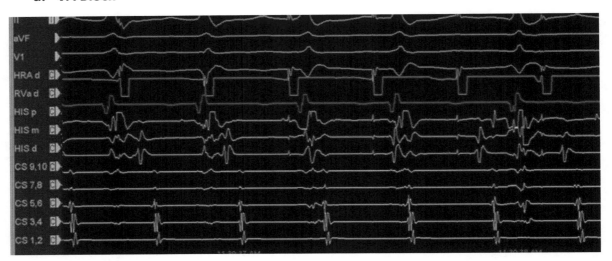

ANSWER: b. AV Wenckebach. Note the fifth V is skipped. AV Block is a normal property of the AV node. Notice how the AV interval continues to get longer and longer until the point of block. This is Wenckebach block, also referred to as AVNERP. Sometimes it
is hard to tell exactly which A goes with which V when it is decremented (stretched out) to this point. HINT: Always start looking at the beginning of the screen (of the drive train if you have that option) and follow through every beat.

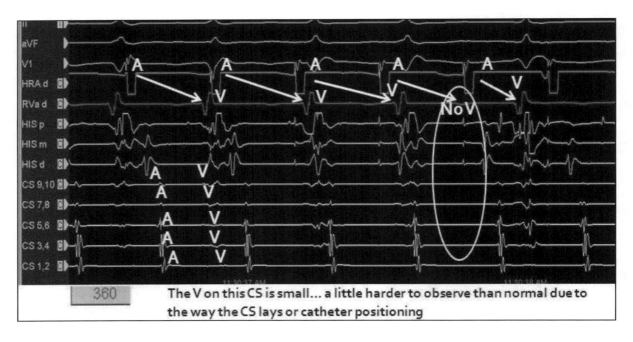

The V on this CS is small... a little harder to observe than normal due to the way the CS lays or catheter positioning

7. In the EGM with decremental CS pacing, what is observed?
   a. **AV Block**
   b. **Initiation of AVNRT**
   c. **VA Block**
   d. **CHB**

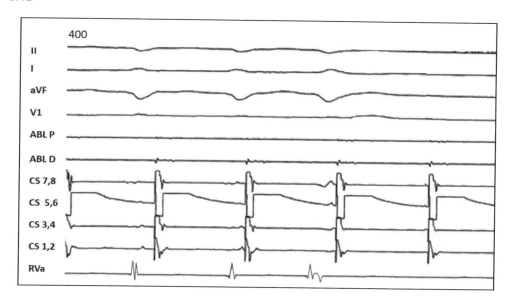

ANSWER: a. AV block. If there was a longer EGM to look at, you would notice the AV progressively lengthened until block occurs. Always start looking at the beginning and walk your way through the EGM to see which A goes with which V. If you jump straight to the end, you may miss valuable information. The ventricular signal in this example is small and harder to visualize. The surface ECG indicates that there is a missing QRS complex in beat 4. A lot of information may be gained from pacing in the atrium such as: assessment of SA nodal automaticity and conductivity, assessment of AV nodal conductivity and refractoriness (such as in this example), assessment of His-Purkinje system conductivity and refractoriness, and induction of atrial arrhythmias. See: Fogoros: chapter on Principles of the Electrophysiology Study

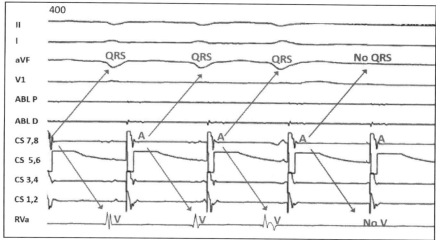

8. **Where is the block located in the first three beats of the displayed example?**
   a. **Above the AV Node**
   b. **Below the AV Node**
   c. **AERP**
   d. **In the Bundle Branches**

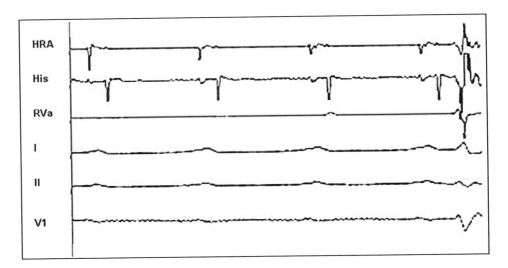

ANSWER: b. Below AV node. Notice the A and His then no V; therefore, it blocks after the HIS infrahisian block. Infrahisian block is more likely than parahisian block to degenerate to CHB. This is an indication for permanent pacing (PPM implantation).

Fogoros says, "In stark contrast to AV nodal block, block occurring distally to the AV node is potentially life-threatening. The potential lethal effect of distal heart block can be attributed to the unreliable, unstable, and slow escape pacemakers that tend to accompany this condition." See: Fogoros chapter on SA Node, AV Node, and His-Purkinje system

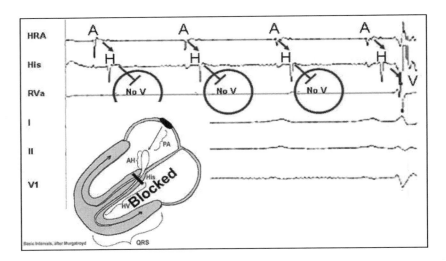

9. On this EGM, RV pacing starts on beat #3. What is the location of the block?
   a. **Above the AV Node**
   b. **Below the AV Node**
   c. **AERP**
   d. **Bundle Branches**

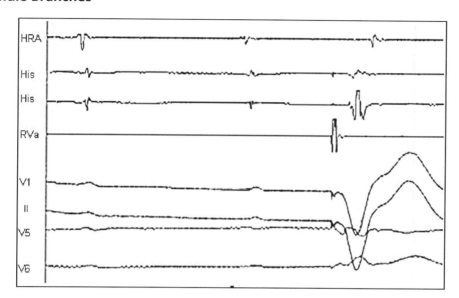

ANSWER: a. Above the AV Node. Notice on the ECG the two P waves with no QRS to follow, which shows block, but you need the EGM to specify at which level it occurred. There are two initial A waves with no following His deflection (assuming the His catheter is in a reliable location). Block above the His, unless symptomatic, typically does not require a PPM (permanent pacemaker). It is unlikely to progress to CHB.

Fogoros says, "conduction disturbances in the AV node most often have acute, transient, and reversible causes. Ischemia or infarction involving the right coronary artery can cause AV nodal block. Acute rheumatic fever and other cardiac inflammatory conditions can also produce transient AV nodal block. While drugs that affect AV nodal function (Digoxin, B Blockers, and Calcium blockers) may produce first-degree AV block; higher degrees of drug-induced AV nodal block suggest underlying intrinsic AV nodal dysfunction. Since AV nodal block is usually reversible, it can frequently be managed simply by dealing with the underlying cause; although sometimes temporary pacing support is required in the meantime." See: Fogoros: chapter on SA Node, AV Node, and His-Purkinje system

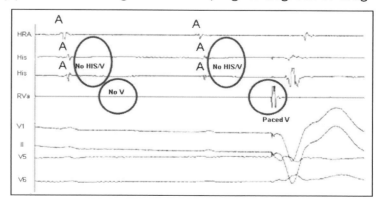

10. On the following patient with suspected AVNRT, what does the third beat suggest?

   a. **Induction of AVNRT**
   b. **VA block**
   c. **AV block**
   d. **AERP**

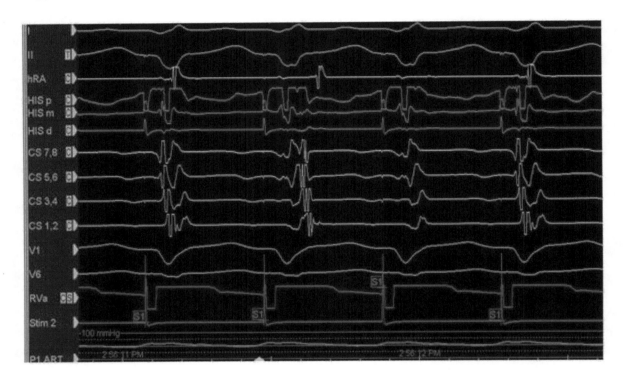

ANSWER: b. VA block. On the stim channel notice the S1, S1, S1. This shows incremental pacing. Ventricular capture is occurring as noted by the wide QRS and the ventricular signals. As the physician continues to pace faster and faster the AV node will eventually block, which is noticed on the third beat. Notice that the first atrial signal is shown on the HIS catheter, followed by CS 7,8 (proximal), CS 5,6 CS 3,4 to CS 1,2 (distal). This is the normal concentric activation; up through the His and spreading concentrically right to left.

Extrastimulus Testing:

1. What do you observe during extrastimulus testing in this example? (The last beat of the drive train and S2 are displayed)

   a. **Infrahisian Block**

   b. **AVNERP**

   c. **AERP**

   d. **APERP**

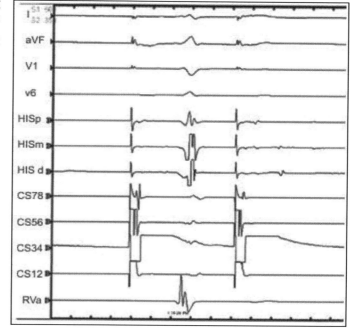

ANSWER: a. Infrahisian Block. The last beat shows an atrial deflection and His deflection, with no ventricular deflection to follow. This shows the block occurred below the level of the compact AV node. This is an important observation because unlike Wenckebach block, block below the AV node will likely progress to complete heart block. This finding that occurred repeatedly was an indication for permanent pacemaker implantation.

Morton F Arnsdorf, MD, says: prolongation of the H-V interval is also not a reliable predictor of sudden death.

Nevertheless, some investigators believe that the symptomatic patient with bifascicular block and an H-V interval equal to or greater than 100 ms is a candidate for permanent pacing." See: (http://cmbi.bjmu.edu.cn)

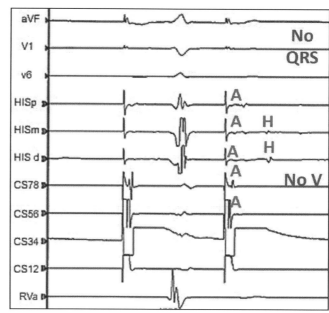

2. On the electrogram below measure the cycle length and coupling interval.

Cycle length= _____, Coupling interval=_____.

   a. 200 ms, 450 ms
   b. 250 ms, 450 ms
   c. 450 ms, 200 ms
   d. 450 ms, 250 ms

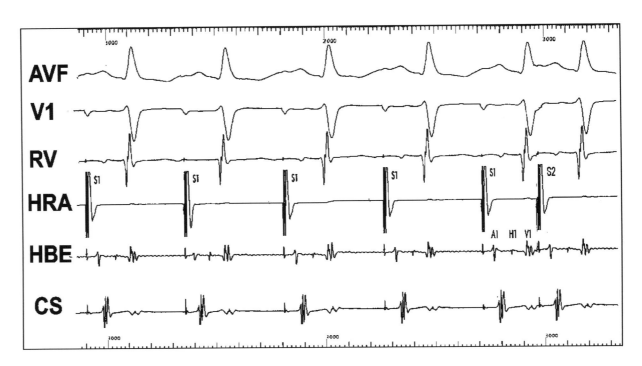

ANSWER: d. CL=450 ms, Coupling Interval = 250 ms. Fogoros says: "Programmed stimulation consists of two general types of pacing: incremental and extrastimulus pacing. Incremental pacing (or burst pacing) consists of introducing a train of paced impulses at a fixed cycle length. The incremental train may last for a few beats or for several minutes.... The extrastimulus technique consists of introducing one or more premature impulses, each at its own specific coupling interval. The extrastimuli are introduced synchronously either from an intrinsic cardiac impulse or following a short train of incrementally paced impulses (traditionally eight beats)."

In the diagram you see the pulse train of rapidly paced beats followed by the even more rapid premature extrastimulus. Measure the RR interval of each type of beat. All the S1 pulse train beats are 450 ms apart, and the extrastimulus S2 is 250 ms from the last S1. S1-S1= 450, S1-S2=250 ms. These are easiest to measure between the clear HRA pacing spikes using a caliper. Note the 4 spikes on the HBE recording S1, A, H and V.
See: Fogoros chapter on Treatment of Arrhythmias

3. Match the refractory period to its definition (Note HPS = His Purkinje System):
   a. **AERP**
   b. **AFRP**
   c. **AVNERP**
   d. **HPS ERP**
   e. **VERP**

   1. **Longest S1-S2 interval that fails to capture the ventricle**
   2. **Longest H1-H2 not propagating to the ventricles**
   3. **Shortest H10H2 in response to any A1-A2**
   4. **Shortest A1-A2 interval recorded at a designated site (often the HB region) before failure of A1-A2 to capture the atrium**
   5. **Longest A1-A2 interval that fails to achieve atrial capture**

CORRECTLY MATCHED ANSWERS ARE:

AERP: 5. Longest A1-A2 interval that fails to achieve atrial capture

AFRP: 4. Shortest A1-A2 interval recorded at a designated site (often the HB region) before failure of A1-A2 to capture the atrium

AVNERP: 3. Shortest H1-H2 in response to any A1-A2

HPS ERP: 2. Longest H1-H2 not propagating to the ventricles

VERP: 1. Longest S1-S2 interval that fails to capture the ventricle

Note in the diagram how stimulation in the relative refractory period (RRP) of beat two causes a slowed and deformed QRS, like a PVC. In the last beat a stimulus falls in the absolute refractory period and does not produce any response. Artificial pacemakers have similar refractory and alert periods. * Indicates pacing. See: Issa, chapter on "EP testing"

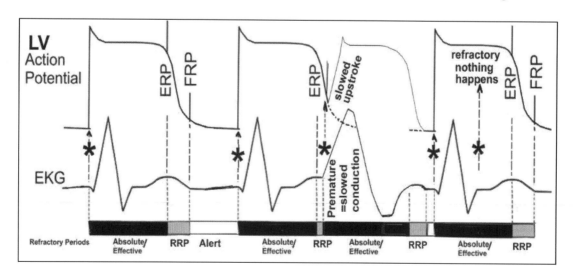

4. What type of pacing maneuver is being performed in these two EGMs?
   a. Ventricular extrastimulus testing
   b. Atrial extrastimulus testing
   c. Burst Pacing
   d. Ramp Pacing

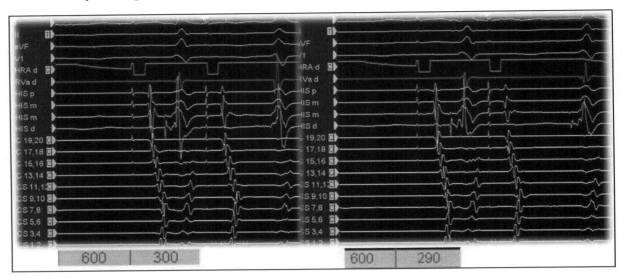

ANSWER: b. Atrial Extrastimulus Testing. The first eight beats of the drive train are at rate of 600 ms (only the last drive train impulse is displayed) with a PAC at 300 ms. The second drive is eight beats at 600 ms with a PAC coming in 290 ms later. We are decrementing the PAC by 10 ms with each drive train.
   - Ventricular Extrastimulus Testing: Drive train in the Ventricle with a PVC
   - Atrial Extrastimulus Testing: Drive train in the Atrium with a PAC
   - Burst: Pacing at a fixed rate faster than the underlying rate
   - Ramp: Pacing that increases during the cycle ex. 360, 350, 340, 330....

5. With the mapping catheter positioned correctly, when is the right bundle branch potential normally seen?
   a. 5-10 ms later than the H, and <40 ms before the V
   b. 15-20 ms later than the H, and <30 ms before the V
   c. 5-10 ms before the H, and <40 ms later than the V
   d. 15-20 ms before the H, and <30 ms later than the V

ANSWER: b. 15-20 ms later than the H, and <30 ms before the V. It may be necessary to ablate the RBB in a patient with BBR VT. Issa says, "The RB potential can be distinguished from the HB potential by the absence of or minimal atrial electrogram on the recording and presence of a sharp deflection inscribed at least 15 to 20 milliseconds later than the His potential. An RB-V interval value of <30 milliseconds may not be a reliable marker of the RB potential in

these patients because disease of the HPS can cause prolongation of the RB-V conduction time."
See: Issa, chapter on BB Reentry

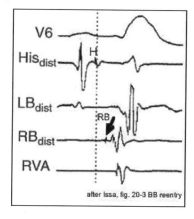

6. In incremental atrial pacing or premature atrial stimuli placed during the relative refractory period, as cycle length decreases, the PR interval normally ____ and the AH interval normally ____.

   a. **Increases, increases**
   b. **Increases, stays the same**
   c. **Decreases, increases**
   d. **Decreases, stays the same**

ANSWER: a. Increases, increases. This is decremental conduction. As incremental pacing rate increases the AV node shows fatigue and begins to decrement and lengthen the AH & PR intervals. The HV interval does not change. Eventually it blocks, first with Wenckebach then with higher degrees of fixed ratio block.

This diagram shows that with exercise or Isuprel the PR & AH intervals initially decrease, #2 & #3 with peeling of refractoriness. Then as you enter the partially refractory period at more rapid paced rates, decremental conduction starts, with longer PR intervals in #4 & #5, and eventually begins to block at ERP #6.

Issa says, "Progressively premature AES (atrial extrastimulus) results in prolongation of PR and AH intervals, with inverse relationship between the AES coupling interval (A1-A2) and the AH interval (A2-H2). The shorter the coupling interval of the AES, the longer the A2-H2 interval. More premature AES can block in the AVN with no conduction to the ventricle (defining AVN ERP). .... The normal response to rate-incremental atrial pacing is for the PR and AH intervals to increase gradually as the pacing CL decreases, until AVN Wenckebach block appears. With further decrease in the pacing CL, higher degrees of AV block

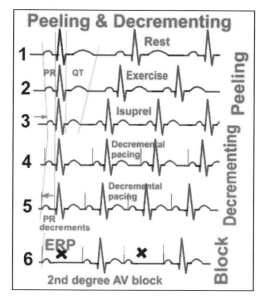

(2:1 or 3:1) can appear. Infranodal conduction (HV interval) remains unaffected...." See: Issa, chapter on EP Testing, Atrial stimulation

7. With Isuprel administration or exercise the PR interval normally_____ the AH interval _____ and the HV interval _____.
   a. Increases, increases, increases
   b. Increases, increases, stays the same
   c. Decreases, decreases, decreases
   d. Decreases, decreases, stays the same

ANSWER: d. Decreases, decreases, stays the same. Fogoros says, "Autonomic tone affects both refractory periods and conduction velocity. An increase in sympathetic tone increases the conduction velocity and decreases the refractory periods throughout the heart. An increase in parasympathetic tone decreases conduction velocity and increases the refractory periods. Here again, there is a differential effect on the AV node, which is far more richly supplied by parasympathetic fibers than most of the heart is. Thus, parasympathetic tone has a disproportionate effect on the AV node." See: Fogoros, chapter on Principles of EP Study

Sympathetic stimulation super-charges everything including increasing the speed of conduction. Likewise, because of neural and hormonal effects, exercise speeds conduction, shortening the PR and AH interval. That is opposite to the effect of rapid pacing, which fatigues the AV node, slows AV conduction, and increases the AH interval. This latter is termed "decremental conduction."

Don't get confused between rapid heart rates due to exercise/Isuprel and rapid heart rates caused by pacing. The first increases conduction, the latter decreases it. See "Peeling & Decrementing" diagram in previous question. Exercise, Isuprel, adrenalin and sympathetic stimulation are similar, they stimulate contraction and conduction. Of course, the parasympathetic being the opposing autonomic system does the opposite, it reduces contraction and conduction, and the AV node is oversupplied with parasympathetic fibers.

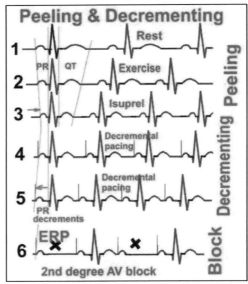

8. In decremental pacing of the RA, as cycle length decreases (faster) in the relative refractory period, the AH interval normally _____ and the HV interval normally _____.
   a. Increases, increases
   b. Increases, stays the same
   c. Decreases, increases
   d. Decreases, stays the same

ANSWER: b. Increases, stays the same. Remember the A2-H2 is a measure of AV node refractoriness. Note in the Response to AES graph how as you get closer to AV ERP the A2-H2 values increase (decremental conduction) but the H2V2 values stay the same. The rapidly rising part of the graph is believed to be due to slow pathway conduction. This is the most common type I of response. In other individuals there may be a jump. Or in rare individuals the H2-V2 may increase due to refractoriness in the HPS system. In all cases the PR interval lengthens because it is the sum of the AH and HV conduction times.

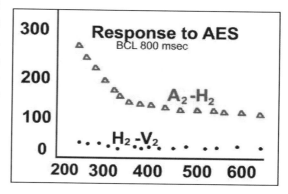

Issa says, "The normal response to rate-incremental atrial pacing is for the PR and AH intervals to increase gradually as the pacing CL decreases, until AVN Wenckebach block appears.... Infranodal conduction (HV interval) remains unaffected." See: Issa, chapter on EP Testing, Atrial stimulation

9. In most cardiac tissue (muscle and purkinje), shorter cycle lengths normally _____ refractory periods. In the AV node shorter cycle lengths normally _____ refractory periods.
   a. Increase, increase
   b. Increase, decrease
   c. Decrease, increase
   d. Decrease, decrease

ANSWER: c. Decrease, increase. Fogoros says, "For most tissue, shorter cycle lengths (i.e., faster heart rates) decrease refractory periods. The glaring exception to this general rule is the AV node, in which shorter cycle lengths increase refractory periods." That is why the QT & PR intervals normally shorten with exercise (until you approach ERP with extrastimulus testing, then PR lengthens). See: Fogoros, chapter on Principles of EP Study

10. What is it called when conduction time of the impulse propagating through cardiac tissue decreases as the tissue cycle length shortens? This is usually true of atrial, His purkinje, and ventricular tissue, but not the AV node.
   a. Increased AVNERP
   b. AVNERP lengthening
   c. Incremental conduction
   d. Decremental conduction
   e. Peeling of refractoriness

ANSWER: e. Peeling of refractoriness. Issa says, "Normally, refractoriness of the atrial, HPS, and ventricular tissue is related to the basic drive CL (i.e., the ERP shortens with decreasing basic drive CL). This phenomenon is termed peeling of refractoriness and is most marked in the HPS." Consider how the PR and QT intervals shorten at faster heart rates, speeding everything up. This is the opposite of decremental conduction. See: Issa, chapter on Programmed Stimulation

Murgatroyd says, "This is the reason that Wenckebach-type conduction indicates block in the AV node, while sudden loss of conduction not preceded by slowing (Mobitz type II) suggests block in the His-Purkinje system." See: Murgatroyd, Basic Electrophysiology Study

11. When conduction time of the impulse propagating through the AVN increases as the atrial cycle length (CL) shortens it is termed:
   a. **Increased AVNERP**
   b. **AVNERP lengthening**
   c. **Incremental conduction**
   d. **Decremental conduction**
   e. **Peeling of refractoriness**

ANSWER: d. Decremental conduction. Issa says that the AV node "exhibits what has been called decremental conduction in which the conduction time of the impulse propagating through the AVN increases as the atrial cycle length (CL) shortens....[In contrast] refractoriness of the atrial, HPS, and ventricular tissue is directly related to the basic drive CL (i.e., the ERP shortens with decreasing basic drive CL). This phenomenon is termed peeling of refractoriness and is most marked in the HPS."

"In contrast, the AVN ERP increases with increasing basic drive CL because of the fatigue phenomenon, which results because AVN refractoriness is time-dependent and exceeds its action potential duration (unlike HPS refractoriness). Additionally, AVN refractory periods are labile and can be markedly affected by the autonomic tone. On the other hand, the response of AVN FRP to changes in pacing CL is variable, but tends to decrease with decreasing pacing CL. This paradox occurs because the FRP is not a true measure of refractoriness encountered by an atrial extrastimulus (AES; A2); it is significantly determined by the AVN conduction time of the basic drive beat (A1-H1); the longer the A1-H1, the shorter the calculated FRP at any A2-H2." See: Issa, chapter on Programmed Stimulation

12. This graph taken during atrial extrastimulus testing, plots the atrial response to a S2 after a drive train. Match the name of each measurement to its point (arrows) on the graph.

   a. **Open circle at 200 ms S2**
   b. **Black circle at 270 ms S2**
   c. **Black circle at 275 ms S2**
   d. **Atrial RRP**
   e. **Atrial ERP**
   f. **Atrial FRP**

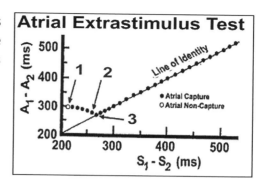

CORRECTLY MATCHED ANSWERS ARE:

1. Atrial ERP (AERP: Atria fails to depolarize) coupling S1-S2 interval of 200 ms. This is a stimulus-to-stimulus measurement i.e., S1-S2 on horizontal axis.

2. Atrial RRP 260 ms (Latent period starts) relative refractory period coupling interval S2 at 260 ms. This is a "stimulus to stimulus" measurement i.e., S1-S2 on horizontal axis.

3. Atrial FRP 270 ms (decremental conduction begins) functional refractory period coupling interval of 270 ms. This is a response-to-response measurement on the vertical axis. Normally atrial tissue does not show decremental conduction, only the AV node does.

This is one way to visualize all 3 atrial refractory periods. I never understood FRP until I saw this graph. It puts the pieces together. ERP is easy because we measure it on every case - where the tissue starts to block. FRP is also easy because it's where the tissue starts to decrement or fatigue. But RRP is more difficult to understand. Note in the diagram that #3 FRP is the LOWEST point or the fastest the atria can respond. It's close to the RRP, but RRP is read off the vertical axis as the heart's response A1-A2. FRP and ERP are read off the horizontal axis as stimulation times as S1-S2.

Here is an analogy. You are a dash-hound chasing a rabbit around the track. You can keep up with the rabbit as it runs faster and faster. Eventually, you can't keep up and the rabbit pulls away. Your fastest speed is your FRP. You keep chasing the rabbit but get slower and slower. Where your response starts to slow is your RRP. But the rabbit's speed (stimulus) where it starts to slow is the FRP. You go slower and slower. Eventually, you tire out and give up. That is your ERP.

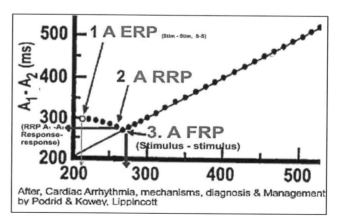

Note: RRP and FRP are seldom measured in the EP lab. We're more interested in what the stimulator settings should be to induce and break arrhythmias.

13. What does this AVN extrastimulus test graph show at 300 ms A1-A2?
- a. Jump to slow pathway
- b. Jump to fast pathway
- c. Infra-His AV block
- d. Supra-His AV block
- e. Eccentric conduction

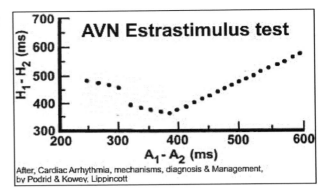

ANSWER: a. Jump to slow pathway, demonstrates dual AV nodal physiology. As premature stimuli get shorter (moving from right to left on the graph) AV conduction can initially match the A1-A2s with equal H1-H2s. AV conduction can speed up for a while. It decreases (just as the PR interval decreases with the decreasing RR interval on exercise). Eventually the AVN begins to fatigue and can no longer conduct as fast as previously. AV decremental conduction begins at the FRP and H1-H2 begins to increase, even as A1-A2 decreases.

You can see this on the AV node extrastimulus response curve shown on a patient with dual AV node physiology. You can plot this type of graph when looking for the A-H jump in AVNRT, as shown.

Initially the response to extrastimuli is a line of identity, where the AV node accurately tracks each atrial stimulus (A1-A2 = H1-H2). But eventually AV conduction begins to decrement or fatigue, and the H1-H2 response starts slowing (here at 380 ms). This is FRP - the inflection point where AV node begins to fatigue and just starts to slow decremental conduction starts. This minimum point on the graph is the lowest H1-H2 achievable for a given pulse train cycle length or extrastimuli.

14. This graph shows the response of three patients to atrial extrastimuli. Match the three patterns of atrial conduction shown with their diagnosis below.
- a. Normal
- b. Accessory pathway
- c. Dual AV node physiology

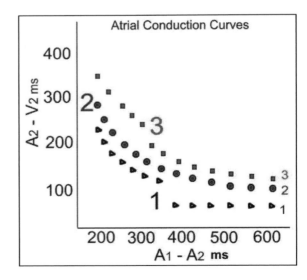

ANSWER: 1.b. Accessory pathway, 2.a. Normal, 3.c. Dual AV node, possible AVNRT.

The curved shape of these lines indicates decremental conduction through the AV node, except in the case of AP conduction, which is a straight line until AV conduction resumes. In patient #3 there is a "jump" in the AV conduction where the second slow pathway takes over conduction through the AV node indicating dual AV node physiology and tendency for AVNRT. Fogoros says, "The normal pattern of gradually increasing AH intervals with progressively premature atrial impulses is shown graphically [#2 circles] ...This AV nodal conduction curve shows the normal smooth and continuous prolongation in AH intervals with progressively premature beats. This normal pattern can be disrupted by two general conditions that produce supraventricular tachycardias: AV nodal pathways, and AV bypass tracts."

"In a patient with an AV bypass tract [1. Triangles lower curve]. At longer coupling intervals, premature atrial impulses are conducted to the ventricles via the bypass tract. Because the bypass tract does not typically display slowing in conduction with premature beats, this portion of the curve is flat. When the refractory period of the bypass track is reached, AV conduction shifts to the normal AV conduction system.... At the point where the curve shifts, the delta wave disappears from the resulting QRS complex. Also, at this point macroreentry is likely to occur." See: Fogoros, chapter on Principles of the EP Study

15. In incremental or EST pacing of the RV, as cycle length decreases, the retrograde VA conduction time normally _____ and the HA interval _____.
   a. **Increases, increases**
   b. **Increases, decreases**
   c. **Decreases, increases**
   d. **Decreases, decreases**

ANSWER: a. Increases, increases. As incremental Ventricular pacing rate increases the VA retrograde conduction shows fatigue and decrements. The VA and HA intervals widen, and VA block eventually starts. Complete VA block defines the AVN Retrograde ERP. However, 25% of people do not conduct retrograde at all, and normal ERP usually occurs at slower pacing rates as compared to antegrade AV conduction. When you see "HA interval" as on this diagram, it means retrograde or VA conduction. Just as in AV decremental conduction, retrograde VA conduction occurs in the AV node.

Issa says, "The normal AVN response to rate-incremental ventricular pacing is a gradual delay of VA conduction (manifest as gradual prolongation of the HA interval) as the pacing CL decreases. Retrograde VA Wenckebach block and a higher degree of block appear at shorter pacing CLS." See: Issa, chapter on EP Testing, Ventricular stimulation

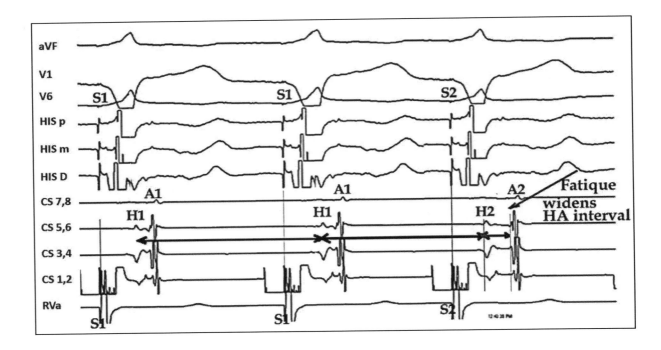

16. During programmed stimulation, following a pulse train of 220 ms, five extrastimuli were given at 190, 180, 175, 170, 165 ms. The first extrastimuli at 190 ms and marked with "?" is termed:

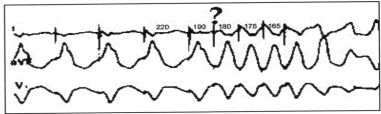

   a. S1

   b. S2

   c. S3

   d. Pulse Train

ANSWER: S2. The incremental pulse train of S1's establishes a base heart rate, then premature extrastimuli are added. Since the S1 beats are the equidistant pulse train, the extrastimuli is labeled S2.

Fogoros says, "The first extrastimulus is introduced at a coupling interval timed either from an intrinsic cardiac impulse or from the last of a short train of incrementally paced impulses. (This train is usually eight beats in duration, owing to tradition rather than to scientific reasons) .... The term S1 (stimulus 1) is used for the incrementally paced impulses or for the intrinsic beat from which the first extrastimulus is timed; S2 is used for the first programmed extrastimulus; S3 for the second programmed extrastimulus, and so forth. This nomenclature (in which e.g., the number 2 is attached to the first extrastimulus) causes a lot of confusion among the uninitiated." See: Fogoros, chapter on "Principles of the Electrophysiology Study"

17. The end of this extrastimulus testing EGM displays _____.
   a. AERP
   b. AP Block
   c. VA Block
   d. Infra-His Block

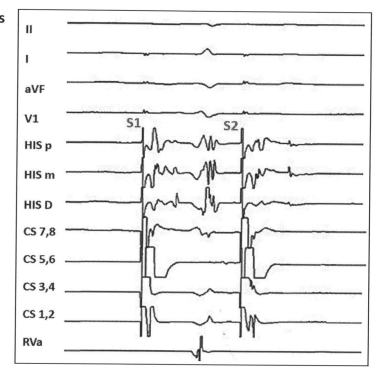

ANSWER: d. Infra-His Block. Notice the A wave and H wave with no V to follow. This shows block below the level of the His bundle. Infrahisian block may be an indication that permanent pacing is needed since block below the AV node is more likely to progress.

Infrahisian block describes block of the distal conduction system. Types of infrahisian block include:

   • 2nd degree type 2 HB (Mobitz II)
   • Left bundle branch block
   • Left anterior fascicular block
   • Left posterior fascicular block
   • Right bundle branch block

Of these types of infrahisian block, Mobitz II heart block is considered most important because of the possible progression to complete heart block."

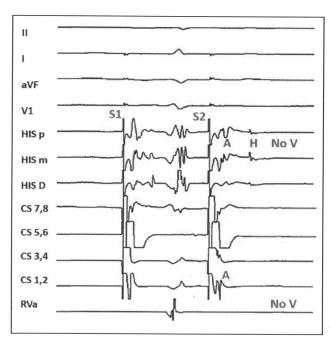

18. What type of conduction occurs here with extrastimulus testing of the atrium via CS 5,6?
  a. AVNERP
  b. AERP
  c. VERP
  d. APERP

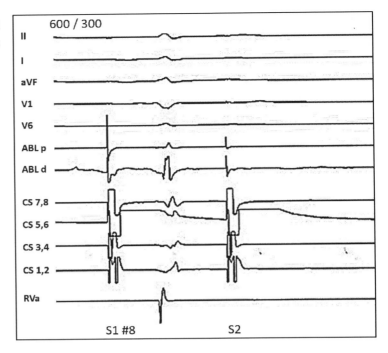

ANSWER: a. AVNERP. AV node effective refractory period. This physician is using the CS catheter for atrial pacing instead of placing an additional line for the HRA. This accomplishes the same thing; however, you are pacing from the low RA at the CS ostium. However, when looking for right sided accessory pathways an HRA catheter can be helpful. Atrial extrastimulus testing is when the physician paces the heart using a drive train of eight paced beats at a fixed cycle length followed by a PAC. The eight drive train impulses are to establish a reasonable steady state.

In AERP, there would be a pacing spike with no atrial deflection to follow. In VERP, pacing would occur in the ventricle and the S2 would show a pacing spike with no ventricular waveform to follow. AP ERP (accessory pathway ERP) would show either the loss of the delta wave or a conduction shift (VA separation on the ablation channel or on the CS if left sided), but there is no pathway in this example.

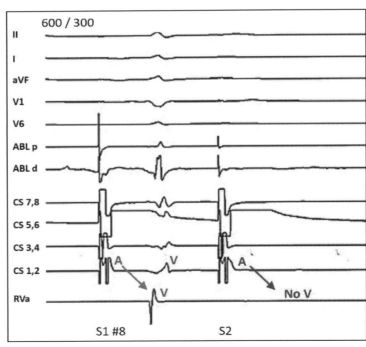

19. On this 56-year-old patient with documented SVT, what occurs in response to atrial extrastimulus testing?

    a. VERP

    b. AERP

    c. Jump w/ Echo

    d. AVNERP

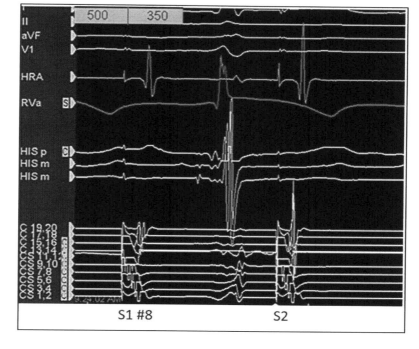

ANSWER: d. AVNERP. AV node effective refractory period. This is like the previous example. Again, the physician is pacing the atrium via the CS catheter. Typically, if an HRA (High right atrial) catheter is used, it would be used to pace the atrium; however, the physician was not getting reliable capture when pacing, so instead of adjusting the catheter they used the CS instead. We are capturing the atrium, as you see by the pacing spike with an A wave following; however, there is no H or V wave to follow. Here, the PAC (S2) was so early that it could not conduct through the AV node (AVNERP).

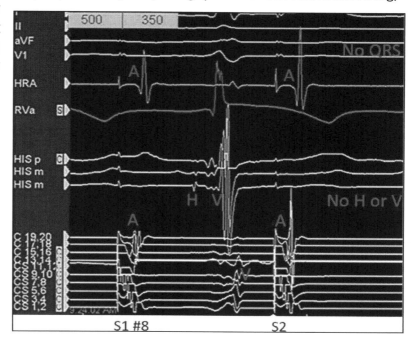

20. During ventricular extrastimulus testing on this patient with a documented wide complex tachycardia, what type of conduction occurs after S2?
  a. **Infrahisian Block**
  a. **VA Jump**
  b. **VERP**
  c. **APERP**

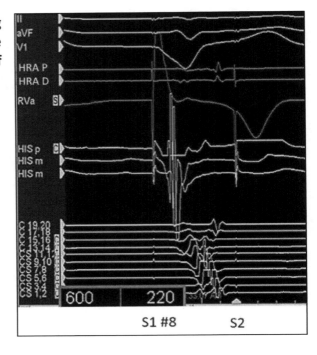

ANSWER: c. VERP. This stands for the ventricular effective refractory period, or the point at which the impulse came in so early that the ventricular myocardium was unable to depolarize (refractory). There is no H because we are pacing the ventricle, so the His is typically hidden within the ventricular signal. After S1, there appears to be a retrograde A on C19,20 & ABL (HRA) catheter. After S2 there is no conduction indicating block.

We were capturing the V during the eight-beat drive train (S1) as apparent by the V signal & the wide QRS. However, the S2 does not capture the Ventricular myocardium whereas the previous run (600/230) did…. It came in too early.

Looking at the ventricular action potential diagram. After our eight-beat drive train if we put a PVC in at #1, Capture occurs (not shown). At #2 pacing a little earlier, Capture occurs (not shown). At #3 a little earlier, (as in the example above) it can no longer capture the ventricular myocardium. This is different than testing thresholds in that you are providing enough voltage to capture. The impulse is in the ERP, and just too early to capture.

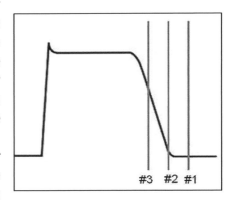

In APERP, VA jump, and Infrahisian block from ventricular extrastimulus testing, there would be capture of the ventricular myocardium. VERP is the only answer in which the ventricular myocardium is not captured.

21. During initial testing on this 56-year-old SVT patient, this EGM shows:
   a. **AVNERP**
   b. **VERP**
   c. **AERP**
   d. **Retrograde AVNERP**

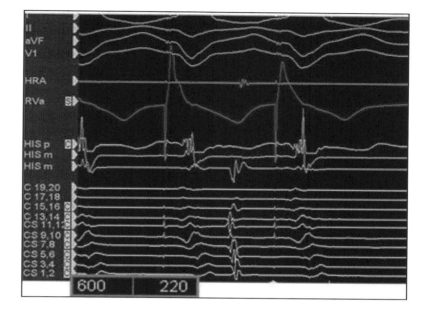

ANSWER: d. Retrograde AVNERP. This a drive train of eight beats at 600ms (only the last impulse of the drive train displayed), then a PVC 220 ms later. The PVC captured the V (wide QRS and a ventricular deflection), but no A wave follows. The previous run at 600/230 did conduct retrograde to the A (not shown). This is referred to as the retrograde AV node ERP, the longest coupling interval that does not produce VA conduction.

Fogoros explains ERP as, "when introducing a premature impulse, the impulse will fail to propagate through the tissue that is refractory. The ERP refers to the latest early impulse that is blocked. If the premature impulse were any later, the tissue would be recovered and would propagate the impulses." Just like antegrade AV conduction (AVNERP), the VA conduction has its own retrograde conduction time (Retrograde AVNERP). Note how the proximal CS electrodes nearest the AV node sense the A before the distal left sided electrodes. Then the HRA electrode senses it last as the A propagates up through the RA. After this S2 the VA conduction is refractory. AVNERP will be measured during atrial pacing, retrograde AVNERP will be measured during V pacing.

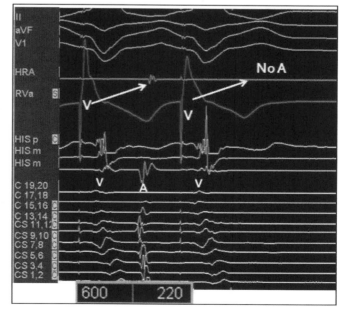

22. These two EGMs were recorded during atrial extrastimulus testing with a drive train of 400ms (the full drive train is not displayed). With a closer S2, what change in conduction happens between #4 & 5? (Small His marked at #5.)
   a. **AVRT starts at 159 bpm**
   b. **AVNRT starts at 159 bpm**
   c. **Jump from slow to fast AVN pathway**
   d. **Jump from fast to slow AVN pathway**

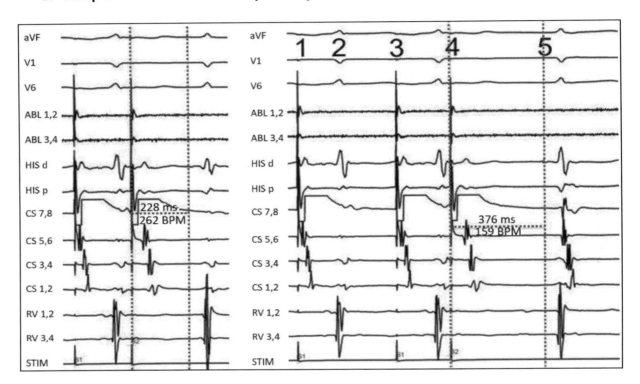

ANSWER d. Antegrade AV conduction switches from the fast to slow pathway. Note the S2-H Jump from 228 to 386 ms, an increase of 158 ms. An echo beat runs retrograde up the fast pathway to initiate atrial contraction. This demonstrates dual AV node physiology and could support AVNRT. Beat five is an echo beat, with retrograde A. Note a small H wave is marked at #5 as conduction passes down the AV node. We see the first echo beat, but there is not enough tracing to diagnose AVNRT. See the ladder diagram below showing the echo beat that may initiate AVNRT.

from http://www.askdrwiki.com/mediawiki/index.php?title=AVNRT_Slow/Fast

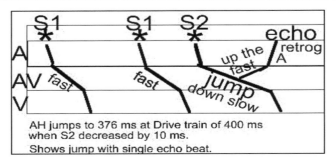

23. In the same patient, atrial extrastimulus testing induces:
   a. AVRT starting at 159 bpm
   b. AVNRT starting at 159 bpm
   c. AVRT starting at 182 bpm
   d. AVNRT starting at 182bpm

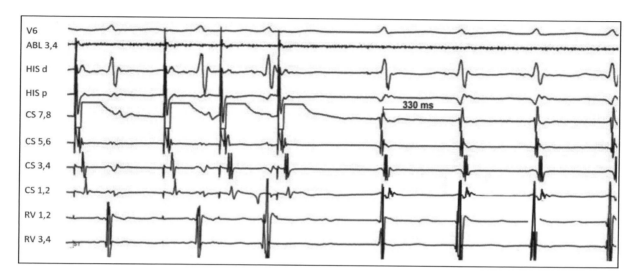

Answer: d. AVNRT starting at 182 bpm. There is a jump in the S2-H interval which starts the narrow complex tachycardia. The A waves are simultaneous with the QRS complexes, typical of AVNRT. Use calipers to measure the tachycardia cycle length at 330 ms, which is 182 bpm. (60,000/330 = 182). Small His signals are seen on HIS distal. The ladder diagram shows how atrial extrastimulus testing induced the jump from the fast to the slow pathway and induction of AVNRT. The first antegrade conduction down the slow pathway passes the AV node and causes a narrow QRS. At the same time the conduction passes up the fast pathway and conducts into the atrium retrograde causing echo beats.

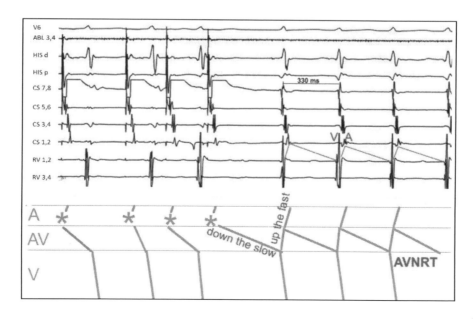

24. Pacing in the CS from the distal electrodes normally initiates a depolarization in the:
   a. RA
   b. LA
   c. RV
   d. LV

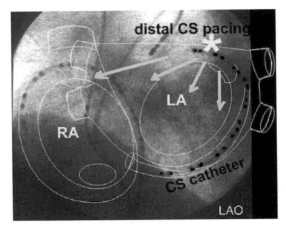

ANSWER: b. LA. Fogoros says: "Pacing and recording from the left atrium are usually accomplished by inserting an electrode catheter into the coronary sinus.... and is most easily entered from the superior approach- only rarely can the left ventricle be paced from this position." Pacing from the proximal electrodes normally initiates RA pacing. Hi RA cath. See: Fogoros chapter on Principles of the EP

25. The His electrogram is normally best recorded when an electrode pair is positioned near the:
   a. Posterior aspect of the tricuspid valve
   b. Anterior aspect of the tricuspid valve
   c. Posterior RV septum
   d. Superior RV septum

ANSWER: a. Posterior aspect of the tricuspid valve. Fogoros says: "To record the His bundle electrogram, an electrode catheter is passed across the posterior aspect of the tricuspid valve (near the penetration of the His bundle into the fibrous skeleton) The catheter is maneuvered while continuously recording electrograms from several electrode pairs (so that the best pair for recording can be selected) .... It straddles the important structures of the AV conduction system and allows one to record the electrical activity of the low right atrium, the AV node, the His bundle, and a portion of the right ventricle - all from one electrode pair."
See: Fogoros chapter on Principles of the Electrophysiology Study

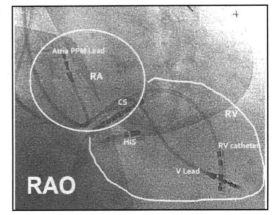

26. When doing incremental atrial pacing, Wenckebach-type AV conduction indicates block in the _____, while sudden loss of conduction not preceded by slowing (Mobitz II) suggests block in the _____.
   a. SA node, Bachman bundle
   b. SA node, His-Purkinje system
   c. AV node, Bachman bundle
   d. AV node, His-Purkinje system

ANSWER: d. AV node, His-Purkinje system. Murgatroyd says, "Wenckebach-type AV conduction indicates block in the AV node, while sudden loss of conduction not preceded by slowing (Mobitz type II) suggests block in the His-Purkinje system." See: Murgatroyd chapter on The Basic EP Study

27. A sudden significant increase in H1-H2 interval in response to a 10-millisecond shortening of A1 suggests:
   a. PAC
   b. AVRT
   c. AVNRT
   d. Atrial Tachycardia

ANSWER: C. AVNRT jump in A2-H2 or H1 - H2 intervals suggests AVNRT. Sometimes you cannot see the A2-H2 interval clearly. Then H1- H2 or V1-V2 can be used to show the same jump. This is only if the HV interval is fixed in length. Also, sometimes people have a clear "jump" and never develop AVNRT. It is just an additional finding. When there are two or more pathways into the AV node it is termed "dual AV Node physiology".

Issa says, "In contrast to the normal pattern of AVN conduction, in which the AH interval gradually lengthens in response to progressively shorter AES (atrial extrastimulus testing) coupling intervals, patients with dual AVN physiology usually demonstrate a sudden increase (jump) in the AH interval at a critical AES coupling interval. Conduction with a short PR or AH interval reflects fast pathway conduction, whereas conduction with a long PR or AH interval reflects slow pathway conduction. The AH interval jump demonstrates block of anterograde conduction of the progressively premature AES over the fast pathway (once the AES coupling interval becomes shorter than the fast pathway ERP) and anterograde conduction over the slow pathway (which has an ERP shorter than the AES coupling interval), with a longer conduction time (i.e., longer A2-H2 interval). A jump in A2-H2 (or H1-H2) interval of 50 milliseconds or more in response to a 10- millisecond shortening of A1-A2 (i.e., AES coupling interval) or of A1-A1 (i.e., pacing CL) is defined as a discontinuous AVN function curve and is considered as evidence of dual anterograde AVN pathways." See: Issa, chapter on "AVNRT"

28. This patient is being ablated for AVNRT. What happens at the question mark?
   a. Jump from fast to slow pathway
   b. Jump from slow to fast pathway
   c. AV block develops
   d. Junctional Tachycardia

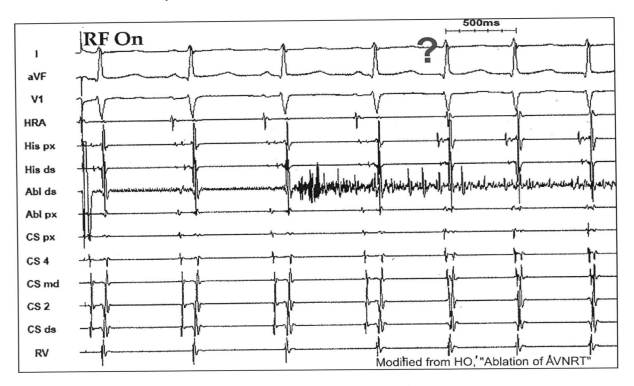

Answer: d. Junctional tachycardia usually develops during this type of RF application. Initially the patient is in sinus rhythm with surface P waves with clear A waves in the HRA catheter. Then the P and A waves disappear, and large but later atrial signals develop on the His proximal and CS proximal channels. This new focus is from the AV junction. It conducts retrograde into the atrium and down the AV node with narrow complex tachycardia with cycle length around 500 ms, thus overdriving the SA node. This is the junctional tachycardia that usually develops during AVNRT ablation. There is no jump or AV block shown. See: Ho, chapter on "Ablation of AVNRT"

Typically, in RF ablation of AVNRT the thermal energy will cause a SLOW junctional response. If a rapid or accelerating junctional response develops, you are too close to the AV node and may be damaging it. Also, since junctional tachycardia looks just like AVNRT you may have just induced AVNRT – in which case you should move to another site looking for the slow pathway. See: Ho, chapter on "Ablation of AVNRT"

29. After placement of the catheters, what is observed after extrastimulus testing? (Only the last two impulses of the drive train are displayed)

a. VAERP
b. AVNERP
c. Echo
d. APERP
e. AV Block
f. VA Block

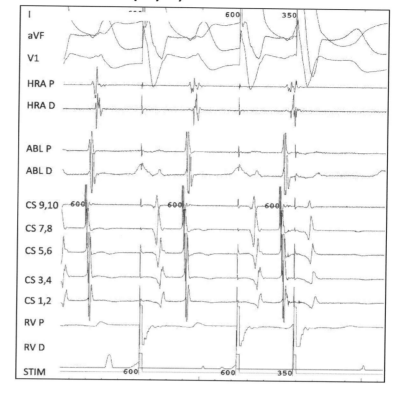

ANSWER: a. VAERP or retrograde AVNERP. VAERP occurs as the AV node blocks the retrograde conduction (conduction from the ventricle to the atrium). The physician is pacing the RV as is evident by the pacing spike on RVd and the wide QRS. Always make sure to see that the drive train captured. If it doesn't capture, it is the VERP (Ventricular Effective Refractory Period), not VAERP.

Start at the beginning and work your way through looking for the missing signal. This shows fusion of the V and A on the distal CS (lateral LA). Atrial conduction proceeds from CS 1,2 to CS 7,8, opposite to the normal concentric activation (eccentric). This will be discussed later but is evidence of an accessory pathway on the left side of the heart.

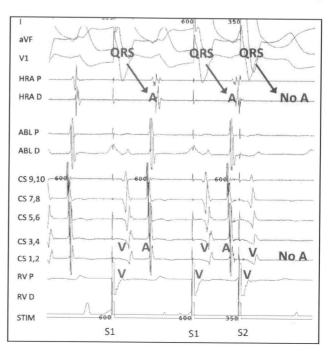

29. **What is observed after extrastimulus testing?**
    (Only the last impulse of the drive train is displayed and two extrastimuli)
    a. **AVNERP**
    b. **Echo**
    c. **AP ERP**
    d. **AV Block**
    e. **VA Block**

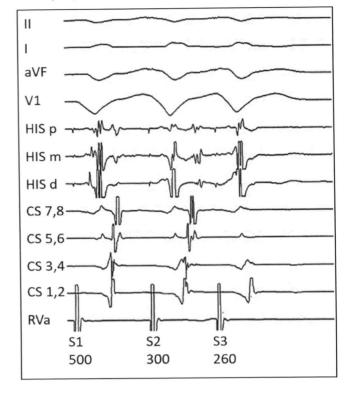

ANSWER: c. AP ERP or accessory pathway ERP. Notice the fusion of the V and A on the distal CS (lateral LA). Atrial conduction proceeds from CS 1,2 to CS 7,8, opposite to the normal activation; therefore, this is an eccentric conduction pattern. This is evidence of an accessory pathway on the left side of the heart. The impulse was unable to travel from the ventricle to the atrium through the AV node or the accessory pathway.

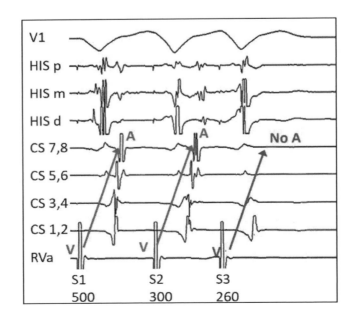

30. What term best describes the conduction after S2?
   a. AERP
   b. VERP
   c. Infranodal Block
   d. Infrahisian Block

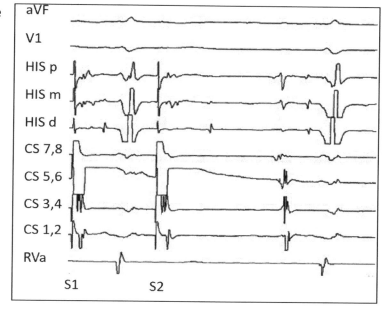

ANSWER: d. Infrahisian block. When looking for block, don't forget to use the surface ECG. If you had more QRS complexes, you would note group beating suggesting Wenckebach.

Kusumoto says, "If complete infrahisian block develops, the patient is dependent on automaticity from ventricular tissue, which is notoriously unreliable. For this reason, evidence of infrahisian block, even in an asymptomatic patient is an indication for permanent pacing." See: Kusumoto chapter on Bradycardia

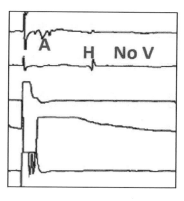

31. In this example, which number on the EGM marks an intrinsic atrial event initiated by the SA node?
   a. 1
   b. 2
   c. 3
   d. 4

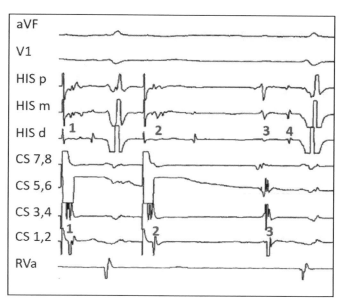

ANSWER: c. #3 is an intrinsic A (not paced) generated by the SA node. After the last paced A that is blocked in the His/Purkinje system, the SA node picks up as pacemaker of the heart. It is followed by normally conduced H (#4) and V waves. This shows concentric atrial activation, meaning high to low, right to left. The 1st atrial deflection is on the His catheter with is higher than the CS catheter which shows high to low conduction. Notice the atrial deflection on CS 7,8 (proximal) which comes first and CS 1,2 (distal) last. This shows right to left activation since the proximal CS originates in the RA and the distal CS lies behind the LA. Eccentric activation is when the impulse does not conduct in this normal pattern.

32. What complication may occur when advancing a catheter into the RV of a patient?
   a. CHB
   b. LBBB
   c. RBBB
   d. 2nd degree HB

ANSWER: c. RBBB. As you pass a catheter into the RV you may bump into the right bundle branch and cause temporary RBBB. This is especially a problem if the patient already has a left fascicular block or LBBB, because then the patient has CHB and bradycardia. In that case be ready to pace the ventricle with an RV electrode. This may occur with placement of a temporary pacemaker, myocardial biopsy, RV lead placement or any right heart cath.

33. When performing extrastimulus testing, if the premature impulse first fails to propagate because the stimulus falls in the refractory period of that tissue it is termed the:
   a. ERP
   b. RRP
   c. FRP
   d. CRP

ANSWER: a. ERP is the first premature stimulus that blocks. EP Essentials says, "A common analogy for discussing ERP is the use of a toilet. Flushing represents tissue depolarization; the tank refilling represents repolarization. Once the toilet is flushed, the tank must refill to a certain level before it may flush again. It does not have to be completely refilled and may be flushed early. However, if there is an attempt to flush again before the required minimum tank level is reached, it will not flush, no matter how hard the handle is pressed: this is ERP. When tissue depolarizes, it needs to repolarize to a certain level before being able to depolarize again. If the extrastimulus is delivered before the tissue has recovered to the appropriate level, the tissue will not depolarize: ERP." See: Understanding EP – A Comprehensive Guide, EP Essentials.

34. The effective refractory period (ERP) is comprised of what phases of a cardiac action potential?
   a. 0 and part of 1
   b. 0, 1, and part of 2
   c. 0, 1, 2, and part of 3
   d. 0, 1, 2, 3, and part of 4

ANSWER: c. 0, 1, 2, and part of phase 3 of the cardiac action potential. As the extrastimulus moved into the first part of the refractory or vulnerable period, the tissue is refractory and cannot conduct. This can be measured for atrial, AV node, His bundle, and ventricular tissue.

Atrial ERP: AERP: Longest A1-A2 interval that fails to achieve atrial capture
AVN ERP: Longest H1-H2 in response to any A1-A2
Ventricular ERP: VERP: Longest V1-V2 interval that fails to achieve ventricular capture

35. In cardiac action potentials, the period in phase 3 between ERP and RRP is termed the:
   a. ERP or Effective Refractory Period
   b. RRP or Relative Refractory Period
   c. FRP or Functional Refractory Period
   d. LP or Latent Period (or Vulnerable Period)

ANSWER: d. LP: Latent Period (or Vulnerable Period)

36. At rest, all cardiac muscle cells are more negatively charged _____ and the resting interior membrane potential is approximately _____?
   a. Outside, -60mV
   b. Outside, -90mV
   c. Inside, -60mV
   d. Inside, -90mV

ANSWER: d. Inside, -90mV. This is the electrical potential across the muscle cell membrane. It is charged like a DC battery that is ready to discharge when stimulated. The positive terminal is outside the cell and the negative is inside.

37. What phase of the ventricular muscle action potential is associated with the QRS complex?
   a. Phase 0
   b. Phase 2
   c. Phase 3
   d. Phase 4

ANSWER: a. Phase 0. The ECG QRS complex is created when thousands of ventricular muscle cells depolarize, going from -90mV to +20mV. This occurs during their phase 0 as Na^+ rushes into the cell making it positively charged.

38. The latent period of a cardiac tissue is important in EP because it:
   a. Determines the time QT interval increases
   b. Is the time of ECG ST depression and elevation
   c. Is the vulnerable period for starting triggered arrythmias
   d. Is the vulnerable period for starting reentrant tachycardias.

ANSWER: d. Is the vulnerable period for starting reentrant tachycardias. This vulnerable period (during phase 3) is where flutter or fibrillation can be most easily induced. As the drive train speeds up, this latent or vulnerable period increases, and it becomes even easier to induce reentrant tachycardias.

39. Which ion flow causes cardiac muscle cells to fire?
   a. Cl^- influx
   b. K^+ influx
   c. Ca^{++} influx
   d. Na^+ influx

ANSWER: d. Na^+ influx.

40. Which ion flow causes the SA and AV nodal cells to depolarize?
   a. Cl^- influx
   b. K^+ influx
   c. Ca^{++} influx
   d. Na^+ influx

ANSWER: c. Ca^{++} influx. The nodal cells utilized the slow calcium influx and as such have a slow rounded appearance to the action potential.

41. What happens across the cell membrane of ventricular muscle cells during phase 4 of the AP?
   a. Systolic Na^+ influx
   b. Systolic Na^- efflux
   c. Diastolic restoration of ionic balance
   d. Diastolic resting phase

ANSWER: c. Diastolic resting phase. Recharging the cell membrane (like recharging a battery to -90mV). The Na-K pump and the Na-Ca pump restore ionic balance. This is often depicted in diagrams as a paddle wheel pushes certain ions out and pulls others in.

42. What two cardiac tissues have a slow action potential and thus a slow conduction velocity? (Select two)
   a. SA node
   b. AV node
   c. Purkinje cells
   d. Atrial muscle
   e. Ventricular muscle

ANSWER: SA node & AV node. Both are slow and sinusoidal in shape. It is the slow upstroke and velocity in the AV node that causes the AV delay. As opposed to this, latent pacemaker cells in the Purkinje and cardiac muscle cells have a rapid phase 0 upstroke due to rapid Na^+ influx.

Chapter 9
Supraventricular Arrhythmias

EP Essentials LLC

Atrial Fibrillation:

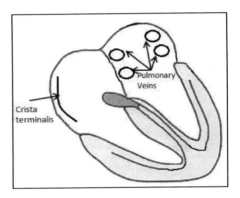

- Most common arrhythmia seen, especially over age 80
- Disorganized atrial activity
- Irregularly irregular ventricular response
- Spontaneous, Persistent or Long Lasting Persistent
- Associated with Hypertension & Mitral Regurgitation
- Multiple reentry circuits
- Often originating in pulmonary veins
- AF begets AF

See, Richard Fogoros – Electrophysiology Testing

1. Which of these patients have the highest recurrence rate of AF after PVI ablation.
   a. High voltage areas within the LA
   b. Pulmonary Vein Stenosis
   c. Aortic Regurgitation
   d. Left Atrial Scarring

ANSWER: d. Left Atrial Scarring. "The pulmonary veins are the dominant triggers of AF initiation. To date, circumferential pulmonary vein isolation (CPVI) is the most common operation for patients with AF. However, it has a lower long-term success rate for paroxysmal AF (PAF) patients, which is only 46.6% at 5 years postoperatively during the follow-up period. Recent studies have reported that patients with low-voltage and scar areas are associated with higher recurrence risks of AF after ablation. Therefore, efforts were made toward AF substrate modification with several non-pulmonary vein targets used as guidance for transcatheter ablation." Zhou, et al, Catheter ablation of paroxysmal atrial fibrillation using

high-density   mapping-guided   substrate   modification. Pacing   and   Clinical
Electrophysiology, 2018.

2. In AF cases, after the pulmonary veins have been isolated and successfully tested for block, to test for other sources of AF you should:
   a. **Perform parahisian pacing**
   b. **Perform rapid RV pacing**
   c. **Administer Isuprel**
   d. **Administer Adenosine**

ANSWER: c. Administer Isuprel to attempt AF induction. "Triggers of AF can also arise from other thoracic veins, such as the superior vena cava, coronary sinus, and vein of Marshall. After the pulmonary veins have been isolated, infusion of isoproterenol is helpful to determine whether any non–pulmonary vein triggers are present." See: Braunwald chapter on AF

"Of the other thoracic veins [besides PVs], the SVC is the most common cause of AF. Previous studies have shown that myocardial fibers connect the right atrium (RA) to the SVC, and electrical activity within these fibers could trigger arrhythmias in a manner like the pulmonary veins…. Several clinical studies have reported that AF or AT could originate in the SVC and demonstrated the safety and efficacy of ablation within this structure. Lin and colleagues have reported that 37% of the non–pulmonary vein triggers were from the SVC….More than 90% of triggers initiating AF have been observed to originate from the pulmonary veins, and the remainder originate from the superior vena cava (SVC), coronary sinus, ligament of Marshall, left superior vena cava (SVC), and scattered other atrial sites (crista terminalis, atrial myocardium, and atrioventricular valves). These thoracic veins appended to the atria have atrial muscle sleeves that extend a variable distance into these structures and have been implicated in the mechanisms of atrial tachycardia (AT) and AF."
See: Braunwald chapter on AF

3. The only absolute contraindication to a PVI ablation procedure for AF is:
   a. **Recent stroke**
   b. **LA thrombus on TEE**
   c. **Asymptomatic AF**
   d. **PFO plug in atrial septum**

ANSWER: b. Atrial thrombus on TEE. Davies says, "There is only one absolute contraindication to AF ablation being the presence of intra-atrial thrombus, typically in the left atrial appendage…." See: Braunwald, chapter on Atrial Fibrillation: When to Ablate - When not, by D. W. Davies 2013

4. PVI ablation is NOT recommended in atrial fibrillation patients with:
   a. **Lone AF**
   b. **Permanent AF with history of stroke**
   c. **Uncompleted antiarrhythmic drug trials**
   d. **Asymptomatic long standing persistent AF**

ANSWER: d. Asymptomatic long standing persistent AF. Davies say, "The only pattern of AF for which ablation is not recommended is asymptomatic long standing persistent AF irrespective of whether antiarrhythmic drugs have failed or not yet been tried.... It is well recognized that increasing duration of persistent AF is associated with progressively reduced success rates for AF ablation. Thus, the threshold for offering ablation increases with AF duration with great difficulty anticipated when ablating patients with AF over 3 years duration...." See: Braunwald, chapter on Atrial Fibrillation: When to Ablate - When not, by D. W. Davies 2013

5. During PVI ablation it is important to not damage the phrenic nerve. How can you mark the location of the Rt. phrenic nerve on the 3D image prior to ablation?
   a. **Have the patient Valsalva while pacing the phrenic nerve in the neck mark the SVC points where diaphragmatic twitching occurs**
   b. **Have the patient Valsalva, while pacing posterior LA wall mark the points where diaphragmatic twitching occurs**
   c. **While high output pacing the posterolateral SVC, mark the points where diaphragmatic twitching occurs**
   d. **While high output pacing the posterolateral LA, mark the points where diaphragmatic twitching occurs**

ANSWER: c. While high current pacing the posterior-lateral SVC, mark the points where hiccups occur. This is the blue line of dots labeled #1 in the 3D image. The right phrenic nerve runs posterolateral to the SVC as shown in the diagram. Caution is required when ablating around the SVC or adjacent right superior pulmonary vein. To map this nerve, move the mapping catheter into superior SVC and pace the distal tip with high output. The mapping catheter is then pulled back, along the poster-lateral wall, until the phrenic nerve is stimulated which in turn stimulates the diaphragm. This can be seen and felt by the physician and can be verified under fluoro. The diaphragm will be seen jumping (hiccupping) at the rate of pacing.

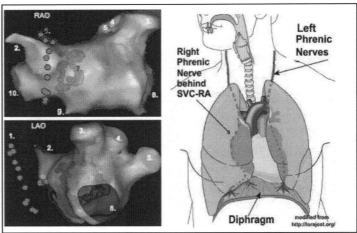

When you see diaphragmatic pacing and twitching, the 3D imaging operator marks a "floating" point (on above map we used blue points to mark the location). This point represents phrenic nerve location. This process is repeated until the mapping catheter drops into the right atrium. The process usually is repeated a couple of times just to make sure that the phrenic nerve location has been mapped. We don't want to damage this vital nerve with ablation. With Ensite imaging, shadowing the entire catheter helps to see if the catheter has moved.

Similar testing is done on the BiV electrode in the LV coronary vein to prevent left phrenic nerve stimulation and hiccups during BiV pacing. It is also done prior to PVI in the RSPV. Botha says, "On the right side it descends immediately lateral or posterolateral to the IVC, though in a few cases it was antero-lateral. The left phrenic nerve lies anterior and far out as it descends over the antero-lateral angle of the pericardial base to reach the diaphragm...." See, Anatomy of the Phrenic Nerve, by Botha, Thorax.bmj.com 2014

6. What treatment frequently causes left atrial "stunning" in AF patients?
   a. **Cardioversion**
   b. **RV apical pacing**
   c. **Transthoracic pacing**
   d. **RA appendage- high voltage pacing**
   e. **Pulmonary vein isolation - high RF energy**

ANSWER: a. Cardioversion causes left atrial "stunning." Dagres says, "Left atrial (LA) stunning is the transient impairment of LA and LA appendage (LAA) mechanical function after successful cardioversion of atrial fibrillation (AF). This dysfunction may last up to a few weeks, is observed after all methods of cardioversion, and is responsible for the increased incidence of thrombus formation and embolic events after cardioversion, despite restoration of sinus rhythm."

"Thus, attenuation of atrial stunning by pharmacological agents would have substantial clinical importance, as it would decrease the thrombo-embolic risk after cardioversion. During AF, an electrical and structural remodeling of the atria takes place. Angiotensin II receptor blockers (ARBs) have been found to significantly attenuate these changes." (This study found that pretreatment with Irbesartan, an ARB, reduced atrial stunning)
"The exact mechanism of atrial stunning after cardioversion of AF is not clear. Several factors are involved in its development, such as tachycardia-induced atrial cardiomyopathy, atrial hibernation, and cytosolic calcium alterations with interplay of more than one mechanism. Recent studies emphasize the role of intracellular calcium homeostasis. It is also proposed that the structural remodeling that takes place during AF and which is characterized by progressive structural changes of the atria, resulting in atrial dilation and interstitial fibrosis, might be a potential mechanism leading to atrial stunning, especially with longer duration of the arrhythmia." See: Pre-treatment with Irbesartan attenuates left atrial stunning after electrical cardioversion of atrial fibrillation at www.ncbi.nlm.nih.gov/pubmed/16891381

7. The only absolute contraindication to a PVI ablation procedure for AF is:
 a. Recent stroke
 b. LA thrombus on TEE
 c. Asymptomatic AF
 d. PFO plug in atrial septum

ANSWER: b. Atrial thrombus on TEE. Davies says, "There is only one absolute contraindication to AF ablation being the presence of intra-atrial thrombus, typically in the left atrial appendage...." See: Braunwald, chapter on Atrial Fibrillation: When to Ablate - When not, by D. W. Davies 2013

8. The only AF patients which PVI ablation procedure is NOT recommended are those with:
 a. Lone AF
 b. Permanent AF with history of stroke
 c. Uncompleted antiarrhythmic drug trials
 d. Asymptomatic long standing persistent AF

ANSWER: d. Asymptomatic long standing persistent AF. Davies say, "The only pattern of AF for which ablation is not recommended is asymptomatic long standing persistent AF irrespective of whether antiarrhythmic drugs have failed or not yet been tried.... It is well recognized that increasing duration of persistent AF is associated with progressively reduced success rates for AF ablation. Thus, the threshold for offering ablation increases with AF duration with great difficulty anticipated when ablating patients with AF over 3 years duration...." See: Braunwald, chapter on Atrial Fibrillation: When to Ablate - When not, by D. W. Davies 2013

9. For patients in AF, electrical cardioversion is contraindicated in patients with:
(Select the best two answers)
 a. Aortic stenosis
 b. Hypokalemia
 c. Hypercalcemia
 d. Digitalis toxicity
 e. Full dose Amiodarone
 f. Recent embolic stroke
 g. Decompensated heart failure

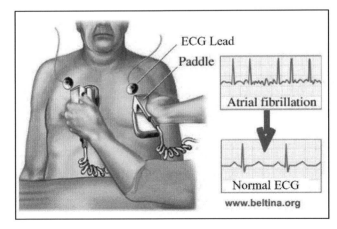

ANSWER: b. Hypokalemia and d. Digitalis toxicity. Hypokalemia makes patients arrhythmia prone. Hypokalemia is often caused by sustained diuretic therapy. ACC/AHA Recommendations for Cardioversion of Atrial Fibrillation say, "Class III (not indicated), Electrical cardioversion is contraindicated in patients with digitalis toxicity or hypokalemia." The presence of an atrial thrombus is of course another contraindication. See: ACC/AHA Recommendations for Cardioversion of Atrial Fibrillation

10. During PVI ablation for AF, the physician has a circular mapping catheter labeled "A" placed in the LSPV. There is an RF ablation catheter and a duodecapolar CS catheter (only 14 poles displayed). What happens after RF ablation of the LSPV?
  a. **Exit Block**
  b. **Entrance Block**
  c. **Far field appendage signal**
  d. **LSPV not isolated**

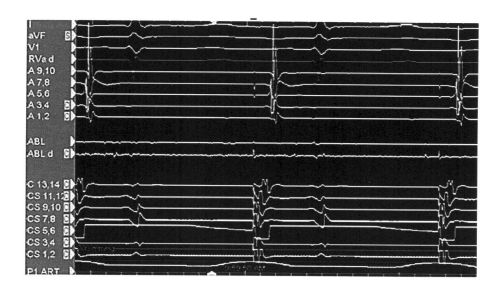

ANSWER: d. LSPV not isolated. Exit block occurs when an impulse spontaneously fires within the pulmonary vein but does not "exit" into the atrium. That would indicate pulmonary vein isolation - not the case in this example. Notice the pacing artifact on CS 5,6 which on this catheter is located on the left side of the LA. This testing is done when the patient is in sinus rhythm to determine if any signal is "entering" into the pulmonary vein. Entrance block is not occurring in this example as noticed by the immediate sharp signal on the lasso catheter. Sometimes you see far field atrial or appendage signals, however, a far field signal would not be a sharp spike as noticed here. In this EGM, the LSPV has not been isolated and further ablation is necessary. Many times, the physician will notice a sharp spike on one

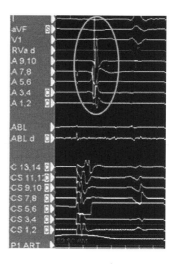

pair of electrodes from the PV catheter, this is beneficial as the physician then knows where to target his ablation.

11. On the same patient after further PVI ablation, this EGM shows:
   a. **Exit Block**
   b. **Entrance Block**
   c. **CHB**
   d. **LSPV not isolated**

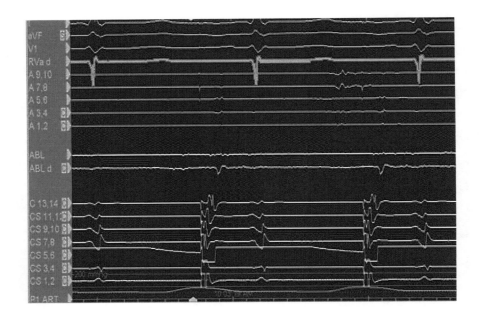

ANSWER: b. Entrance Block. Pacing is still occurring on CS 5,6 on the left side of the heart near the left sided veins. If assessing the right sided veins, the physician would want pacing on the right side of the CS (proximal CS) which is closer to the RSPV and RIPV. When pacing here, no signal enters the vein. This is a good sign of successful vein isolation; however, this does not tell anything about exit block. The best example of exit block is when the pulmonary vein fires by itself. Other physicians may try to pace within the pulmonary vein with high output to capture the pulmonary vein itself and to see if that impulse exits to the LA. David S. Frankel, MD and Michael P. Riley, MD, PhD says, "Entrance block in the absence of exit block has been reported to occur in 40% of pulmonary veins following ablation. There are explanations for the occurrence of entrance block without exit block. First, bidirectional conduction may be present between the pulmonary vein and atrium, but the operator may mistakenly conclude entrance block is present. It can be difficult to distinguish pulmonary vein potentials from far-field potentials recorded from adjacent structures, such as the right atrium or left atrial appendage.

Second, both entrance and exit block may be truly present, but pacing the circular mapping catheter at high output may directly capture the right atrium or left atrial appendage. This can be recognized by examining the P-wave morphology and intracardiac activation sequence." See: "Entrance without Exit Block" September 2011 Innovations in Cardiac Rhythm Management.

12. These two images were recorded during RF application during PVI on a patient with atrial fibrillation, Catheter tracing PV 7,8 shows:
   a. **Atrial fibrillation**
   b. **Failure to capture**
   c. **Patient movement**
   d. **RF catheter touching PV catheter**

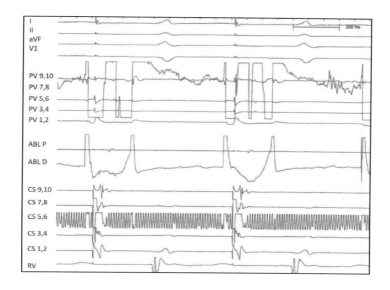

ANSWER: d. RF catheter touching the pulmonary vein circular mapping catheter near pole 7,8. Both catheters show simultaneous large squared off artifacts. Note how close they are on the Xray.

A second type of high frequency artifact is seen on the middle CS channel. You may see this on open pacing channels during ablation. Any pacing channels not being utilized should be turned off so as to not get this artifact. The patient is not moving, he is under general anesthesia. Once ablation ceases the channels return to a baseline state.
The patient is not currently in atrial fibrillation as seen by distinct A waves with 1:1 AV conduction and all pacing impulses from the CS appear to capture the atrial tissue as seen by the A wave following the pacing spike on the CS channels.

13. This EGM was recorded during wide area circumferential ablation of the RSPV. A Lasso catheter records from the RSPV. What happens at #1 and #2 in the electrogram below?
   a. **#1 AFL rhythm terminates, #2 AFL signals in RSPV terminate.**
   b. **#1 AFL rhythm terminates, #2 AFL reentry signals isolated in LA isthmus**
   c. **#1 AF rhythm terminates, #2 AF signals in RSPV terminate.**
   d. **#1 AF rhythm terminates, #2 AF reentry signals isolated in LA isthmus**

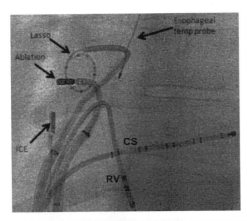

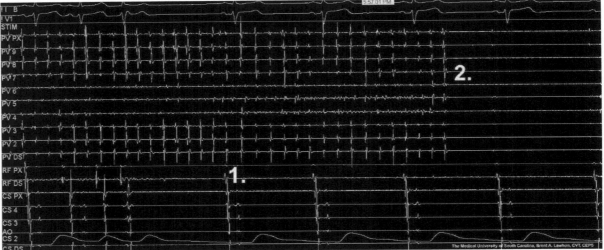

ANSWER: c. #1 AF rhythm terminates, #2. AF signals in RSPV terminate. This electrogram starts with AF originating in the RSPV. After a wide area circumferential ablation (WACA) a circular mapping catheter was placed into the right superior pulmonary vein. As seen at #1 the surface ECG shows termination of atrial fibrillation on V1 during ablation. The CS leads also show normal A waves and AV interval. The regular PV signals are too fast for AFL. AF often shows as rapidly occurring regular impulses in a PV. Even though the patient has converted to sinus rhythm the RSPV mapping catheter still shows frequent AF signals. Finally at #2, all AF signals terminate. (This case submitted by Brent Lawhorn, from Med. Univ. of SC.)

14. The following EGM shows the surface ECG, RV catheter, circular mapping catheter (labeled LA) positioned in the RSPV, RF ablation catheter in the LA, and the CS catheter. This EGM taken during PVI (pulmonary vein isolation) for AF shows:

    a. Exit Block

    b. Entrance Block

    c. Intermittent Heart Block

    d. Unsuccessful AF Ablation

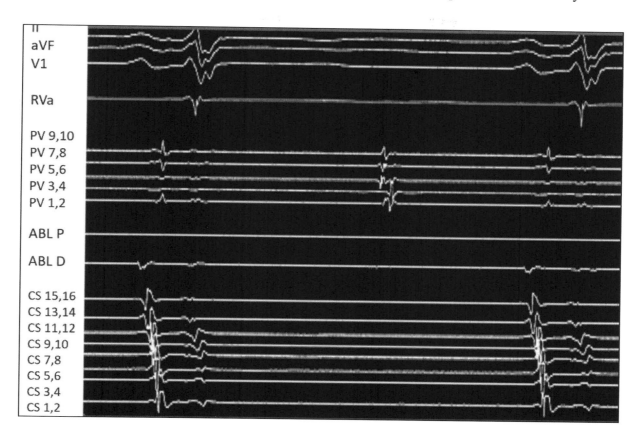

ANSWER: a. Exit Block. Spontaneous firing of the pulmonary veins is not always seen, but when it is it is an excellent sign of successful pulmonary vein isolation. Other examples may show entrance block, where LA or CS pacing does not enter the pulmonary vein. Exit block like this, is more challenging to prove.

With this patient the pulmonary vein was firing by itself. This is quite possibly what initiates his atrial fibrillation. Notice the circled signal on the PV Lasso channel, showing activation or firing within the vein. The earliest (only) signal was in the pulmonary vein, and it did not exit to the left atrium. If it did exit there would be a signal on the CS catheter running along the AV groove between the left atrium and left ventricle. This proves that the vein is isolated. According to AF.com, "An AF signal is blocked by ablation lesions from leaving the pulmonary veins and affecting the rest of the left atrium. This is a goal of a successful AF ablation, along with entrance block. Entrance and Exit Block are called Bidirectional Block."

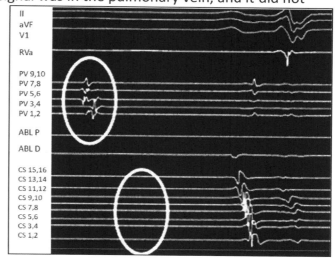

15. This patient was brought into the EP lab for an AF ablation. What is recorded here after initial catheter placement?

    a. VF defibrillation

    b. VT Defibrillation

    c. Successful Cardioversion

    d. Unsuccessful Cardioversion

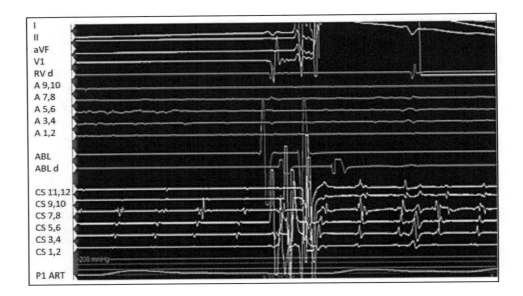

ANSWER: e. Unsuccessful Cardioversion. First, one must understand which channels are displayed. The first four are the surface ECG, followed by the RVa, the next five channels labeled A are in the LA. This is from a circular mapping catheter used for AF ablation. The physician will place this at the entrance of the pulmonary vein for mapping and to confirm entry and exit block in the pulmonary vein during a PVI (pulmonary vein isolation) ablation. The next two channels are the ablation channels followed by the CS catheter.

From this EGM you are unable to determine exact placement of the ablation and circular mapping catheter. From the frequent A's seen, the patient is clearly in an atrial rhythm. The start of the strip resembles AF or AFL. If more of the strip was displayed, you would see the irregular R-to-R intervals. The atrial activity in atrial fibrillation is very chaotic, whereas in atrial flutter the atrial impulses are more organized. It is not VT... notice more A's than V's. This is unsuccessful cardioversion because AF continues.

16. Further into the procedure the same patient was cardioverted a second time, now at 250J. The EGM below shows:

    a. Successful Cardioversion

    b. Unsuccessful Cardioversion

    c. Conversion to Atrial Flutter

    d. Degeneration to VT

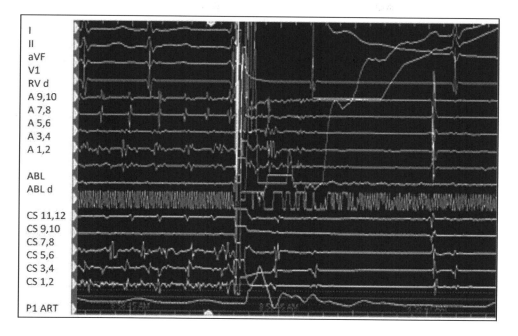

ANSWER: a. Successful Cardioversion. At the beginning of the slide the patient is clearly in AF. Note chaotic atrial activity on the CS channel. It is not VT, because there are many more A's than V's and a very narrow QRS on the surface ECG. AF is successfully converted to sinus rhythm. The 5th-9th channels show the circular mapping catheter in the LSPV, and the 10th and 11th channels show the ablation catheter which was disconnected. This CS channels clearly show the conversion to sinus rhythm. After cardioversion, each atrial deflection is followed by a ventricular deflection and the chaotic atrial activity is gone.

Atrial Flutter:

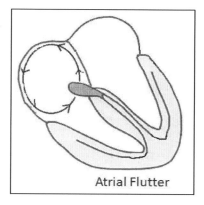

- Macro reentrant
- Can typically be terminated by pacing
- Usually accompanied by AV block
- Most common in the right atrium with counterclockwise propagation
- May also be located around areas of scar as well, such as post AF ablations

Atrial Flutter

1. A patient with prior AF ablation returns with AFL. What is the most common form of AFL seen in returning PVI patients?
  a. **Typical AFL**
  b. **Perimitral AFL**
  c. **Pulmonary vein AFL**
  d. **Cavotricuspid AFL**

ANSWER: b. Perimitral Atrial Flutter around the Mitral Annulus. Issa says, "This circuit involves reentry around the mitral annulus in a counterclockwise or clockwise fashion. This arrhythmia is more common in patients with structural heart disease; however, it has been described in patients without obvious structural heart disease but, in these patients, electroanatomical voltage mapping often shows scar or low-voltage area(s) on the posterior wall of the LA as a posterior boundary of this circuit. Perimitral AFL Is the most common macroreentrant AT in patients with prior LA ablation procedures for AF" See: Issa, chapter on Atypical (Non-isthmus dependent) AFL

Besides perimitral AFL other atypical left sided AFL macroreentry circuits can involve the PVs, LA scar from valve surgery, Left Septal wall (Fossa), and post-Maze procedure scars.
See: 3D activation video of Mitral annular reentry AFL at:
http://drwes.blogspot.com/2014/01/case-study-mitral-annular-left-atrial.

2. This EGM is continuous recording while pacing the atrium (via the CS catheter) during ablation of the cavotricuspid isthmus for typical atrial flutter The ABL catheter shows:
   a. **Successful ablation with AV block**
   b. **Successful ablation with increased pace to A time**
   c. **Unsuccessful ablation, AH still prolonged**
   d. **Unsuccessful ablation, possible AV node destruction**

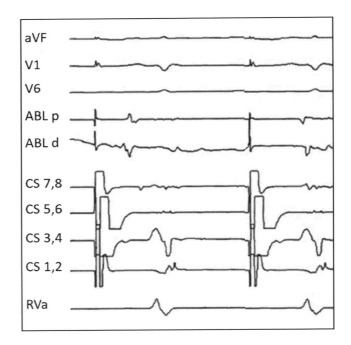

ANSWER: b. Successful Ablation with increased pace to A time. This is nice to see during isthmus ablation because it shows block. The impulse can no longer take the short cut through the isthmus but must go all the way around the atrium before it is seen on the ablation catheter. However, you must still complete the ablation line (typically from the IVC ring to the TV annulus). If there is any leak in the line, Atrial flutter (macro-reentry) may still occur.

The following diagram is a simplified description of this concept. To prove bidirectional block; the physician would also pace from the ablation catheter to see how long the impulse takes to travel to the CS catheter on the opposite side of the line. If the pace to A time is short, then the impulse was able to take a "short cut" across the isthmus and further ablation would be necessary. Not all physicians use this method for bidirectional block, many physicians use a duodecapolar catheter in the right atrium.

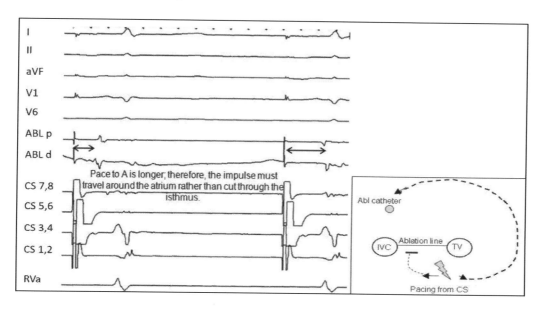

3. This EGM was recorded while mapping the isthmus after the initial ablation of atrial flutter. The arrow points to:

   a. **Persistent Flutter**
   b. **Bidirectional Block**
   c. **Counterclockwise Flutter**
   d. **Double potential**

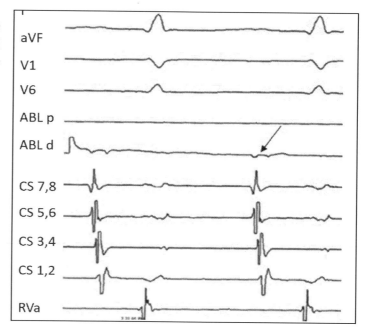

ANSWER: d. Double potential. A double potential is when you see the local A then a far field A from the other side of the ablation line. "Transmural ablation lesions in the isthmus can be recognized during flutter by double potentials separated by an isoelectric interval. Post ablation recurrent flutter is usually due to a single discrete recovered gap" (Circulation. 1997; 96:2505-2508)

According to Fogoros, for ablation of Atrial flutter, "the ablation catheter is introduced from the femoral vein and advanced into the right atrium and across the tricuspid valve. The tip of the catheter is rotated so that it is inferior to the ostium of the coronary sinus and is then pulled back to the tricuspid annulus. RF energy is then applied as the catheter is slowly drawn back from the annulus to the inferior vena cava. The linear lesion thus created must produce a complete electrical blockade between the inferior vena cava and the tricuspid annulus."
See Fogoros, Chapter on "Transcatheter Ablation"

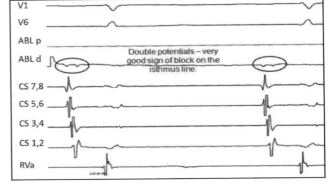

4. These four images show testing for bidirectional block after an AFL ablation. From top to bottom, each image shows a 3D activation map and EGM from a duodecapolar catheter in the RA with proximal CS pacing (CS not displayed).

Which set of images best depicts successful ablation of AFL? (Note: TA = Tricuspid annulus)

    a. #1
    b. #2
    c. #3
    d. #4

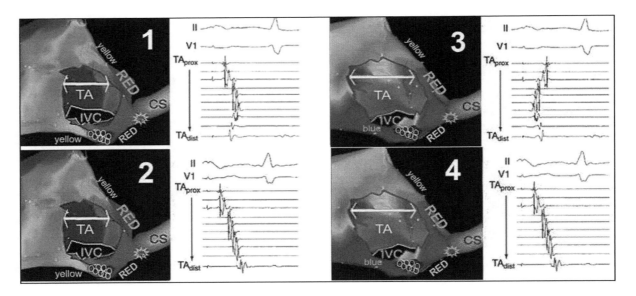

ANSWER: d. #4 indicates successful AFL ablation.

The 3D map at #1 & #2 depicts an incomplete CTI block because the yellow activation proceeds around both sides of the tricuspid annulus, indicating an incomplete block at the isthmus.

#3 & #4 maps show the activation proceeding only counterclockwise and being blocked at the isthmus.

The #1 & #3 EGMs show the impulse starting at the distal and proximal ends and meeting in the center of the duodecapolar catheter indicating incomplete block.

The EGMs #2 & #4 show the impulse rotating counterclockwise in one direction indicating complete block at the isthmus.

Pacing from CS should show activation along the duodecapolar from proximal to distal as one downward slanting line (\), not as in #1 & #2 with a (>) shaped sequence. Pacing from tip of Duo should show activation in the opposite direction from distal to proximal, as one upward slanting line (/), not shown. Images modified from Issa, chapter on AFL

5. This patient with atrial flutter has a RA surgical scar. How would you describe the macroreentry loops shown in the diagram?
   a. **Typical RA flutter with CW periatriotomy loop & CCW bystander peritricuspid loop**
   b. **Atypical RA flutter with CCW peritricuspid loop & CW bystander periatriotomy loop**
   c. **Figure-8 RA reentry with CCW periatriotomy loop, coexisting CW peritricuspid loop**
   d. **Figure-8 RA reentry with CW periatriotomy loop, coexisting CCW peritricuspid loop**

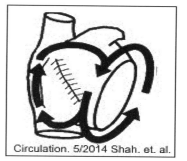

Circulation. 5/2014 Shah. et. al.

Answer d. Figure-8 RA reentry with clockwise periatriotomy loop, coexisting counterclockwise peritricuspid loop. Bystander loops are not an essential part of the reentrant circuit. Here both macroreentry loops are essential and linked by a common pathway. If only one loop is ablated, the other will continue. If the common pathway is ablated the macroreentry tachycardia stops. Otherwise, both loops must be ablated separately.

Shah says, "This article describes the characteristics of dual-loop, figure-8 atrial reentry. All occurred in patients previously operated on for surgical closure of an ostium secundum atrial septal defect and required ablation of two isthmuses to be curative.... conclusions—Figure-8 double-loop tachycardias mimicking the ECG pattern of a common atrial flutter occur in some patients after a surgical atriotomy. Ablation of one loop produces a sudden transformation to a new reentrant tachycardia formed of the remaining loop that requires ablation at a second isthmus." See: http ://circ.ahajournals.org/content/101/6/631.full

Two reentry loops may circle around a scar in opposite directions and meet on the other side of the scar, as shown in the diagram. This is most common in scar mediated VT. This shows a narrow isthmus within the scar that allows the two activation loops to meet, pass through and exit the isthmus, divide, and reenter myocardium again. Other loops and bystander circuits may exist within the scar. It is important to realize there are two loops in the figure 8 reentry, and if only one is ablated, the other may predominate; best to target the isthmus. Some physicians describe this VT ablation process as "breaking the small rocks (scars) into one big rock (scar)."

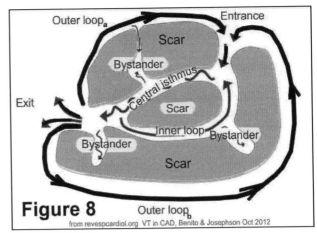

Figure 8 Outer loop_b
from revespcardiol.org VT in CAD, Benito & Josephson Oct 2012

See:http://www.revespcardiol.org/en/ventricular-tachycardia-in-coronary-artery/articulo/90155075/

6. From this EGM and LAO Xray in the following image, what is the most likely diagnosis?
   a. CW Atrial flutter with 3:1 block
   b. CW Atrial flutter with 2:1 block
   c. CCW Atrial flutter with 3:1 block
   d. CCW Atrial flutter with 2:1 block

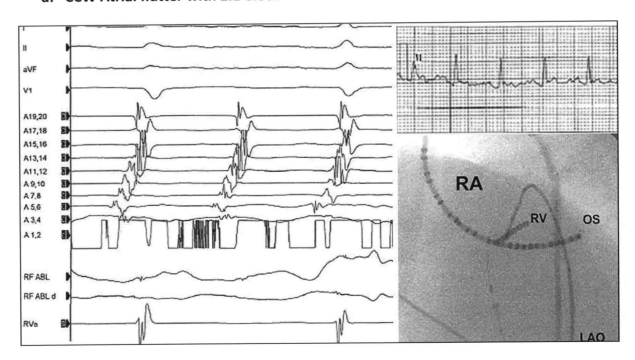

ANSWER: b. CW (clockwise) Atrial flutter with 2:1 block. In the EGM, the A channels are from a duodecapolar RA catheter, there is no CS catheter. The channel A1,2 is located near the CS ostium. The EGM shows two A signals for every QRS – a 2:1 flutter ratio. The flutter waves are not well seen on the surface ECG.

Notice how the wave of depolarization goes from the low right atrium at A5,6 and progresses clockwise up to the HRA at A 19,20. This example is during ablation, which is causing the disturbance on A1,2. This atrial flutter is isthmus dependent, just not in the usual counterclockwise direction. Whether it is clockwise or counterclockwise, typical Atrial Flutter ablations are still performed by drawing a line of block from the TV to the IVC through the CTI (Cavotricuspid isthmus). Left sided flutter was ruled out with a CS catheter that is now removed.

7. Identify this 12-lead ECG rhythm?
    a. **Typical CCW AFL with 3:1 AV block**
    b. **Typical CW AFL with 2:1 AV block**
    c. **Typical CCW AFL with 3:1 AV block**
    d. **Typical CW AFL with 2:1 AV block**
    e. **Atypical CCW AFL with 3:1 AV block**
    f. **Atypical CW AFL with 2:1 AV block**

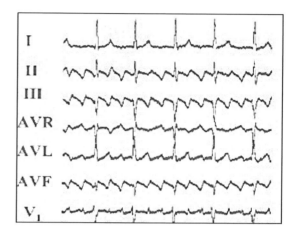

ANSWER: c. 3:1 typical CCW Atrial flutter with counterclockwise rotation. It is CCW because the flutter waves point down in inferior leads (II, III & aVF). Note one F wave buried in each QRS. This buried wave may be unmasked by vagal maneuvers or adenosine.

Issa says, "Counterclockwise AFL will always have a negative deflection preceding the positive deflection in the inferior leads.... Clockwise AFL has broad positive deflections in the inferior leads and wide negative deflections in V1."

Clockwise AFL will be positive in V1. See: Issa, chapter on Isthmus-dependent AFL

8. These three activation maps and EGMs are from a duodecapolar catheter placed normally in the RA with extremely limited geometry creation.
Match each 3D map with its corresponding atrial flutter EGM (below).

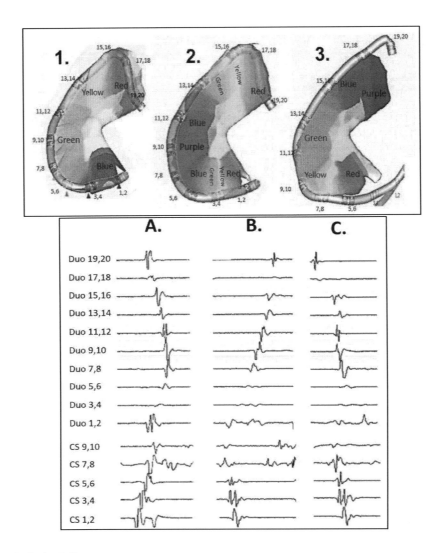

ANSWERS: 1-C, 2-A, 3-B,

2-A: The flutter in EGM A (corresponds with #2) is a left sided flutter passively activating the RA. Notice that the first A signals on the duodecapolar catheter is 1,2 (distal) and 19-20 (proximal) appear around the same time. Duo 9,10 is late.

3-B. The flutter in B (corresponds with #3) is an atrial flutter moving in the counterclockwise direction in the RA. The earliest A signal is on the duodecapolar distal (Duo 1,2) and moves to the proximal duodecapolar (Duo 19,20).

1-C. The flutter in C (corresponds with #1) is an atrial flutter moving in the clockwise direction. The earliest A signal is on the duodecapolar proximal (Duo 19,20) and moves to the distal duodecapolar (Duo 1,2).

All three of these examples could be left sided flutter showing how the wavefront propagates around the right atrium. In A, the wavefront activates the RA via Bachmann's bundle and the

CS. In B, the RA activation is coming from LA via the CS. In C, the RA is activated from the LA via Bachmann's bundle.

A key feature to help differentiate RA vs LA flutter is to see if the **entire cycle length** is accounted for in the RA. We can't determine this here as all the cycle lengths accounted for from the duodecapolar are not displayed. Depending on your reference point, there should be an early-meets-late phenomenon (dog chasing its tail) on the duodecapolar in typical RA flutter. If referencing the proximal CS, this is normally observed on the low lateral RA wall. Another way to see if your catheter is in the correct chamber is to try entrainment from various pacing sites.

9. Your patient is in atrial flutter. After entrainment of the flutter, to be sure the pacing electrodes are within the reentry circuit the post pacing interval (minus the TCL) should be:
   a. **>50 ms longer than CL of the original AF**
   b. **>50 ms longer than the entrainment pacing interval**
   c. **The same CL as the original AF (or within 30 ms)**
   d. **The same CL as the entrainment pacing interval (or within 30 ms)**

ANSWER: c. The same CL as the original AF (or within 30 ms). This confirms an isthmus dependent flutter, so the site of ablation is between the tricuspid annulus and the IVC. If the PPI is >50 ms longer than the AF CL, then it is atypical and usually needs further mapping to find the reentry loop and the best ablation site.

"The PPI is the time interval from the last pacing stimulus that entrained the tachycardia to the next non-paced recorded electrogram at the pacing site. During entrainment from sites within the reentrant circuit, the orthodromic wave front from the last stimulus propagates through the reentry circuit and returns to the pacing site, following the same path as the circulating reentry wavefronts. The conduction time needed is the revolution time through the circuit. Thus, the PPI (measured from the pacing site recording) should be equal (within 30 milliseconds) to the tachycardia CL if the conduction velocities and the reentrant path did not change during pacing;" See: Issa, chapter on "Mapping and Navigation"

AVNRT (AV Node Reentrant Tachycardia):

- Most common reentrant SVT: 60%
- AV Node: micro-reentrant
- Dual AV Nodal Physiology (slow and fast)
- In typical AVNRT, a premature impulse enters the circuit when the fast pathway (FP) is still refractory (impulse blocks in the FP fig. 2), but the slow has recovered. By the time this impulse reaches the distal connection, the FP has recovered, and the impulse conducts retrograde to the atrium while simultaneously going down the ventricle (fig. 3).
- Block in the atrium or in the ventricle does not affect the tachycardia
- AV nodal blocking agents are effective
- Treatment of choice: slow pathway ablation

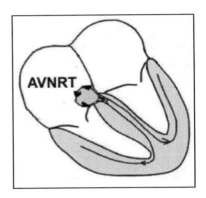

AVNRT: Jumps and Echo Beats

1. Dual AV node physiology is found in approximately___ % of normal adults.
   a. 0.1-1%
   b. 1-3%
   c. 5-10%
   d. 15-25%

ANSWER: d. 15-25%. The incidence of dual AV node physiology in normal adult's ranges from 37% to 13%. This high incidence of dual AV node physiology is why AVNRT is the most common form of SVT in adults. AVNRT requires dual AV node pathways with different ERPs (slow and fast). Note that dual AV node physiology does not necessarily mean the patient will develop AVNRT. That is why when you find a "jump" during extrastimulus testing, it is followed with attempted induction of AVNRT arrhythmia. See: D'Este, et.al., "Electrophysiological properties of the atrioventricular node and aging: evidence of a lower incidence of dual nodal pathways in the elderly," D'Este, et.al., JACC, 3, 2001

2. What happens in the second EGM with a 320 ms atrial extrastimuli?
   a. **Jump w/ Echo**
   b. **RVOT**
   c. **AV Block**
   d. **AH Jump**

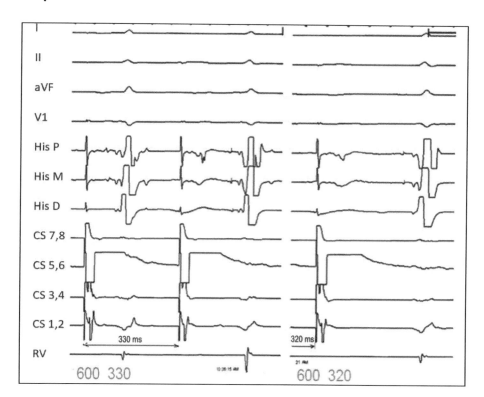

ANSWER: d. AH jump. During AEST the AV conduction appears normal until you reach the 320 ms extrastimuli. Then, note how the AH jumps to a much longer interval - over the 50 ms allowed. The AV node normally decrements with faster rates, i.e., increases AH intervals. But here, it is excessive - over 100 ms increase. The fast path blocks, and the slow path conducts down; the fast recovers and conducts up - down the slow / up the fast. It can form an endless reentry loop tachycardia termed AV nodal reentry tachycardia (AVNRT).

A jump occurs during extrastimulus testing the A to H interval "jumps" out more than 50 ms when going down in 10 ms increments. The impulse then travels down to the V via the slow pathway to the ventricle. If it were to travel back up the fast pathway to the atrium that would be termed and echo beat. So, the impulse through the slow pathway causes a long AH, followed by V, which is passed retrograde up the now recovered fast pathway, followed by an A (echo) that is often simultaneous with the V. This simultaneous atrial and ventricular contraction is characteristic of AVNRT. This is the point at which the fast pathway is refractory, so the impulse jumps to the slow pathway.

This patient is said to have dual AV nodal physiology. These two pathways lie within the triangle of Koch. Roughly 20% of the normal population has dual AV nodal physiology; however, not all these patients are able to conduct fast enough to induce AVNRT.

A similar tachycardia can happen in DDD pacing when the paced V wave passes retrograde up the AV node which is sensed as an A, and then the V is paced too soon. This circus movement may lead to pacer mediated tachycardia (PMT), like AVNRT.

See: Fogoros: chapter on Supraventricular tachycardia

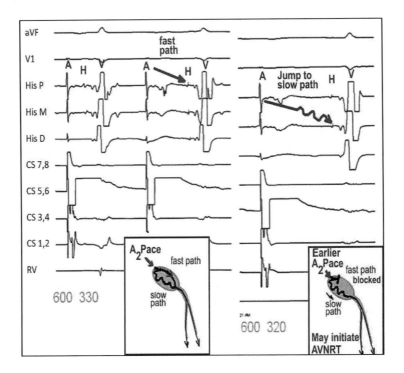

3. This patient came to the EP lab for presyncopal episodes. From this EGM taken during extrastimulus testing, what happened?

 a. VA Block
 b. AV Block
 c. Jump with Echo
 d. AP Potential

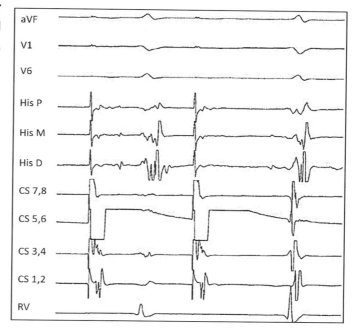

ANSWER: c. Jump with Echo. An echo is like one beat of nonsustained AVNRT. First, you will notice an AH jump, in which the fast pathway is refractory and the impulse "jumps" to the slow pathway. The impulse traveled down to the V and now it can travel back up to the A because the fast pathway has now recovered.

At times it may be difficult to distinguish an echo beat from a junctional beat which looks the same. Normally one would see an A and V deflection with a short VA interval; however, in this example notice that the CS channel V deflection is small on the first beat therefore is not seen well on the echo beat. This is still seen though by looking at the RVa catheter and the QRS complex. Junctional beats are commonly seen with patients on Isuprel, which is commonly used to help induce SVTs (slicks" up the AV node).

Isoproterenol's effects on the cardiovascular system (non-selective) relate to its actions on cardiac β1 receptors and β2 receptors on skeletal muscle arterioles. Isoproterenol has positive inotropic and chronotropic effects on the heart. In skeletal muscle arterioles it produces vasodilation. It's inotropic and chronotropic effects elevate systolic blood pressure, while its vasodilatory effects tend to lower diastolic blood pressure.

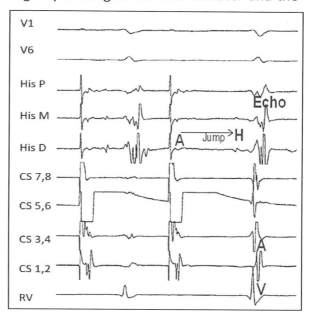

The adverse effects of isoproterenol are also related to the drug's cardiovascular effects. Isoproterenol can produce an elevated heart rate (tachycardia), which predisposes patients to cardiac dysrhythmias. This makes it an excellent choice for EP procedures).

4. During cryoablation of the slow pathway, testing was performed. With extrastimulus testing at 600/320, the circle beat was observed. This was unable to be reproduced on additional attempts. What is this beat?
   a. **Junctional**
   b. **Initiation of AVNRT**
   c. **VA block**
   d. **CHB**
   e. **AP Echo**

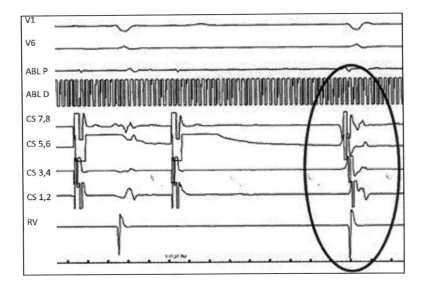

ANSWER: a. Junctional. Slow pathway ablation is the main treatment for AVNRT.
This looks just like an echo beat; however, this is a little too far out to be a jump w/ echo and on additional attempts this was not reproducible. Junctional beats are a normal finding, and no further ablation is necessary.

A junctional escape beat is a delayed heartbeat originating not from the atrium but from an ectopic focus somewhere in the AV junction. It occurs when the rate of depolarization of the sinoatrial node falls below the rate of the atrioventricular node. This dysrhythmia also may occur when the electrical impulses from the SA node fail to reach the AV node because of SA or AV block. It is a protective mechanism for the heart, to compensate for the SA node no longer managing the pacemaker activity and is one of a series of backup sites that can take over pacemaker function when the SA node fails to do so.

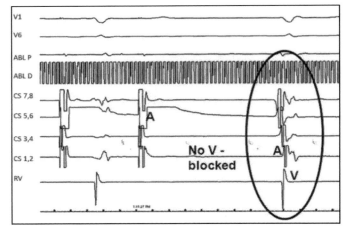

5. This 42-year-old patient was brought to the EP lab with complaints of palpitations and a wide complex tachycardia on the Holter monitor. What happens to this EGM during preliminary testing?

   a. **VA Block**
   b. **Jump with Echo**
   c. **AV Block**
   d. **VT**

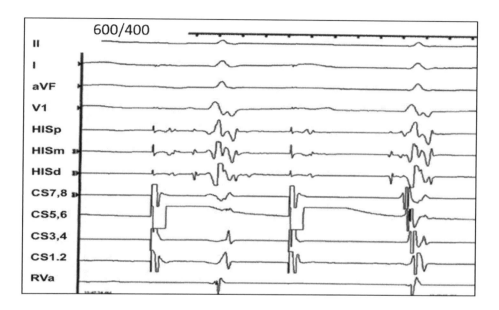

ANSWER: b. Jump with Echo. This shows dual AV nodal physiology or evidence of a slow pathway with at least one beat of tachycardia (echo). Since her tachycardia was a wide complex, further detailed testing is needed. Her tachycardia could be AVNRT with a rate related bundle branch block. Or her documented wide complex tachycardia on the Holter monitor could be ventricular tachycardia. The echo beat could just be an additional finding. Some patients may have a single echo beat but are unable to produce tachycardia. Further testing is needed to make sure the clinical tachycardia is not VT.

According to The Anatomy of the Atrioventricular Node by Robert H. Anderson, BSc, MD, FRCPath and Siew Yen Ho, PhD, "A short-coupled atrial stimulus may be blocked in the fast pathway (anterior septal input) while successfully propagating via the slow pathway (posterior input) toward the bundle of His. If this propagation is slow enough, the impulse may reenter the atrium retrogradely via the

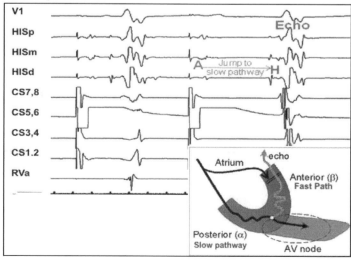

sufficiently recovered fast pathway, producing an echo-beat. The latter may then continue the same process leading to AVNRT."

6. In this 45-year-old patient with a history of palpitations, what happened with this atrial pacing maneuver after the 330 ms S2 in the following electrogram?
(Middle four channels are the CS; bottom channel is the RVa)
   a. Jump
   b. AVNERP
   c. AV Nodal Echo Beat
   d. CHB

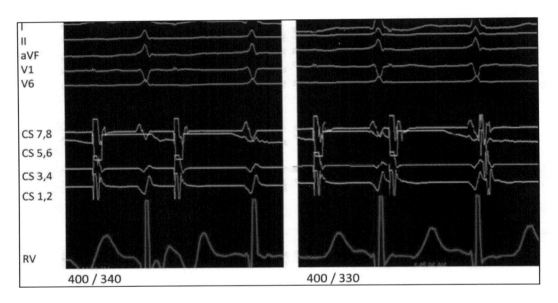

400 / 340   400 / 330

ANSWER: c. Echo. Typically, you would measure the AH interval. On this patient not His catheter was used, but since the HV interval is typically fixed we can measure from the A to the V. The A and V may seem to be simultaneous or fused. However, the A goes to the V in the next beat as noted by the arrows. Always start at the beginning of the slide and work your way through. This patient's jump was from 285 to 344 ms. (More than the 50 ms step-up allowed)

The channels are not labeled, but you should be able to determine what they are. Since you can see the A and V but no His on the middle 4 channels, one would assume that they are the CS. The bottom channel has a ventricular signal that lines up with the QRS. A jump is when the AH interval increases by >50 ms when S2 goes down in 10 ms increments (400, 340 to 400, 330...). The beat also "echoed" back up to the atrium.

When an early impulse initiates reentry, this impulse is blocked in the fast pathway and instead conducts via the slow pathway. A beat that initiates reentry is commonly accompanied by conduction delay. The electrophysiologist must pay particular attention to the occurrence of conduction delay during the onset of tachycardia. The site of this delay virtually always points to one of the pathways within the reentrant circuit. Fogoros: Supraventricular Tachyarrhythmias.

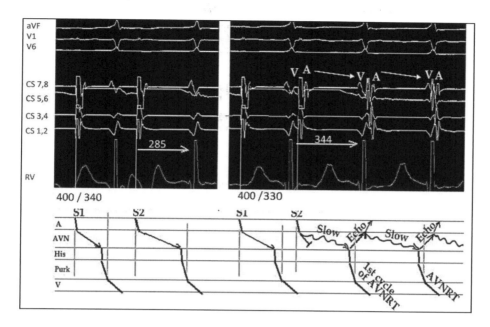

7. When looking for AVNRT with extra-stimulus testing, as you shorten the coupling interval by 10 ms, what type of jump is diagnostic for AVNRT?
   a. 25 ms prolongation of the A-H interval
   b. 50 ms prolongation of the A-H interval
   c. 75 ms prolongation of the H-V interval
   d. 100 ms prolongation of the H-V interval

ANSWER b. 50 ms prolongation of the AH interval. Purves says, "As you perform extra-stimulus testing (the S1-S2 extra-stimulus study), continue to measure the AH interval generated by the S2. You will notice the AH interval gradually lengthening as the fast AV nodal pathway decrements. A sudden, abrupt prolongation of the AH interval signals a block in the fast pathway and transition to the slow pathway. This jump is an indication that we have reached the ERP of the fast pathway and conduction to the ventricles is now occurring via the slow pathway. By arbitrary definition we consider at least a 50 ms prolongation in the AH interval with a 10 ms shortening of the S1-S2 coupling interval to be a significant jump." See: Purves, chapter on AVNRT

8. Diagnosis of dual AV node pathways relies on atrial extrastimuli (PACs) to diagnose a jump in the AH interval. If the H is unclear or obscured, how can a significant jump be identified?
   a. A2-V2 interval of >25 ms
   b. A2-V2 interval of >50 ms
   c. V2-A3 interval of >25 ms
   d. V2-A3 interval of >50 ms

ANSWER: b. A2-V2 interval of >50 ms. Note that as the H jumps out, the V jumps by the same amount, as shown. So, as commonly happens the H is not clear, you can measure the A2-V2 jump, or even V1-V2 jump which is the same as the AH jump. This is best seen on the CS tracing.

Issa says, "Patients with dual AVN physiology usually demonstrate a sudden increase (jump) in the AH interval at a critical AES (A1-A2) coupling interval. Conduction with a short PR or AH interval reflects fast pathway conduction, whereas conduction with a long PR or AH interval reflects slow pathway conduction. The AH interval jump demonstrates block of anterograde conduction of the progressively premature AES over the fast pathway (once the AES coupling interval becomes shorter than the fast pathway ERP) and anterograde conduction over the slow pathway (which has an ERP shorter than the AES coupling interval), with a longer conduction time (i.e., longer A2-H2 interval). A jump in A2-H2 (or H1-H2) interval of 50 milliseconds or more in response to a 10- millisecond shortening of A1-A2 (i.e., AES coupling interval) or of A1-A1 (i.e., pacing CL) is defined as a discontinuous AVN function curve and is considered as evidence of dual anterograde AVN pathways." See: Issa, chapter on "AVNRT"

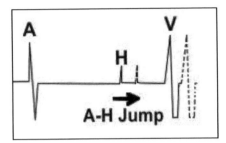

9. The current cure for typical AVNRT in patients who do not wish to take drugs is to ablate the:
   a. **Slow pathway to the AV node, along the tricuspid annulus**
   b. **Slow pathway to the AV node, along the tendon of Todaro**
   c. **Fast pathway to the AV node, along the tricuspid annulus**
   d. **Fast pathway to the AV node, along the tendon of Todaro**
   e. **Entire AV node and implant a pacemaker**

ANSWER: a. Slow pathway to the AV node, along the tricuspid annulus. Fogoros says, "During the past decade, RF ablation has become the treatment of choice for AV nodal reentrant tachycardia. The ablation of AV nodal reentry in recent years has been accomplished by ablating the slow pathway. Since the slow pathway is posterior, it is distant from the AV node, and thus ablation of this structure yields a low incidence of complete heart block.... In patients with AV nodal reentrant tachycardia, the fast and slow pathways can be visualized as two tracts of atrial fibers that coalesce to form the compact AV node. The fast pathway is...located along the tendon of Todaro. The slow pathway is a posterior and inferior tract of fibers, located along the tricuspid annulus near the ostium of the coronary sinus." See: Fogoros, chapter on "Transcatheter Ablation"

10. What are the two approaches to ablating AVNRT in the triangle of Koch? (Select two answers)

a. Use the ablation catheter to locate and ablate low amplitude potentials along the atrial aspect of the tricuspid annulus

b. Use the ablation catheter to locate and ablate low amplitude potentials along the tendon of Todaro

c. Use the ablation catheter to locate and ablate the earliest A

d. Gradually advance and ablate as you move anteriorly

e. Gradually pull back and ablate as you move inferiorly

ANSWER: (a & d) a. Use ablation electrode to search for and ablate low amplitude potentials along the atrial aspect of the tricuspid annulus (slow pathway) and d. Gradually advance and ablate as you move anteriorly along the atrial aspect of the tricuspid annulus. You do not want to damage the AV node, so you ablate starting inferiorly and moving anteriorly watching for block. "The target site can be mapped using the anatomical or electroanatomical approach. Large-tip and irrigated-tip catheters have no role in catheter ablation of the slow pathway, because the larger lesions they create can increase the risk of AV block." See Issa chapter on AVNRT

11. In a patient with typical AVNRT, your physician wishes to ablate using the electroanatomic approach. As he moves the catheter below the ostium of the CS as shown, this EGM was recorded. Which letter designates the slow-path late-potential closest to the AV node?

a. A
b. B
c. C
d. D
e. E
f. F

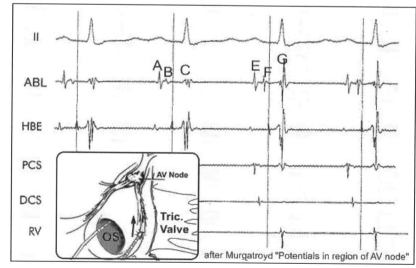

after Murgatroyd "Potentials in region of AV node"

ANSWER: f. The slow potentials B & F indicates you are on the slow pathway, and a good place to ablate. The slow potentials precede the His. The His is marked here with calipers. As you move closer to the AV node the slow potential becomes closer to the His. Depolarization

F is closer to the His than B, suggesting it is closest to the AV node. A & E are the atrial signals, B & F are the slow potentials, and C & G are the V signals.

The fast pathway is not usually ablated because it is the normal conduction pathway. Murgatroyd says, "A mapping catheter exploring the posterior part of the triangle of Koch can often record potentials that are separate from both the local atrial EGM and the His potential. These have been termed "slow pathway" potentials, but their exact cause is unclear. Near the CS the atrial electrogram may be sharp but the SP potential may be of low frequency and amplitude. At a slightly more anterior location the SP potential may become discrete, even if smaller, and the atrial EGM may become less well defined. At an even more anterior location, neither the SP nor the His potential can be recorded; this is the approximate location of the AV node [which you do not wish to ablate]. If the catheter is advanced beyond the His location, a RBB potential can often be recorded." See Murgatroyd, chapter on "Dual AV Node Pathways and AV Nodal Reentry"

12. In dual AV node physiology, what are the usual electrical properties of the abnormal tract?
   a. **Rapid depolarization & rapid repolarization**
   b. **Rapid depolarization & slow repolarization**
   c. **Slow depolarization & slow repolarization**
   d. **Slow depolarization & rapid repolarization**

ANSWER: d. Slow depolarization & rapid repolarization. Reentry requires a branching circuit, each with opposite electrical conduction properties - one fast and one slow conduction. This diagram shows how the two actions potentials differ. Remember, a fast depolarization upstroke (phase 0) means the potential is fast moving; a slow upstroke (phase 0) means slow moving wave front. The doughnut image shows how the fast action potential beats the slow potential out of the loop and its partially refractory tail has already exited the doughnut allowing the slow potential to turn around and pass up the fast path. This may occur in dual AV node physiology. Then all you need is a premature beat to start a continuous reentry loop circus movement.

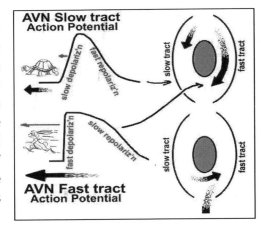

View the link below to a YouTube animation of an AVNRT micro-reentry. Dr Seedy explains, "The slow passage of current through the diseased tract allows enough time for the normal path to repolarize, and current arriving at the distal end of the abnormal tract is propagated not only into the AV node and into the ventricles but also in a retrograde direction up the normal fast path. By the time the current reaches the proximal end of the normal tract, the rapidly repolarizing diseased section is ready to conduct again. In this way a cycle of circulating current is established. In a small area of the junctional region the combination of an unfortunately timed atrial ectopic and the existence of tissues with opposite electrical conduction properties has established a rapidly discharging self-sustaining reentry loop of depolarizing current which is discharging distally into the ventricle by the bundle of His and in a retrograde fashion into the atrium. This is a micro-reentry circuit of AVNRT. The rapid atrial rate overrides SA node discharge." See ECG Teacher tutorial, by Dr. Seedy& Ryan https://www.youtube.com/watch?feature=player_embedded&v=PtM58hjSkIw

13. A patient with dual AV node physiology is in normal sinus rhythm. In NSR the action potential in the slow track _____ and the action potential in the fast track _____.
   a. Is extinguished, continues through the AV node
   b. Is extinguished, cycles retrograde up the slow path
   c. Continues through the AV node, is extinguished,
   d. Continues through the AV node, cycles retrograde up the slow pathway

ANSWER: a. Slow, is extinguished, fast continues through the AV node. This diagram shows what happens normally in NSR with dual AV node pathways. Normally the fast pathway dominates conduction, and the slow path is extinguished. The slow path action potential is met head-on and is cancelled out by the fast action potential in the distal end of the loop (#2 & 3). Meanwhile the fast impulse exits the loop in a normal manner. If there are no premature beats the slow path is suppressed by the fast path.

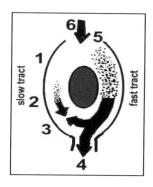

14. These four diagrams show the initiation sequence of typical common AVNRT. The fast path is on the right, slow on the left. Match the numbered locations on the diagram with their role and sequence in reentry. Black arrows are depolarizing tissue, dotted areas are repolarizing tissue, white areas are repolarized. Match all four.
   a. Reentry and an echo beat
   b. Retrograde conduction via fast path
   c. Antegrade conduction via slow path
   d. PAC with Unidirectional block

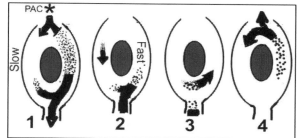

CORRECTLY MATCHED ANSWERS ARE:
d. PAC with unidirectional block
c. Slow antegrade conduction in slow path
b. Retrograde conduction in fast path
a. Reentry and echo beats start

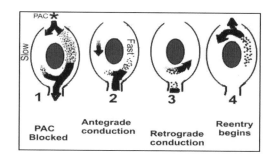

A PAC finds the fast path refractory causing unidirectional block. The premature beat cannot propagate down this fast side of the loop because of the refractoriness of this tissue. So, it activates only the slow path.

The slow tract conducts this PAC antegrade while the previous beat exits to the AV node. At the distal end of the loop the premature beat finds the fast track repolarized and ready to conduct because the preceding beat has exited the loop and entered the AV node. The premature beat jumps to the fast path conducts up the right side retrograde.

At the proximal end of the loop, the premature beat finds the slow path repolarized and ready to conduct downward. Reentry begins and continues around the loop. There is usually an echo beat in the atrium as the premature beat crosses the proximal end of the loop and depolarizes the atrium retrograde. This echo beat P wave is usually buried in the QRS from the previous beat. This slow-fast reentry cycle takes longer than the normal fast conduction, so we see a jump in the conduction time as that first beat comes around. Consecutive beats will have a much shorter cycle length than that of the SA node, thus a nodal reentry tachycardia continues. Thus, the saying "Down the slow, up the fast."

This describes common (slow-fast) counter-clockwise AVNRT. If it were clockwise (fast-slow) AVNRT the sequence would be the same except rotating the other direction from fast to slow in a clockwise direction. See:
https://www.youtube.com/watch?feature=player_embedded&v=PtM58hjSklw

15. You are doing an AVNRT ablation with RF energy. The physician is worried about ablation damage to the AV node. The rhythm changes from NSR to a junctional rhythm. You should inform the physician and:
   a. Stop ablating, AV block is immanent
   b. Stop ablating, and start atrial pacing
   c. Say, "It broke" and ask if he wishes to continue ablating
   d. Reduce the ablation power until NSR returns
   e. Continue ablating, and start atrial pacing

ANSWER: e. Continue ablating and start atrial pacing. Junctional rhythm is desirable and expected as it shows you are on the AV node pathway. But you need to monitor AV conduction to be sure you are not damaging the AV node. Since in junctional rhythms the P wave is not usually seen, pacing at a faster rate allows monitoring of AV conduction, as shown. Also, be ready to pace the ventricle and stop ablation, in case AV block develops.

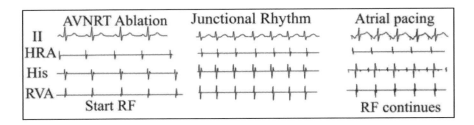

Issa says, [In AVNRT ablation] "An accelerated junctional rhythm typically develops within a few seconds of RF delivery at the effective ablation site.... The occurrence of this rhythm is strongly correlated to and sensitive for successful ablation sites; it occurs more frequently ... and for a longer duration... during successful compared with unsuccessful RF applications. Such a rhythm is, however, not specific for slow pathway ablation and is routinely observed during unintentional fast pathway and AVN ablation. Junctional tachycardia, on the other hand, is probably caused by thermal injury of the HB and heralds impending AV block." For this reason, if the junctional rhythm continues to accelerate - stop ablation. You may be damaging the fast pathway.

"When an accelerated junctional rhythm occurs, careful monitoring of VA conduction during this rhythm is essential and atrial pacing should be performed to ensure maintenance of 1:1 anterograde AV conduction. Occasionally, atrial pacing at a rate fast enough to override the junctional rhythm results in AV Wenckebach block at baseline, even before the onset of RF energy delivery; in this case, isoproterenol can be used to shorten the AV block CL and maintain 1:1 AV conduction during pacing."

[In AVNRT] "Ablation should be performed during NSR, when it is easier to maintain a stable catheter position. When ablation is carried out during AVNRT, sudden termination of the tachycardia during RF delivery can result in dislodgment of the ablation catheter, inadvertent AV block, and an incomplete RF lesion."

"The absence of junctional rhythm during RF application corresponds to an unsuccessful ablation site, and when an accelerated junctional rhythm does not develop within 10 to 20 seconds of RF delivery, RF application is stopped, and the catheter tip is repositioned to a slightly different site or better contact is verified and a new RF application attempted."

"Typical RF settings consist of a maximum power of 50 W and a maximum temperature of 55° to 60°C, continued for 30 to 60 seconds, or until the junctional rhythm extinguishes...." See Issa, chapter on "AVNRT"

16. This patient's AVNRT was approximately 190 to 200 beats per minute. Post AVNRT ablation, what does the last beat of the atrial extrastimulus testing show?
   a. **Fast pathway conduction**
   b. **Slow pathway conduction**
   c. **Complete AV block**
   d. **Wenckebach Conduction**

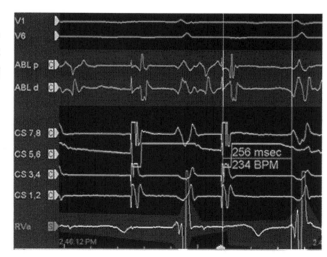

ANSWER: a. Fast pathway conduction. Since this patient's particular tachycardia was around 200 beats per minute this extrastimulus is conducted much faster. Since this A to V interval measures 234 bpm, it is unlikely to be slow pathway conduction. Slow pathways typically cannot conduct that fast. If it did, the patient's tachycardia would be able to go at 234 bpm…. Very fast!!

If the AV was longer showing slow pathway activation, then further ablation would be necessary depending on the end point desired. Younger patients may not be ablated as aggressively as older patients due to the risk of PPM if you damage the fast pathway.

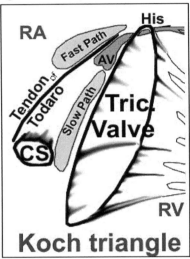

Koch triangle

Fogoros says, "Originally, the fast pathway was the target for ablation, but with the high chance of complete heart block, today physicians target the slow pathway. To visualize the dual AV nodal pathways as currently conceptualized, one must be familiar with the anatomy of Koch's triangle. The three sides of Koch's triangle are defined by the tricuspid annulus, the tendon of Todaro, and the ostium of the coronary sinus. The AV node is located at the apex of Koch's triangle. The apex of Koch's triangle is an anterior structure, and the CS is a posterior structure. The fast pathway is an anterior and superior tract of fibers, located along the tendon of Todaro. The slow pathway is a posterior and inferior tract of fibers, located along the tricuspid annulus near the ostium of the coronary sinus. Once the two pathways are localized, one can be ablated." See: Fogoros – Transcatheter Ablation: Therapeutic Electrophysiology

17. Typically, to initiate sustained AVNRT the VA Wenckebach ERP must be _____ ms in the slow pathway, and the AV Wenckebach ERP must be _____ms in the fast pathway.
   a. <100 ms, <500 ms
   b. <200 ms, <450 ms
   c. <300 ms, <400 ms
   d. <400 ms, <350 ms

ANSWER: d. <400 ms, <350 ms. Issa says, "The ability to initiate sustained AVNRT also requires the capability of the slow pathway to sustain repetitive anterograde conduction. Typically, for AVN reentry to occur, the fast pathway should be able to support 1:1 VA conduction at a ventricular pacing CL less than 400 milliseconds (i.e., retrograde Wenckebach CL less than 400 milliseconds) and the slow pathway should be able to support 1:1 AV conduction at an atrial pacing CL less than 350 milliseconds (i.e., antegrade Wenckebach cycle length less than 350 milliseconds). The shorter the AH interval with anterograde conduction over the fast pathway, the better the

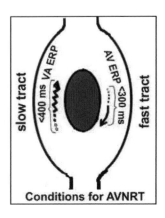

Conditions for AVNRT

retrograde conduction over the same pathway (i.e., the shorter the HA interval), and the better inducibility of AVNRT" See: Issa, chapter on AVNRT

18. In typical AVNRT, the initiating PAC finds the abnormal or slow tract (depolarized, repolarized) and the normal or fast tract (depolarized, repolarized).
   a. **Depolarized, Depolarized**
   b. **Depolarized, Repolarized**
   c. **Repolarized, Depolarized**
   d. **Repolarized, Repolarized**

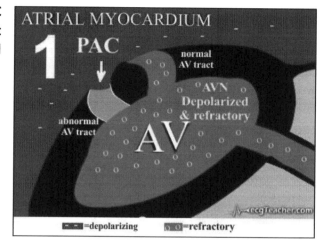

ANSWER: c. Repolarized, depolarized. The lower abnormal slow tract is repolarized and ready to conduct, while the upper or fast tract is depolarized or refractory so it will not conduct. Meanwhile, the slow conduction continues down the abnormal tract toward the AV node. See: https://www.youtube.com/watch?feature=player_embedded&v=PtM58hjSkIw

19. In AVNRT, when the slow abnormal tract depolarization reaches the AV node, the AV node is (depolarized, repolarized) and the normal fast pathway is (depolarized, repolarized).
   a. **Depolarized, depolarized**
   b. **Depolarized, repolarized**
   c. **Repolarized, depolarized**
   d. **Repolarized, repolarized**

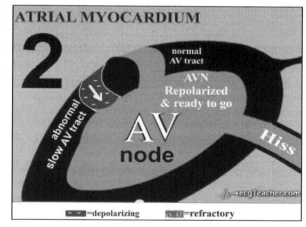

ANSWER: d. Repolarized, repolarized and ready to fire again. So, when the impulse from the slow tract arrives in the AV node, The node is ready to fire and conduct again. The other normal tissues, the fast track and His bundle are also ready to fire. Although it is too early, these tissues will conduct this irregular impulse and create a premature beat. See: https://www.youtube.com/watch?feature=player_embedded&v=PtM58hjSkIw

20. In diagram 4, what happens at the distal end of the reentry circuit in slow-fast AVNRT? After the abnormal tract depolarizes the AV node, the impulse passes (antegrade, retrograde) through the normal tract and it finds the atrium (depolarized, repolarized), and the abnormal tract (depolarized, repolarized).

    a. Antegrade, depolarized, depolarized
    b. Antegrade, depolarized, repolarized
    c. Retrograde, repolarized, depolarized
    d. Retrograde, repolarized, repolarized

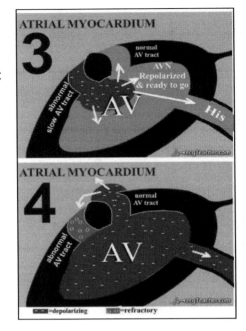

ANSWER: d. Retrograde, repolarized, repolarized. The signal passes up the fast tract retrograde, and up into the atrium which is also repolarized and read to fire again. Thus, we see retrograde atrial echo beats in AVNRT. As the impulse loops around in the atrium it finds the slow track repolarized and ready to conduct down the AV node again. This starts the reentry cycle again. The Depolarized AV node conducts down the His bundle into the ventricle, resulting in a narrow complex QRS. In AVNRT, since the impulse is also firing the atrium retrograde at the same time, the A and V are often superimposed. See: https://www.youtube.com/watch?feature=player_embedded&v=PtM58hjSkIw

21. On this EGM, what happens in the fourth beat?

    a. **Retrograde P wave**
    b. **Orthodromic AVRT**
    c. **PAC with 1st degree block**
    d. **Dual AV node, jump to slow pathway**
    e. **2nd degree AV block with 2:1 conduction**

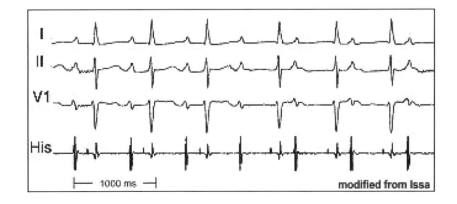

ANSWER: d. Jump to slow AV node pathway. Dual AV node physiology, diagnosed by a large jump in AH interval from 176 ms to 402 ms. The sudden increase or jump in the PR interval suggests dual AV node physiology, where AV conduction switches from the fast pathway to the slow pathway. AVNRT does not necessarily develop. Note that the PR interval lengthens proportionately.

Issa says, "Dual atrioventricular node (AVN) physiology manifests as two different PR intervals during normal sinus rhythm (NSR). Note the shift in AV conduction from the fast to the slow AVN pathway ... occurs without any changes in the sinus cycle length (CL) (680 ms). This phenomenon indicates that the fast pathway anterograde effective refractory period (ERP) is long relative to the sinus CL." See: Issa, chapter on EP Testing

22. AVNRT usually has a heart rate _____ while junctional tachycardia has a heart rate _____.

   a. 100 bpm, <60 bpm
   b. 140 bpm, <130 bpm
   c. 150 bpm, <150 bpm
   d. 160 bpm, <120 bpm

ANSWER: b. > 140 bpm is AVNRT, <130 bpm is junctional tachycardia.
AVNRT generates a heart rate greater than 140 beats per minute or faster. AVNRT and junctional tachycardia look similar and arise from the same area of the heart, the AV junction. But junctional tachycardia arises from an automatic focus with a slower heart rate between 100 and 130 beats per minute. Tachycardia must have a heart rate over 100 bpm.

In the online video Dr. Seery says, "Heart rate allows us to assume about the mechanism generating the arrhythmia. A tachycardia originating in the junctional region with a rate greater than 140 is certainly AVNRT. While, if the rate is less than 130 bpm the tachycardia is labeled junctional. There is a gray area, between 130 and 140." See: ECG Teacher tutorial, by Dr. Seery& Ryan

https://www.youtube.com/watch?feature=player_embedded&v=PtM58hjSkIw
See: AHA, ACLS Provider Manual, chapter on "Stable Tachycardias"

23. You are monitoring the AVNRT patient's EGM during slow pathway ablation. This EGM shows:
   a. Wenckebach
   b. Jump to fast pathway
   c. VA prolongation
   d. Junctional rhythm like this is normal

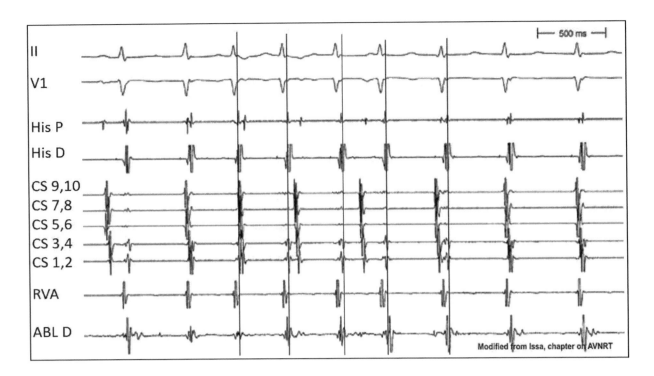

ANSWER: c. VA prolongation is a sign of AV node damage, and you should inform the physician. In this EGM notice the A shows clearly on the CS catheter. The A initially merges with the V in a junctional rhythm and in the third beat starts to fall behind the V and eventually dissociate from the V, indicating AV block.

At the first sign of VA prolongation ablation should be stopped. This is everyone's job in the control room. A junctional rhythm like this during AVNRT ablation is a good sign. But you must notify the electrophysiologist to stop when the His or CS catheters show the A splitting off from the V as shown here.

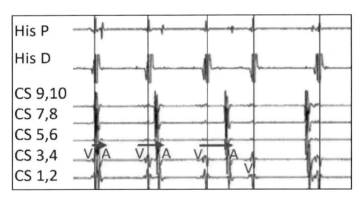

Nakagawa says, "The loss of 1:1 retrograde fast pathway conduction during junctional rhythm may indicate injury to the AV node or fast pathway, and the RF application should be terminated immediately." See: "Catheter Ablation of Paroxysmal Supraventricular Tachycardia,"

Nakagawa, et. Al., Circulation, 2007, http://circ.ahajournals.org/content/116/21/2465.full

"A number of markers of impending AV block have been suggested, ... It is important to terminate the RF application if short cycle length junctional tachycardia occurs to confirm 1:1 AV conduction without prolongation of the PR interval. The anatomic location of the ablation is important.... The most useful sign is the presence of varying degrees of VA block in junctional rhythm during the application. It is important to carefully monitor the VA relationship during the RF application because any increase in the VA interval or sudden development of VA block might signify imminent heart block." See: Zipes, chapter on Ablation of SVT

24. Your patient is having a slow pathway RF ablation for typical AVNRT. The anesthesiologist has the patient asleep with all muscles relaxed. During RF ablation the anesthesiologist stops the patient's breathing - WHY?
   a. To increase CO_2 levels and parasympathetic tone (slow AV conduction)
   b. To decrease O_2 levels and sympathetic tone (speed AV conduction)
   c. To minimize risk of tamponade
   d. To minimize catheter motion
   e. To minimize risk of air embolism

ANSWER: d. To minimize catheter motion and create an effective lesion. Zipes says, "The risk of AV block during slow pathway ablation has varied according to the reported series but, in general, is less than 1%. In cases where catheter stability is difficult to achieve and when the distance between the anterior and posterior inputs is small, several measures can be taken to avoid inadvertent damage to the fast pathway and compact AV node. We prefer the routine use of a long vascular sheath, and, in some cases, we use general anesthesia with muscle relaxation to allow cessation of respiration during the RF application. This latter technique has proved very useful to ensure catheter stability during difficult cases." See: Zipes, chapter on AVNRT

25. Your patient has typical AVNRT inducible with atrial extrastimulus testing and Isuprel infusion. Isuprel was stopped and the SVT terminated after RF ablation.
To see if this ablation effectively cured the AVNRT, this should be done prior to ending the procedure.
   a. Try to reinitiate AVNRT with Isuprel
   b. Try to reinitiate AVNRT with Isuprel and atrial extrastimulus testing
   c. Wait 10 minutes, then try to reinitiate AVNRT with Isuprel
   d. Wait 30 minutes, then try to reinitiate AVNRT with Isuprel and atrial extrastimulus testing

ANSWER: d. Wait 30 minutes, then try to reinitiate AVNRT with Isuprel and atrial extrastimulus testing. Waiting for 30 minutes allows for acute tissue inflation from the RF to resolve. Issa says, "The optimal endpoint for slow pathway ablation is the complete elimination of slow pathway conduction and dual AVN physiology without impairing the fast pathway. This [endpoint] is evidenced by loss of conduction over the slow pathway.... However, elimination of all evidence of slow pathway conduction is not a necessary requirement for a successful slow pathway ablation procedure. It suffices to eliminate inducibility of AVNRT and 1:1 anterograde conduction over the slow pathway, with and without isoproterenol infusion.... Reassessment of inducibility should be repeated 30 minutes after the last successful RF application.... If isoproterenol was required for initiation of SVT prior to ablation, isoproterenol should be discontinued during ablation and readministered afterward to assess the efficacy of ablation."

Tip: Note how you jumped to select answer a. It is correct - but only partially. Answer d is more correct because it includes the obligatory 30-minute wait period. Be sure to evaluate all answers carefully before selecting the correct one. See: Issa, chapter on AVNRT

26. AVNRT was induced on this patient during catheter placement. Is this an appropriate position to begin cryoablation?
   a. **Yes, fractionated signal on ABL catheter**
   b. **Yes, His spike seen on ABL catheter**
   c. **No, not until AVNRT induced**
   d. **No, not until you are in the fast pathway**

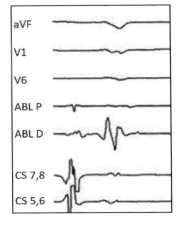

ANSWER: a. Yes, fractionated signal on ABL catheter. Slow pathway potentials are small fractionated electrograms. According to the Division of Cardiology, University of Michigan Medical Center, Ann Arbor, "Atrial electrograms recorded from target sites during radiofrequency catheter ablation of the slow atrioventricular (AV) nodal pathway are often fractionated and may be associated with a late, high frequency component (the slow pathway potential)." This is thought to be the impulse going through the actual slow pathway and is an ideal ablation location.

This is an ideal spot for ablation. Some physicians ablate anatomically... starting posterior and working anterior. Some map slow pathway potentials, while most do a combination of both. Always look to be sure there is not His deflection before ablating to make sure you will not inadvertently induce CHB.

Cardiac Dictionary says,
"Fractionated electrogram: prolonged, low amplitude, high frequency myocardial recordings thought to be related to the zone of slow conduction in a reentrant circuit."
See: Hayes, Dictionary of Pacing, Defibrillation, Resynchronization & Arrhythmias.

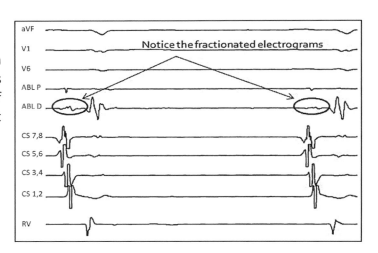

27. This EGM was recorded during AVNRT ablation. Why did the physician start atrial pacing?
   a. **Monitor AV conduction**
   b. **Monitor for vagal nerve damage**
   c. **Reduce risk of ventricular arrhythmia**
   d. **Break the junctional tachycardia (ATP)**

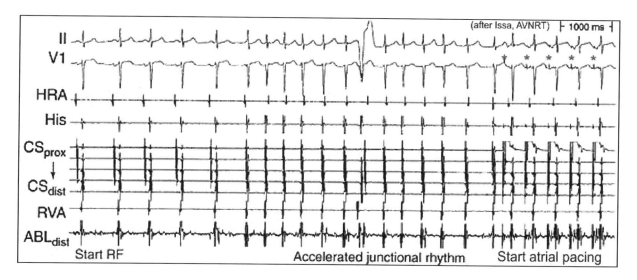

ANSWER: a. Monitor AV conduction because prolongation as a sign of AV node damage. The appearance of a junctional rhythm like this during ablation of a slow pathway is a good sign. It is such a good sign that some Drs. continue ablation until the junctional rhythm stops. In this EGM example ablation started in sinus rhythm, that soon turned to a Junctional rhythm, which is good. But, because the junctional rhythm is fast, there is concern that the AV node is being damaged, so atrial pacing was started to better monitor AV conduction.

Issa says, "An accelerated junctional rhythm typically develops within a few seconds of RF delivery at the effective ablation site. The mechanism of this rhythm is unclear ... Occurrence of this rhythm is strongly correlated to and sensitive for successful ablation sites; it occurs more frequently (94% versus 64%) and for a longer duration (7.1 versus 5.0 seconds) during successful compared with unsuccessful RF applications.... Typical RF settings consist of a maximum power of 50 W and a maximum temperature of 55° to 60°C, continued for 30 to 60 seconds, or until the junctional rhythm extinguishes.".
See: Issa, chapter on AVNRT, See Also Huang pp. 336-337; McGavigan Et. Al. Pacing Clinical Electrophysiology 2005; 28:1052-54

28. Which EGM shows the best place to apply RF energy for an AVNRT slow pathway ablation on this 26-year-old patient?

    a. A

    b. B

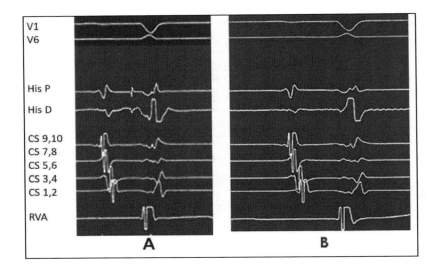

ANSWER: B. Notice the small fractionated atrial signal on the distal ablation channel. This is an ideal spot for slow pathway ablation. The slow pathway gives the best outcome for AVNRT ablations. If the fast pathway were ablated then the patient would be dependent on using the slow pathway for their underlying rhythm which is slower and unreliable; however, this was the treatment of choice in the past. Fast pathway ablations have an elevated risk for CHB. If the physician were to apply RF energy at location A, this patient may have CHB. Notice the small, sharp His deflection on the ablation channel in between the atrial and ventricular deflections.

29. The electroanatomical approach to ablate AVNRT usually involves mapping the:

    a. Fast pathway for slow potentials

    b. Fast pathway for fast potentials

    c. Slow pathway for slow potentials

    d. Slow pathway for fast potentials

ANSWER: c. Slow pathway for slow potentials. Issa says, "Electroanatomical Approach: The (AVNRT slow pathway) target site is identified by slow pathway potentials. Initially, the triangle of Koch is mapped from the apex of the triangle (where the HB is recorded) and then moved toward the CS ostium.... Slow pathway potentials are usually recorded at the mid anteroseptal position, where they are in the middle of the isoelectric line connecting the atrial and

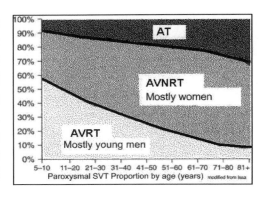

ventricular electrograms. Moving the mapping catheter inferiorly, the slow pathway potential moves towards the atrial electrogram, and when the optimal site for slow pathway ablation is reached, it merges with the atrial electrogram... using the HB

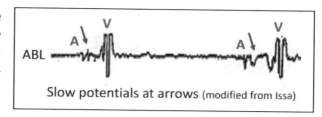

Slow potentials at arrows (modified from Issa)

and CS ostium positions (as defined by the HB and CS catheters) as landmarks, the most common area where the slow potentials are recorded is in the posterior third of the line connecting those two landmarks." Don't confuse these slow potentials with the His signal. See: Issa, chapter on AVNRT

AVRT (AV Reentrant Tachycardia)

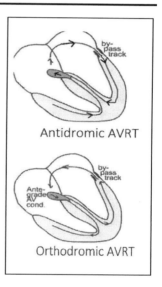

Antidromic AVRT

Orthodromic AVRT

- Macro reentrant circuit involving the atrium, AV node, His/Purkinje system, ventricle, and accessory pathway.
- Block in the A or V will terminate the tachycardia
- WPW is an ECG finding that shows evidence of an antegrade conducting accessory pathway. A patient may have an accessory pathway without WPW on the ECG.
- Reentrant circuit during tachycardia:
  o Antidromic (Delta waves): Down the pathway / up the node –
  o Orthodromic: down the AV node / up the pathway
    ▪ Orthodromic is more common
- Treatment: Ablation of pathway

Accessory Pathways & AVRT

1. AVRT is most common in _____.
   a. Young men
   b. Young women
   c. Older men
   d. Older women

ANSWER a. Young men. More men have AVRT than women and this develops at an early age because anatomic APs are genetically transmitted. The diagram above shows AVRT mostly in young men. Issa says, "a minority of patients have late onset of symptoms associated with

AVRT and thus continue to account for a small proportion of ablations in older patients. Men account for a higher proportion of AVRT at all ages." See Issa, chapter on PSVT, Epidemiology

2. Most patients with AVRT have a normal QRS because their AP can only conduct retrograde. This is termed:
   a. **Manifest: Orthodromic AVRT**
   b. **Manifest: Antidromic AVRT**
   c. **Concealed: Orthodromic AVRT**
   d. **Concealed: Antidromic AVRT**

ANSWER: c. Concealed: Orthodromic AVRT. Concealed pathways travel down the AV node and up the accessory pathway; therefore, the QRS activation is narrow and does not have a delta wave. "In orthodromic AVRT, the AVN-HPS serves as the anterograde limb of the reentrant circuit (i.e., the pathway conducts the impulse from the atrium to the ventricle), whereas an AV BT serves as the retrograde limb. Approximately 50% of BTs participating in orthodromic AVRT are manifest (able to conduct bidirectionally) and 50% are concealed (able to conduct retrogradely only). Therefore, a WPW pattern may or may not be present on surface ECG during NSR. When preexcitation is present, the delta wave seen during NSR is lost during orthodromic AVRT, because anterograde conduction during the tachycardia is not via the BT (i.e., the ventricle is not preexcited) but over the normal AV conduction system. Orthodromic AVRT accounts for approximately 95% of AVRTs and 35% of all paroxysmal supraventricular tachycardias (SVTs)." See: Issa, chapter on "AVRT"

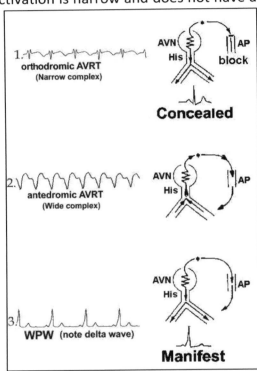

3. Parahisian pacing helps to differentiate:
   a. **Septal AVRT from AVNRT**
   b. **VT from SVT with aberrancy**
   c. **His bundle from AV node**
   d. **WPW from RBBB**

ANSWER: a. Septal AVRT from AVNRT. Issa says, "This maneuver helps exclude the presence of a septal AV-BT, which can mediate an orthodromic AVRT with retrograde atrial activation sequence like that during AVNRT. Overdrive ventricular pacing is performed at a long pacing CL (more than 500 milliseconds) and high output from the pair of electrodes on the HB catheter that record the distal HB potential. During pacing, direct HB capture is indicated by shortening of the width of the paced QRS complex. The pacing output and pulse width are then decreased until the paced QRS widens, indicating loss of HB capture. The pacing output is increased and decreased to gain and lose HB capture, respectively, while local ventricular capture is maintained." Since the HB is deep within the RV septum, it takes more energy to pace than the myocardium (wide LBB complex). This is opposite to threshold testing, where you must increase the voltage to get the ventricular wide complex; here you decrease it. See: Issa chapter on "EP Testing"

4. What is a maneuver used to distinguish retrograde atrial activation occurring over a septal accessory pathway from that occurring over the normal VA conduction system?
  a. **Valsalva maneuver**
  b. **Isuprel infusion**
  c. **Atrial extrastimulus testing**
  d. **Ventricular extrastimulus testing**
  e. **Parahisian pacing**
  f. **Atrial overdrive pacing**

ANSWER: e. Parahisian pacing. "Parahisian pacing: A maneuver used to distinguish retrograde atrial activation occurring over septal accessory pathway from that occurring over the normal VA conduction system. An electrode catheter is placed near the His bundle and pacing occurs at a constant cycle length with decreasing pulse amplitude, beginning at a high output. The His bundle is captured initially, but then capture is lost, and ventricular capture occurs as the output is reduced." Changes in the Pace-A intervals are assessed. In the presence of an accessory pathway, the AP does all the retrograde conducting, and the Pace-A time is constant when pacing the His or the Ventricle. See: Hayes, EP Dictionary

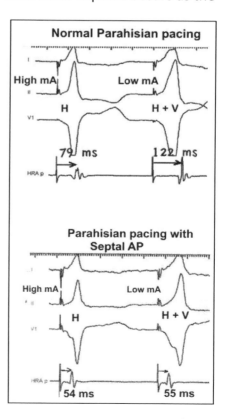

This diagram shows parahisian pacing normally and with a septal accessory pathway. While pacing the His first at high output and the turning down mA, if normal VA conduction is present (upper picture) the time from pacing spike to A will be longer at the lower paced output. But if a septal pathway is present (lower diagram) that AP will conduct up to the atrium rapidly and with equal timing both at high and low pacing outputs. The EGMs show how when the H is captured (it requires higher mA) the QRS is narrow, but at lower mA when mostly the V is captured the QRS is broad. Note how the second H+V is broader in both the normal and AP EGMs. The difference between the normal and AP patient is how rapidly it conducts to the atrium. Retrograde conduction up the AP will be constant no matter whether the H or V is paced.

5. In this patient with manifest WPW, his basic cycle length measures 850 ms. The RF ablation catheter is placed near the His. What can be done to measure the true HV interval with antegrade AV nodal conduction?

    a. **Reposition the His catheter**
    b. **Pace the RV at 800 ms**
    c. **Pace the HRA at 1000 ms**
    d. **Pace the proximal CS at 700 ms**

ANSWER: d. Pace the proximal CS at 700 ms. The RF ablation catheter is already at the level of the His / AV node. Repositioning the His catheter will not help. In manifest WPW there is a delta wave, here best seen in lead I. Conduction to the ventricle occurs rapidly through the AP and slower through the AV node. There is only one waveform on the RF channel (His channel) because the impulse is conducting through the accessory pathway causing a short PR interval and fusing with AV conduction. This results in the delta wave on the surface ECG.

In EGM #1, you cannot see the His at all; it is buried in the delta wave. Pacing the CS at a faster rate can help to differentiate the waveforms and convert to pure antegrade AV conduction, as in the second EGM. Now, by pacing the atrium at a rate faster than the accessory pathway ERP you lose the delta wave and can easily see the A, H, and V waves.

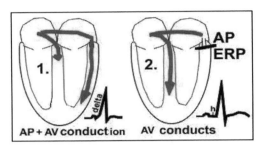

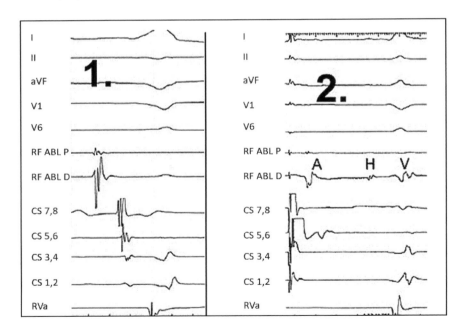

6. In this example of ventricular extrastimulus testing, what is the best explanation for the change in conduction with S2?
   a. **AERP**
   b. **AP ERP**
   c. **VA Block**
   d. **AV Block**

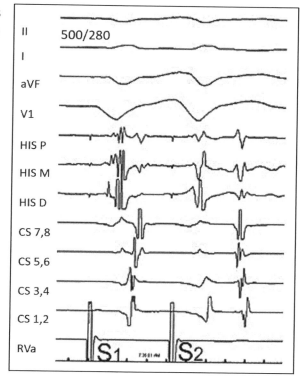

ANSWER: b. AP ERP. A left-sided accessory pathway effective refractory period is reached. In S2 note the longer VA interval and change from eccentric to concentric conduction. A left sided accessory pathway could act like this. S1 shows retrograde conduction via a left sided accessory pathway with eccentric conduction on the CS channel. In S1 the V and A fuse at CS1,2. But with S2 the V and A separate and conduct concentrically (proximal to distal CS electrodes).

In the second beat, S2 is so early that the accessory pathway fails to conduct retrograde into the atrium; AP ERP is reached. With S2, slower VA conduction moves up the AV node. It reaches the atrium late and results in concentric (distal to proximal) CS conduction.

Ventricular extrastimulus testing is performed the same way as atrial extrastimulus testing except we are pacing the ventricle with a drive train of eight beats and adding a PVC from the same location. Then this PVC is brought in a little closer (typically 10 to 20 ms) with each consecutive drive train.

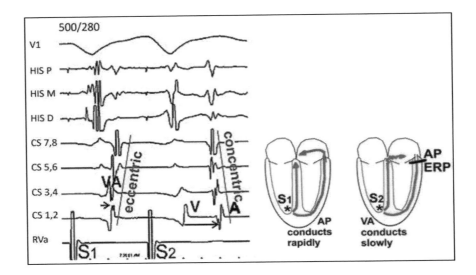

7. During atrial extrastimulus testing in this patient with suspected accessory pathway, what type of conduction occurs after S2?

    a. AERP
    b. VA Block
    c. AP ERP
    d. AV Block

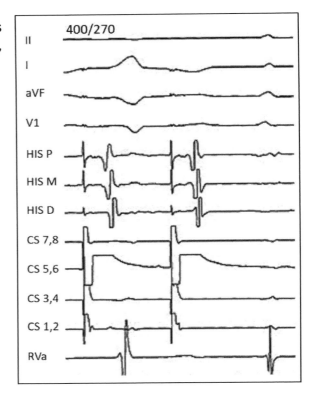

ANSWER: c. AP ERP. In this example notice the loss of the delta wave. When there is a delta wave it is referred to as WPW which demonstrates the ventricle is preexcited. WPW is a form of AVRT. Note that after S2, the AV interval jumps from about 80 ms to 200 ms as preexcitation stops.

"The effective refractory period of the accessory pathway in the A-V direction is defined as the shortest atrial premature stimulus interval showing block in A-V conduction over the accessory pathway from the atrial stimulation site closest to the atrial end of the accessory pathway." See: Dutch EP pioneer Hein J. J. Wellens.

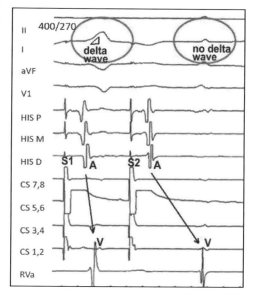

It is important to understand how fast the patient's pathway can conduct in the antegrade direction (down the pathway from atrium to ventricle) to classify them for sudden cardiac death (SCD). Patients, whose pathways conduct at 250 ms or faster, are at greatest risk of SCD. If that patient went into atrial fibrillation, their bypass tract would send all the impulses down to the ventricles at 250 ms cycle length which could lead to VF and SCD. See: Wellens: 33 years of Cardiology and Arrhythmology.

8. On this 35-year-old patient, the physician is performing decremental pacing. The physician stopped decrementing the pacing train when it reached 300 ms. What type of conduction occurs throughout?

   a. **VERP**
   b. **Bundle Branch**
   c. **Block**
   d. **AERP**
   e. **VA conduction**

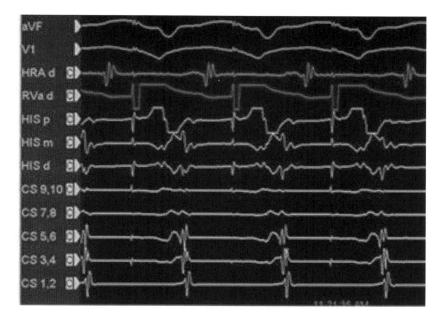

ANSWER: d. VA conduction. There is an A following every paced V indicating retrograde VA conduction. This may be normal. At the point of 300 ms many physicians stop pacing. Pacing the ventricle any faster may induce VT or VF. Some physicians pace faster than 300 ms; this is up to physician discretion. This is also a good example of why it is essential to have the patient connected to the defibrillator during the entire study. It is also recommended to have a second defibrillator in the room as backup in case of failure. Notice the wide QRS complex, which is normal with V pacing. This does not necessarily mean the patient has an underlying BBB.

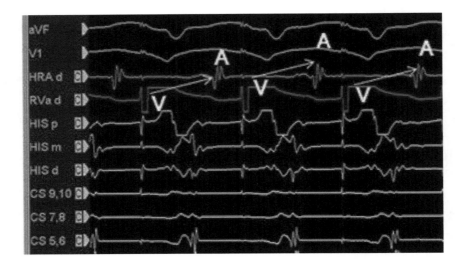

9. In this patient with WPW what type of conduction occurs in the last beat?
   a. **AP block**
   b. **Fast pathway block**
   c. **First degree block**
   d. **Second degree block**

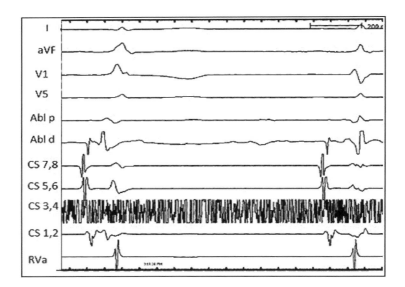

ANSWER: a. AP block. Block in the accessory pathway is evident by the loss of preexcitation (delta wave) and the AV interval that was fused now separates. When the AV interval is fused, then the impulse goes through the accessory pathway, it is not slowed down by the AV node. In this example, block did not occur during programmed stimulation (pacing), but preexcitation would come and go in sinus rhythm. In this example, there is a lot of interference on CS 3,4; it is just a poor connection or cable.

Wolff–Parkinson–White syndrome (WPW) is one of several disorders of the conduction system of the heart that are commonly referred to as pre-excitation syndromes. While many individuals with WPW remain asymptomatic throughout their entire lives, there is a risk of sudden cardiac death associated with the syndrome.

WPW is caused by the presence of an abnormal accessory electrical conduction pathway between the atria and the ventricles. Electrical signals traveling down this abnormal pathway may stimulate the ventricles to contract prematurely, resulting in a specific type of supraventricular tachycardia referred to as an atrioventricular reentrant tachycardia (AVRT). The incidence of WPW is between 0.1% and 0.3% in the general population. People with WPW are usually asymptomatic. However, the individual may experience palpitations, dizziness, shortness of breath, or syncope (fainting or near fainting) during episodes of supraventricular tachycardia.

The telltale "delta wave" may sometimes—but not always—be seen on an electrocardiogram. WPW is commonly diagnosed based on the electrocardiogram in an asymptomatic individual. In this case it is manifested as a delta wave, which is a slurred upstroke in the QRS complex that is associated with a short PR interval. The short PR interval and slurring of the QRS complex is the impulse making it through to the ventricles prematurely (across the accessory pathway) without the usual delay experienced in the AV node.

This diagram shows the blocked AP which allows normal AV conduction to occur. The next page shows a similar diagram where the AP does conduct - with A and V wave fusion.

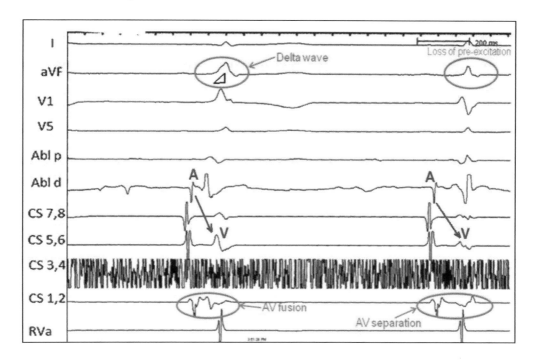

10. In this patient with suspected WPW, what type of conduction occurs with an atrial coupling interval of 270 ms?
   a. AERP
   b. AP ERP
   c. VA Block
   d. Retrograde AP block

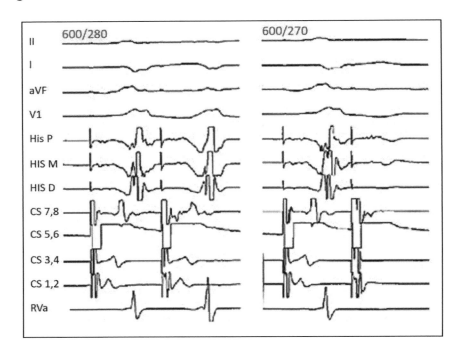

ANSWER: b. AP ERP. Notice the fused AV interval in the first slide, then in the second slide there is an A with no V. This AP becomes refractory (AP ERP) when forced to conduct with a PAC this premature (270 ms). This is an important number to document.... If the refractory period is less than approximately 250 ms in an antegrade conducting pathway, it may be very dangerous. This is because if the patient goes into AF the pathway will conduct the impulse at that rate down to the V causing VT.

Accessory pathways do not decrement or slow down the impulses like the AV node does. The AV node was built by design to decrement or slow down these impulses. It is like a gate keeper for the ventricles. This is to allow only properly timed impulses through to not overwhelm the ventricle. This has not proceeded to AVRT yet, but if it did "antidromic" AVRT proceeds antegrade down the AP and retrograde up the AV node. "Orthodromic" AVRT (which is the most common form) proceeds antegrade (from atrium to ventricle) down the AV node and retrograde up the accessory pathway. Note in this example, the ventricular conduction moves from the distal CS in a medial direction (note slanted line) to the central His catheter, suggesting a left sided bypass track (AP). This is noticed with the AV fusion on CS 1,2. The first part of the signal is the A wave, and the second (triangular part) is the V wave. Notice on the second EGM only the first part of the waveform (A wave) is present.

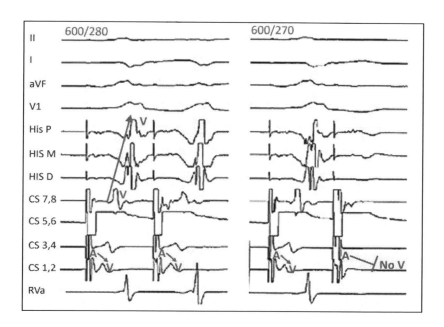

11. In atrial extrastimulus testing on this patient with suspected WPW, what type of conduction occurs after S2?
   a. AVNERP
   b. VERP
   c. AP ERP
   d. AERP

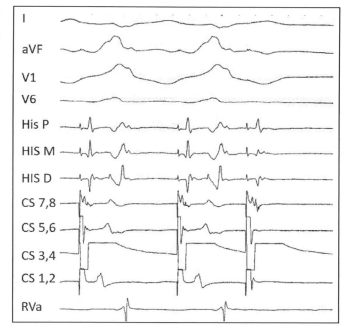

ANSWER: c. AP ERP. The use of atrial extrastimulus testing is a common maneuver to demonstrate this finding. In this example, the physician used a drive train of 8 beats followed by a PAC. The rate at which pacing occurs is not displayed, but it is quite clear that the final beat came in earlier.

The first two beats go through the left sided pathway as seen by the AV fusion on CS 1,2. In the third beat there is atrial capture with the CS pacing; however, no impulse gets to the ventricles. You may wonder in the extrasystole why the AV node did not conduct normally and caused a narrow QRS. This is because the AV node with its longer refractory period would have blocked before the accessory pathway finally blocked.

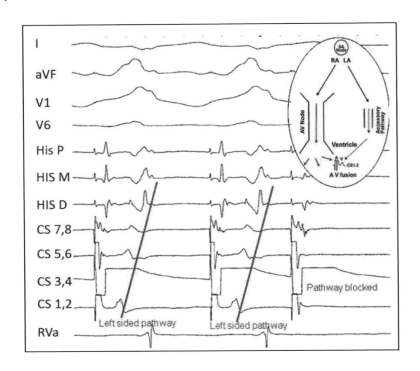

12. When an A progresses from the proximal to the distal electrodes on the CS catheter it is termed _____. When the CS channels are displayed with proximal electrodes (CS 9,10) on top, the signal will normally proceed _____.

    a. Eccentric conduction, diagonally downward to right
    b. Eccentric conduction, diagonally upward to right
    c. Concentric conduction, diagonally downward right
    d. Concentric conduction, diagonally upward to right

ANSWER: c. Concentric conduction, diagonally downward to right. Concentric conduction is normal and occurs from RA to LA diagonally down the stacked CS channels as shown (Proximal to distal on CS catheter). Electrode CS 9,10 represent the RA and are normally the first to activate, followed by the septum and finally the lateral LA.

Eccentric conduction is the opposite and would occur from LA to RA moving diagonally up the CS channels, with a line of activation sloping up (not shown). In WPW patients, this is a very handy way to identify the presence of a left-sided accessory pathway (AP). With either orthodromic AVRT (conducting down the AV nodal pathway and back up to the atrium through the accessory pathway) or ventricular pacing with retrograde conduction through the AP, activation on the CS activation will appear eccentric. For example, if CS 3,4 was earliest to activate and all other electrodes followed, the EGM would have a < shape, suggesting an accessory pathway from the lateral LV. Be aware that, some labs chose to stack the CS channels with the distal electrodes first (CS 1,2).

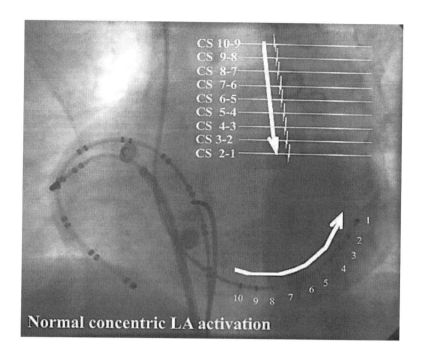

Normal concentric LA activation

13. This EGM was recorded during ventricular pacing prior to RF ablation on a 17-year-old patient with AVRT. The ablation catheter is located on the lateral side of the LA. What do the arrows point to?

    a. Right & left bundle branch signals
    b. Echo beat
    c. Slow pathway potential
    d. AP (Accessory pathway) potential

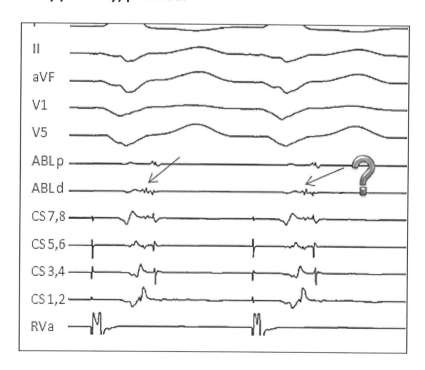

ANSWER: d. AP potential. With the location of the ablation catheter, we know that the signal is not the His. The term slow pathway is utilized when describing AVNRT. Seeing AP potentials along with VA fusion is a good target for ablation.

According to Fogoros, "There are several considerations for successfully mapping and ablating these accessory pathway bypass tracts. Mapping can be conducted on either the atrial or ventricular aspects of the AV groove. When mapping on the ventricular aspect, antegrade conduction over the bypass tract is mapped."
"When the mapping catheter is located near the bypass tract, the interval between the atrial and ventricular depolarizations will be short. (No greater than 60 ms and sometimes the A and V signals are virtually continuous. When the mapping catheter is near the bypass tract and preexcitation is occurring; the local ventricular depolarization should be earlier than the earliest ventricular depolarization seen on any surface ECG lead."

"Loss of preexcitation when pressure is applied with the tip of the mapping catheter is an excellent indication that the site of the bypass tract has been localized. In many patients, a localized potential from the bypass tract itself can be recorded. These bypass tract potentials tend to be low in amplitude, but tend to have discrete, sharp onsets." See Fogoros, chapter on SVT.

14. Your physician has located a septal AP and asks you to begin RF ablation at the catheter position shown on this EGM. You recommend:
   a. **"Not here, you are on the His," or possibly suggest cryoablation**
   b. **"Not here, you are near the SA node," also suggest irrigated RF**
   c. **"Start at low power 15 W while dragging the catheter back"**
   d. **"Do further mapping, you are not on the AP"**

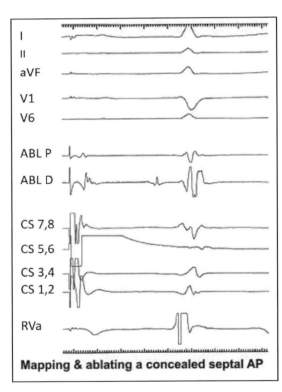

Mapping & ablating a concealed septal AP

ANSWER: a. "Not here, you are on the His," also possibly suggest cryoablation. Note the His spike in the distal ABL channel. This is spot is dangerous to ablate and may result in complete heart block. Cryoablation reduces the chance of damage to the AV node, but it is still a possibility. Issa says, "The ability of cryoablation to suppress local cardiac electrical activity, by cooling to -30° C without producing an irreversible lesion (ice mapping), reduces the risk of inadvertent permanent AV block when ablating in septal locations. Pooled data from

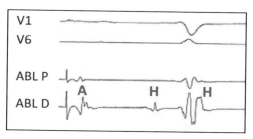

three case series of cryoablation for septal accessory pathways (45 patients) showed an initial success rate of 96% for no cases of permanent AV block, with a recurrence rate of 16%." See: Issa, chapter on "Challenging Ablation Targets"

15. When a roving catheter touches the site of the accessory pathway on the AV ring, the preexcitation may suddenly stop. This is termed: (select two answers)
   a. **Bump Mapping**
   b. **Fascicular block**
   c. **Mechanical ablation**
   d. **Catheter induced AP block**
   e. **Peeling back of Refractoriness**

ANSWER: a. Bump Mapping & d. Catheter induced AP block. "Mapping Sites of Mechanically Induced Loss of Preexcitation: Atypical BTs are particularly sensitive to mechanical trauma, and catheter manipulation along the tricuspid annulus during mapping of the BT may result in loss of BT function, even because of gentle pressure from the catheter tip. When mapping is performed during preexcited atrial pacing or SVT, damage to the BT is indicated by a sudden, transient loss of preexcitation. This phenomenon can be used to localize the BT precisely (bump mapping) .... Block usually lasts from a few beats to a few minutes but can last for hours, after which preexcitation resumes. This method can be used during any consistently preexcited rhythm (atrial pacing, AF, and antidromic AVRT). "See, Issa, chapter on "Variants of Preexcitation"

16. While placing catheters in a patient with suspected WPW, we observed this EGM? Note the small delta wave on the first beat. What occurs on the first beat?
   a. **Initiation of tachycardia**
   b. **Block in the accessory pathway**
   c. **Antegrade AP conduction**
   d. **Retrograde AP conduction**

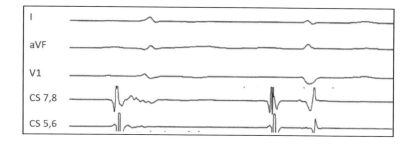

ANSWER: c. Antegrade AP conduction. Accessory pathways conduct so fast that you see AV fusion near the pathway. There is virtually no delay through an accessory pathway. The fusion will be the "tightest" at the electrodes closest to pathway. Notice the fusion at CS 1,2 – this is the distal electrode pair on the CS catheter which is located on the left lateral location: a left sided pathway.

Also, notice the delta wave on the first QRS that is gone on the second beat. When a delta wave is present it is called WPW or manifest WPW. It is termed Antidromic (going down the pathway and up the AV node). If there is no delta wave it is termed orthodromic or concealed AVRT (going down the AV node and up the pathway). If tachycardia develops with this pattern, it would be a wide complex tachycardia termed antidromic AVRT.

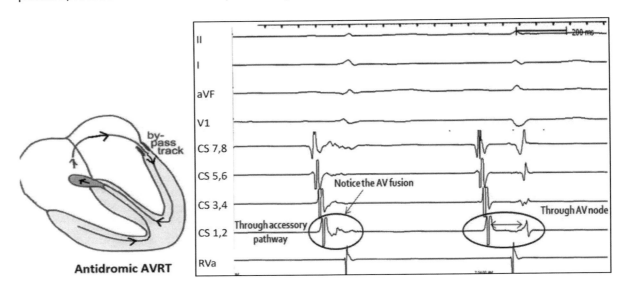

Antidromic AVRT

17. For a successful AVRT ablation, your ablation catheter needs to be on the accessory pathway. Which ablation catheter location shown on the EGM would be the most likely to ablate the active accessory pathway shown?
   a. **Diagram A**
   b. **Diagram B**

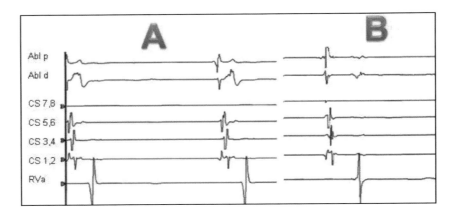

ANSWER: a. Diagram A. Notice the AV fusion in A. This is a good spot for ablation. When ablating with RF the AV interval should separate within the first 10 to 15 seconds. If it is not, you may be close, but not right on the pathway, and you should try a different spot. Note in the heart diagram that ABL catheter B is closer to the AP than ABL catheter A. Fogoros says, "When the mapping catheter is located near the bypass tract (whether on the atrial or ventricular aspect of the AV groove), the interval between the atrial and ventricular depolarizations (assuming that either antegrade or retrograde conduction of impulses is occurring across the bypass tract) will be short. Generally, the localized AV interval is no greater than 60 ms, and sometimes the atrial and ventricular depolarizations are virtually continuous." See Fogoros, Chapter on "Transcatheter Ablation"

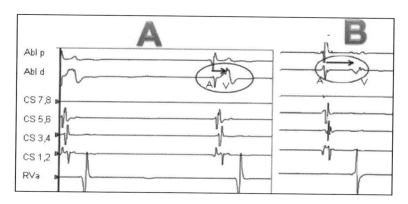
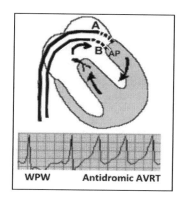

18. This is an EGM recorded during an RF ablation. What does the widening AV interval in CS 7,8 suggest?

    a. **Successful burn for WPW**
    b. **Successful burn for AVNRT**
    c. **Junctional Escape**
    d. **Unsuccessful burn …. Move the catheter**

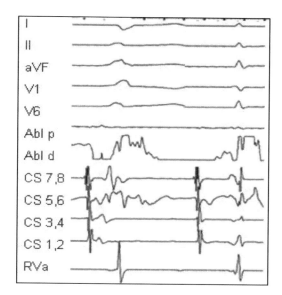

ANSWER: a. Successful burn for WPW. There is no longer AV fusion and loss of delta wave.

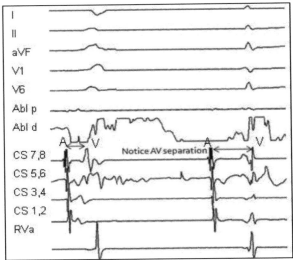

The physician would like to see this happen within the first 10 to 15 seconds of the ablation. This is a particularly good sign that you are right on the pathway.

Incorrect answers are:

- A successful RF burn of AVNRT would show slow junctional beats.
- During AVNRT cryoablation the AVNRT will be non-inducible while testing.
- With all ablations near the AV node watch for AV prolongation. If you see this, come off immediately, because you may be damaging the AV node (fast pathway) which could lead to complete heart block.

19. This patient is having an SVT ablation for WPW. What does the arrow point to on the distal ablation electrode?

a. **Slow pathway potential**
b. **Fast pathway potential**
c. **AP potential**
d. **His**

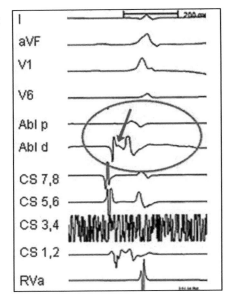

ANSWER: c. AP potential. This patient has an accessory pathway. Notice the Delta wave and the AV fusion. This is a good ablation spot for AVRT with fusion of A, V, and the accessory pathway potential in the middle. Within 15 seconds of RF energy the AV interval should split apart.

20. What happens in this AVRT patient's EGM when pressure is applied to the ablation catheter after the second beat?

   a. **Induced PAC with RBBB**
   b. **Induced PAC with LBBB**
   c. **Bump blocks preexcitation**
   d. **Bump mapping initiates preexcitation**

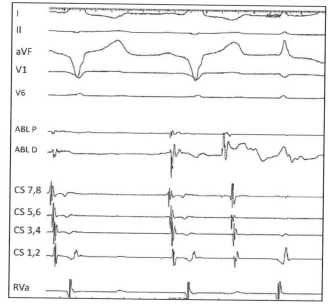

ANSWER: c. Bump blocks preexcitation. Note the third beat in this EGM. The first two beats show antegrade conduction over the accessory pathway as seen by the AV fusion on the ablation catheter and the delta wave of the surface ECG. When catheter pressure is applied to the AV ring on the third beat, the A and V separate, and the delta wave is lost. This may be referred to as a "bump ablation." Further ablation at this location is needed for a successful cure; however, with the disappearance of the delta wave and the AV separation, mapping is not possible. Energy must be applied at this location right away before the catheter moves off the pathway. Sometimes the pathway will present itself again; however, it may not be until the patient goes home. Using 3D mapping, the physician may mark the exact location where this bump ablation happened so they can go back and ablate further.

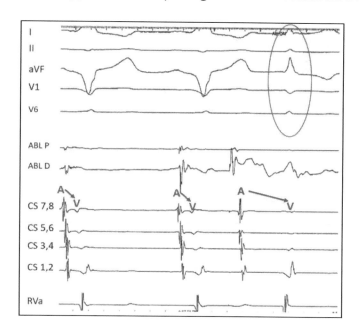

21. This EGM was recorded on a patient with WPW. Pressure is applied to the ablation catheter on the second beat causing _____.

    a. **A PVC**

    b. **A PAC**

    c. **Damage to AP**

    d. **Damage to FP**

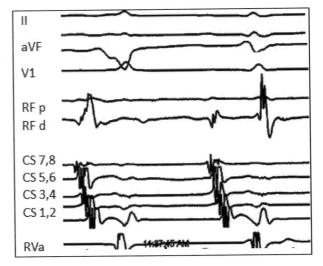

ANSWER: c. Damage to the accessory pathway. On the first beat the distal ablation catheter shows AV fusion and a delta wave on the surface ECG. AV fusion on the distal ablation electrodes indicates that our catheter is at the location of the accessory pathway where ablation should be performed. With pressure, the delta wave disappeared, and the AV interval spread out. This is a "bump ablation." However, the AP conduction will most likely return. Ablation should be performed before the catheter moves.

Inadvertent damage to the fast pathway, which is part of the normal conduction system, would show PR and AV lengthening. It is also observed frequently with rapid junctional beats.

Huang says, "Some pathways are sensitive to mechanical trauma. If a catheter bumps into it, there may be pause of accessory pathway activity, which can be from minutes to hours. Thus, the ability to relocate the accessory pathway is confounded by the time it takes to recover. Three-dimensional mapping and noncontact mapping may be used to mark the position of the catheter when accessory pathway conduction is lost after bumping and to anatomically guide ablation of the accessory pathway." See: Catheter Ablation of Cardiac Arrhythmias by Huang, Wood, and Miller.

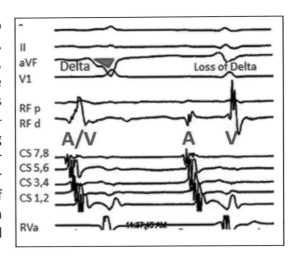

22. Which of the following observations would essentially rule out AVRT?
   a. SVT continues with AV dissociation/block
   b. SVT continues with Bundle Branch Block
   c. SVT is initiated by Ventricular Pacing
   d. SVT is terminated with an A

ANSWER: a. SVT continues with AV dissociation/block. AVRT is a macro-reentry circuit which includes the atrium and ventricle. Since the A and V are both in the circuit, the tachycardia would not continue if they were dissociated from one another. That is why adenosine blocks AVRT and AVNRT.

With BBB, tachycardia may continue. However, it may be slowed depending on the site of the block. It could be induced (not always) with various pacing maneuvers from the A or the V. It may terminate with either an A or V.

23. Where is the accessory pathway (AP) in each AVRT patient? Match each EGM to its AP location.
   a. **Right free wall**
   b. **Anteroseptal**
   c. **Left free wall**
   d. **Posteroseptal**

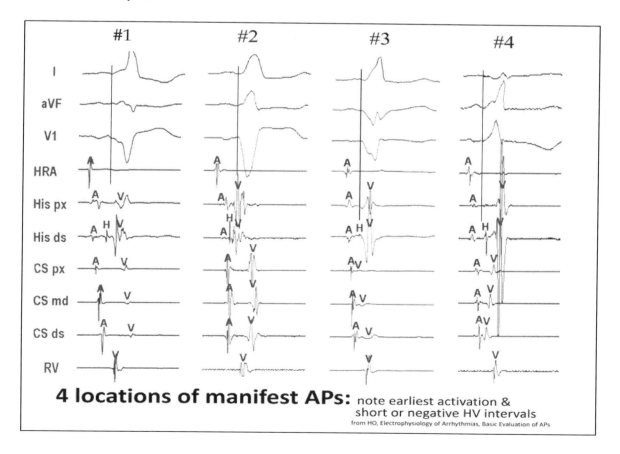

4 locations of manifest APs: note earliest activation & short or negative HV intervals
from HO, Electrophysiology of Arrhythmias, Basic Evaluation of APs

ANSWERS:
1. a. Right free wall
2. b. Anteroseptal
3. c. Posteroseptal
4. d. Left free wall

In manifest WPW there is a short PR and delta wave.
#1 Right Free wall: The slightly +Delta wave in aVF and +Delta wave in I suggest a right free wall location for the AP. For right free wall pathways, there is a +Delta wave in V1, but a right anterolateral location for the AP could explain the findings in the example EGM. The relationship among the A, H, and V waves appears normal.

#2 is Anteroseptal: The -Delta wave in V1 indicates a septal AP location, and the +Delta wave in aVF indicates a superior/anterior location. The short AV interval in the distal His catheter is indicative of an anteroseptal AP.

#3 Posteroseptal AP: The -Delta wave in V1 indicates a septal AP location, and the -Delta wave in aVF suggests an inferior/posterior location. The earliest V occurring at CS proximal is also indicative of a posteroseptal pathway as the proximal CS is a posterior structure.

#4. Left free wall. The initial isoelectric Delta wave in I and R>S in V1 is both indicative of a left free wall AP. The +Delta wave in aVF allows one to further localize the site of the AP to a more superior/anterior location. Further, the earliest ventricular activation on the electrograms occurs at the distal CS which further proves the presence of a left free wall AP. Note how the earliest V in this example is in CS distal, which is on the LV free wall.

Localizing the AP for the 12-lead ECG depends on identifying the initial delta wave vector direction. E.g., Positive delta wave in V1 indicates a left sided pathway. Zipes says, "The electrocardiogram may be helpful for localizing manifest accessory pathways. An analysis of the delta wave vector can predict the general location of an accessory pathway to 1 of 10 sites around the tricuspid and mitral annuli or at subepicardial locations with an overall sensitivity of 90% and specificity of 99%. Precise pathway localization, however, depends on detailed mapping at EP study. Broadly, two electrophysiologic approaches may be used alone or in combination to precisely localize an accessory pathway."
"The first approach is to map the earliest local ventricular or atrial electrogram. The site of earliest ventricular activation, prior to delta wave onset, usually identifies the location of the ventricular insertion of a manifest accessory pathway.... During anterograde conduction, an accessory pathway potential is usually assumed if a distinct bipolar potential preceding the delta wave is recorded between the local atrial and ventricular potentials." See: Zipes, chapter on Ablation of SVT/WPW

24. This 28-year-old patient was brought into the EP lab with complaints of palpitations. Concealed AVRT was induced. Looking at the EGM on the right, where is the location of the bypass tract?

a. RV free wall
b. LV free wall
c. Anterior septum
d. Posterior septum

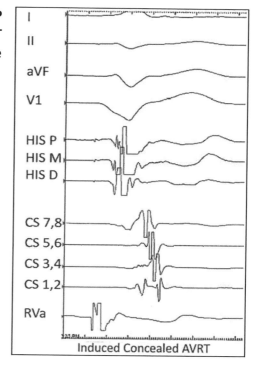

Induced Concealed AVRT

ANSWER: c. Anterior septal track. The first atrial signal is early on the His catheter and last on CS 1,2. The bundle of His is an anterior septal structure, while the CS ostium (CS 7,8) is a posterior septal structure. The atrial signal on His d, is slightly earlier than CS 7,8.

This pathway moves concentrically from the anterior septum to lateral LA (\). If it were a lateral AP, it would show eccentric conduction from the lateral wall toward the septum (/). Parahisian pacing may be used to further define its location.

25. In typical WPW, what causes the delta wave on ECG?

a. WPW bundle short circuiting the AV node
b. Kent bundle short circuiting the AV node
c. AP bypassing AV node and pre-exciting the ventricles
d. Retrograde Mahaim fibers bypassing AV node and pre-exciting the ventricles

ANSWER: c. AP bypassing AV node and pre-exciting the ventricles. WPW is commonly diagnosed based on electrocardiograms. In this case it is manifested as a delta wave, which is a [triangle shaped] slurred upstroke in the QRS complex that is associated with a short PR interval. The short PR interval and slurring of the QRS complex is the impulse making it through to the ventricles prematurely (across the accessory pathway) without the usual delay experienced in the AV node.... The definitive treatment of WPW is a destruction of the abnormal electrical pathway by radio-frequency catheter ablation. See: http://en.wikipedia.org/WPW

Issa says, "Bypass tracts (BTs) are remnants of the atrioventricular (AV) connections caused by incomplete embryological development of the AV annulus and failure of the fibrous separation between the atria and ventricles. There are several types of BTs. Atrioventricular BTs are strands of working myocardial cells connecting atrial and ventricular myocardium across the electrically insulating fibrofatty tissues of the AV junction bypassing the atrioventricular node–His-Purkinje system (AVN-HPS) .... In the older literature, these BTs were called Kent bundles, although incorrectly .... Thus, the use of the term bundle of Kent should be discouraged."

"Atypical BTs include various types of Hisian-Fascicular pathways.... Mahaim fibers, a term to be discouraged because it is more illuminating to name the precise BT according to its connections." See Issa, chapter on Types of Preexcitation Syndromes

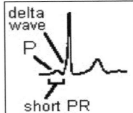

26. In WPW preexcitation, the AP conduction travels from _____ across the _____.
  a. **Ventricle to atrium, AV node**
  b. **Ventricle to atrium, AV ring**
  c. **Atrium to ventricle, AV node**
  d. **Atrium to ventricle, AV ring**

ANSWER: d. Atrium to ventricle, AV ring. In WPW Abedin says, "Most APs travel from the atrium to the ventricle across the AV ring... The location of the pathway is identified by the shortest local AV (preexcited) or VA interval and by recording pathway potentials. [activation mapping] Ventricular or atrial insertion sites can be identified by ventricular and atrial pacing and the earliest atrial or ventricular conduction.... The presence of antegrade conduction results in a short PR interval, slurring of the initial component of the QRS call delta wave and increase in the duration of the QRS. These ECG features are due to preexcitation of the ventricles and if accompanied by tachycardia are characteristic of WPW syndrome." See: Abedin, chapter on Supraventricular Tachycardia

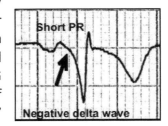

27. What is the chief cause of sudden cardiac death associated with WPW?
  a. **Myocardial Infarction**
  b. **Development of VT**
  c. **Development of AF**
  d. **Stroke**

ANSWER: c. Development of AF with rapid conduction through the bypass tract. Issa says, "Paroxysmal AF occurs in 50% of patients with WPW. In most cases, VF occurring in patients with the WPW syndrome results from the rapid ventricular response during AF. If the BT has a short antegrade effective refractory period (ERP < 250 milliseconds), a rapid ventricular response can occur with degeneration of the rhythm to VF. A short preexcited RR interval during AF of 220 milliseconds or less appears to be a sensitive clinical marker for identifying patients at risk for sudden death in children," See, Issa, chapter on AVRT

28. Which wide complex tachycardia typically proceeds antegrade down an accessory pathway and retrograde up the AV node?
   a. **Orthodromic AVNRT**
   b. **Antidromic AVNRT**
   c. **Orthodromic AVRT**
   d. **Antidromic AVRT**

ANSWER: d. Antidromic AVRT. Antidromic AVRT can occur with electrical conduction of the sinus impulse via the preexcited accessory pathway (antegrade fashion), and then retrograde via the normal AV node to create a circuit reentry rhythm. This form of SVT leads to a wide-complex fast heart rhythm and is much less common than the narrow form of orthodromic AVRT"

"If the refractory period is less than approximately 250 ms in antidromic AVRT it may be dangerous. This is because if the patient goes into AF, the pathway will conduct the impulse at that rate down to the ventricle causing VT or VF. Accessory pathways do not decrement or slow down the impulses like the AV node does, they conduct rapidly, all or none. The AV node was built by design to decrement or slow down these impulses.

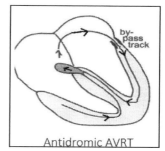

Antidromic AVRT proceeds antegrade down the AP and retrograde up the AV node. Orthodromic AVRT (which is the most common form) proceeds antegrade (from atrium to ventricle) down the AV node and retrograde up the accessory pathway." See: http://www.washingtonhra.com/38.html

29. This diagram shows surface ECGs from patients with different accessory pathway conduction. Match each ECG to its type of ventricular activation.
   a. **Orthodromic AVRT (ORT)**
   b. **WPW preexcitation**
   c. **Antidromic AVRT**

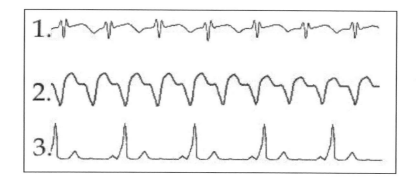

CORRECTLY MATCHED ANSWERS:

1.a. Orthodromic (ortho means straight or normal conduction) "orthodromic atrioventricular reciprocating tachycardia (AVRT) with a reentrant circuit consisting of two limbs. The forward or antegrade limb involves the normal AV nodal system (and thus a narrow QRS), and the reverse, or retrograde, limb involves the accessory pathway."

2.c. Antidromic AVRT passes antegrade down both the accessory, where it conducts slowly through the ventricle, creating a broad QRS. Then the impulse passes up the AV node retrograde to re-stimulate the atria and passes rapidly down the AP. This creates the circus (reentry) movement and tachycardia. "The forward, or antegrade, limb involves the accessory pathway, and the reverse, or retrograde, limb involves the normal AV nodal conduction system. This type of SVT leads to a wide-complex rhythm on the ECG as seen above."

3. b. WPW, where conduction passes antegrade down both the accessory pathway (delta wave) and the AV node (RS wave). "Electrical conduction from the atria to the ventricles can occur via the normal AV nodal system and the accessory pathway simultaneously. This leads to the creation of the slurred upstroke, or delta wave, seen on the surface ECG lead and denoted by arrows in the tracing seen here." See: http://www.washingtonhra.com/38.html

30. While performing atrial extrastimulus testing, a tachycardia develops with a "similar" narrow QRS. This is due to:
   a. **Orthodromic AVRT (ORT)**
   b. **Antidromic AVRT (ART)**
   c. **Idiopathic VT**
   d. **RVOT**

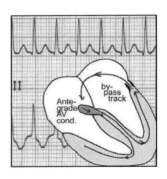

ANSWER: a. Orthodromic AVRT. Since AV conduction is normal ("ortho") the QRS is narrow unless aberrant conduction is present. Zipes says "Atrioventricular (AV) reentry accounts for approximately one third of the cases of paroxysmal supraventricular tachycardia among patients referred for catheter ablation. It is a macro-reentrant tachycardia that uses both the normal conduction system and an accessory pathway. Most instances of AV reentrant tachycardia (AVRT) involve the AV node and the accessory pathway for anterograde and retrograde conduction, respectively. The result is a regular, narrow complex rhythm referred to as orthodromic reciprocating tachycardia (ORT). Less commonly, a wide-complex rhythm may be observed when anterograde conduction occurs over the accessory pathway and retrograde conduction occurs over the AV node, referred to as antidromic reciprocating tachycardia (ART)." See, Zipes, chapter on SVT - AV Reentry

31. With extrastimulus testing, the majority of AV accessory pathways conduct:
   a. Antegrade only
   b. Retrograde only
   c. With decremental conduction
   d. Both antegrade and retrograde

ANSWER: d. Both antegrade and retrograde, although in tachycardia (AVRT) most will be orthodromic with retrograde accessory pathway conduction. Issa says, "Although the majority (approximately 60%) of AV BTs conduct both anterogradely and retrogradely (i.e., bidirectionally), some AV BTs are capable of propagating impulses in only one direction. BTs that conduct only in the anterograde direction are uncommon (less than 5%), often cross the right AV groove, and frequently possess decremental conduction properties. On the other hand, BTs that conduct only in the retrograde direction occur more frequently, with an incidence of 17% to 37%." A BT that conducts only antegrade would only support antidromic AVRT, while one that conducts only retrograde would only support orthodromic AVRT. See: Issa, chapter on AVRT

32. AV Accessory Pathways that cause ventricular preexcitation during NSR conduct____ and are termed____.
   a. Antegrade, manifest
   b. Antegrade, concealed
   c. Retrograde, manifest
   d. Retrograde, concealed

ANSWER: a. Antegrade, manifest. Issa says, "If the accessory pathway is capable of anterograde conduction, the resting electrocardiogram demonstrates a short PR interval and a slurred upstroke of the QRS complex that constitutes the delta wave—the hallmarks of ventricular preexcitation. The accessory pathway is thus termed manifest. BTs capable of retrograde only conduction are referred to as concealed." See: Issa, chapter on AVRT

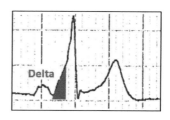

33. Conduction over most BTs is caused by____ and conduction over AV node is caused by____.
   a. Slow inward K current, rapid inward Na current
   b. Slow inward K current, rapid inward Ca current
   c. Rapid inward Na current, slow inward K current
   d. Rapid inward Na current, slow inward Ca current

ANSWER: d. Rapid inward Na current, slow inward Ca current. Issa says: "Because working myocardial cells make up the vast majority of AV BTs, propagation is caused by the rapid inward sodium current, like normal His-Purkinje tissue and atrial and ventricular myocardium.... In contrast, the AV node depends on the slow inward calcium current for generation and propagation of its action potential...." See: Issa, chapter on AVRT

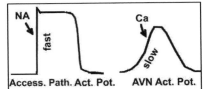

This means accessory pathways conduct rapidly - all or none, unlike the AV node which has decremental conduction. See: Issa, chapter on AVRT

34. How does conduction rate through most bypass tracts change at shorter cycle lengths?
   a. It decreases with decremental conduction as it approaches ERP
   b. It increases with peeling of refractoriness as it approaches ERP
   c. It is constant until it completely blocks conduction at ERP
   d. It is virtually instantaneous through short non-diagonal BTs

ANSWER: c. It is constant with non-decremental conduction. Issa says, "AV BTs (bypass tracts) have constant anterograde and retrograde conduction at all rates until the refractory period is reached, at which time conduction is completely blocked (non-decremental conduction). Thus, conduction over the AV BT usually behaves in an all-or-none fashion. In contrast, the AVN, exhibits what has been called decremental conduction in which the conduction time of the impulse propagating through the AVN increases as the atrial cycle length (CL) shortens." AP conduction normally does not change. When its ERP is reached it usually blocks completely. Then AV conduction may shift to the AV node. Its conduction is "all or none." See: Issa, chapter on AVRT

35. In patients with an AV bypass tract showing preexcitation an orthodromic macroreentry tachycardia can usually be initiated with a premature atrial impulse when the bypass tract is ___ and the AV node is ____.
   a. Refractory, recovered
   b. Refractory, refractory
   c. Recovered, recovered
   d. Recovered, refractory

ANSWER: a. Refractory, recovered. Fogoros says, "a macroreentry rhythm can then often be started simply by introducing an atrial impulse at a time when the bypass track is still refractory from the previous impulse but when the AV node has recovered. The macroreentry tachycardia has a normal QRS complex because antegrade conduction is via the normal AV conduction system. Orthodromic AVRT like this accounts for about 95% of AVRTs and requires a manifest WPW pattern, where the BP is capable of bidirectional conduction. At least this type of AVRT is limited by the protective decremental conduction of the AV node and won't be too fast. Because the retrograde AP conduction causes the P wave, we say the P follows the QRS. The P is not caused by normal sinus node stimulation. But the P also precedes and causes the normal AV conduction. In such a cycle it's hard to say what comes first - the chicken or the egg. See: Fogoros chapter on SVT

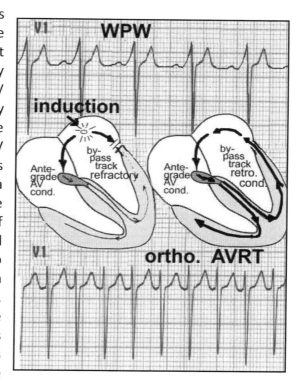

36. In orthodromic macroreentry tachycardia where are the P waves usually located?
   a. **Prior to the QRS with a short PR interval**
   b. **Prior to the QRS with a long PR interval**
   c. **After the QRS, with a short RP interval**
   d. **Within the QRS**

ANSWER: c. After the QRS, with a short RP interval less than halfway to the next R wave.

Fogoros says, "As opposed to AV nodal reentry, in which the atria and ventricles are being depolarized nearly simultaneously, in macroreentry, the atria and ventricles are being depolarized sequentially. Thus, distinct P waves are virtually always seen. P waves tend to be less than halfway between successive QRS complexes. (The RP interval is shorter than the PR interval) because retrograde conduction via the bypass track tends to be faster than antegrade conduction via the normal AV conducting system. Because atrial stimulation is in the retrograde direction, the P wave axis is superior- the P waves will be negative in the inferior leads (II,

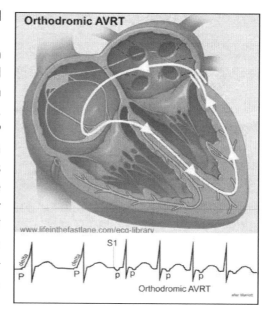

III, and AVF)" Good whiteboard video at www.lifeinthefastlane/ecglibrary See: Fogoros chapter on SVT

37. What treatment would you recommend to an 80-year-old WPW asymptomatic patient with no history of arrhythmia?
   a. Beta and/or Ca channel blockers
   b. EP study and AP ablation
   c. Recommend ICD implant
   d. No treatment

ANSWER: d. No treatment. Issa says, "For the low risk [WPW] patient, no measures are advised other than an explanation to the patient of the ECG findings. . .. Esophageal pacing can be performed to determine the anterograde ERP of the BT and the ability to induce sustained arrhythmias. If arrhythmias can be induced, the benefits and risk of an invasive investigation and catheter ablation should be based on individual considerations such as age, gender, occupation, and athletic involvement. . .. If an EP study is performed for risk stratification, the combination of inducible AVRT and a shortest preexcited RR interval during AF of less than 250 milliseconds provide the most compelling indications for ablation. . .. Certain patients such as athletes and those in higher risk occupations will generally choose ablation. Others, especially older patients..., may prefer the small risk of a conservative strategy." AV nodal blocking agents (beta & CA blockers) are contraindicated as they eliminate the slowing influence of the AV node. In these patients AF rapidly conducted through the bypass tract may degenerate into VF and sudden death. See: Issa chapter on AVRT.

Oabeyesekere, et.al., say about WPW, "The evolution of curative catheter ablation has clearly become the treatment of choice in the patient with substantive symptoms. A continuing controversy has been the use of this therapy in the asymptomatic or less symptomatic individual, and the central looming theme is the incidence of SCD as part of the natural history of this entity and our ability to predict it.... [but] the incredibly low mortality in general in the WPW syndrome, even in patients with a short ERP.... supports the contention that both medical therapy and no therapy are reasonable options, even in the symptomatic patient who is clearly told of the therapeutic options, along with the pros and cons of ablation, and who elects not to have ablation." http://circ.ahajournals.org/content/125/5/659 2012

38.The EGM below was taken on a child with an AP. Why are the VA conduction times so different between RV apex and RVOT pacing?
   a. Orthodromic verses Antidromic conduction
   b. Eccentric verses concentric Atrial conduction
   c. Accessory Pathway is closer to RV apex than RVOT
   d. Slanted Accessory Pathways

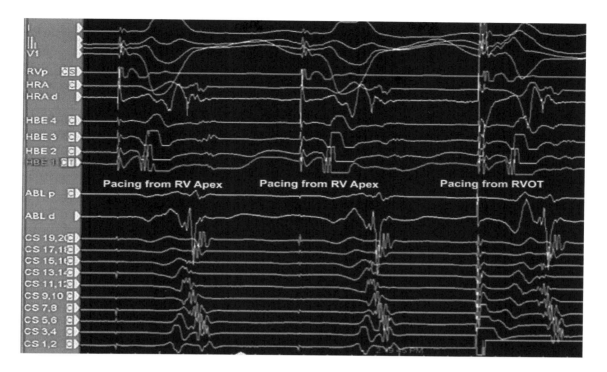

Pacing from RV Apex   Pacing from RV Apex   Pacing from RVOT

ANSWER: d. Slanted or oblique Accessory Pathway. Note on CS 13,14 how much slower the VA conduction time is when pacing from RVOT. This is because the ventricular activation passes CS 15,16 and then travels upward against the slant to enter the atrium later.

Note the diagram by Huang & Wood demonstrating this. Study the diagram at right while considering a driving analogy. The gray bar is the AP, with ventricular insertion at C3, atrial insertion at C1. Imagine 2 cars on a divided freeway. Car A is driving north (RV post. Paced V signal); car B is driving South (RV-OT V paced signal). Each car takes an off ramp (through the AP) at milepost 3 (the ventricular insertion site). Car A turns off a slight left turn and passes into the Atrium at milepost 5 and enters the atrium at milepost 3; whereas car B must go past milepost 3 to milepost 5 before he turns off and backtracks to milepost 3 before entering the atrium. It will take longer for car B to get there, because he had to pass milepost 3 before he could turn off at milepost 5. In the diagram note that car A passes into the atrium prior to CS 3 electrode, and car B passes C3 to C5 before entering the AP into the atrium. Thus, the greater VA time at C 3 in the RVOT paced beat.

Asirvatham says of the original black background EGM: "pathway slant with intracardiac electrograms during ventricular pacing. The first two beats represent ventricular pacing from the right ventricular apex with the third paced beat from the right ventricle outflow tract region. Note the sudden reversal in the ventricular activation sequence. The pacing rate has not changed, yet the local V-A interval in the mid-coronary sinus is vastly different. With the V-A interval shorter when there is a septal to lateral ventricular wave front, suggests that the ventricular insertion if closer to the septum with the atrial insertion located more laterally."

"Accessory pathways are rarely perpendicular to the atrioventricular annulus. Since annular mapping catheters (coronary sinus catheters) are parallel to the annulus, a unique phenomenon regarding the atrioventricular interval (with antegrade conduction) occurs when pacing on either side of the accessory pathway and is referred to as pathway slant. One would expect that the atrioventricular interval at the site of the accessory pathway should be fixed and independent of the pacing site (assuming the rate is constant).

However, this is not often the case. When an antegrade conducting pathway has its atrial insertion septal to its ventricular insertion at the pathway site, the coronary sinus electrode will record an atrial electrogram while pathway conduction is already occurring (along the slant) resulting in a short A-V interval. When pacing from a lateral location, the atrial

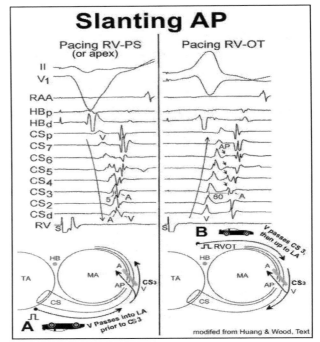

electrogram will be inscribed first even before the atrial insertion of the pathway has been activated, thus giving rise to a long A-V interval. A thorough understanding of this phenomenon is important for two reasons, 1, mapping for an accessory pathway potential with the wave front against the slant (long AV interval) maximizes the chance of seeing the pathway potential, and 2, understanding the actual direction of the slant may allow the electrophysiology to specifically target the ventricular insertion if that insertion is further away from a sensitive area such as the conduction system or a coronary artery."

Asirvatham, Difficulties with Ablation for Arrhythmias in Children,
http://www.ipej.org/0802S/asirvatham.pdf

Atrial Tachycardia:

- Focus (origin) may be in the right or left atrium
- Often located at the crista terminalis or pulmonary veins - paroxysmal or persistent
- Ablation: use of activation mapping to identify the earliest atrial deflection.
- Ventricular Overdrive Pacing Response: VAAV
- Usually terminates with a V, termination with an atrial event if AV block is at the same time (uncommon)
- AV block may occur, and the tachycardia will be unaffected.

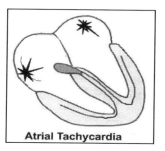

Atrial Tachycardia

1. The most common site of origin for focal atrial tachycardias is:
    a. **RA, IVC**
    b. **RA, Crista Terminalis**
    c. **LA, LSPV**
    d. **LA, Atrial septum**

ANSWER: b. RA, Crista terminalis. Issa says, "Most focal ATs (83%) arise from the RA, about 2/3 of which are distributed along the long axis of the crista terminalis from the sinus node to the coronary sinus (CS) and atrioventricular (AV) junction (called the line of fire) ...." See, Issa, chapter on Focal AT

2. What is the typical observed with RF ablation of the atrial tachycardia focus?
    a. **Abrupt termination of AT**
    a. **Junctional rhythm with later inability to induce AT**
    b. **Gradual slowing of the AT rate leading to sinus bradycardia**
    c. **Speeding of the AT rate, with later inability to induce AT**

ANSWER: a. Abrupt termination of AT. Issa says, "The response of the AT focus to a successful RF application should be rapid, typically within a few seconds of RF energy delivery. The most common response to successful ablation is abrupt termination." See, Issa, chapter on Focal AT
AVNRT

Chapter 10
Ventricular Rhythms

1. Sudden Cardiac Death (pg. 407)
2. Ventricular Ablation (pg. 412)

EP Essentials LLC

Sudden Cardiac Death (SCD)

1. The most common arrhythmia found in patients recovering from MI is:
   a. **Ventricular Tachycardia**
   b. **Ventricular Fibrillation**
   c. **PACs**
   d. **PVCs**

ANSWER: d. PVCs are most common, especially in the setting of myocardial ischemia. Ischemic tissue may set up a reentry loop which causes unifocal PVCs or multifocal PVCs. Runs of 3 or more PVCs are called Ventricular Tachycardia. Runs are obviously more serious than single PVCs.

Treatment for MI includes: O2, pain relief, and alteration of hemodynamics with nitroglycerine and beta blockers. Routine lidocaine is no longer routinely recommended for patients with frequent PVCs post MI. Treat the patient not the monitor. See: ACLS chapter on "Evaluation and treatment of arrhythmias associated with MI."

2. The most common dysrhythmia leading to sudden death in patients is:
   a. **Polymorphic Ventricular Tachycardia**
   b. **Ventricular Fibrillation**
   c. **Complete Heart Block**
   d. **Asystole**

ANSWER: b. Ventricular fibrillation. Most sudden deaths are cardiovascular and of these 62% are attributed to Ventricular Fibrillation (VF) in patients following myocardial infarction. A smaller percentage of SD is due to asystole or severe bradyarrhythmias. Most VF is believed to start as VT and deteriorate to VF. Most Ventricular Tachycardia (VT) is slow enough to sustain a pulse, but it may degenerate into Ventricular Fibrillation (VF), which, of course, cannot sustain a pulse. The mechanism of death in most patients dying of sudden cardiac death is ventricular fibrillation; consequently, there may be no prodromal symptoms associated with the death. See: ACLS Manual, chapter on "Sudden Death."

3. What is the most powerful predictor of sudden cardiac death in all patients?
   a. **Coronary Artery disease (Three-vessel)**
   b. **EP inducible monomorphic VT**
   c. **EP inducible polymorphic VT**
   d. **Ejection fraction <30%**
   e. **History of prior MI**

ANSWER: d. Ejection fraction <30%. Braunwald says, "A marked reduction in left ventricular ejection fraction is the most powerful of the known predictors of SCD in patients with chronic ischemic heart disease, as well as those at risk for SCD from all causes....An ejection fraction equal to or less than 30 percent is the single most powerful independent predictor for SCD, but has a low specificity." See Braunwald chapter on Arrhythmias, Sudden Death & Syncope. Issa says, "The severity of left ventricular dysfunction is the most powerful predictor of mortality in patients with DCM and CHF.... Programmed electrical stimulation has not been shown to be an accurate predictor of sudden death in patients with nonischemic DCM...In the asymptomatic patient with DCM, ejection fraction and the presence of ventricular tachycardia on Holter monitoring remain the only clinically useful predictors of sudden cardiac death." See Issa, chapter on Ventricular Arrhythmias.

4. How many leads should match when pace mapping VT morphology?
   a. **36/36**
   b. **12/12**
   c. **10/12**
   d. **8/12**
   e. **6/6**

ANSWER: b. 12/12. Ideally all 12 of the surface leads should match in contour and timing. Pacing from an arrhythmias site of origin generates an identical surface ECG. Pacing other sites gives a different ECG morphology. Issa says: "The greater the degree of concordance between the morphology during pacing and tachycardia, the closer the catheter is to the site of origin of the tachycardia. Pace maps with identical or near-identical matches of the tachycardia morphology in all 12 surface ECG leads are indicative of the site of origin of the tachycardia." See: Issa, chapter on focal atrial tachycardia

5. Your patient becomes hemodynamically unstable in VT. How can you map the site of origin while the patient is stable? (Select the two best answers.)
   a. **Entrainment map**
   b. **Propagation map**
   c. **Activation map**
   d. **Isochronal map**
   e. **Pace map**
   f. **Voltage map**

ANSWER: e. Pace map and f. Voltage map. Issa say: "For the unmappable VT (because of hemodynamic intolerance, inconsistent induction, altering QRS morphology, and/or nonsustained duration), pace mapping is the predominant mapping technique and is directed to the scar border zone as defined by voltage mapping." Since the patient can't tolerate the VT use pace mapping to identify areas where the V morphology is identical to that in VT. Once identified, you can ablate that area and avoid the unstable VT. See: Issa, chapter on "Other VT"

6. What is the most ordinary form of idiopathic left ventricular tachycardia?
   a. **Verapamil sensitive fascicular VT**
   b. **Focal left posterior fascicle VT**
   c. **Ischemic/scar reentry VT**
   d. **LVOT VT**

ANSWER: a. Verapamil sensitive fascicular VT. Left posterior fascicle VT is due to abnormal automaticity, LVOT VT may be triggered, reentry or due to automaticity, and verapamil sensitive fascicular VT is believed to be due to reentry. Verapamil sensitive VT is seen in patients without structural heart disease, RBBB, and left-axis deviation. It may also be induced with atrial pacing. Idiopathic means of unknown cause. Huang says, "Some data suggest that the tachycardia may originate from a false tendon or fibromuscular band in the ventricle." Catheter Ablation of Cardiac Arrhythmias by Huang and Wood.

7. Which is the most common form of verapamil-sensitive ventricular tachycardia?
   a. **Left upper septal fascicular VT**
   b. **Left posterior fascicular VT**
   c. **Left anterior fascicular VT**
   d. **Bundle branch reentry**

ANSWER: b. Left posterior fascicular VT. Bundle branch reentry is a different type of ventricular tachycardia utilizing the right and left bundle branches. Left anterior fascicular VT is uncommon, left upper septal fascicular VT is exceedingly rare, and left posterior fascicular VT is the most common form.
Huang says, "The mechanism of verapamil-sensitive left VT is reentry, because it can be induced, entrained, and terminated by programmed ventricle or atrial stimulation." Catheter Ablation of Cardiac Arrhythmias by Huang and Wood.

8. A physician puts an electrophysiology catheter into the coronary sinus or pericardium because he was unable to normally map and stimulate a VT. What category of mapping is this?
   a. **Electromagnetic mapping**
   b. **Noncontact mapping**
   c. **Epicardial mapping**
   d. **Pace mapping**
   e. **Cryomapping**

ANSWER: c. Epicardial mapping. According to Fogoros, "Some reentrant circuits (especially VT) may be subepicardial, making the endocardial approach to mapping difficult. In these cases, epicardial mapping may be of use." This is accomplished by placing a catheter in the CS which runs along the outside of the heart in the posterior AV groove. Epicardial mapping may also be done by inserting a catheter directly into the pericardial space by using the subxiphoid puncture approach. See: Fogoros: Transcatheter Ablation: Therapeutic Electrophysiology.

9. This patient has dilated cardiomyopathy with a wide complex tachycardia. The EGM shows an H (but no A) before each V.
This EGM demonstrates:
   a. **Idiopathic LV outflow tract VT with RBBB**
   b. **Idiopathic RV outflow tract VT with LBBB**
   c. **Post Infarction polymorphic VT**
   d. **Bundle Branch Reentry VT**

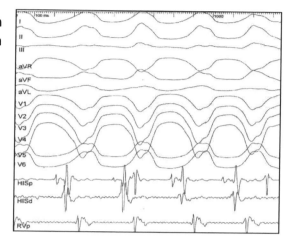

ANSWER: d. Bundle Branch Reentry VT. There is AV dissociation, and an H before each V. Bundle Branch Reentry Ventricular Tachycardia is a reentry loop around the 2 main septal bundle branches. It is conducted through the His on top and the ventricular septum on the bottom. This one has a LBB morphology (negative QRS in V1).

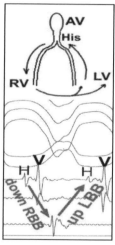

Braunwald says about BBRVT, "Retrograde conduction over the left bundle branch system and anterograde conduction over the right bundle branch create a QRS complex with a left bundle branch block contour and constitute the most common form.... Bundle branch reentry is a form of monomorphic sustained VT usually seen in patients with structural heart disease, such as dilated cardiomyopathy."

Issa says, "BBR VT can only be diagnosed using intracardiac recording. AV dissociation is typically present, EP criteria for the diagnosis of BBR VT include the following: (1) the His potential precedes the QRS; and (2) ...the HV interval is usually 55 to 160 milliseconds. [here it is around 60 ms. Remember, the range of HV intervals in normal subjects is narrow, 35 to 55 ms]... Twelve-lead ECG documentation of BBR VT is usually unavailable because the VT is rapid and hemodynamically unstable [This patient's rate is 200 bpm.]....The ablation target is either the RB or LB; however, RB ablation is easier and usually is the method of choice." This case submitted by Brent Lawhorn, from Med. Univ. of SC.

10. In patients with structural heart disease, ventricular tachycardia usually originates as:
   a. **Automaticity in the RV**
   b. **Automaticity in the LV**
   c. **Reentry in the RV**
   d. **Reentry in the LV**

ANSWER: d. Reentry in the LV. Fogoros says: "Left ventricular catheterization is also required for mapping of ventricular tachycardia, since most ventricular reentrant circuits reside in the left ventricle." Ventricular reentry circuits usually originate around scar tissue from old MIs. See: Fogoros chapter on Principles of the Electrophysiology Study

11. This is a 12 lead pacemap & ventricular mapping catheter EGM on a patient with ischemic VT? What does it suggest?
   a. **Complete Heart Block**
   b. **Diastolic potentials**
   c. **10 out of 12 match**
   d. **A & F waves**

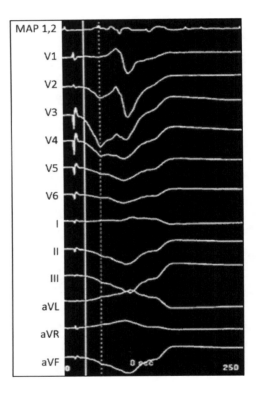

ANSWER: b. Diastolic potentials. We are unable to determine whether the pacemap is 10 out of 12 matching as the clinical PVC or VT is not shown. It may look like CHB on the mapping catheter (top line); however, those are not atrial deflections. These small deflections are diastolic potentials which are small, fractionated signals in the ventricle. During VT, the slow zone of conduction produces an activation signal that occurs after one surface QRS complex and before the next (that is, when the bulk of normal ventricular myocardium is in diastole – therefore, the signal is called a "diastolic potential"). Usually there are other areas in the scar that also conduct slowly and show diastolic potentials during VT, even though they do not participate in the re-entry circuit. Therefore, diastolic potentials are not a specific finding. To figure out if a site with diastolic potentials is part of the re-entry circuit, pacing stimuli are delivered through the mapping/ablating catheter at a rate slightly faster than the tachycardia. If the site is within the re-entry circuit, the pacing stimuli should produce paced QRS complexes with similar morphology as the QRS complexes during VT; and, during pacing, the interval from stimulus to the onset of the paced QRS should be identical to the interval from the diastolic potential to the QRS during VT." See: Management of Complex Cardiovascular Problems. By Nguyen, Hu, Kim, and Grines.

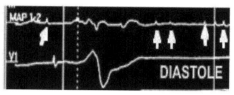

Ventricular Ablation

1. While placing the His electrode, you advance the catheter into the RV so that the distal electrodes show a small spike just before the V, but no preceding A signal. The explanation is that you went:
    a. **Way too deep into RV, recording Left bundle**
    b. **Not far enough, recording AV bundle**
    c. **Appropriate recording of His bundle**
    d. **Too far, recording of Right bundle**

ANSWER: c. Too far, recording of Right bundle. "The RB potential can be distinguished from the HB potential by the absence of or minimal atrial electrogram on the recording and presence of a sharp deflection inscribed at least 15 to 20 milliseconds later than the His potential. An RB-V interval value of <30 milliseconds may not be a reliable marker of the RB potential in these patients because disease of the HPS can cause prolongation of the RB-V conduction time." See EGM on next question. See: Issa, chapter on "Bundle Branch Reentrant Tachycardia"

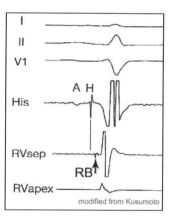

2. A patient has bundle branch reentry VT with a LBBB pattern. Where should the ablation catheter be placed?
    a. **LV well below the AVN (mid septum)**
    b. **RV His bundle below the AV node**
    c. **High LV septum below aortic root**
    d. **RV septum below the His bundle**

ANSWER: d. RV septum below the His bundle. "The baseline rhythm is usually normal sinus rhythm (NSR) or atrial fibrillation (AF). ...The most common ECG abnormality is nonspecific intraventricular conduction delay (IVCD) of a LBBB pattern and PR interval prolongation.... Twelve-lead ECG documentation of BBR VT is usually unavailable because the VT is rapid and hemodynamically unstable.... QRS morphology during VT is a typical BBB pattern or can be identical to that in NSR. BBR VT with LBBB pattern is the most common VT morphology, The ablation target is either the RB or LB; however, RB ablation is easier and usually is the method of choice."

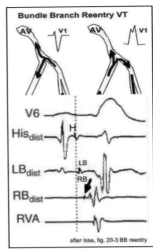

"The RB is a long, thin, and discrete structure that courses down the right side of the interventricular septum near the endocardium in its upper third, ... The RB does not divide throughout most of its course, the RB potential can be distinguished from the HB potential by the absence of ...an atrial electrogram on the recording and presence of a sharp deflection inscribed at least 15 to 20 milliseconds later than the His potential...." Note the RB signal in diagram.

"RF delivery is usually started at low levels (5 W) and gradually increases every 10 seconds, targeting a temperature of 60°C. In general, RBBB develops at 15 to 20 W. Successful ablations will result in clear development of RBBB in V1. Occasionally, an accelerated rhythm from the RB is observed during ablation (analogous to accelerated junctional rhythm with HB ablation..." Be sure there is no underlying LBBB, or after ablating the right bundle, you will have complete heart block. See Issa, chapter on Bundle Branch Reentry VT

3. Where is the typical ablation site for a patient with Bundle Branch Reentry?
   a. **AV node, followed with pacemaker implant**
   b. **Left common bundle branch**
   c. **Right bundle branch**
   d. **Anterior left fascicle**

ANSWER: c. Right Bundle Branch. Typically, BB Reentry uses the right bundle branch in the downward direction and the left bundle branch in the upward direction. It may be cured by ablating the right bundle branch which is easier to access. This cures the reentrant arrhythmia, but RBBB remains.

4. The following ECG shows what abnormality?
   a. **Posterior Myocardial Infarction**
   b. **Anterior lateral infarction**
   c. **Brugada syndrome**
   d. **Delta wave**

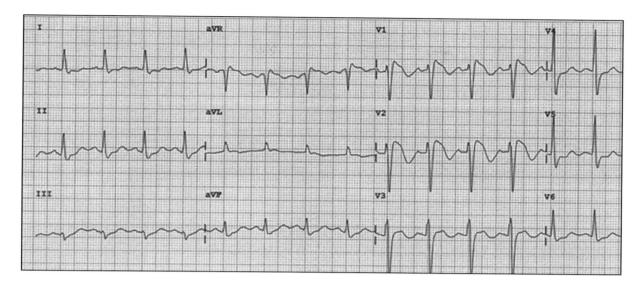

ANSWER: c. Brugada syndrome. Note the ST elevation in leads V1 and V2.
Antzelevich says, "The electrocardiographic manifestations of the Brugada syndrome when concealed can be unmasked by sodium channel blockers, a febrile state, or vagotonic agents. Three types of repolarization patterns in the right precordial leads are recognized. Type 1 is diagnostic of Brugada syndrome and is characterized by a coved ST segment ≥2mm (0.2 mV) followed by a negative T wave. Type 2 has a saddleback appearance with a high take-off ST segment elevation of ≥2mm followed by a trough displaying ≥1mm ST elevation followed by either a positive or biphasic T wave. Type 3 has either a saddleback or coved appearance with an ST segment elevation of <1mm. These three patterns may be observed sequentially in the same patient or following the introduction of specific drugs." See: The Brugada Syndrome: From Bench to Bedside by Charles Antzelevich.

5. This 3D voltage map was taken of the left ventricle post MI. Purple represents >1.5 mV. Where is the physician ablating?
   a. **Channel between low voltage**
   b. **Along the scar border areas**
   c. **VT entrant site**
   d. **VT exit site**

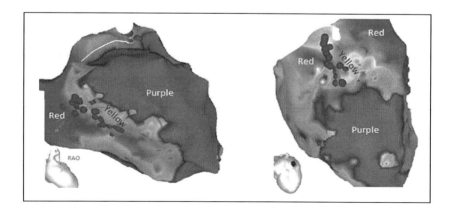

ANSWER: a. Channel between low voltage areas. Purple is designated as healthy tissue (typically >1.5 mV), Red is low voltage and yellow is in-between. In the example below, the physician is ablating along the scar border. Methods to ablating ischemic VT may include connecting scar areas, at the entrant or exit site, or modifying the substrate which is shown in these examples.

Huang says, "The electrophysiologic substrate for VT gradually develops during the first 2 weeks after MI, and once established, it appears to remain indefinitely. During the infarct healing process, necrotic myocardium is replaced with fibrous tissue. ... Endocardial recordings from sites of VT origin during sinus rhythm consistently demonstrate low-amplitude, prolonged, multicomponent potentials."

"Substrate mapping strategy: *anchor points* for linear lesions are determined by pace mapping to match VGT morphologies in the infarct border zone. Linear ablation is applied through these anchor points from the dense scar (<0.5 mV) to normal tissue (>1,5 mV) or anatomic barrier." See: Catheter Ablation of Cardiac Arrhythmias by Huang and Wood's chapter on Ablation of Ventricular Tachycardia in Coronary Artery Disease.

6. While mapping out a sustained, hemodynamically stable ventricular, the following point was acquired. The vertical line represents the point of reference for mapping.
Should you suggest ablation at this site?
   a. **Depends on VA conduction time**
   b. **Depends on VERP**
   c. **Yes**
   d. **No**

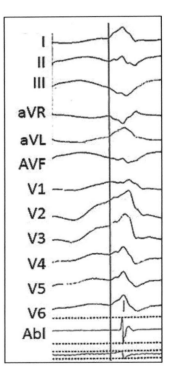

ANSWER: d. No. Notice how much later the signal appears on the ablation channel. It is very delayed (no calipers shown) from the reference line. The catheter is not close to the origin of the ventricular tachycardia. Huang says, "The site of earliest ventricular activation typically is >30 ms before QRS onset" Catheter Ablation of Cardiac Arrhythmias by Huang and Wood.

7. For the following ventricular arrhythmias match the definition with the correct label.
   a. Ventricular fibrillation
   b. Torsades de pointes
   c. Monomorphic VT
   d. Pleomorphic VT
   e. Polymorphic VT
   f. Sustained VT
   g. Focal VT
   h. PVC

1. A form of polymorphic VT with continually varying QRS complexes that appear to spiral around the baseline of the ECG lead in a sinusoidal pattern.
2. A chaotic rhythm defined on the surface ECG by undulations that are irregular in both timing and morphology, without discrete QRS complexes.
3. More than one morphologically distinct QRS complex occurs during the same episode of VT, but the QRS is not continuously changing.
4. A continuously changing QRS configuration from beat to beat, indicating a changing ventricular activation sequence.
5. A point source of earliest ventricular activation with a spread of activation away in all directions from that site.
6. Continuous VT for 30 seconds, or which requires an intervention for termination.
7. An early ventricular depolarization with or without mechanical contraction.
8. A similar QRS configuration from beat-to-beat.

CORRECTLY MATCHED ANSWERS:

2, a. Ventricular fibrillation - A chaotic rhythm defined on the surface ECG by undulations that are irregular in both timing and morphology, without discrete QRS complexes.

1, b. Torsades de pointes - A form of polymorphic VT with continually varying QRS complexes that appear to spiral around the baseline of the ECG lead in a sinusoidal pattern.

4, c. Monomorphic VT - A similar QRS configuration from beat to beat.

5, d. Polymorphic VT - A continuously changing QRS configuration from beat to beat, indicating a changing ventricular activation sequence.

7, e. Pleomorphic VT - More than one morphologically distinct QRS complex occurs during the same episode of VT, but the QRS is not continuously changing.

6, f. Sustained VT - Continuous VT for 30 seconds, or which requires an intervention for termination.

8, g. Focal VT - A point source of earliest ventricular activation with a spread of activation away in all directions from that site.

3, h. PVC - An early ventricular depolarization with or without mechanical contraction.

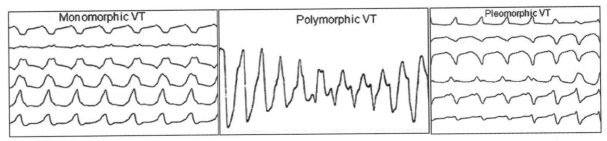

2019 HRS/EHRA/APHRS/LAHRS expert consensus statement on catheter ablation of ventricular arrhythmias. Journal of Arrhythmia

8. This is the triangular region of the most superior part of the LV epicardial surface bounded by the circumflex, LAD, and an approximate line from the first septal coronary artery laterally to the left AV groove.
   a. Sinuses of Valsalva
   b. LV outflow tract
   c. LV false tendon
   d. LV summit

ANSWER: d. LV Summit. The great cardiac vein (GCV) bisects the triangle. An area superior to the GCV is considered to be inaccessible to catheter ablation due to the proximity of the coronary arteries and overlying epicardial fat.

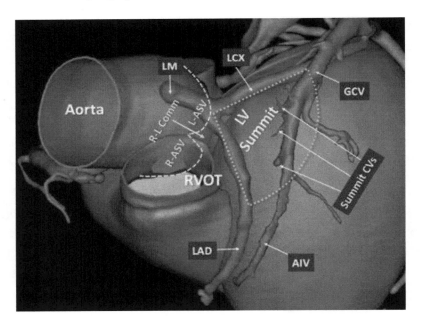

"The left ventricular (LV) summit (dotted outline) is shown on a 3-dimensional rendering of a cardiac computed tomography scan with coronary angiography and venography in a cranial right anterior oblique view. It is defined as an epicardial triangular structure whose apex is formed by the bifurcation of branches of the left coronary artery. The basal extent of the triangle is formed by the arc drawn from the origin of the first septal perforator of the left anterior descending artery (LAD) to the left circumflex artery (LCX). The right and left ASV are outlined (light yellow dashed line). AIV = anterior interventricular vein; GCV = great cardiac vein; LM = left main coronary artery; R-L comm = commissure between right and left ASV; RVOT = right ventricular outflow tract; summit-CV = communicating veins of the GCV"

Cheung, et al, Catheter Ablation of Arrhythmias Originating from the Left Ventricular Outflow Tract. JACC: Clinical Electrophysiology. 2019

9. Which three procedures are recommended to detect or reduce significant ischemia before catheter ablation of a patient with ischemic VT?
   a. **Electrophysiology Study**
   b. **Coronary Angiography**
   c. **Revascularization**
   d. **Holter Monitor**
   e. **Stress testing**

ANSWER: b, c, & e. In patients with suspected ischemic ventricular arrhythmias, stress testing and/or coronary angiography and subsequent revascularization can be beneficial before catheter ablation. This will aid in avoiding significant ischemia during induced VT.

2019 HRS/EHRA/APHRS/LAHRS expert consensus statement on catheter ablation of ventricular arrhythmias. Journal of Arrhythmia

10. Which of the following is the recommended treatment for a symptomatic patient with frequent PVCs originating from the RVOT in a structurally normal heart?
   a. **Cardiac Resynchronization Therapy**
   b. **ICD Implantation**
   c. **Cardiac Ablation**
   d. **Propafenone**
   e. **Metoprolol**

ANSWER: c. Cardiac Ablation. This is a Class I (strong) indication with a level (quality) of evidence at a level B-NR (Nonrandomized). Level B-NR shows that there is moderate-quality evidence from 1 or more well-designed, well-executed nonrandomized studies, observational studies, or registry studies. The level of evidence will most likely not be tested on, but it is valuable information to understand the recommendation.

Level (Quality) of Evidence Level A	
High-quality evidence from more than 1 RCT (randomized controlled trial) Meta-analyses of high-quality RCTs	
Level B-R (Randomized)	Level C-LD (Limited Data)
Moderate-quality evidence from 1 or more RCTs Meta-analyses of moderate-quality RCTs	Randomized or nonrandomized observational o registry studies with limitation of design or execution Meta-analyses of such studies Physiological or mechanistic studies in human subjects
Level B-NR (Nonrandomized)	Level C-EO (Expert Opinion)
Moderate-quality evidence from 1 or more well-designed, well-executed nonrandomized studies, observational studies, or registry studies Meta-analyses of such studies	Consensus of expert opinion based on clinical experience

2019 HRS/EHRA/APHRS/LAHRS expert consensus statement on catheter ablation of ventricular arrhythmias. Journal of Arrhythmia

11. What is the recommended class of cardiac ablation for a symptomatic patient with a structurally normal heart and left ventricular VT in which antiarrhythmic medications are ineffective?

    a. Class I
    b. Class IIa
    c. Class IIb
    d. Class III

ANSWER: a. Class I. Class I: Is recommended, is indicated/useful/effective/beneficial, should be performed/administered/other Level of Evidence – B-NR: Moderate-quality evidence from 1 or more well-designed, well-executed nonrandomized studies, observational studies, or registry studies, Meta-analyses of such studies.

2019 HRS/EHRA/APHRS/LAHRS expert consensus statement on catheter ablation of ventricular arrhythmias. Journal of Arrhythmia

12. **Which three of the following will have a Class I recommendation?**
    a. Ablation in patients with ischemic heart disease who experience recurrent monomorphic VT despite chronic amiodarone therapy
    b. Ablation in a patient with repaired Tetralogy of Fallot & sustained monomorphic VT
    c. Patient with ischemic heart disease with a single event of monomorphic VT
    d. Revascularization alone to prevent VT recurrence
    e. Ablation of bundle branch reentrant VT

ANSWER: a, b, & e. Revascularization alone to prevent VT recurrence is Class III
A patient with ischemic heart disease with a single event of monomorphic VT is Class IIb

2019 HRS/EHRA/APHRS/LAHRS expert consensus statement on catheter ablation of ventricular arrhythmias. Journal of Arrhythmia

13. **Which medication is recommended when performing a VT ablation in the left ventricle?**
    a. 2B/3A inhibitor
    b. Metoprolol
    c. Adenosine
    d. Heparin

ANSWER: d. Heparin. Anticoagulation is recommended for any left-sided ablation to reduce the risk of clot and associated complications. Isoproterenol (Isuprel) may be utilized to induce VT in some patients; however, this is not needed to perform a left ventricular ablation.

2019 HRS/EHRA/APHRS/LAHRS expert consensus statement on catheter ablation of ventricular arrhythmias. Journal of Arrhythmia

14. **Which two of the following are often performed during an outflow tract PVC ablation?**
    a. Entrainment Mapping
    b. Activation Mapping
    c. Substrate Mapping
    d. Pace Mapping

ANSWER: b & d. Activation mapping and pace mapping are commonly utilized during outflow tract ablations. Entrainment mapping is utilized during ischemic VT ablations to help determine the proximity of the ablation catheter to the VT circuit. Substrate mapping is also used during ischemic VT ablations to identify areas of scar and potential channels within it.

2019 HRS/EHRA/APHRS/LAHRS expert consensus statement on catheter ablation of ventricular arrhythmias. Journal of Arrhythmia

15. An LV summit VT site may require ablation at which three of the following sites?
   a. Anterolateral papillary muscle
   b. Ligament of Marshall
   c. Sinuses of Valsalva
   d. RVOT
   e. LVOT

ANSWER: c, d, & e. The LV summit is often a challenging site to ablate. It is the highest site of the LV. The summit is a triangular portion of the epicardial LVOT bounded by the bifurcation between the LAD (left anterior descending artery) and the CX (Circumflex artery). It is transected laterally by the great cardiac vein (GCV) at its junction with the anterior interventricular vein (AIV). Ablation may need to be performed from the RVOT, LVOT, Sinuses of Valsalva, the coronary venous system, or even in epicardial space. The basal portion may be inaccessible due to a thick overlying endocardial fat pad.

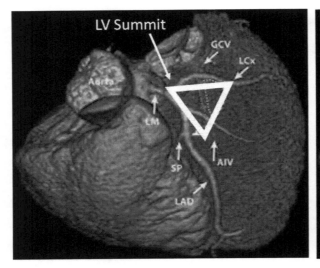 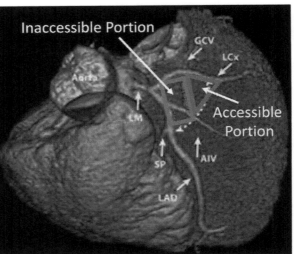

2019 HRS/EHRA/APHRS/LAHRS expert consensus statement on catheter ablation of ventricular arrhythmias. Journal of Arrhythmia

16. Ventricular arrhythmias associated with the papillary muscles are most commonly found in a:
   a. Anterolateral LV papillary muscle
   b. Posteromedial papillary muscle
   c. Ruptured papillary muscle
   d. RV papillary muscles

ANSWER: b. Posteromedial papillary muscle. This is the most common papillary muscle for a VT origin. They are also more commonly found at the tip of the muscle rather than the base.

2019 HRS/EHRA/APHRS/LAHRS expert consensus statement on catheter ablation of ventricular arrhythmia. Journal of Arrhythmia. 2020

17. Which of the following ablation sites will cure bundle branch reentrant VT?
   a. **Both right and left bundle branches must be ablated**
   b. **Right bundle branch**
   c. **Mahiam fibers**
   d. **AV node**

ANSWER: b. Right Bundle Branch. Ablation of either the right or left bundle branch will cure bundle branch VT. The right bundle is usually ablated due to easier access. Neither the AV node nor accessory pathways are part of the circuit; therefore, ablation will not terminate the VT or prevent its recurrence.

2019 HRS/EHRA/APHRS/LAHRS expert consensus statement on catheter ablation of ventricular arrhythmias. Journal of Arrhythmia

18. After a successful ischemic VT ablation procedure, symptomatic recurrence of VT usually involves the:
   a. **Papillary Muscles**
   b. **Endocardium**
   c. **Epicardium**
   d. **Fascicles**

ANSWER: c. Epicardium. Epicardial ablation is not usually required; however, it may need to be performed on a patient with recurrent VT. This may be performed via ablation through the cardiac veins, subxiphoid approach, or even an ethanol ablation.

2019 HRS/EHRA/APHRS/LAHRS expert consensus statement on catheter ablation of ventricular arrhythmias. Journal of Arrhythmia

19. Which three of the following may function as a barrier for a ventricular tachycardia circuit?
   a. **Patch material from a prior repair of a sinus venous defect**
   b. **Repair of atrioventricular canal type septal defect**
   c. **Scar from previous MI**
   d. **Ventricular Resection**
   e. **Prior atriotomy**

ANSWER: b, c, & d. Each of these options will create a boundary or barrier for a ventricular tachycardia circuit. The VT isthmuses are located between anatomical barriers. This isthmus may be identified during sinus rhythm with 3D mapping. Entrainment mapping is also utilized to identify the critical components of the VT circuit.

- Ventricular resection is used to treat heart failure by reshaping or reducing an over-sized left ventricle.
- Atrioventricular canal type (inlet) VSD is located underneath the tricuspid and mitral valves.
- An atriotomy is a surgical opening within the atrium. So, a prior atriotomy may lead to atrial flutter, but not VT. A sinus venous defect is a septal defect within the atrium; therefore, it would not lead to VT. The various locations for septal defects are displayed in the following images.

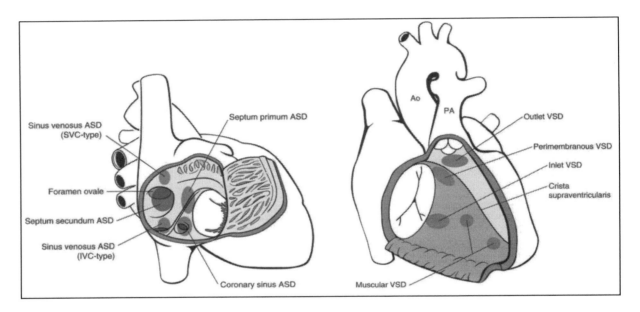

Images from obgynkey.com: Atrial, Ventricular, and Atrioventricular Septal Defects.
2019 HRS/EHRA/APHRS/LAHRS expert consensus statement on catheter ablation of ventricular arrhythmias. Journal of Arrhythmia

20. If catheter stability is difficult to maintain during a VT ablation on a papillary muscle, the physician may utilize:
- a. A contact force sensing catheter
- b. An irrigated RF catheter
- c. Cryoablation
- d. ICE

ANSWER: c. Cryoablation. All these options may be utilized during a VT ablation on a papillary muscle. An irrigated RF catheter will give a deeper lesion whereas contact force and ICE (intracardiac echo) will help the physician know if they are in contact with the tissue.

However, the only option that will increase stability is a cryoablation catheter. When cooled, the tip will adhere to the tissue and move in tandem with the papillary muscle.

2019 HRS/EHRA/APHRS/LAHRS expert consensus statement on catheter ablation of ventricular arrhythmias Journal of Arrhythmia, 2020

21. Which of the following may be utilized in VT ablation if the arrhythmogenic substrate is unable to be reached/ablated?
   a. **Contact force sensing RF catheter**
   b. **Ethanol ablation**
   c. **Cryoablation**
   d. **Stereotaxis**

ANSWER: b. Ethanol ablation. A cardiac ablation with ethanol may generate lesions in areas that may otherwise not be reached with the standard approach. To utilize this technique, there must be a suitable target vessel in the arrhythmogenic substrate area such as a septal perforator on a VT in the septum that was unable to be ablated from either the right or left ventricle. Ethanol ablation is also used in the EP lab to ablate hypertrophied areas of the LV that cause outflow tract obstruction in HOCM.

2019 HRS/EHRA/APHRS/LAHRS expert consensus statement on catheter ablation of ventricular arrhythmias Journal of Arrhythmia, 2020

22. Which of the following catheters would be the best choice for a VT substrate map?
   a. **2-10-2 electrode spacing**
   b. **2-2-2 electrode spacing**
   c. **2-5-2 electrode spacing**
   d. **5-5-5 electrode spacing**

ANSWER: b. 2-2-2 electrode spacing. This example is a duodecapolar (20 electrodes) catheter with tightly spaced electrodes that may be utilized for this purpose. "A multielectrode mapping catheter with a high number of small, and closely spaced electrodes increases the mapping speed, EGM density, and the ability to recognize low amplitude near-field EGMs in ventricles with healed infarction." Barkagan, et al, A novel multielectrode catheter for high-density ventricular mapping: electrogram characterization and utility for scar mapping. EP Europace, 2020

A substrate map is a 3D mapping technique in which the voltage of the myocardium is acquired. The different voltages are displayed with a designated color. With this type of map, low voltage channels within the ventricular myocardium may be observed. A commonly used catheter is a 2-2-2 spaced decapolar catheter. Now newer high-density mapping catheters are now more commonly utilized such as the HD Grid by Abbott.

23. Which type of mapping would you recommend in a hemodynamically unstable VT.
   a. **LAT Mapping (local activation time)**
   b. **Entrainment Mapping**
   c. **Reentrant Mapping**
   d. **Substrate Mapping**

ANSWER: d. Substrate Mapping. Substrate or Voltage mapping may be performed during sinus rhythm or pacing. Entrainment, LAT, and Reentrant maps all require the patient to be in tachycardia for adequate VT mapping. If the patient is unable to tolerate tachycardia, the physician may utilize an Impella to maintain patient stability.

24. This rhythm is from an asymptomatic Asian man, referred because his father recently experienced sudden unexpected nocturnal death syndrome (SUNDS). What is the rhythm?
   a. **Bundle Branch Reentry**
   b. **LV Fascicular VT**
   c. **RV dysplasia**
   d. **Brugada**

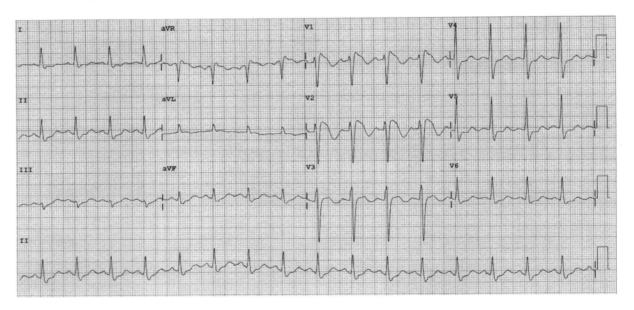

ANSWER: d. Brugada. This may also be referred to as SUNDS or "sudden unexpected nocturnal death syndrome" which is most common in Asian males in their sleep. Brugada syndrome is treated with the implantation of an ICD. Approximately 20% of the cases of Brugada syndrome have been shown to be associated with mutation(s) in the gene that encodes for the sodium ion channel. It is a genetic abnormality involving the SCN5A gene.

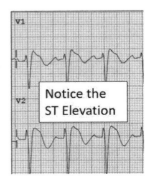

Notice the ST Elevation

25. Match the ventricular heart rate range with the correct ventricular arrhythmia.

a. <40 bpm
b. 50-110 bpm
c. 110-250 bpm
d. 150-300 bpm
e. 400-600 bpm

1. Ventricular Tachycardia
2. Ventricular Flutter
3. Ventricular Fibrillation
4. Accelerated Idioventricular Rhythm
5. Idioventricular Rhythm with AV Block

MATCHED RATE RANGES FOR VENTRICULAR ARRHYTHMIAS:
Ventricular tachycardia: 110-250 bpm
Ventricular flutter: 150-300 bpm
Ventricular fibrillation: 400-600 bpm
Accelerated idioventricular rhythm: 50-110 bpm
Idioventricular rhythm with AV block: <40 bpm

Braunwald says, "The electrocardiographic diagnosis of ventricular tachycardia is suggested by the occurrence of a mature ventricular complex whose duration exceeds 120 ms, with the ST-T vector pointing opposite to the major QRS deflection" Ventricular rates range from 110 to 250 bpm," ICDs use these rate zones to determine therapy, defibrillate VF and attempt ATP on VT. See: Braunwald, chapter on "Specific Arrhythmias: Diagnosis and Treatment."

26. What is the rhythm in the Lead II ECG recording of this asymptomatic patient?

a. Atrial Fibrillation with VT
b. Torsade de Points
c. Initiation of VT
d. Artifact

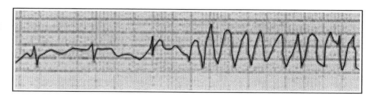

ANSWER: d. Artifact. Don't forget to check the patient…. Always check the patient and confirm on another ECG lead. Many times, with patient movement or placement of sheaths in the groin, this type of artifact is seen. If you look closely, you can see QRS spikes marching through.

27. PVC complexes are distinguished from simple supraventricular QRS complexes in that in PVCs the QRS complexes are _____ and the T waves are usually _____.

a. Narrow and negative in polarity, asymmetrical and positive in polarity
b. Broad and bizarre in shape, asymmetrical and positive in polarity
c. Broad and bizarre in shape, large and in the opposite direction
d. Narrow and inverted, large and in an opposite direction

ANSWER: c. Broad and bizarre in shape and the T waves are large and in the opposite direction. A premature ventricular complex is characterized by the premature occurrence of

a QRS complex that is bizarre in shape and has a duration usually exceeding the dominant QRS complex, greater than 120 ms. The T wave is commonly large and opposite in direction to the major deflection of the QRS. The QRS is not preceded by a premature P wave.

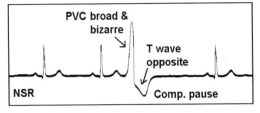

28. **Ventricular tachycardia may be mimicked by:**
    a. **Mobitz II block with rapid ventricular response**
    b. **Supraventricular Tachycardia with aberrancy**
    c. **Paroxysmal Atrial Tachycardia**
    d. **Disconnected leads**

ANSWER: b. Supraventricular Tachycardia with aberrancy. An ongoing problem for CCU nurses is to distinguish SVT with aberrancy from VT. Both are wide complex tachycardias, but with different implications and treatments. This diagram compares Ventricular Tachycardia and Supraventricular tachycardia with aberrant conduction. Although the look similar on ECG, the Ladder diagram below clearly shows the different origins of the rhythms. Marriott suggests using lead V1 or MCL1 to distinguish the QRS morphology. VT mimicked by SVT with aberrancy Supraventricular aberrant beats resemble triphasic (rabbit ears rSR') RBBB pattern. Ventricular ectopic beats are more likely to be monophasic R or biphasic (QR). See: Marriot, chapter on "Ventricular Tachyarrhythmias."

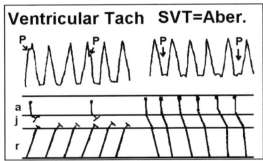

29. **The arrhythmias shown on this ECG (consecutively) are:**
    a. **VF & VT**
    b. **VT & VF**
    c. **PVCs & VT**
    d. **VFL & VT**

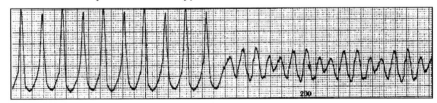

ANSWER: b. Ventricular Tachycardia & Ventricular Fibrillation. The ventricular tachycardia (VT) may deteriorate to Ventricular Fibrillation (VF) as it does here. That is the problem with VT, it may lead to lethal VF. See: ACLS manual chapter on "Arrhythmias."

30. **An 80-year-old man comes to your lab in NSR with a prolonged QT interval. Before an EP procedure starts, he develops the tachy-arrhythmia shown. He is conscious but complains that his heart is pounding. His BP drops from 120/80 to 100/70. What is the rhythm?**

a. Ventricular fibrillation (VF)
b. Ventricular flutter
c. Monomorphic VT
d. Torsade de pointes

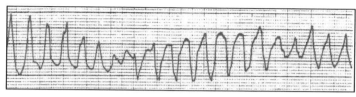

ANSWER: d. This is Torsade de pointes, a type of VT which tends to increase then decrease in amplitude in an envelope as shown. The QRS complexes point up, then down. In this tracing, note how the first 6 beats point up; the next 8 beats point down. When the patient is in NSR they may have long QT intervals and electrolyte disorders. Commonly treated with IV magnesium or overdrive pacing in 10 second bursts at a rate slightly faster than tachycardia. Cardioversion may be necessary if the patient becomes unstable. Braunwald says: "The term torsades de pointes refers to a VT characterized by QRS complexes of changing amplitude that appear to twist around the isoelectric line and occur at rates of 200 to 250 bpm. . .. Torsades de pointes can terminate with progressive prolongation in cycle length and larger and more distinctly formed QRS complexes and culminate in a return to the basal rhythm, a period of ventricular standstill, and a new attack of torsade des pointes or ventricular fibrillation." See: Braunwald, chapter on Specific Arrhythmias: Diagnosis and Treatment

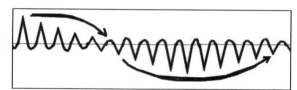

31. **The third beat on this V1 recording is an:**

a. RV-PVC
b. LV-PVC
c. RA-PAC
d. LA-PAC

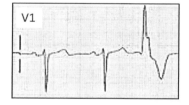

ANSWER: b. LV-PVC (Left Ventricular Premature Contraction). PVCs are broad and bizarre with a compensatory pause. If PVCs originate in the LV, the impulse travels anteriorly making a large positive "R" wave on lead V1. RV PVCs show negative (rS) waves on lead V1. Left sided PVCs are more likely to precipitate ventricular fibrillation and are more often associated with heart disease. LV-PVC is also termed LVPCs. The MCL1 monitoring lead is especially helpful in distinguishing RVPCs from LVPCs. Note in the diagram how the RV-PVCs form a broad QS pattern in lead V1, while LV-

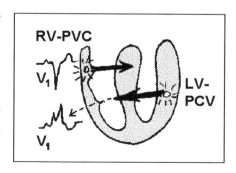

PVCs are in the opposite direction, and resemble a RBBB pattern. Remember the turn signal rule: V1 distinguishes RV PVCs from LV PCVs down=Left turn= LBBB pattern, like RV-PVC. See: Marriot, chapter on "Premature Beats."

32. Long QT syndrome is associated with:
   a. **Bundle Branch Reentry**
   b. **Torsades de pointes**
   c. **LV Fascicular VT**
   d. **RV dysplasia**
   e. **Brugada**

ANSWER: b. Torsades de pointes. Zipes says, "The tachyarrhythmia most encountered in congenital and acquired long QT syndrome is torsade de pointes, an atypical polymorphic ventricular tachycardia.... An EAD-induced extrasystole [after depolarization] is believed to be responsible for the premature beat that initiates torsade de pointes, but the maintenance of the arrhythmia is thought to be due to circus movement reentry." See Zipes, chapter on Drug induced Channelopathies

33. A man occasionally goes into wide complex tachycardia and faints on exercise. His resting HR=60, PR=0.18 sec, QRS=0.11 sec, QT=0.52 sec. This patient has _____ with _____.
   a. **Long QT syndrome, SVT with aberrant conduction**
   b. **Brugada syndrome, SVT with aberrant conduction**
   c. **Long QT syndrome, Torsades de pointes**
   d. **Brugada syndrome, Torsades de pointes**

ANSWER: c. Long QT syndrome, Torsades de pointes. This man has long QT syndrome. QTc = 0.52 which is high. His VT is most likely Torsade de Pointes, which is associated with long QT. Normal QTc= 0.45 sec. Ellenbogen says, "The typical features of LQTS are prolonged corrected QT (QTc) interval in the 12-lead electrocardiogram (ECG), T-wave abnormalities, and symptoms that vary from syncope to SCD. Symptoms are secondary to torsades de pointes, a rapid polymorphic VT that may be self-limited or may degenerate into VF .... The arrhythmic episodes are often triggered by adrenergic stimuli (e.g., exercise, emotion)" See: Ellenbogen, chapter on "Channelopathies"

34. Which type of ventricular tachycardia typically has an RBBB morphology?
   a. **Bundle Branch Reentry**
   b. **Idiopathic LV VT**
   c. **RVOT VT**
   d. **ARVD**

ANSWER: b. Idiopathic LV ventricular tachycardia has a RBBB pattern whereas all the rest usually display a LBBB morphology. TIP: To determine the site of the BBB look at V1. Imagine driving your car if you are turning left, you push the blinker down, if you're turning right, you turn the blinker up. Same with BBB, if the V1 QRS has a negative deflection it is LBBB, and a positive deflection is RBBB. RBBB typically has a "rabbit –ear" morphology.

35. The ectopic beats recorded in this example with an arterial blood pressure are:

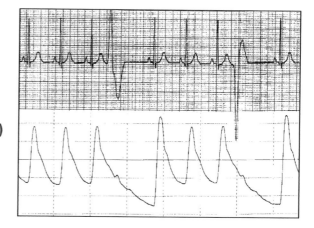

    a. **Multifocal premature ventricular contractions (PVCs)**
    b. **Unifocal premature ventricular contractions (PVCs)**
    c. **Premature junctional contraction (PJC)**
    d. **Premature atrial contraction (PAC)**

ANSWER: a. Multifocal PVCs. The two premature beats are broad and different in shape. This indicates each comes from a different focus in the ventricle, and that ventricular conduction is slow since it must go through the ventricular muscle, not the faster Purkinje system. If this were lead V1, the first PVC would be an LV PVC and the second an RV PVC. Note that these PVCs occurred too early to generate any significant blood pressure.
See: Marriot, chapter on "Premature Beats."

36. The premature beats above are followed by a _____ pause.
    a. **Non-compensatory**
    b. **Compensatory**
    c. **Interpolated**
    d. **Aberrant**

ANSWER: b. Compensatory. The PVCs are not usually conducted retrograde into the atria and do not reset the SA node. The normal sinus P wave usually falls in the refractory period of the AV node and is not conducted. This makes the long compensatory pause following most PVCs. These beats can occur while manipulating a catheter in either ventricle.
See: Marriot, chapter on "Premature Beats."

37. This arrhythmia recorded with an arterial pressure shows:
   a. Couplet
   b. Interpolated PVCs
   c. Multifocal PVCs
   d. Ventricular Bigeminy

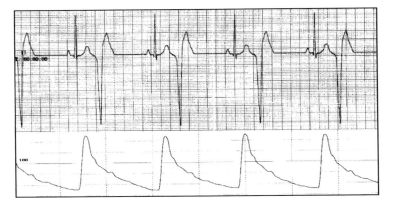

ANSWER: d. Ventricular Bigeminy. A PVC follows each Sinus beat. Constant coupling intervals occur between each pair of normal sinus and premature beats. Note that the PVCs are too early to generate any significant blood pressure.
See: Marriot, chapter on "Premature Beats."

38. In the ECG and pressure displayed, why is the pulse rate half the ECG heart rate?
   a. Electromechanical dissociation occurs
   b. Pulsus alternans occurs due to CHF
   c. PVCs too early to allow filling
   d. PVCs do not contract the heart

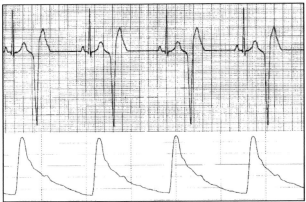

ANSWER: c. PVCs too early to allow filling. The ECG shows ventricular bigeminy with a rate of 70 bpm. The pulse rate is only 35 bpm. Note. The PVCs do cause a small contraction, seen near the dicrotic notch. These premature beats have just barely enough pressure to open the aortic valve. Premature beats have less diastolic filling time than slower beats. Depending on how early the beat is, there may not be enough blood in the ventricle to pump effectively. The reduced preload diminishes their contractile force and resulting blood pressure. With premature beats an apical pulse rate is more accurate than a radial pulse rate because you can feel each LV contraction, including PVCs. See: Marriot, chapter on, Premature Beats.

39. Match the type of VT with its ECG.
  a. **Monomorphic VT**
  b. **Polymorphic VT**
  c. **Ventricular Flutter**
  d. **Ventricular Fibrillation**

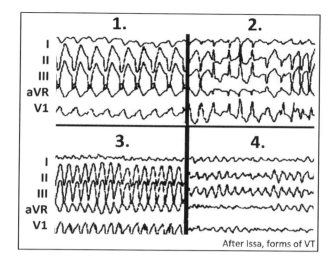

After Issa, forms of VT

CORRECTLY MATCHED ANSWERS:
1. Monomorphic VT
2. Polymorphic VT
3. Ventricular Flutter
4. Ventricular Fibrillation

Issa says, "Monomorphic ventricular tachycardia (VT) has a single stable QRS morphology from beat to beat, indicating repetitive ventricular depolarization in the same sequence. Polymorphic VT has a continuously changing or multiform QRS morphology (i.e., no constant morphology for more than five complexes, no clear isoelectric baseline between QRS complexes, or QRS complexes that have different morphologies in multiple simultaneously recorded leads), indicating a variable sequence of ventricular activation and no single site of origin. Torsades de pointes is a polymorphic VT associated with a long QT interval, and electrocardiographically characterized by twisting of the peaks of the QRS complexes around the isoelectric line during the arrhythmia.... Ventricular flutter is a regular (cycle length [CL] variability less than 30 milliseconds), rapid (approximately 300 bpm) ventricular arrhythmia with a monomorphic appearance but no isoelectric interval between successive QRS complexes. Ventricular fibrillation (VF) is a rapid, usually more than 300 bpm, grossly irregular ventricular rhythm with marked variability in QRS CL, morphology, and amplitude" See: Issa, chapter on VT

40. Match each Arrhythmia to its ECG in the diagram below:
   a. **Sustained polymorphic VT**
   b. **Sustained monomorphic VT**
   c. **Nonsustained polymorphic VT**
   d. **Nonsustained monomorphic VT**
   e. **Ventricular Flutter**

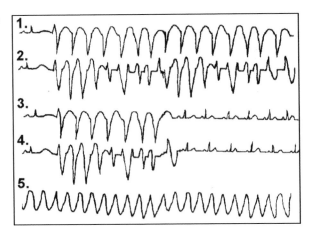

CORRECTLY MATCHED ANSWERS ARE:
   a. Sustained monomorphic VT
   b. Sustained polymorphic VT
   c. nonsustained types of ventricular tachycardia/flutter monomorphic VT
   d. Nonsustained polymorphic VT
   e. Ventricular Flutter

Sustained monomorphic Ventricular Tachycardia (VT). If the VT complexes are all NOT identical, they are multifocal (most dangerous type). And if the run of VT lasts over 30 seconds is termed sustained. See: Marriot, chapter on "Ventricular Tachycardia."

41. What rhythm is illustrated in this example?
   a. **Nonsustained Ventricular Fibrillation**
   b. **Nonsustained Ventricular Tachycardia**
   c. **A run of Ventricular Fibrillation**
   d. **A run of Ventricular Flutter**

ANSWER: b. Nonsustained Ventricular Tachycardia. A short run of PVCs becomes VT after consecutive beats. If the run lasts less than 30 seconds it is termed "Nonsustained VT", longer and it is termed "sustained VT." If the ventricular complexes are identical in shape (morphology), as these are, it is termed a monomorphic or uniform VT. If the VT complexes vary, they are termed polymorphic or multiform. See: Marriot, chapter on "Ventricular Tachycardia."

42. Electromechanical dissociation (PEA) is defined as:
   a. **Visible ECG but no detectable pulse**
   b. **Ventricular fibrillation**
   c. **Complete heart Block**
   d. **Asystole**

ANSWER: a. Visible ECG but no detectable pulse. PEA is pulseless electrical activity. It is a state in which organized cardiac electrical depolarization, but mechanical contractions are absent or undetectable. The ECG may look like any rhythm (usually bradycardia), but no pulse is detectable. The most common cause of PEA is hypovolemia, which can usually be corrected with fluid administration. Pulseless Electrical Activity or PEA was previously called electro-mechanical dissociation (EMD). See: ACLS Manual, chapter on Essential of ACLS.

43. What arrhythmia may mimic asystole on the ECG monitor?
   a. **Pulseless Ventricular Tachycardia**
   b. **Electromechanical Dissociation**
   c. **Fine Ventricular Fibrillation**
   d. **Complete Heart Block**

ANSWER: c. Fine Ventricular Fibrillation may appear as a flat line unless the gain is increased. The monitoring lead should be switched to the one that shows the largest QRS. This is because if your lead is perpendicular to the mean QRS axis, the QRS will be exceedingly small. Lead II is usually best. See: ACLS Manual, chapter on "Arrhythmias."

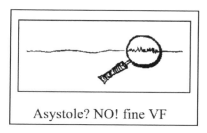

Asystole? NO! fine VF

44. All the following are TRUE about ventricular fibrillation (VF) EXCEPT:
   a. **VF causes cardiovascular collapse**
   b. **VF is a disorganized tachycardia**
   c. **VF has no QRS complexes**
   d. **VF leads to pulseless VT**
   e. **VF leads to asystole**

ANSWER: d. VF leads to pulseless VT - false. The opposite is true: VT leads to VF. Fogoros says: "Ventricular fibrillation is a completely disorganized tachyarrhythmia without discrete QRS complexes. This arrhythmia causes instant hemodynamic collapse and rapid loss of consciousness since the heart immediately ceases to contract meaningfully. When ventricular fibrillation begins, it is associated with a course electrical pattern. As the heart becomes less viable (over a period of a few minutes), the fibrillation becomes fine, and then all electrical activity ceases (flat line)." The usual sequence of events in sudden death is an increase in ventricular ectopy (PVCs), ventricular tachycardia, course ventricular fibrillation, fine ventricular fibrillation, then within 5-7 minutes to no electrical activity (asystole) and death. See: Fogoros, chapter on EP Testing for Cardiac Arrhythmias

45. The ECG and arterial pressure displayed shows PVCs leading to:
   a. **Polymorphic Ventricular Tachycardia**
   b. **Pulseless Ventricular Tachycardia**
   c. **Pulseless Ventricular Fibrillation**
   d. **Electromechanical Dissociation**

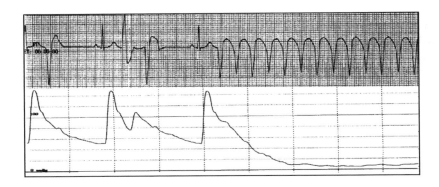

ANSWER: d. Pulseless Ventricular Tachycardia. The Multifocal PVCs trigger VT and the blood pressure falls to zero. The patient will be unconscious within 10 seconds. Defibrillation and Basic life support resuscitation are needed. VT patients often have a pulse and may not need emergency treatment. See: Marriott, chapter on "Ventricular Tachyarrhythmias."

46. You are alone in the EP lab with a patient post PVI and coronary sinus angiography. You are ready to remove the arterial line when you hear a snoring sound. Then the patient's eyes roll back. You look at the monitor and see the ECG and arterial tracing above. The defib pads have been removed. After calling for help you should:
   a. Apply an external transthoracic pacemaker
   b. Apply Oxygen by nasal cannula 5 L/min
   c. Administer 0.5 mg Epinephrine IV
   d. Administer a precordial thump
   e. Begin endotracheal intubation

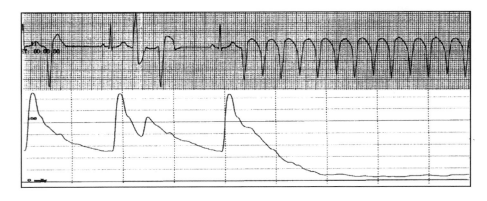

ANSWER: d. Precordial thump. Only recommended for witnessed VT by health professionals. This rhythm shows Multifocal PVCs leading to a lethal arrhythmia pulseless VT. After checking the pulse, A forceful precordial thump is administered by "hammering" your fist from 1 foot above the patient's sternum. It generates 10-20 joules of energy and may convert VT into a perfusing arrhythmia in (successful in 11%-25% of cases). It is recommended only immediately in monitored VT when a defibrillator is not available. If the precordial thump proves ineffective, the patient will require CPR and defibrillation. Beware that a precordial thump may make VT deteriorate into VF. The Precordial thump is NOT likely to convert VF.

The definitive treatment is defibrillation. Your lab will have a defibrillator, but as here, it may not be readily available. Other options to consider are begin airway management, begin CPR, defibrillate with paddles, and to record the ECG so it will be documented. See: ACLS manual chapter on "VF/VT algorithm" and "Defibrillation"

47. Which is most likely to be hemodynamically stable and not need defibrillation/cardioversion?
   a. **Monomorphic VT (CL>300)**
   b. **Monomorphic VT (CL<300)**
   c. **Polymorphic VT (CL>300)**
   d. **Polymorphic VT (CL<300)**

ANSWER: a. Monomorphic VT (CL>300). Remember that cycle length decreases as the heart rate increases. CL 200 is 300 bpm, while CL of 300 ms is 200 bpm. The formula is CL=60,000/HR. Polymorphic VT has a greater tendency to degenerate into VF. Because in polymorphic there are multiple reentry loops. It will be less stable than monomorphic VT. Issa says, "The ability to terminate SMVT (Sustained Monomorphic Ventricular Tachycardia) by rapid ventricular pacing and/or VES is influenced most importantly by the tachycardia CL (50% of VTs with CLs less than 300 milliseconds will require electrical cardioversion), but also by the local ERP at the pacing site, conduction time from the stimulation site to the site of origin of the VT, duration of the excitable gap, and presence of antiarrhythmic agents."
"Monomorphic ventricular tachycardia (VT) has a single stable QRS morphology from beat to beat, indicating repetitive ventricular depolarization in the same sequence. Polymorphic VT has a continuously changing or multiform QRS morphology (i.e., no constant morphology for more than five complexes, no clear isoelectric baseline between QRS complexes, or QRS complexes that have different morphologies in multiple simultaneously recorded leads), indicating a variable sequence of ventricular activation and no single site of origin." See: Issa, chapter on Postinfarction Sustained Monomorphic VT

48. Frequent bouts of VT and VF occurring in close succession requiring numerous ICD shocks is termed a/an:
   a. **Ventricular Exacerbation**
   b. **Reperfusion Arrhythmia**
   c. **Torsade de Pointes**
   d. **Electrical Storm**

ANSWER: d. Electrical Storm. "A frequent example of the vicious cycle responsible for electrical storms is ventricular fibrillation occurring as a result of myocardial ischemia, provoking further ischemia and further induction of ventricular fibrillation. Without urgent intervention, electrical storms are fatal despite the presence of a normally functioning cardiac defibrillator." Cohen says, "electrical storm refers to incessant ventricular tachycardia or fibrillation that results in numerous ICD shocks."
See: Hayes and Sirvatham, Dictionary or Cohen Chapter on Preoperative checklist

49. **The most common form of idiopathic VT in patients with no structural heart disease is:**
   a. Long QT syndrome
   b. Brugada syndrome
   c. RVOT
   d. LVOT

ANSWER: c. RVOT. "Outflow tract ventricular tachycardias (OT VT) comprise a subgroup of idiopathic VT that are localized in and around the right and left ventricular outflow tracts. OT VT are the most common form of idiopathic VTs and originate, in more than 80-90% of cases, from the right ventricular outflow tract. They manifest at an early age (30-50 years) ..." See: http://www.escardio.org/Idiopathic-Ventricular-Tachycardia-Brugada.aspx#

Issa says, "Most forms of outflow tract VTs are adenosine-sensitive, and are thought to be caused by ... (cAMP)–mediated delayed afterdepolarizations (DADs) and triggered activity" See: Issa, chapter on idiopathic VT

50. **Right ventricular outflow tachycardia manifests as:**
   a. Monomorphic nonsustained VT with RBBB & anterior axis
   b. Monomorphic nonsustained VT with LBBB & inferior axis
   c. Polymorphic VT with RBBB & anterior axis
   d. Polymorphic VT with LBBB & inferior axis

ANSWER: b. Monomorphic nonsustained VT with LBBB & inferior axis. RVOT is "Nonsustained, repetitive, monomorphic VT. This is the most common form (60-90%). It is characterized by frequent ventricular ectopy, right ventricular couplets, and salvos of non-sustained ventricular tachycardia (NSVT) with left bundle branch block morphology and inferior QRS axis. These extrasystoles occur more often during the day than at night, at rest or following a period of exercise and are transiently suppressed by sinus tachycardia. They may diminish or disappear with exercise during stress testing." See: http://www.escardio.org/Idiopathic-Ventricular-Tachycardia-Brugada.aspx#

Issa says, "RVOT VTs have LBBB morphology with precordial QRS transition (first precordial lead with R/S ratio >1) that begins no earlier than lead V3 and more typically occurs in lead V4. The frontal plane axis, precordial R/S transition, QRS width, and complexity of the QRS morphology in the inferior leads can pinpoint the origin of VT in RVOT. Most RVOT VTs originate from the anterosuperior aspect of the septum, just under the pulmonic valve." See: Issa chapter on Idiopathic VT

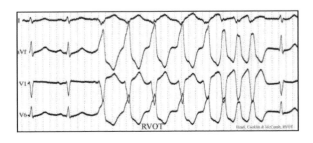

51. Patients who present with VT but have no CAD, myopathy or other obvious structural heart disease have:
   a. Verapamil sensitive VT
   b. Non-sustained VT
   c. Polymorphic VT
   d. Idiopathic VT
   e. Aberrant VT

ANSWER: d. Idiopathic VT. Idiopathic means of unknown cause. Issa says, "Ventricular tachycardia (VT) is usually associated with structural heart disease, with coronary artery disease and cardiomyopathy being the most common causes. However, about 10% of patients who present with VT have no obvious structural heart disease (idiopathic VT). Absence of structural heart disease is usually suggested if the ECG, echocardiogram, and coronary arteriogram collectively are normal." However, the Brugada syndrome and long-QT syndrome forms of idiopathic VT will have abnormal ECGs." See: Issa, chapter on idiopathic VT

52. This patient's ECG starts with sinus bradycardia with _____ and ends with _____.
   a. Type II block and Long QT, Monomorphic VT
   b. Type II block and Long QT, Torsade de Pointes
   c. Hypercalcemia, Monomorphic VT
   d. Hypercalcemia, Torsade de Pointes

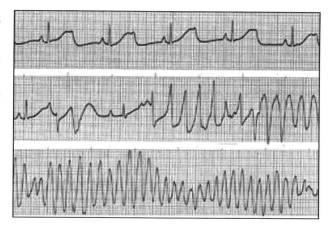

ANSWER: b. Type II block and Long QT, Torsade de Pointes VT. Note a second P wave buried in each T wave. This shows how long QT syndrome may lead to Torsade de pointes. The sinus bradycardia rate (41 bpm) has giant and delayed T waves, with superimposed p waves indicating second degree type II AV block.

The RR=1.46 sec (square root=1.20), QT int. = .77 sec, QTc=0.64 sec. which is much higher than the 0.45 allowed. This is slow brady. rhythm with long QT syndrome that leads directly to rapid Torsade de Pointes VT. Note the initial VT shows the changing of points (torsade de pointes) then degenerates into an oscillation VT where the wave envelope widens and thins all characteristics of TdP (torsades de pointes) type polymorphic VT. Note that incorrect answer "hypercalcemia" causes short QT interval, not long QT as we see here.

Issa says, "Torsade de pointes is a polymorphic VT associated with a long QT interval and electrographically characterized by twisting of the peaks of the QRS complexes around the isoelectric line…. In long-QT syndrome (LQTS) with a long QT interval, functional block between the HB and ventricular muscle caused by prolonged ventricular refractoriness can lead to 2:1 AV block and severe bradycardia." See: Issa chapter on AV Conduction Abnormalities

53. Bundle branch reentry VT is a _____ associated with the pathology of _____.
   a. **Monomorphic VT, Ischemic ventricular scar tissue**
   b. **Polymorphic VT, Ischemic ventricular scar tissue**
   c. **Monomorphic VT, dilated cardiomyopathy**
   d. **Polymorphic VT, dilated cardiomyopathy**

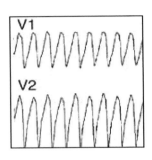

ANSWER: c. Monomorphic VT, dilated cardiomyopathy. Since it cycles down one bundle branch and up the other it is a monomorphic VT. The long macro-reentry path is usually associated with a dilated ventricle. Braunwald says, "Bundle branch reentry is a form of monomorphic sustained VT usually seen in patients with structural heart disease, such as dilated cardiomyopathy." See: Braunwald, chapter on Ventricular Rhythm Disturbances

54. Typical Bundle Branch Reentry VT (BBRVT) cycles in a _____ direction and shows a _____ morphology.
   a. **Counterclockwise, RBBB**
   b. **Counterclockwise, LBBB**
   c. **Clockwise, RBBB**
   d. **Clockwise, LBBB**

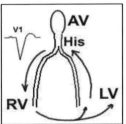

ANSWER: b. Counterclockwise, LBBB. A macroreentry VT, circling around with the most common form moving retrograde up the left bundle branch system and anterograde conduction down the right bundle branch, [counterclockwise] creating a QRS complex with a left bundle branch block contour.

Zipes says, "In the most common form of bundle branch reentry (BBR) VT, ventricular activation begins as the impulse exits from the right bundle branch and thereafter spreads as it does during typical LBBB. The ECG thus has an LBBB configuration…." See: Zipes, chapter on differential diagnosis of wide QRS complex tachycardia

55. A run of PVCs lasts for one minute and then reverts to sinus rhythm, it is termed:
   a. **Sustained VT**
   b. **Nonsustained VT**
   c. **Monomorphic VT**
   d. **Polymorphic VT**

ANSWER: a. Sustained VT. If the run lasts more than 30 seconds, it is termed sustained VT, shorter than 30 seconds is nonsustained. See: Marriot, chapter on "Ventricular Tachycardia."

56. The 12 lead ECG below was taken on this 93-year-old ER patient. What is the most likely arrhythmia?
   a. **AF with an accessory pathway**
   b. **SVT with an aberrancy**
   c. **AVNRT**
   d. **VT**

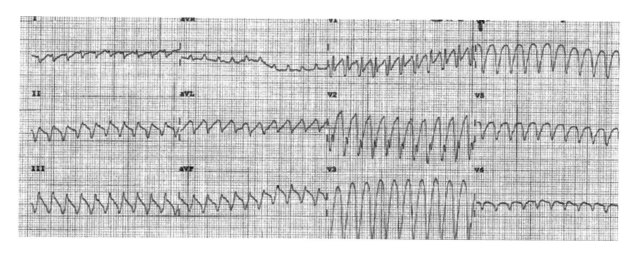

ANSWER: a. VT. Why is this called ventricular tachycardia?
   1. The patient is 93 years old: most likely VT
   2. Precordial lead concordance (all the V leads are pointing the same direction unifocal)
   3. Extreme right axis deviation = No man's land (- in I and – in aVF)
   4. Occasional P waves, but not 1:1 conduction

If unstable ALWAYS treat like VT! If there was an old ECG to view – look for delta waves or an underlying BBB which could then lead you more to SVT with aberrancy.
Answer a (AF) is incorrect because AF should show an irregular rhythm. In AVNRT, the P wave is typically buried within a narrow QRS complex.

57. During an SVT study, your RV catheter causes PVCs and sustained VT at a rate of 175 bpm. He is still wide awake. Expect to:
   a. **Let the patient continue in asymptomatic VT**
   b. **Defibrillate (Sync mode is off)**
   c. **Cardiovert (Sync mode is on)**
   d. **Administer Amiodarone IV**

ANSWER: c. Cardiovert (Sync mode is on). If the QRS complex can trigger the defibrillator, it is safer to shock in synchronized mode. This avoids shocking on the vulnerable period on the T wave which could result in VF. However, the awake patient will not appreciate this shock, and the patient should be sedated, unless he becomes unconscious first. It is usually possible to terminate a VT episode with a direct current shock across the heart. This is ideally synchronized to the patient's heartbeat. As this is quite uncomfortable, shocks should be delivered only to an unconscious or sedated patient. A patient with pulseless VT or ventricular fibrillation will be unconscious and treated as an emergency on an ACLS protocol and given high energy biphasic defibrillation. Patients with a stable VT are given cardioversion if the tachycardia exceeds 150 bpm.

58. What is the rhythm?
a. CHB with Ventricular Escape
b. Idioventricular Rhythm
c. Ventricular Paced
d. Junctional Escape

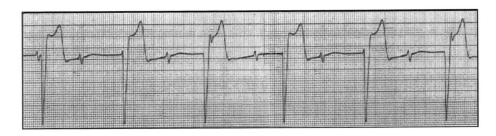

ANSWER: b. Idioventricular Rhythm, slow ventricular with wide QRS complex (>0.12 sec.). P waves are unrelated to QRS and are completely blocked by the AV node. Many QRS complexes contain P waves. The R-to-R interval = 40 mm = 1.6 sec = 38 bpm
If the ventricle does not receive triggering signals at a rate high enough, the ventricular myocardium itself becomes the pacemaker (escape rhythm). This is called Idioventricular Rhythm. Ventricular signals are transmitted cell-to-cell between cardiomyocytes and not by the conduction system, creating wide sometimes bizarre QRS complexes (> 0.12 sec). The rate is usually 20-40 bpm. If the rate is >40 bpm, it is called accelerated idioventricular rhythm.

60. Which of the following are characteristics of bundle branch reentry VT? (Select all that apply)
a. V-to-V drives the H-to-H
b. H-to-H drives the V-to-V
c. RBBB Morphology
d. LBBB Morphology
e. Monomorphic
f. Polymorphic

ANSWERS: b, d, e. The circuit for bundle branch reentry is from the His, down the right bundle, and up the left; therefore, the His is "driving" the V. The preceding H-to-H interval will be the same as the following V-to-V. The target of ablation is the right bundle branch.

References:

- 300th Cryoballoon Ablation At Our Unit. (2016, Feb 17) Image retrieved from http://www.capetownafcentre.co.za/news/300th-cryoballoon-ablation
- Abedin, Z, Essential Cardiac Electrophysiology: The Self-Assessment Approach, Blackwell Publishing, 2013
- Aibolita (Retrieved July 2018) Bundle Branch Reentrant VT. Retrieved from http://aibolita.com/heart-and-vessels/50757-bundle-branch-reentrant-vt.html
- Allmers, Nancy M., and Verderame, Joan A., Appleton, and Lange's Review for Surgical Tech. Exam, Appleton and Lange, Fourth Edition, 1996
- American Heart Association, Textbook of ADVANCED CARDIAC LIFE SUPPORT, 2010
- American Heart Association. Atrial Fibrillation. Watch, Live and Learn. Video retrieved from http://watchlearnlive.heart.org
- American Heart Association. Ventricular Fibrillation. Watch, learn and live. Animation retrieved from http://watchlearnlive.heart.org
- Anand, R. (Nov 2011) EP Lab Digest, Volume 11, Issue 11. Key Consideration for Designing an Electrophysiology Laboratory in a Community Hospital.
- Antzelevitch, C. & Burashnikov, A. (2011, Mar 1) Overview of Basic Mechanisms of Cardiac Arrhythmia. Retrieved from https://www.ncbi.nlm.nih.gov/pmc/articles/PMC3164530/
- Asirvatham, S. J., Mayo Clinic Electrophysiology Manual, Mayo Clinic Scientific Press, 1dst Edition, 2014
- Baim, D. S and Grossman W.., Cardiac Catheterization, Angiography, and Intervention, 7th Ed., Lea and Febiger, 2006
- Basicmedical Key: Fastest Basicmedical Insight Engine. AV Nodal Reentrant Tachycardia: Atypical. (2017, Mar 25) Retrieved from https://basicmedicalkey.com/av-nodal-reentrant-tachycardia-atypical/
- Berne, R. M. and Levy, M. N., Cardiovascular Physiology, 8th Ed., Mosby Yearbook, 2001
- Biosense Webster, http://www.biosensewebster.com/
- Braun, Nemcek, and Vogelzang, Interventional Radiology Procedure Manual, Churchill Livingstone, 1997
- Braunwald, Eugene, Ed., HEART DISEASE A Textbook of Cardiovascular Medicine, 9th Ed., W. B. Saunders Co., 2012
- Browning, T. (2013, Nov 19) Class II antiarrhythmics. Retrieved from https://www.youtube.com/watch?v=2uUj05KaVyo
- Burns, E., (2018) Life in the Fastlane: Brugada Syndrome. Retrieved from https://lifeinthefastlane.com/ecg-library/brugada-syndrome/
- Burns, E., (2018) Life in the Fastlane: VT versus SVT. Retrieved from https://litfl.com/vt-versus-svt-ecg-library/
- Chinitz, J., Michaud, G. Stephenson, K. (Oct 2017) The Journal of Innovations in Cardiac Rhythm Management. Impedance-guided Radiofrequency Ablation: Using Impedance to Improve Ablation Outcomes. Retrieved from

http://www.innovationsincrm.com/cardiac-rhythm-management/articles-2017/october/1100-impedance-guided-radiofrequency-ablation

- Cleveland Clinic (2011, Oct 5) Catheter Ablation For Atrial Fibrillation. Animation retrieved from https://youtu.be/SZ_uIfj-hIQ
- Cleveland Clinic (2019, Apr 23) Arrhythmogenic Right Ventricular Dysplasia (ARVD) Retrieved from https://my.clevelandclinic.org/health/diseases/16752-arrhythmogenic-right-ventricular-dysplasia-arvd (2019, Oct 3)
- Cohen, Todd, Practical Electrophysiology, HMP Publications, 2005
- Craig, Gloria P., Clinical Calculations Made Easy, Solving Problems Using Dimensional Analysis, 2nd Ed., Lippincott, 2001 Curry, Dowdey, and Murry, Christensen's Introduction to the Physics of Diagnostic Radiology, 3rd Ed., Lea & Febiger Publishers
- Crawford, M. & DiMarco, J. (2003, Dec 1) Cardiology
- Daily, E. K., and Schroeder, J. S., Techniques in Bedside Hemodynamic Monitoring, 4th Edition
- Dave Droll, Cath Lab Digest, Clipping versus Shaving: Who Wins in the End? Infection Risk and Hair Removal Guidelines, Sept 2005
- Deisenhofer, I., Zrenner, B., Yin, Y., Pitschner, H., Kuniss, M., GroBmann, G., Stiller, S., Luik, A., Veltmann, C., Frank, J., Linner, J., Estner, H., Pflaumer, A., Wu, J., Von Bary, C., Ucer, E., Reents, T., Tzeis, S., Fichtner, S., Kathan, S., Karch, M., Jilek, C., Ammar, S., Kolb, C., Liu, Z., Haller, B., Schmitt, C., & Hessling, G., (2010, Nov 15) Cryoablation Versus Radiofrequency Energy for the Ablation of Atrioventricular Nodal Reentrant Tachycardia (the CYRANO Study) Results From a Large Multicenter Prospective Randomized Trial. Retrieved from http://circ.ahajournals.org/content/122/22/2239
- DiMario, et. al., "Clinical application and image interpretation in intracoronary ultrasound" in European Heart Journal, 1998
- Dubin, Dale, RAPID INTERPRETATION of EKG's, 3rd Ed., Cover Publishing Co., 1982
- ECGPedia contributors. (2013, May 22) Brugada Syndrome. In ECGPedia, Part of Cardionetworks.org. Retrieved from http://en.ecgpedia.org/wiki/Brugada_Syndrome
- Ellenbogen, K, A, and Wood, Cardiac Pacing and ICDs, Blackwell Publishing, 5th Edition, 2008
- Ellenbogen, Kay, Lau, Wilkof, Clinical Cardiac Pacing, Defibrillation, and Resynchronization Therapy, 4th Edition, 2011
- Endosonics Company Literature and Web Site (Endosonics.com), 1999
- EP Europace Vol. 7, Issue 6 (2005, Nov 1) Electroanatomic mapping characteristics of ventricular tachycardia in patients with arrhythmogenic right ventricular cardiomyopathy/dysplasia.
- Fernandez-Armenta, J. & Berruezo, A. (May 2014) How to Recognize Epicardial Origin of Ventricular Tachycardias. Retrieved from https://www.researchgate.net/publication/262339568_How_to_Recognize_Epicardial_Origin_of_Ventricular_Tachycardias
- Fogoros, R. (2012, Sept 17) Electrophysiology Testing
- Fogoros, R., MD, Practical Cardiac Diagnosis, Electrophysiologic Testing, Blackwell Scientific Pub.,4th Edition, 2006

- Function of the Atrioventricular and Semilunar Valves. Retrieved from http://antranik.org/function-of-the-atrioventricular-and-semilunar-valves-and-fibrous-skeleton/
- Garcia and Holtz, 12-Lead EKG, The Art of Interpretation, Jones, and Bartlett Publishers, 2001
- Gardner, D. and Anderson-Manz E. (2001, May 1) How to Perform Surgical Hand Scrubs. Retrieved from http://www.infectioncontroltoday.com/articles/2001/05/how-to-perform-surgical-hand-scrubs.aspx
- Gruendemann and Meeker, Alexander's Care of the Patient in Surgery, CV Mosby Co., 1987
- Highlights of the 2010 American Heart Association Guidelines for CPR and ECC, http://static.heart.org/eccguidelines/pdf/ucm_317350.pdf
- Ho, R. (2008, Aug 18) Electrophysiology of Arrhythmias: Practical Images for Diagnosis and Ablation.
- Ho, R.T., Electrophysiology of Arrhythmias: Practical Images for Diagnosis and Ablation, Published by Lippincott, 1st Edition, 2010
- https://ghr.nlm.nih.gov/condition/brugada-syndrome#synonyms
- https://ghr.nlm.nih.gov/condition/jervell-and-lange-nielsen-syndrome#resources
- Huang, S.K. and Wood, M. A., Catheter Ablation of Cardiac Arrhythmias, Saunders Elsevier, 2nd Edition, 2011
- Huen, M. (2018) 10 Fact About Retroperitoneal Hematoma. Retrieved from http://www.thrombocyte.com/retroperitoneal-hematoma/
- Images retrieved from https://www.sjm.com and https://www.sjm.com/en/professionals/disease-state-management/cardiac-arrhythmias/integrated-lab
- Intravascular Ultrasound, An interactive Learning Tool With CME Credit, J.M. Hodgson, Senior Editor, Technology Solutions Group, Ltd., Ed. Div.
- Isa, Miller and Zipes, Clinical Arrhythmology and Electrophysiology, A Companion to Braunwald's Heart Disease, Saunders/Elsevier Publishers, 2009
- Issa, Z.F., Miller, J.M., & Zipes, D.P., (Philadelphia: Saunders Elsevier, 2009) Clinical Arrhythmology and Electrophysiology
- J.B. Lippincott Co., 1989
- Joseph, J.P. & Rajappan, K. (2011, Nov 12) Radiofrequency ablation of cardiac arrhythmias: past, present, and future. Retrieved from http://qjmed.oxfordjournals.org/content/105/4/303
- Kern, M. J., Ed., The Cardiac Catheterization Handbook, 4th Ed., Mosby-Yearbook, Inc., 2003
- King, & Yeung, Interventional Cardiology, McGraw-Hill Co., 2007
- Kirkorian, G., Moncada, E., Chevalier, P., Canu, G., Claudel, JP., Bellon, C., Lyon, L. & Touboul, P. (1994, Dec 1) Radiofrequency ablation of atrial flutter. Efficacy of an anatomically guided approach. Circulation: Vol. 90, No. 6 Retrieved from https://www.ahajournals.org/doi/abs/10.1161/01.cir.90.6.2804

- Kiser, A., Wimmer-Greinecker, G., Kapelak, B., Bartus, K., Sadowski, J. (Image modified on July 2018) Paracardioscopic Ex-Maze Procedure for Atrial Fibrillation. Image retrieved from http://ismics.org/abstracts/2008/V13.cgi

- Klabunde, R. (2008, Dec 13) Cardiovascular Physiology Concepts: Sinoatrial Node Action Potentials. Retrieved from http://www.cvphysiology.com/Arrhythmias/A004

- Kusukmoto, F., Understanding Intracardiac EGMs and ECGs, Wiley-Blackwell Publishers, 1st Edition 2010

- Loebl, Suzanne, and Spratto, George, and Heckheimer, Estelle, The Nurses Drug Handbook, 2nd Ed., Wiley Medical Pub., 1980 Ed., Lippincott Williams & Wilkins, 2002

- Makhija, A., Thachil, A., Sridevi, C., Rao, B., Jaishankar, S. & Narasimhan, C. (2009) Indian Pacing and Electrophysiology Journal. Substrate Based Ablation of Ventricular Tachycardia Through an Epicardial Approach.

- Mann, Roger, Edwards, and Scott, Electrophysiology Board Review (Board Review for Electrophysiology Book 1), Published by Knowledge Testing. Com

- Marriott, Henry J., and Conover, Mary H., Advanced Concepts in Arrhythmias, The C.V. Mosby Co., 1983

- Matthews, R. (Retrieved July 2018) Cardiology Explained and Presented by Robert Matthews, MD. The Wolff-Parkinson_White Syndrome. Retrieved from http://www.rjmatthewsmd.com/Definitions/wolff_parkinson_white_syndrome.htm

- McGowan, A. (2004, Dec 14) Iatrogenic Arteriovenous Fistula. Retrieved from http://www.medscape.com/viewarticle/494434

- Medical Expo. The Online Medical Device Exhibition. (2018) Ultrasound Catheter / Vascular. Retrieved from http://www.medicalexpo.com/prod/st-jude-medical/product-70886-446852.html

- Medical Expo. The Online Medical Device Exhibition. (2018) Vascular Access Sheath / Steerable. Retrieved from http://www.medicalexpo.com/prod/st-jude-medical/product-70886-518094.html

- Medical Multimedia Laboratories. Heart Sounds and Cardiac Arrhythmias. SVT Tutorial. Retrieved from www.Blaufuss.org

- Medtronic, The ECG Workbook, Medtronic Inc.1996, Medtronic.com

- Michaud, GF., Tada, H., Chough, S., et al. (2001) Differentiation of atypical atrioventricular node re-entrant tachycardia from orthodromic reciprocating tachycardia using a septal accessory pathway by the response to ventricular pacing.

- Moses, K. Weston, et al., A Practical Guide to Cardiac Pacing, 4th Ed., Little and Brown Co., 1995

- Moulton, Kreigh, Electrophysiology Review Course Book 1 & 2, 2002

- Murgatroyd & Krahn, Handbook of Cardiac Electrophysiology, Remedica, 2002

- Murgatroyd, F & Krahn A. (2003, Jan 5) Handbook of Cardiac Electrophysiology: A Practical Guide to Invasive EP Studies and Catheter Ablation.

- Musa, K. (2014, Dec 15) Anatomy of the heart. Retrieved from http://www.slideshare.net/Abomustafa/anatomy-of-the-heart-42723933

- NanoDomino (2014, Feb 14) Domino Heart. Retrieved from https://www.youtube.com/watch?v=hu59C1K5stM

- Nantou, Taiwan, 2010 http://homepage.vghtpe.gov.tw/~jcma/73/9/471.pdf

- Nazarian, S., Kolandaivelu, A., Zvimuan, M., Meininger, G., Kato, R., Susil, R., Roguin, A., Dickfeld, T., Ashikaga, H., Calkins, H., Berger, R., Bluemke, D., Lardo, A., & Halperin, H. (2008, Jun 23) Feasibility of Real-Time Magnetic Resonance Imaging for Catheter Guidance in Electrophysiology Studies. Retrieved from http://circ.ahajournals.org/content/118/3/223
- NIBIB gov (2015, Jun 5) How Ultrasound Works. Retrieved from https://youtu.be/I1Bdp2tMFsY
- NIH. U.S. National Library of Medicine. Genetics Home Reference. Published 2019, Oct 1. Retrieved from https://ghr.nlm.nih.gov/condition/romano-ward-syndrome#resources
- Nogami, A. (2018) European Cardiology Review: Vol. 6, Issue 4. Diagnosis and Ablation of Fascicular Tachycardia.
- Nordkamp, L. (2013, Mar 25) Textbook of Cardiology. LQTS. Retrieved from https://www.textbookofcardiology.org/wiki/LQTS (2019, Oct 3)
- Nordkamp, L. (2014, Mar 26) Textbook of Cardiology. SQTS. Retrieved from https://www.textbookofcardiology.org/wiki/SQTS (2019, Oct 3)
- Opie, Lionel H., Drugs for the Heart, 4th Edition, W. B. Saunders, 2005
- PACES. The Pediatric & Congenital Electrophysiology Society. Cardiac Channelopathies. Retrieved from http://pediatricepsociety.org/Patient-Resources/Cardiac-Channelopathies.aspx (2019, Oct 3)
- Parikh, V. & Kowalski, M. (2015, Dec 31) Journal of Atrial Fibrillation. Comparison of Phrenic Nerve Injury during Atrial Fibrillation Ablation between Different Modalities, Pathophysiology and Management.
- Patel, V. (2017, Jan 4) TheHeart.org Medscape: Digitalis Toxicity Treatment & Management. Retrieved from http://emedicine.medscape.com/article/154336-treatment
- Permanent Pacemaker Implantation. (2016, July 28) Peel-away of Right Ventricular Lead Sheath. Retrieved from https://youtu.be/i9iaVBxAng8
- Popovic, D. (Retrieved July 2018) Noise in ECG and how to deal with it. Retrieved from http://www-classes.usc.edu/engr/bme/620/LectureECGNoise.pdf
- Protonotarios, N., Tsatsopoulou, A. (2006, Mar 13) Orphanet Journal of Rare Diseases. Naxos disease: Cardiocutaneous syndrome due to cell adhesion defect.
- Published by Cardioelectric, 1st Edition, 2012
- Purves, Klein, Leong-Sit, Yee, Skanes, Gula, & Krahn, Cardiac Electrophysiology, A Visual Guide for Nurses, Techs, and Fellows, 2012
- Quallich, S., Goff, R. & Iaizzo, P. Journal of Medical Devices: Vol. 8/Issue 2. High-Speed Visualization of Steam Pops During Radiofrequency Ablation. Retrieved from http://medicaldevices.asmedigitalcollection.asme.org/article.aspx?articleid=1876472
- Rafla, S. (2013, July 12) Technique of Ablation of AVNRT and case presentation. Retrieved from https://www.slideshare.net/SamirRafla/samir-rafla-technique-of-ablation-of-avnrt-and-case-presentation
- Raza, S. (2006, Oct) Radiation Exposure in the Cath Lab – Safety and Precautions. Retrieved from http://www.priory.com/med/radiation.htm

- Reddy, VY., Shah, D., Kautzner, J., Schmidt, B., Sadodi, N., Herrera, C., Jais, P., Hindricks, G., Peichl, P., Yulzari, A., Lambert, H., Neuzil, P., Natale, A. & Kuck, KH. (Nov 2012) Heart Rhythm. The relationship between contact force and clinical outcome during radiofrequency catheter ablation of atrial fibrillation in the TOCCATA study. Retrieved from https://www.ncbi.nlm.nih.gov/pubmed/22820056

- Retrieved from https://www.ncbi.nlm.nih.gov/pmc/articles/PMC1435994/ (2019, Oct 3)

- Reynolds, Terry, RDCS, BS, ULTRASOUND PHYSICS, A Registry Exam Preparation Guide, School of Cardiac Ultrasound, Arizona Heart Institute Foundation, Phoenix, AZ 1996

- Roberts-Thomson, Kurt & Kistler, Peter & M Kalman, Jonathan. (2005). Atrial Tachycardia: Mechanisms, Diagnosis, and Management. Current problems in cardiology. 30. 529-73. 10.1016/j.cpcardiol.2005.06.004. Retrieved from https://www.researchgate.net/publication/7582173_Atrial_Tachycardia_Mechanisms_Diagnosis_and_Management

- Saint Jude Medical, http://professional.sjm.com/

- Saksena, S. (2015, May 1) Interventional Cardiac Electrophysiology: A Multidisciplinary Approach.

- Schneider, Peter, Endovascular Skills, Guidewire and Catheter Skills for Endovascular Surgery, 2nd Edition, Marcel Dekker, Inc., 2003

- Schotten, U., Verheule, S., Kirchhof, P. & Goette, A. (2011, Jan 1) American Physiological Society: Physiological Reviews. Vol. 91, No. 1 Pathophysiological Mechanisms of Atrial Fibrillation: A Translational Appraisal.

- Sheikh, M., Bruhl, S., Foster, W., Grubb, B. & Kanjwal, Y. (Jan 2011) EP Lab Digest, Volume 11, Issue 1. Premature Ventricular Contractions May Not Be All That Benign: The Role of Radiofrequency Ablation.

- Siemens.com AcuNav instruction manual online, //www.medical.siemens.com/siemens/en_US/gg_us_FBAs/files/brochures/AcuNav/Instructional_Guide.pdf

- Smith, S. (2016, June 3) Dr. Smith's ECG Blog: Instructive ECGs in Emergency Medicine Clinical Context. Wide Complex Tachycardia with Fusion and Capture Beats. Not what you think. Retrieved from http://hqmeded-ecg.blogspot.com/2016/06/wide-complex-tachycardia-with-fusion.html

- Sorgente, A., Chierchia, G., Asmundis, C., Sarkozy, A., Capulzini, L., Brugada, P. (2011, July 21) EP Europace. Complications of Atrial Fibrillation Ablation: When Prevention Is Better Than Cure.

- Steinberg J.S, and Suneet, M, Electrophysiology: The Basics: A Companion Guide for the Cardiology Fellow during the EP Rotation, Published by Lippincott, 1st Edition, 2009

- Stevenson, W. & Soejima, K. (2018, Nov 25) Recording Techniques for Clinical Electrophysiology. Medscape. Retrieved from https://www.medscape.com/viewarticle/512810_2

- Tabatabaei, N., & Asirvatham, S. (2009, Jun 1) Circulation: Arrhythmia and Electrophysiology. Vol. 2, No. 3. Supravalvular Arrhythmia: Identifying and Ablating the Substrate.

- Tadvi, N. (2013, Sep 25) Antiarrhythmic drugs. Retrieved from https://www.slideshare.net/nasertadvi/antiarrhythmic-drugs-26524937
- Taiwan Heart Rhythm Society (2013, Apr 11) Electrophysiology Study: Pacing Methods & EP Testing. Retrieved from http://www.slideshare.net/thrs/electrophysiologic-study
- Taiwan Heart Rhythm Society (2013, Apr 11) Intracardiac Electrograms. Retrieved from https://www.slideshare.net/thrs/intracardiac-electrograms
- Tipp, Alice, Basic Pathophysiological Mechanisms of Congestive Heart Failure, McGraw-Hill, 1979 Torres, Basic Medical Techniques and Patient Care for Radiologic Technologists,
- Underhill, S. L., Ed., CARDIAC NURSING, 2nd Ed., J. B. Lippincott Co., 1989 Wiggers diagram:
- Valves of the Heart. Retrieved from http://www.apsubiology.org/anatomy/2020/2020_Exam_Reviews/Exam_1/CH18_Valves_of_the_Heart.htm
- Vitulano, N., Pazzano, V., Pelargonio, G. & Narducci, ML (2014, Sept 19) Dovepress: Medical Devices: Evidence and Research Vol 8. Technology update: intracardiac echocardiography – a review of the literature. Retrieved from https://www.dovepress.com/technology-update-intracardiac-echocardiography-ndash-a-review-of-the--peer-reviewed-fulltext-article-MDER#F2
- Waksman and Ajani, Pharmacology in the Catheterization Laboratory, Wiley-Blackwell, 2010 Watson, Sandy, Ed., Invasive Cardiology, A manual for Cath Lab Personnel, 2nd Ed., Physicians Press, 2005 Wilson, J.H., Cardiac EP Exam Preparation: A review for allied professionals,
- Watson, L. (2009) EP Studies in Bradyarrhythmias. Retrieved from http://slideplayer.com/slide/230395/
- Webber, J., Jang, J., Gustavson, S. & Olin, J. (2007, May 22) Contemporary Management of Postcatheterization Pseudoaneurysms. Retrieved from http://circ.ahajournals.org/content/115/20/2666
- WebMD, LLC. (2018, May 9) Vagal Maneuvers to Slow Heart Rate. Retrieved from http://www.webmd.com/heart-disease/atrial-fibrillation/tc/vagal-maneuvers-for-a-fast-heart-rate-topic-overview
- Wells, P. (2018) Heart Racing: RF vs. Cryoablation. Retrieved from http://www.heartracing.com/patients/rf.vs.cryoablation.asp
- Wikipedia contributors. (2018, Oct 23) Antiarrhythmic Agent. In Wikipedia, The Free Encyclopedia. Retrieved from https://en.wikipedia.org/wiki/Antiarrhythmic_agent
- Wikipedia contributors. (2018, Oct 29) Long QT Syndrome. In Wikipedia, The Free Encyclopedia. Retrieved from https://en.wikipedia.org/wiki/Long_QT_syndrome
- Wikipedia contributors. (2018, Sept 10) Fluoroscopy. In Wikipedia, The Free Encyclopedia. Retrieved from https://en.wikipedia.org/wiki/Fluoroscopy
- Wong, M., Edwards, G., Spence, S., Kalman, J., Kumar, S., Joseph, S. & Morton, J. (2013, Oct 17) Circulation: Arrhythmia and Electrophysiology: Vol. 6, No. 6 Characterization of Catheter – Tissue Contact Force During Epicardial Radiofrequency Ablation in an Ovine Model

- Wu, J., Ding, W., Horie, M. (2016, Jan 27) Journal of Arrhythmia. Molecular pathogenesis of long QT syndrome type 1. Retrieved from https://www.ncbi.nlm.nih.gov/pmc/articles/PMC5063268/ (2019, Oct 3)
- Yaniga, Leslie, RCIS, Cath Lab Pharmacology, Smith Notes, 1998
- Yetkin, U., Ozelci, A., Akyuz, M., Goktogan, T., Yurekli, I. & Gurbuz, A. (2009 Volume 8 Number 2) Surgical Approach To A Giant Post Cardiac Catheterization Pseudoaneurysm After unsuccessful Duplex Ultrasound-Guided Compression. The Internte Journal of Cardiology. Retrieved from http://ispub.com/IJC/8/2/5346
- Yock, Fitzgerald, and Popp, Intravascular Ultrasound, in Scientific American, Science and Medicine, 1995
- Your Pericardium. Retrieved from http://www.cardiachealth.org/your-pericardium
- Zipes, D. & Jalife, J. (2013) Cardiac Electrophysiology: From Cell to Bedside.
- Zipes, D.Z. and Jalife, J., Cardiac Electrophysiology, from Cell to Bedside, published by, Saunders-Elsevier, 5th Edition, 2009
- Петр Иванов (2015, Mar 24) Seldinger Technique. Retrieved from https://www.youtube.com/watch?v=a3pLVr8jShQ&feature=youtu.beguidelines-for-cpr.html